MICROCOMPUTER ACCOUNTING

TUTORIAL AND APPLICATIONS

FOR PEACHTREE COMPLETE ® ACCOUNTING RELEASE 8.0

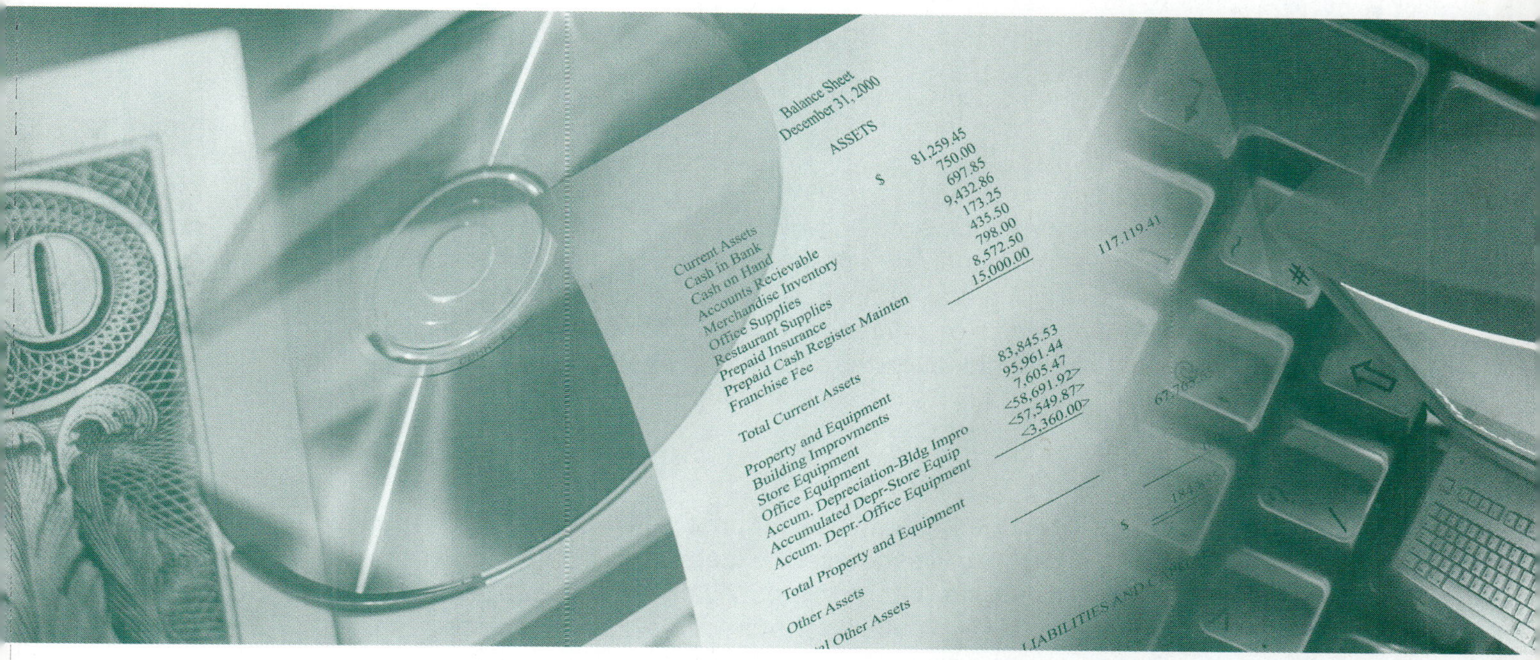

FOURTH EDITION

Dr. Gregory E. Anders
Adjunct Professor
University of Phoenix
Orlando, Florida

Dr. EmmaJo Spiegelberg
Adjunct Professor
University of Wyoming

Sally Nelson
Iowa Northeast Community College

Glencoe McGraw-Hill

New York, New York Columbus, Ohio Woodland Hills, California Peoria, Illinois

Library of Congress Cataloging-in-Publication Data

Anders, Gregory E.
Microcomputer accounting: tutorial and applications for Peachtree Complete® Accounting, release 8.0/Gregory E. Anders, EmmaJo Spiegelberg, Sally Nelson. -- 3rd ed.
p. cm.
Includes index
ISBN 0-07-825035-8 (student text, CD-ROM).
-- ISBN 0-07-825036-6 (instructors manual)
1. Peachtree complete accounting. 2. Accounting--Computer programs. I. Spiegelberg, EmmaJo. II. Nelson, Sally (Sally J.) III. Title.
HF5679.A597 2001
657'.0285' 5369--dc21 99-40025
CIP

Printed in the United States of America.

Send all inquiries to:
Glencoe/McGraw-Hill
21600 Oxnard Street, Suite 500
Woodland Hills, CA 91367

ISBN 0-07-825035-8

3 4 5 6 7 8 9 10 079 05 04 03 02

Preface

After you have learned accounting principles, what's next? Applying this knowledge to accounting software is an important next step. Computers and accounting software, once the exclusive domain of large organizations, have become indispensable tools used by all types and sizes of businesses. Today, a business may choose from a diverse range of computer hardware and software accounting tools.

Learning to combine computer technology with an understanding of accounting is an important part of the development of your academic skills. This text/workbook (with *Peachtree Complete Accounting 8.0* software and the accompanying template student disks) provides a comprehensive package for learning automated accounting procedures.

ORGANIZATION OF THIS TEXT/WORKBOOK

This book consists of fourteen chapters that provide extensive coverage of accounting topics. You will find a balanced approach between reading and hands-on activities. The chapters include learning objectives, step-by-step instructions, computer practice activities, review questions, and computer application problems that reinforce the accounting principles taught in the chapter. Additionally, each chapter contains a vignette; these explore topics such as securing data. Scattered throughout the body of the text are notes that are intended to recall an accounting procedure or alert students to computer procedures that should be followed.

Chapters 1, 2, and 3 of the text explain setting up and maintaining *Peachtree*. Chapters 4 through 9 give instructions for using the software and recording transactions involving the General Ledger, sales and accounts receivable, purchases and accounts payable, cash receipts, cash disbursements, and job costing.

Chapter 10 provides instructions for generating financial reports. Setting up and processing payroll is explained in Chapters 11 and 12. Chapter 13 explains the process for estimating budgets for revenue and expense accounts. The Business Analysis chapter provides the opportunity to analyze accounting information such as projected and actual cash flow, forecast for cash collecting, collecting accounts receivable and payment aging. Ratios (such as profitability and working capital) are calculated in the financial manager component. Analysis information can be presented in numeric or graphic form.

Three capstone business simulations are provided following the tutorial chapter. The simulations are designed to give you the opportunity to apply your accounting and computer skills by entering business transactions for the final month of the fiscal period for a small merchandising business. Creamy Delight is a sole proprietorship; The Book Worm, a partnership; and The Floor Store, a corporation. After completing a simulation, an analysis test is provided. The Tumbleweed simulation gives you experience in payroll procedures.

There is a glossary of accounting and computer terms. The Appendix contains a list of the icons used in *Peachtree*.

FEATURES OF THE SOFTWARE

Peachtree, a commercial accounting package, has been designed to be easy to learn and easy to teach. Features of the software include:

- Navigation aids
- Menus and submenus
- Invoicing
- Budgeting
- Business analysis
- Sales
- Purchasing
- Job costing
- Payroll
- Drill-down feature in reports, for ease in editing and auditing
- Help
- Drop down menus
- Lookup boxes

COMPUTER PRACTICE AND END-OF-CHAPTER PROBLEMS

Practice activities are spread throughout the chapters, and comprehensive application problems are at the end of each chapter. Premier Fitness Club, Inc. is the corporation used in Chapters 4 through 14 of the tutorial.

José Garcia is the president and principal stockholder of Premier Fitness Club, Inc., a fitness and exercise club located in Chicago, Illinois. Premier is a small corporation, with annual sales of approximately $1 million. The company employs five full-time persons and hires part-time employees on an as-needed basis.

The club sells individual memberships for $30.00 and offers $25.00 memberships to a single group or organization. Premier has a pro shop on the premises where sports clothing and exercise tapes are sold. Through the pro shop, the business deals with several vendors and customers.

INSTRUCTOR'S RESOURCES

The instructor's manual includes a broad range of useful resources. Teaching suggestions and solutions for the Review and Application exercises are also included.

HARDWARE REQUIREMENTS

Peachtree is designed to run on IBM PC and compatibles using Windows 95 or 98. The hardware requirements are the following:

- IBM (or 100% compatible) computer, 386 or higher
- MS-DOS 3.13 (or higher) and Windows 3.1 or higher
- Color or monochrome VGA monitor
- Printer that can print 132 characters in compressed or expanded mode and supported by Windows
- 4 MB RAM; minimum 11 MB free disk space
- Mouse

Dr. Gregory E. Anders
Dr. EmmaJo Spiegelberg
Sally Nelson

Contents

Chapter 1

Navigating Through Peachtree

OBJECTIVES

When you have completed Chapter 1, you should be able to:

1. Discuss the benefits of using computer technology in business accounting.
2. Open a file for a sample company.
3. Launch *Peachtree Complete Accounting 8.0* functions from the Peachtree Today screen.
4. Use the menus to open task windows.
5. Use the Navigation Aids to open task windows.
6. Use shortcut keys to perform accounting and windows functions.

Accounting is the process of recording, processing, and reporting financial events or transactions. Generally accepted accounting principles apply whether accounting transactions are recorded manually in a journal and ledger or electronically with a computer and software like *Peachtree Complete Accounting 8.0*.

Three main steps are involved in processing business transactions: financial information is collected, verified, and analyzed; transactions are recorded; and reports that analyze and summarize the financial information are produced. The primary goal of an accounting system is to provide information needed to manage activities on a day-to-day basis. This text will help you learn to process business transactions electronically—that is, quickly and efficiently.

COMPUTERIZED VERSUS MANUAL ACCOUNTING

Accountants realized early in the computer revolution how electronic accounting would benefit them in terms of the speed and accuracy of data entry. The primary differences between manual and computerized accounting are the methods used for recording data and generating reports. Although the same generally accepted accounting principles are followed, computerized accounting performs many of the manual functions behind the scenes without additional input.

A source document contains pertinent information about a business transaction. Purchase orders, invoices, and receipts are examples of source documents. In both manual and electronic accounting, source documents related to the daily operation of the business must be analyzed and recorded. Determining which accounts are affected by the transactions is a critical component of that analysis.

In a manual system, data is recorded by entering the account information and amounts in a journal. The information is then posted to the appropriate accounts in the ledger, and eventually financial statements are prepared that provide information about the condition of the business and whether it has earned a profit or experienced a loss. Each time data is entered (journal, ledger, financial statements, etc.), there is a possibility of error.

Whether you are currently learning accounting or are already familiar with basic accounting principles, your knowledge can be applied to a computerized system. *Peachtree* will use the same concepts you learn in an accounting class. You will follow the same basic steps to analyze and initially record the information. The behind-the-scenes work that *Peachtree* performs for you will speed up your work.

In an electronic system, data is entered one time. The computer is able to classify and summarize data rapidly and to report the results in a number of ways and as often as needed by decision makers. The flow of accounting information is the same in both manual and computerized accounting. The following chart illustrates the processes that are completely or partially automated in a computerized accounting system. An **M** indicates that the step is performed manually; **A** indicates that the step is automated.

Accounting Cycle	*Manual Accounting*	*Computerized Accounting*
1. Analyze business transactions using source documents	M	M
2. Enter transactions in the journal (journalize)	M	M
3. Post journal entries to the general and subsidiary ledgers	M	A
4. Prepare a Trial Balance	M	A
5. Analyze accounts to determine required adjusting entries	M	M
6. Journalize and post adjusting entries	M	M/A

Accounting Cycle	*Manual Accounting*	*Computerized Accounting*
7. Prepare financial statements	M	A
8. Journalize and post closing entries	M	A
9. Prepare a post-closing trial balance	M	A
10. Create analysis reports	M	A

INSTALLATION OF THE SOFTWARE

If you are working in a networked computer laboratory, *Peachtree* will most likely have been installed for you. If you need to install the software on your classroom or personal computer, a CD with an educational version of the software is included with this text. To install *Peachtree* insert the CD and the program will begin the self-install process. Unless you want to alter the suggested program or data pathways or make other changes in the default installation, you will simply click the **Next** button as each screen appears. After the installation is complete, restart your computer, and you are ready to begin exploring and learning about *Peachtree*.

INSTALLATION OF SAMPLE TAX TABLE

You must install a tax table in order to complete the payroll activities for Chapters 11 and 12 and the Tumbleweed Fast Food simulation. All other chapters and simulations can be completed without the tax tables.

After *Peachtree* has been installed, use the Windows Explorer program to install the tax table.

Step 1 Close *Peachtree*.

Step 2 From the Start menu, select Programs and then Windows Explorer.

Step 3 Insert the *Peachtree* CD included with this text.

Step 4 Display the contents on the CD.

Step 5 Click on the last file on the CD (win0101.exe).

Step 6 Choose **Yes** to begin the installation.

Step 7 Choose **Next** on subsequent screens to install in the recommended locations.

Step 8 Choose **Finish** to complete the installation.

OVERVIEW OF PEACHTREE 8.0

All types of businesses can use *Peachtree*. During this course you will have the opportunity to enhance your accounting skills by applying what you have learned as you become acquainted with the various components of *Peachtree*.

Peachtree has two sample companies that you can explore to learn how to navigate through the various components of the software. Bellwether Garden Supply is a sales and service company, and Pavilion Design Group is a service company. Since you will be recording transactions for a sales and service company later in this text, we will use Bellwether Garden Supply. Throughout this text, a computer symbol will indicate practice activities within the chapter. You should complete these activities as well as those at the end of the chapter.

Step 1 Open *Peachtree* by clicking on the shortcut icon on the desktop or from the **Start** menu.

Step 2 Browse through each feature as it is explained.

Step 3 From the opening screen (Figure 1–1), select *Explore a sample company*. You can use the *Open an existing company* option after you have worked in the sample company.

Step 4 Choose Bellwether Garden Supply.

Step 5 Click **OK**.

When the file for a company has been opened, you can perform accounting tasks using one or a combination of three methods to move among the various data entry windows: the Action Center of *Peachtree* Today's Welcome screen, the Navigation Aids, or the menus. When you open the Bellwether files, the first screen will be *Peachtree* Today.

Figure 1–1 Peachtree's opening screen

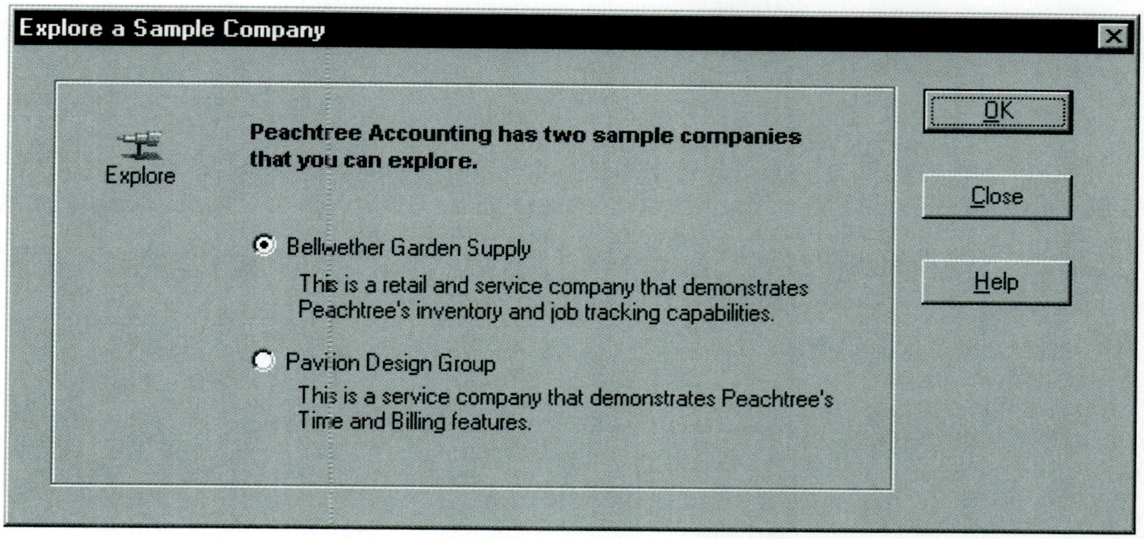

Figure 1–2 Select the sample company file to open

PEACHTREE TODAY

Peachtree Today is a new feature in version 8.0. The default setting is to display this window automatically when you open a company. *Peachtree* Today is an information center that allows you to access key functions and monitor your business activity. It also provides helpful information about using the software more efficiently. It is one of several methods of navigating through *Peachtree Accounting*.

If the *Peachtree* Today window is not displayed, select *Peachtree* Today from the **Online** menu, or click the **Today** button on the status bar at the bottom of the screen. If you do not want the *Peachtree* Today window open as you enter accounting information, simply click on the **Minimize** or **Close** button at the top of the window.

Below *Peachtree* Today's toolbar are your company's name, the *Peachtree* system date, and a ticker tape section that displays *Peachtree* product and service announcements. The **Welcome** section, illustrated in Figure 1-3, displays the Action Center on the left and Product Tips on the right. The shortcut keys will be discussed later in this chapter. From the Action Center you can launch major areas of the software. You also can access *Peachtree's* Help features from several points on this screen.

Peachtree Today is essentially a Web browser within *Peachtree Accounting*. The toolbar buttons at the top of the window allow you to navigate through the areas of *Peachtree* Today and Web pages the same way that you would in any Web browser. An Internet connection is not required to open or run *Peachtree* Today or to launch functions from the Action Center, but a connection is required to utilize the **My Business** or **My Resources** sections or to click on the ticker tape for product updates, service, etc. Clicking on **Preferences** allows you to customize the appearance and features of *Peachtree* Today.

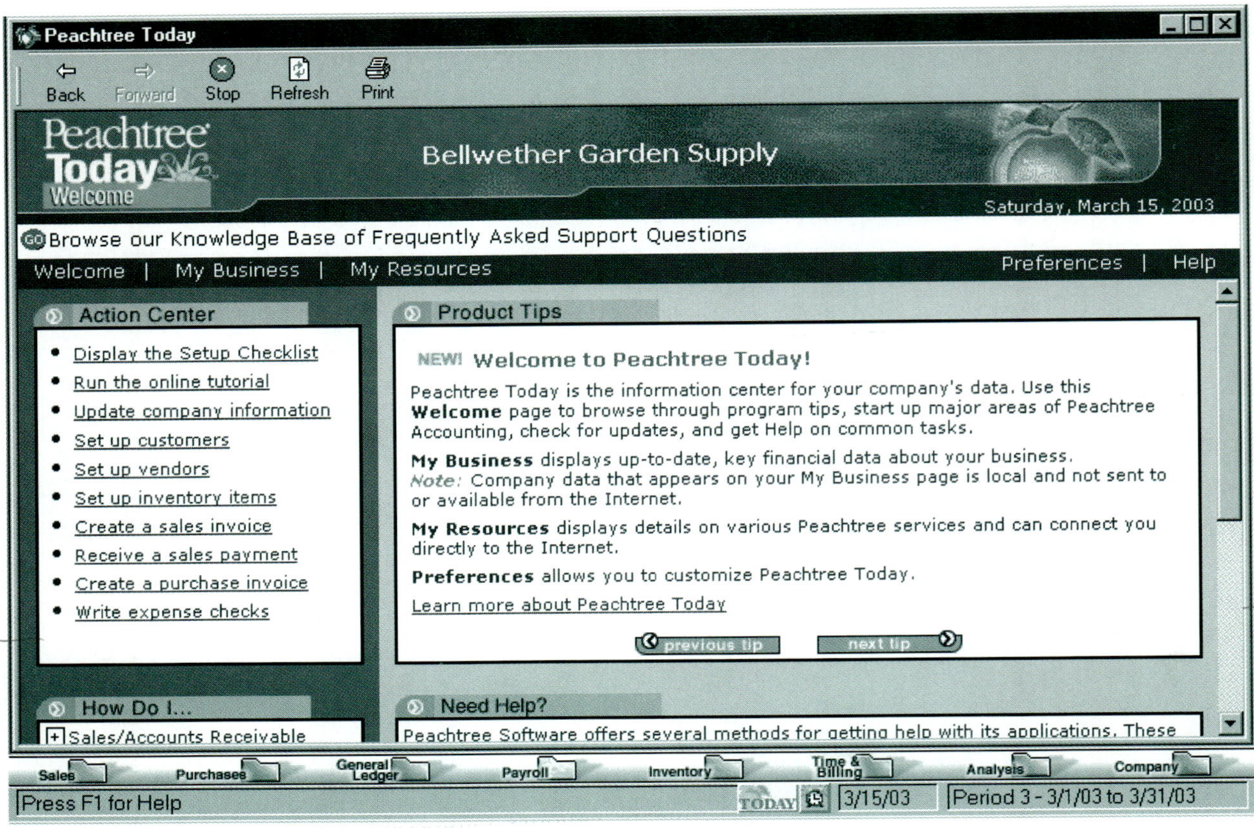

Figure 1–3 Peachtree Today information center

The instructions in this text will use the Navigation Aids or the menus to navigate through *Peachtree,* rather than *Peachtree* Today's Action Center. All of the methods will be explained, however, and you can choose the one that you prefer to use.

Explore the various aspects of the *Peachtree* Today window in the Bellwether Garden Supply file.

Step 1 For example, click on *Create a sales invoice* in the Action Center. The Sales/Invoicing data entry window will open. You will use this window in Chapter 5 when you record sales to customer.

Step 2 Click the **Close** toolbar button to close the Sales/Invoicing window.

Step 3 Click on **next tip** in the Product Tips section.

Step 4 Close or minimize the *Peachtree* Today window.

Step 5 Reopen *Peachtree* Today from the status bar.

Step 6 Open the Help menu by clicking **Help** on the welcome screen of *Peachtree* Today.

Step 7 Close the Sales/Invoicing and Help windows.

Step 8 Close *Peachtree* Today.

MENUS

You can open any of *Peachtree's* menus by using the mouse or the ALT key and the underlined letter in the menu name. A right arrow on the submenu (i.e., *Quotes/Sales Orders*) indicates that a second menu will open if that menu option is selected. An ellipsis (*Sales/Invoicing...*) indicates that a data entry window will open if you select that menu item.

Using the menus,

Step 1 Open the **Tasks** menu.

Step 2 Select *Sales/Invoicing.*

Step 3 Browse through each menu as it is explained below.

The same data entry window opens from the menu as when you used the Peachtree Today screen.

The **File** menu is used to set up and open companies within *Peachtree Accounting*. You will also use this menu to back up (**Save**) your accounting files at the end of a work session and to restore your files the next time you are ready to enter data. The **Edit** menu allows you to work with information in records, transactions, reports, or forms. The options within the **Edit** menu differ according to the window that is open.

You will use the **Maintain** menu to set up and change information about your customers, vendors, employees, etc. The **Tasks** menu will be used for entering your accounting transactions. As you can see in Figure 1-4, you can open a task window for each type of accounting

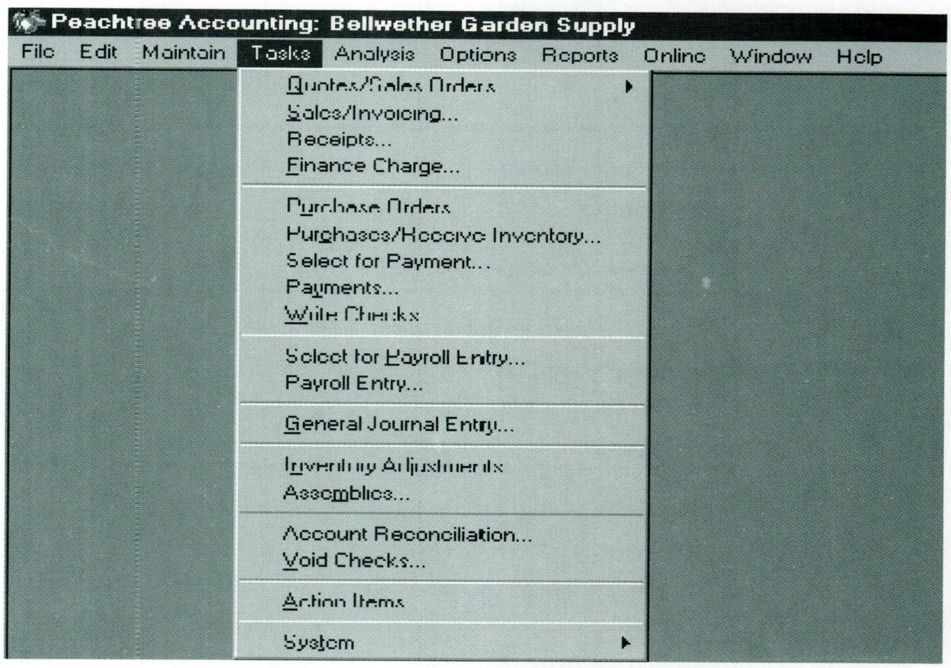

Figure 1–4 Menu bar with Tasks submenu

transaction. The **Analysis** and **Reports** menus are valuable decision-making tools that will be explained in subsequent chapters.

The **Options** menu allows you to set certain defaults that let you work the way you want. For example, you decide how *Peachtree* will enter decimals in the numbers you enter.

Step 1 Open the *Global* submenu.

Step 2 Indicate how you want decimals inserted in numbers. The default setting is to automatically enter two decimal places in numbers. This means that if you enter 20 in an amount field, *Peachtree* will enter it as .20. If you change the setting to manual and enter 20, *Peachtree* will record the amount as 20.00.

Step 3 Choose **OK** to close the Global Options window.

Peachtree includes a comprehensive **Help** menu where you can find the answers to questions about the program, technical support, and products and services. The first time you encounter tasks in this tutorial, you will be given step-by-step instructions. In subsequent chapters and in the simulations, you will be directed only to complete the tasks. You can always refer to the step-by-step directions in the appropriate chapter, but it will be more efficient to use the **Help** menu to find the explanations and instructions.

When you open the **Help** menu, you can select from the Contents listing or open the Index tab and key in a term or phrase that will scroll

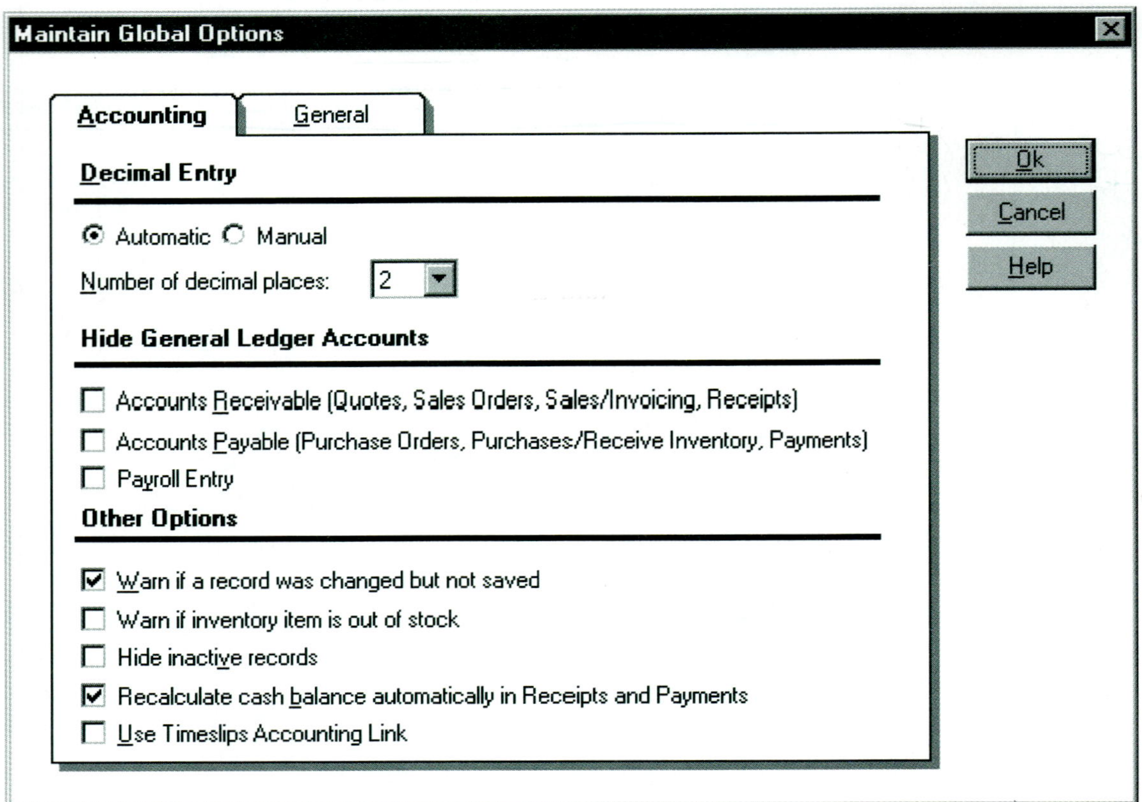

Figure 1–5 Default settings for Global Options

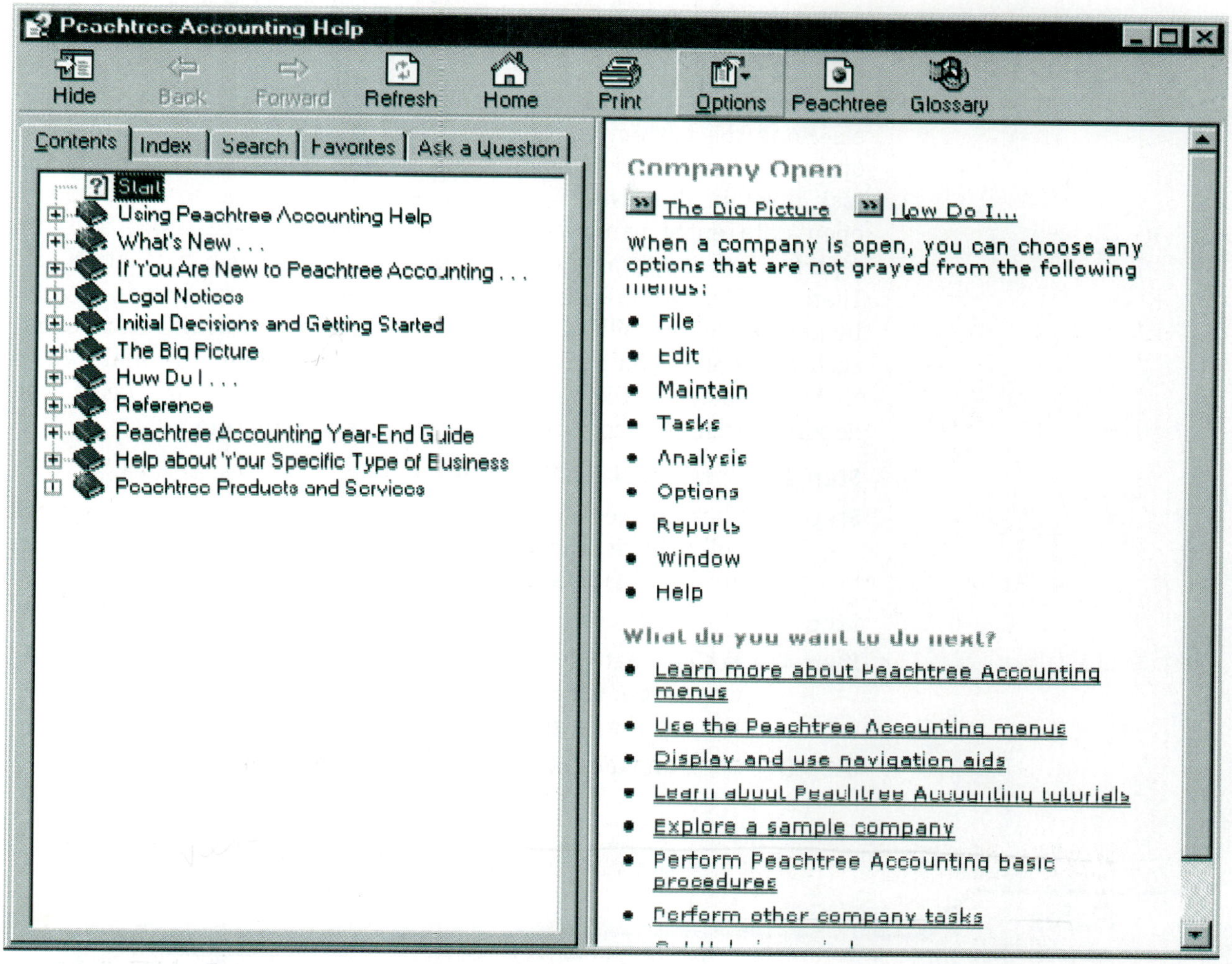

Figure 1–6 A sample Peachtree Help screen

the index forward to the alphabetic listing closest to the one you enter. Click on a link on the right side of the screen for additional information.

Step 1 Drop down the **Help** menu.

Step 2 Choose *Peachtree Accounting Help.*

Step 3 Explore one of the topics on the right side of the screen.

Step 4 Click on the *Index* tab on the left side of the Help window. The first time you open this tab, you will see a *preparing index* message. Wait until that box disappears from your screen.

Step 5 Key *sales invoices* in the keyword field at the top.

Step 6 Choose *enter* from the choices under sales invoices.

Step 7 Read the Help screens that explain how to enter a product sales invoice.

Step 8 Close the Help screens.

NAVIGATION AIDS

The Navigation Aids (when turned on) appear as a row of file folders along the bottom of the screen (see Figure 1–3). When a folder is open, the Navigation Aid contains a graphic representation of common task flows in *Peachtree*. Navigation Aids can be used as a method to open data entry windows, maintain records, initiate tasks, and run reports. Each major area of *Peachtree Accounting* has a navigation aid. There are Navigation Aids for Sales, Purchases, General Ledger, Payroll, Inventory, Time & Billing, Analysis, and Company. You will learn about each of these as you work through the chapters of this tutorial. Notice that the folder is divided into three sections—Maintain, Tasks, and Reports—that correspond to *Peachtree*'s menu structure.

Step 1 Open the Sales Navigation Aid.

Step 2 Click on the *Sales/Invoicing* icon. The same data entry window will open as when you used the Peachtree Today Action Center and the **Tasks** menu.

Step 3 Close the Sales/Invoicing window.

Step 4 Notice that the Sales Navigation Aid automatically closed when you made a selection from the icons in the folder. Reopen the Sales Navigation Aid.

Step 5 Click on *Sales Orders*.

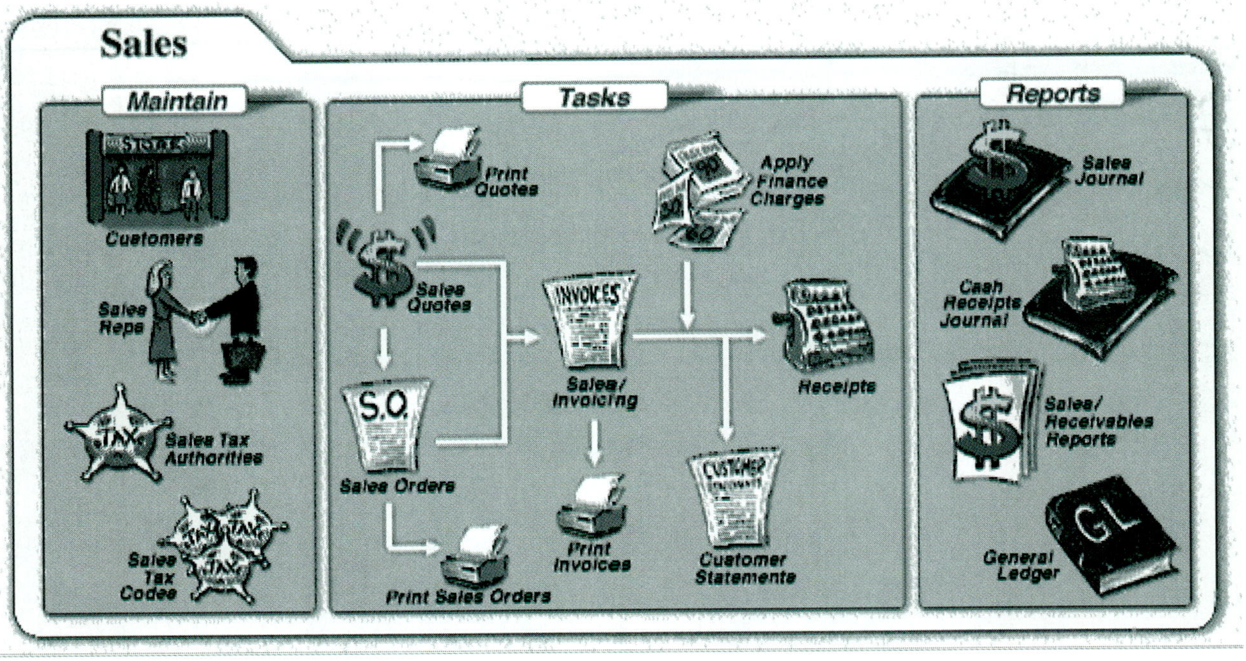

Figure 1–7 Sales Navigation Aid

PARTS OF THE DATA ENTRY WINDOW

The windows in *Peachtree* have several major areas with shortcuts designed to make data entry fast and easy. Explanations for window components that have not been explained previously follow Figure 1–8.

Step 1 Open the Sales/Invoicing window.

Step 2 Click in each field or area of the window as it is explained.

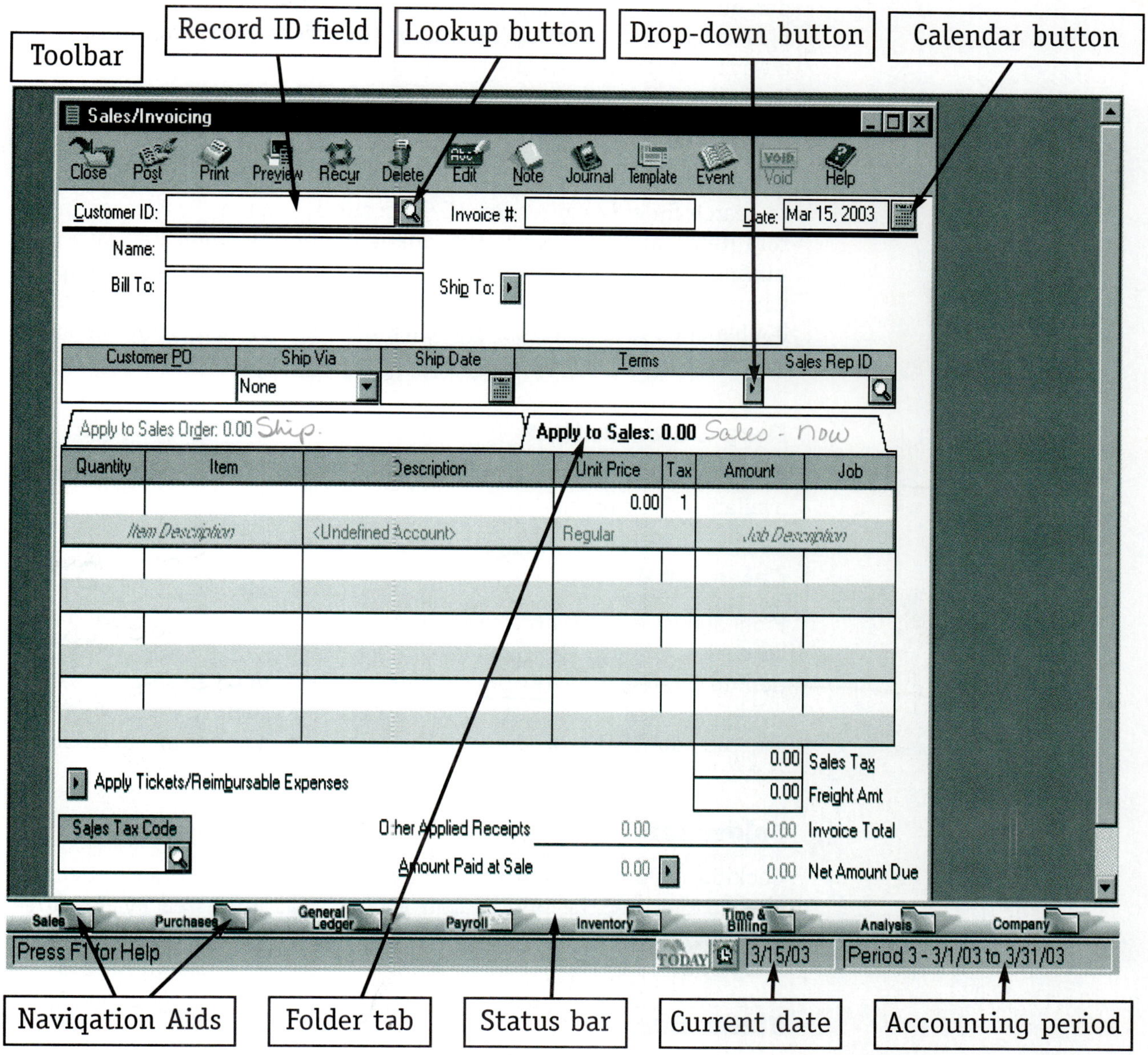

Figure 1–8 Components of a data entry window

Toolbar

The toolbar is at the top of the window. It contains icons representing the types of commands you can execute in this window. You can select any of the buttons to perform a function. See the Appendix for descriptions of all buttons.

Record ID Field

In some record ID fields, you will see +? next to the I-bar cursor: The plus sign indicates that you can add a record such as a customer, vendor, employee, and so on. The question mark indicates that you can display a list of all existing records of this type. The plus sign may not always appear; this means that you cannot add a record in this area. You will add records in Chapters 2 and 3. Record IDs are case sensitive.

Lookup Button

To search for existing records (G/L accounts, vendors, customers, inventory items, and so on), use the lookup list button (indicated by a magnifying glass). A list of available records for that data type will appear when you click on the lookup button. To choose a record from the list, double-click it or select it, and click **OK.** You can also open the list by right clicking in the field or by typing a ?.

Drop-Down Button

An arrow next to a field indicates that a drop-down list of choices is available. Click on the arrow to open the list.

Calendar Button

From almost every *Peachtree* window, you need to select or enter a date. Whenever you see the calendar button next to a date field, click it to pop up a calendar. After the calendar displays, you can select a date. If you right click in any date field, the pop-up calendar will also appear. The calendar that pops up is for the accounting period (displayed in the status bar).

Folder Tab

Clicking on a folder tab in a window will display additional fields or change the way the information you enter is processed by *Peachtree*. You will use the different tabs on the Sales/Invoicing window in Chapter 5.

Status Bar

The status bar is at the bottom of the window. It displays useful information about a field when you click on a field with the mouse. It also shows the current date and the accounting period that *Peachtree* is in.

SHORTCUT KEYS

It is up to you whether you want to use the mouse or the keyboard to select things in *Peachtree*. Shortcut keys enable you to perform common operations with a minimum of keystrokes. For example, for any Windows program, if there is an underlined letter in the menu or option you want to select, hold down the ALT key and the underlined letter to select the item. If the ALT and letter shortcut opens additional options, simply press the underlined letter to select an item. The shortcut feature is not case sensitive.

The following list gives you additional shortcuts to use in *Peachtree Accounting*.

CTRL + Letter Shortcuts

CTRL+X	Cut
CTRL+C	Copy
CTRL+V	Paste
CTRL+E	Delete Record
CTRL+F	Find
CTRL+D	Find Next
CTRL+N	New Company
CTRL+O	Open Company
CTRL+B	Back Up Company
CTRL+R	Restore Company
CTRL+P	Print what is displayed

Note

Pressing CTRL in conjunction with another key (for example, CTRL+O) will behave differently when the Peachtree Today window is open and active. In these cases, the shortcut keyboard combination will behave as it would in Microsoft Internet Explorer.

Function Keys

F1	Displays online Help topic for the current window
SHIFT+F1	Changes mouse pointer to What's This Help selector
F5	Saves records and posts (or saves) transactions in certain windows
F10	Toggles between the open window and menu bar
CTRL+F4	Closes current document window
ALT+F4	Closes the application window
CTRL+F6	Moves to next window
SHIFT+CTRL+F6	Moves to the previous window

Computer Shopping

Walk into any discount or retail electronics outlet or an office supply store and you will see a proliferation of computers and "peripherals." Where do you start figuring out what your company needs? Open any computer publication and you will encounter a barrage of advertisements and an unlimited amount of computer jargon. With names like IBM Aptiva, Presario, iMac, OptiPlex, and Gateway G6-450, how do you decide what to buy? Should you buy at the store, or buy mail order? Should you sign on to the Internet and purchase directly from a manufacterer, an online distributor, or retailer?

To make a wise investment, consider three essential questions: How fast is the processor speed? How big is the memory and hard disk? How expensive is the price tag? Computers with more memory and faster speed are going to cost the most. Peripherals (an extra-large monitor, DVD-ROM, etc.) will add more cost. However, if you are going to use the computer for more than three hours a day, a 17-inch screen or a high-resolution display will increase your comfort level and justify the increased cost. So you can see that how you are going to use the computer is the basis for making your decision.

Consider, too, what your future updating needs might be. Each new year comes with a fresh lineup of faster processors, larger hard drives, and "who-would-have-thought-it" features. Buy, then, as much processing power as you can afford, thus adding to the life of your machine and increasing its ability to be upgraded. Or plan on replacing your system totally again in two or three years. It is clear that in this industry, a top machine will remain top for no more than a year.

Name ______________________________ Date ______________

SUMMARY OF KEY POINTS

1. Accounting is the process of recording and reporting financial data.
2. *Peachtree Complete Accounting* allows you to perform all the steps in the accounting cycle, from recording business transactions to generating reports.
3. In a computerized accounting system, data is entered only one time.
4. You can navigate the various components of *Peachtree* by using Peachtree Today, the menu system, or the Navigation Aids.
5. Shortcut buttons in each information window, as well as keyboard shortcuts, enable you to work more efficiently.

CHAPTER REVIEW AND APPLICATIONS

Completion

In the space provided, write the word or words that best complete each statement.

1. Accounting is the process of recording, processing, and reporting financial events of a business.
2. The record of a business transaction is referred to as a Source document.
3. The keyboard shortcut to open the **File** menu is alt & F4.
4. To change the way decimals are entered in the data you enter in *Peachtree*, open the Options menu.
5. To search for existing records, use the lookup button next to the record ID field. Cust vendors.
6. An arrow next to a field indicates that a dropdown list is available. A/R payments
7. The accounting period is identified in the Status bar.
8. The F1 function key displays the **Help** topic for the open window.
9. The toolbar contains icons that represent commands you can perform in the open window.
10. In date fields, you can type in a date or use the Calendar button.

Chapter 2

New Company Setup

OBJECTIVES

When you have completed Chapter 2, you should be able to:

1. Set up accounting files for a company.
2. Back up *Peachtree* files.
3. Enter beginning balances for accounts in the General Ledger.
4. Display and print a trial balance.

In Chapter 1, you explored some of the components of *Peachtree Complete Accounting 8.0* using a sample company that *Peachtree* provides just for that purpose—getting acquainted with the software. However, before a company can enter its accounting data in *Peachtree* or any other computerized accounting program, the company files must be created. This is called setting up the company.

When you set up a company, you provide *Peachtree* with basic information such as name and address. You also create the chart of accounts, establish the accounting periods, and choose when transactions will be posted.

SET UP A NEW COMPANY

The computer practice activities in this chapter will lead you through the setup process in Peachtree and will also review fundamental acconting principles as you make choices about how the company's accounting data will be handled. Be sure to complete each of the following steps to set up files for Anderson Consulting Company.

Step 1 Start Peachtree Accounting if it is not already running.

Step 2 Choose *Set up a New Company* from the Peachtree Accounting Startup menu. If Peachtree is already running, select *New Company* from the **File** menu.

Step 3 Read the basic information on the Welcome screen of the New Company Setup wizard.

Step 4 Select the **Next** button to continue with the setup. The Company Information window will open.

In this window you will enter basic information such as your company name, address, and phone numbers. In the *Business Type* field, use the drop-down list to identify whether your company is a corporation, sole proprietorship, etc. The *Federal Employer ID* is the ten digit number that identifies your company when you pay federal taxes. You will also specify the numbers that identify your company for state taxes and state unemployment.

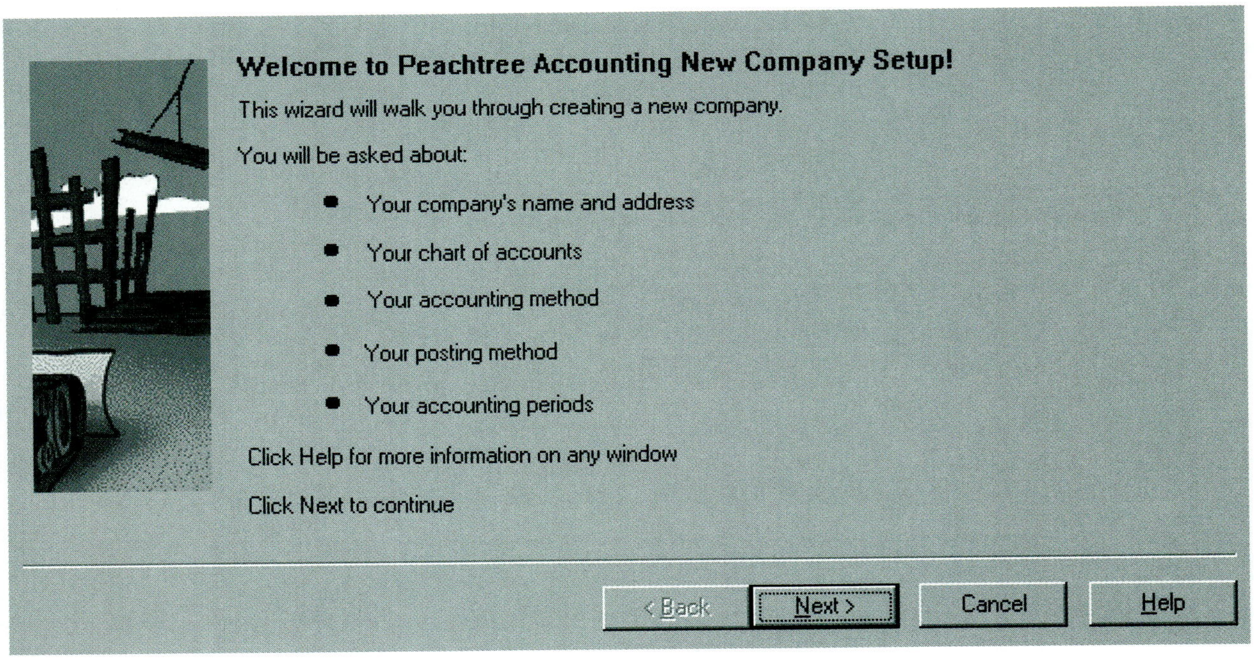

Figure 2–1 New Company Setup wizard

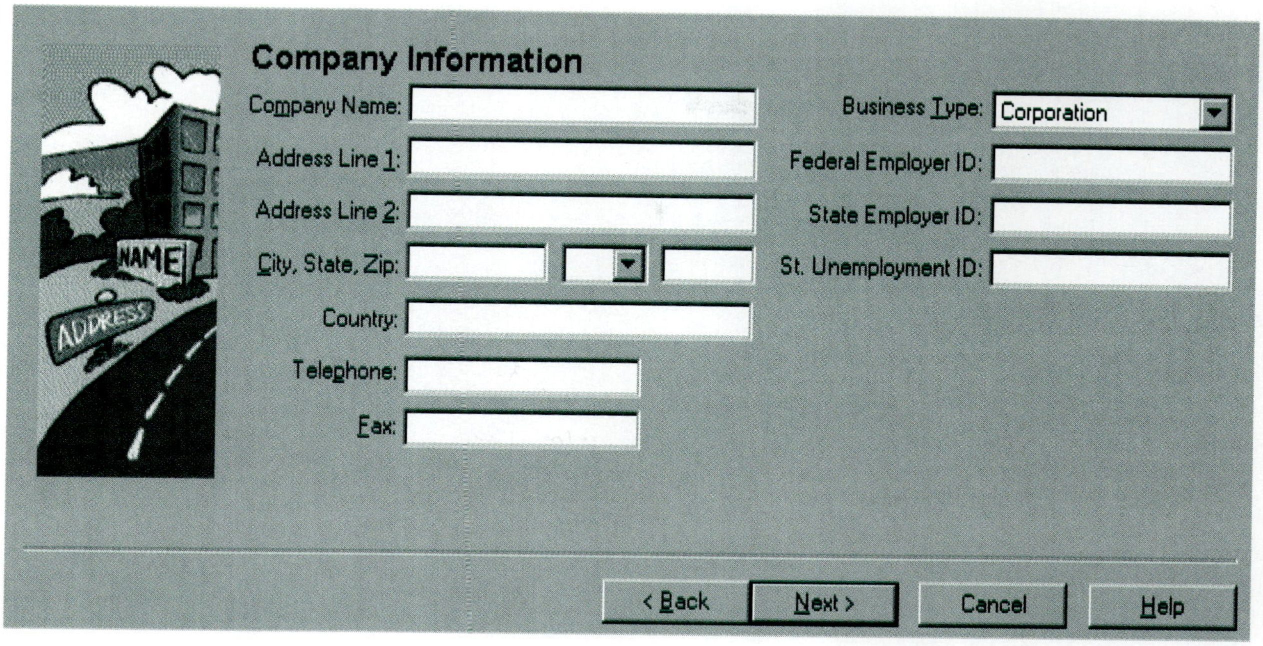

Figure 2–2 Company Information window

Step 5 Set up the accounting files for the following business. Use either the Tab key or the Enter key to move to the next field.

Name and Address:	Anderson Consulting Company 4465 Oakland Boulevard Indianapolis, IN 46236
Telephone	318-555-8647
Fax	318-555-6955
Business Type	Sole Proprietorship
Federal Employer ID	35-7788588
State Employer ID	34-1258887
St. Unemployment ID	34-6575

Step 6 After you have entered information in each field of the Company Information screen, select **Next.**

You can choose to copy one of the many sample charts of accounts in *Peachtree*, or you can create your own. Most companies choose to copy one of the samples and then add and/or delete accounts after the setup has been completed.

Note

If you make a mistake, go back one or more steps by using the **Back** button.

Step 7 Be sure that *Set up a new company based on one of several sample companies* is active.

Step 8 Select **Next.**

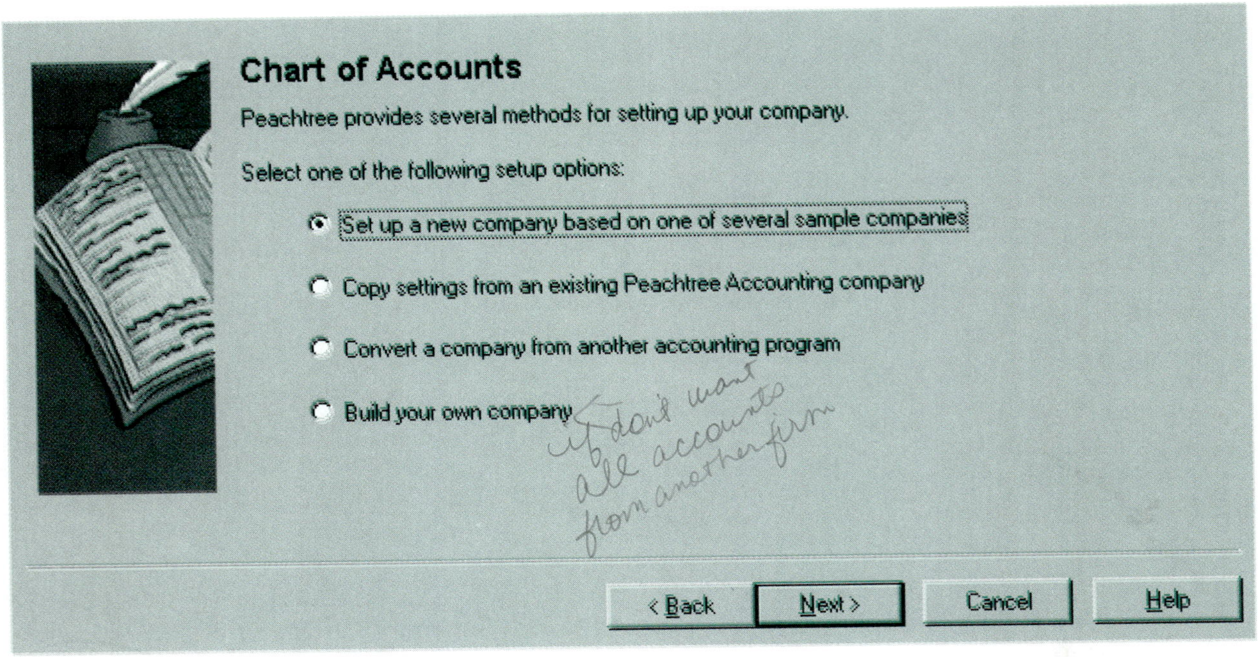

Figure 2–3 Setting up the Chart of Accounts

Since the company you are setting up is a consulting company, scroll through the available Charts of Accounts list and select *Consulting Company*. Notice that you can choose to learn more about consulting companies as an industry and view the sample Chart of Accounts.

Step 9 Select Consulting Company from the *Available Charts of Accounts* list.

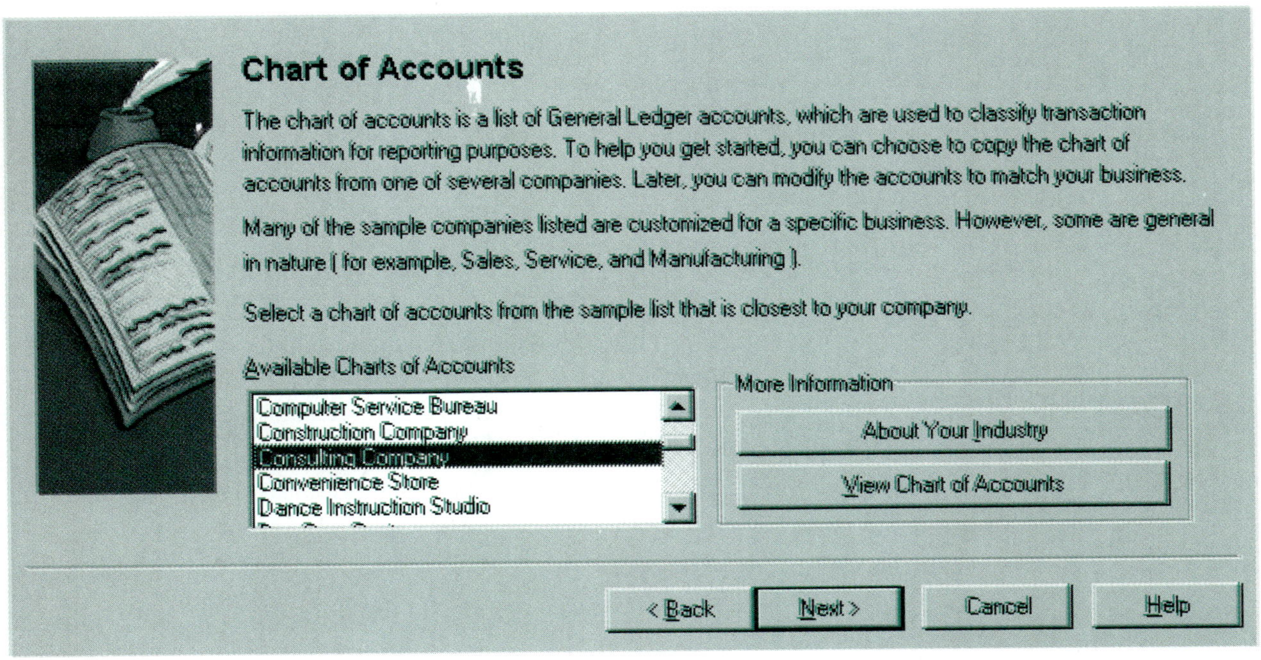

Figure 2–4 Select a Chart of Accounts

Step 10 Select **About Your Industry** and read about the services a consulting company provides to its customers.

Step 11 Select **Next.**

The next step in setting up a company is to select the accounting method. Most companies use the accrual method. Accrual method means that you record income when earned (generally when you invoice customers) and expenses when incurred (generally when you receive bills). If you choose the cash method, you would not record income until you received the cash from the customer, nor would you record expenses until you actually paid them.

Up to this point, the choices you have made in the setup process can be changed. The accounting method, however, cannot be changed after you finish the setup.

Step 12 Choose *Accrual.*

Step 13 Choose **Next.**

Peachtree gives you a choice between real-time posting and batch posting. If you choose real-time posting, transactions will be posted when you save them. Batch posting is more like what you would do in manual accounting, when transactions are posted at a specified time rather than when each transaction is journalized. Most companies use real-time posting. Transactions can be edited or corrected after they have been posted in either method.

Step 14 Choose *Real Time.*

Step 15 Choose **Next.**

On this screen you will indicate how you want to divide your fiscal year. Most companies divide the fiscal year into monthly accounting periods.

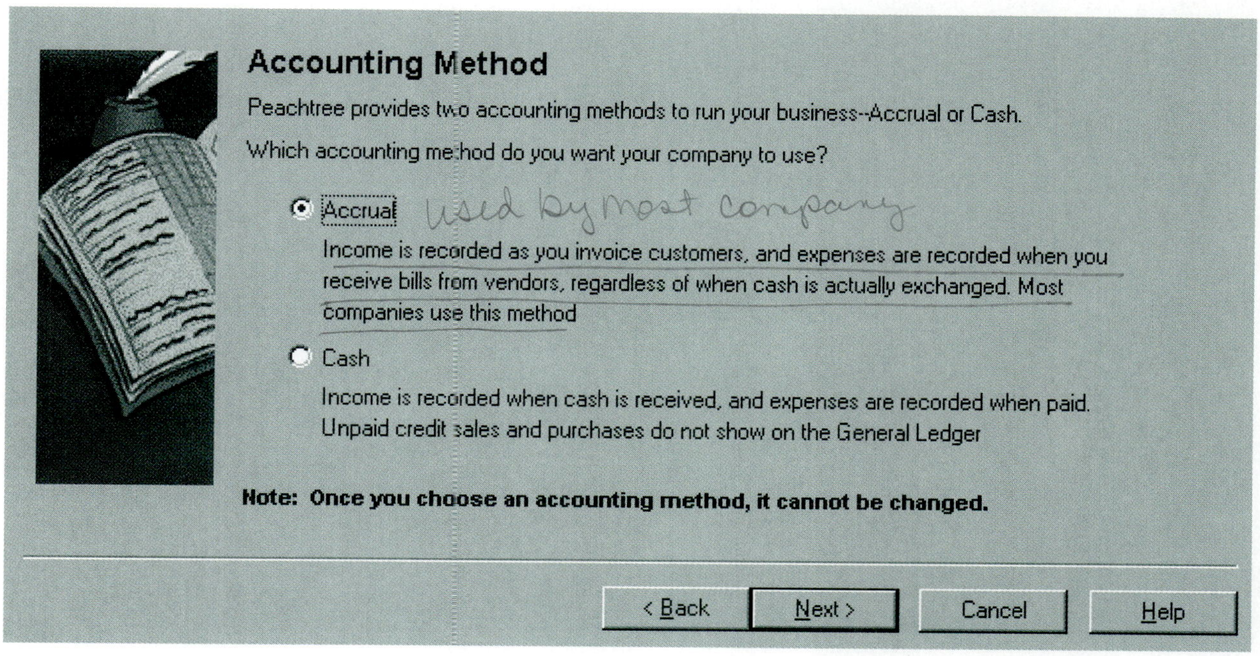

Figure 2–5 Select an accounting method

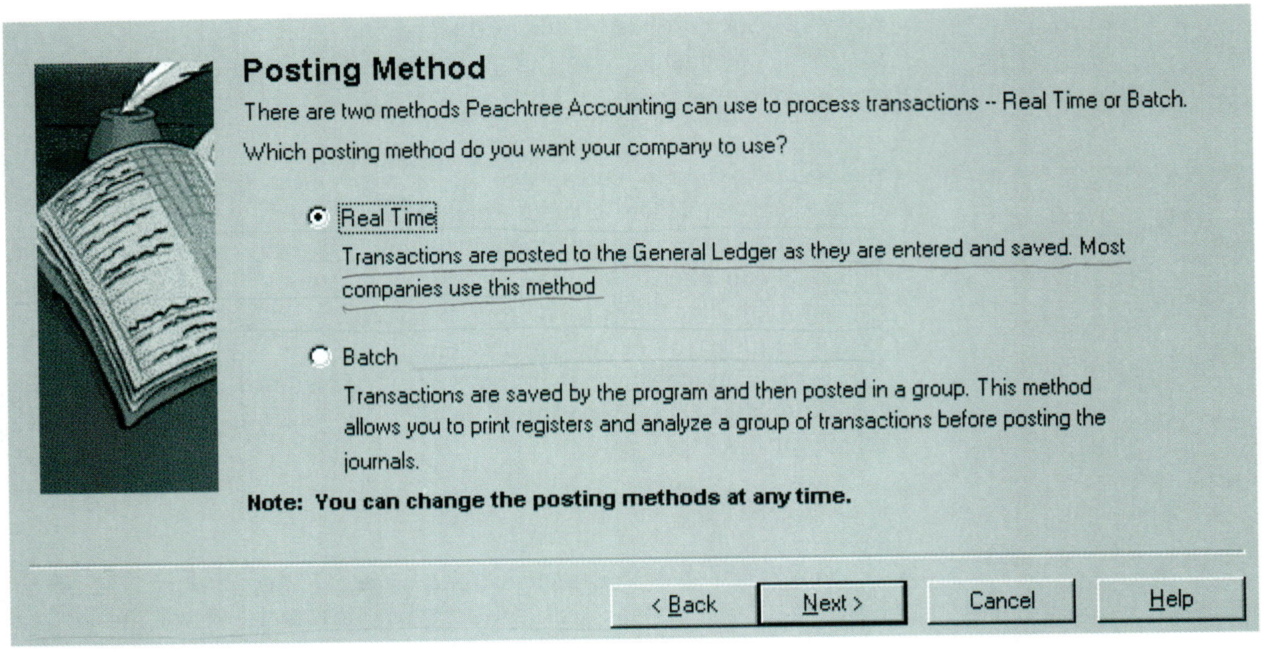

Figure 2–6 Select a posting method

Step 16 Choose to use *12 monthly accounting periods.*

Step 17 Choose **Next.**

A company will not necessarily begin using Peachtree Accounting at the beginning of a fiscal year. On the Monthly Accounting Periods screen, you will indicate when the fiscal year begins and indicate when you will begin entering data in *Peachtree*.

Step 18 Choose January of the current year as the beginning of the fiscal year and the first month in which you will enter data.

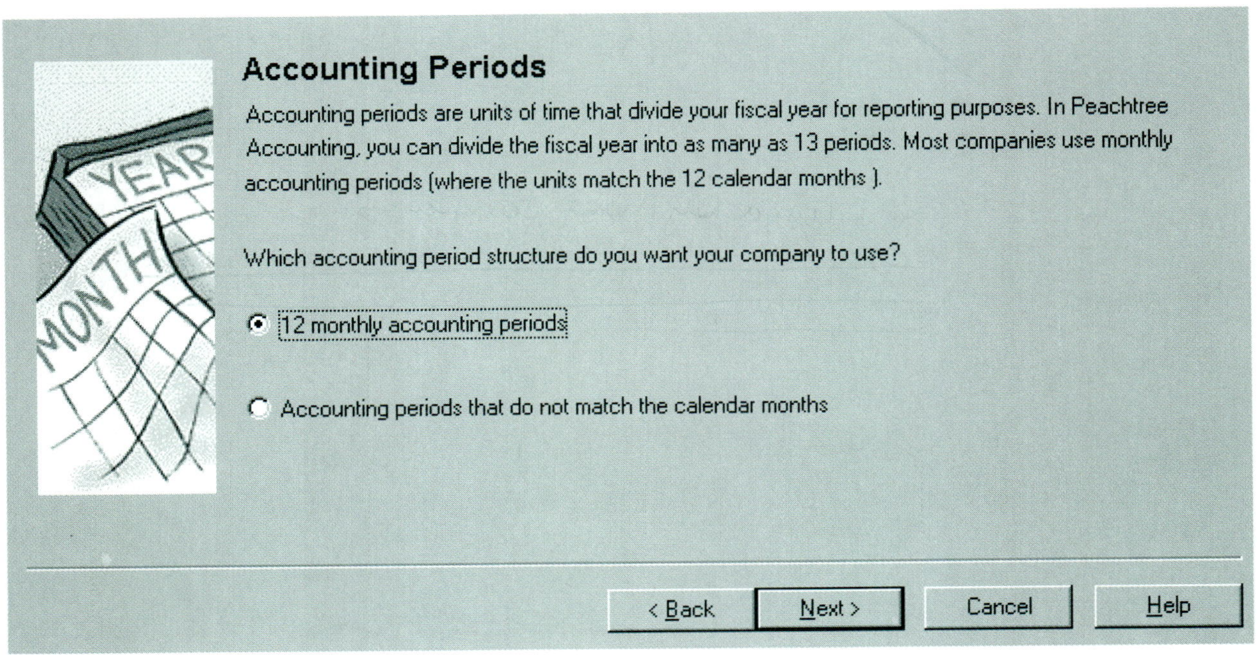

Figure 2–7 Choose 12 monthly accounting period

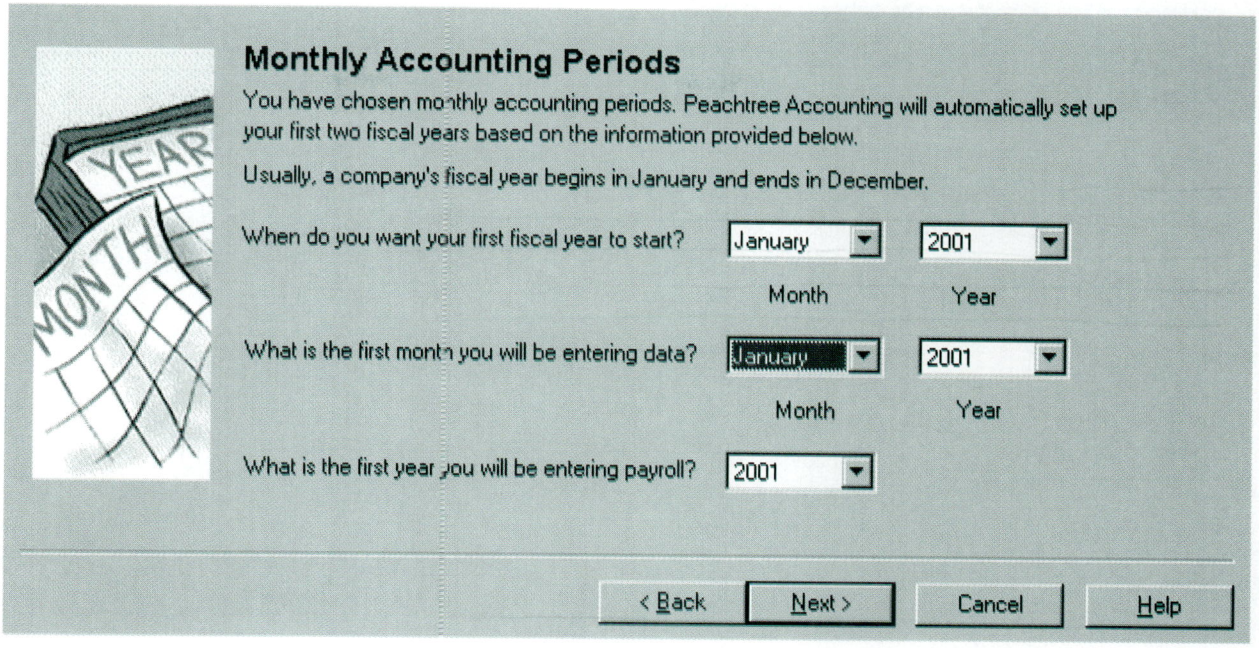

Figure 2–8 Choose when you will begin entering data

Step 19 Use the current year as the first year in which you will enter payroll information.

Step 20 Select **Next.**

Step 21 In the Defaults window, accept the standard defaults. You can change these at any time. You will have an opportunity to change some of these in later chapters of this text.

Step 22 Choose **Next** to complete the new company setup process.

Step 23 Choose to follow the Setup Checklist.

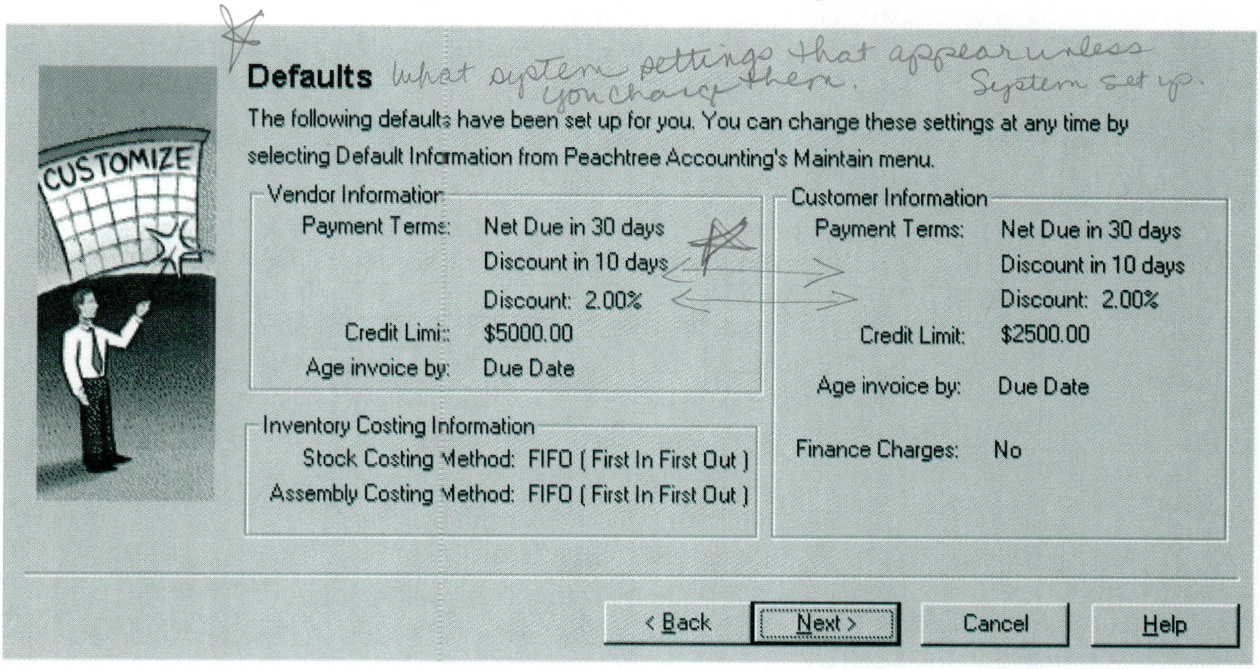

Figure 2–9 Default settings for vendors, inventory, and customers

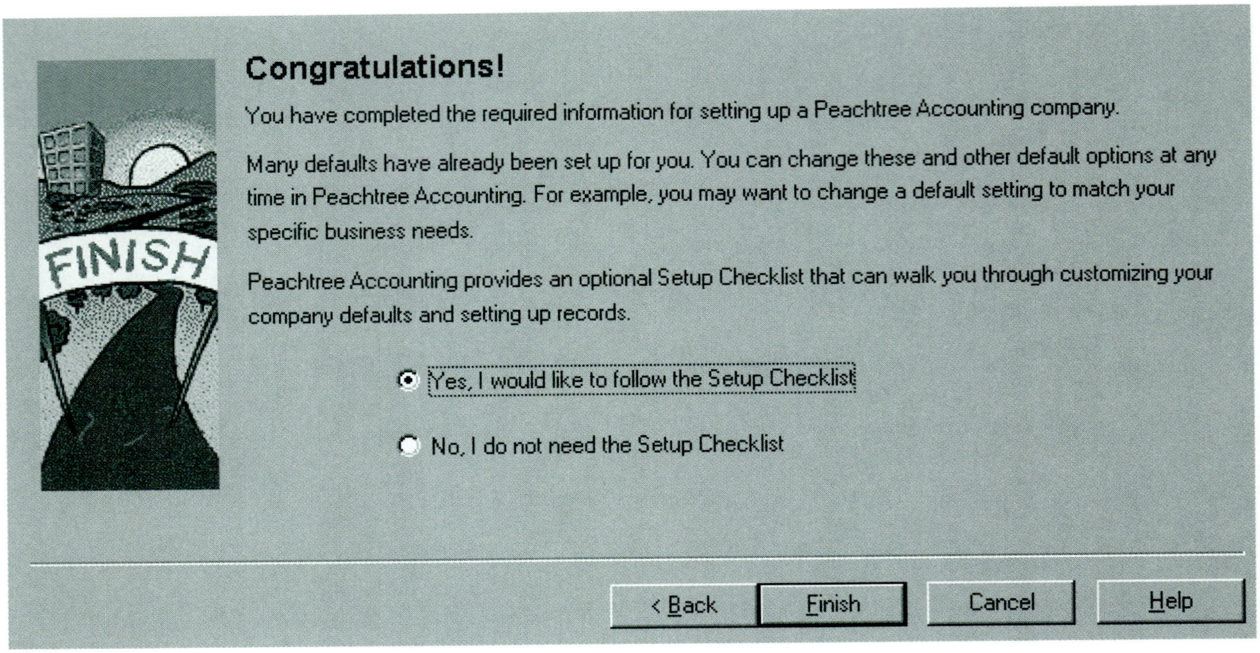

Figure 2–10 Completion of setup

Step 24 Choose **Finish.**

After you indicate that you are finished with the new company setup, you will be asked to wait while files are created that reflect the choices you made during the setup. Several windows will flash on your screen during the automatic file creation. When the files are complete, the Setup Checklist (Figure 2–11) will open.

Once the New Company Setup is complete, you can start entering default information, or you can start using *Peachtree* to enter accounting data and change the standard defaults, as you need to. You will use the Setup Checklist to guide you through the process of setting up company default information as you learn about the various functions in *Peachtree* (such as employee, vendor, and customer records, as well as beginning balances). The checklist will track your progress by marking each task when you complete it.

Notice that the defaults you accepted during the setup process have a check mark next to them. Each time you select a function from the setup checklist, you will be asked whether you want to mark the task as complete when you exit the task. If you select the Yes button, a check mark is placed next to the task. You can still access options that are check marked. The check marks merely track your progress toward setting all the defaults that are specific to your company.

Step 25 Select **Close** at the bottom of the Checklist window.

Step 26 Click **OK** when the reminder appears that you can return to the checklist at any time.

Step 27 Close the Peachtree Today welcome screen.

You should set up the Chart of Accounts and beginning balances for the General Ledger accounts first, but after that it is not important in

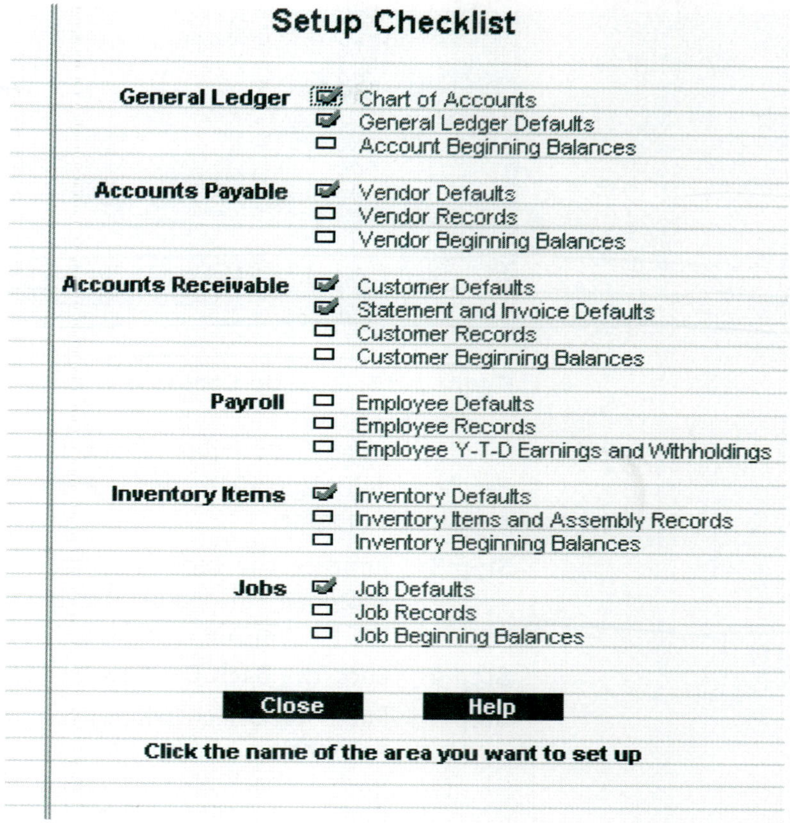

Figure 2–11 Setup Checklist

what order you complete the other items on the checklist. This text will present Accounts Receivable after you have learned to enter beginning balances for the General Ledger accounts and edit your Chart of Accounts.

Back Up

The files for Anderson Consulting Company that you created in this chapter will remain on the hard drive of the computer you used during the setup process. It is important that you also back up your company data files on a regular basis in case hard drive information is accidentally deleted or corrupted. You can then restore your data, if necessary. In this tutorial, be sure to back up at the end of each work session.

There are several methods for backing up your company data. You can back up company data within *Peachtree Accounting,* and your company data files and customized forms will be backed up using the *Peachtree* format. As a student, you will most likely save your *Peachtree* backup to a diskette.

Back up your file for Anderson Consulting Company.

Step 1 From the **File** menu, select Back Up. *Peachtree* displays the Back Up Company window.

Step 2 Select the reminder check box if you want to be prompted to back up in a specified number of days.

Note

You can move a dialog box on the screen, but you cannot size it or use the menu while a dialog box is open.

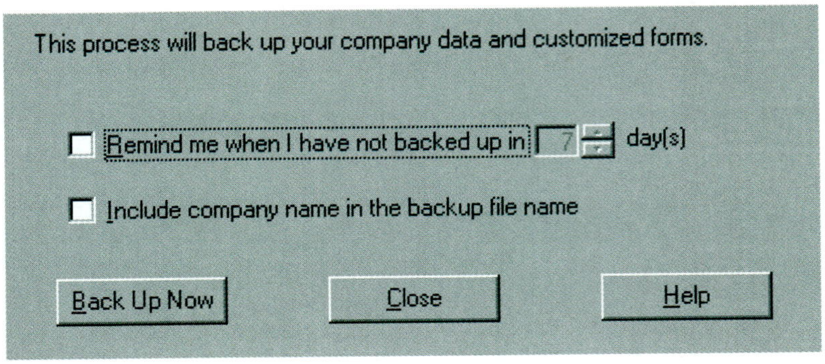

Figure 2–12 Back Up Company window

If the specified number of days has elapsed since your last backup, *Peachtree* will display a reminder message when you close the company or exit the program.

Step 3 Activate the *Include company name* check box if you want *Peachtree* to incorporate the company name in the name of the backup file it creates.

Step 4 Click the **Back Up Now** button.

Step 5 Enter or select where you want to save your *Peachtree* Accounting backup file (your floppy drive). If you are not ready to back up your data at this point, you can simply click **Close** and return to *Peachtree*.

> **Note**
> Depending on the quantity of data, the backup process may take a while to complete. Be patient and do not interrupt the process. If you interrupt the backup process, you might corrupt the data.

Step 6 In the *File name* field, enter the name for the backup copy. If you chose to include the company name (Figure 2–12), Peachtree will use the company name and the current system date. The extension .ptb is added to all backup files. You can change the file name if you want to.

Step 7 Click the **Save** button. *Peachtree* will tell you how much space is needed for the backup.

Step 8 Click **OK.** You will be prompted to insert your disk.

Step 9 Click **OK.** The system displays the progress of the backup until it is complete.

ENTER BEGINNING BALANCES

During the new company setup procedure, you chose to use a sample chart of accounts for Anderson Consulting Company. When you open the Maintain Chart of Accounts window and you have not yet posted any transactions, *Peachtree Accounting* assumes that you are entering beginning balances for your accounts when you select the Beginning Balances button. If you have previously posted transactions, *Peachtree* assumes that you are entering adjustments to your accounts for a period in a prior year.

During the new company setup procedure, you chose to use a sample chart of accounts for Anderson Consulting Company. You will enter beginning balances for Anderson Consulting Company in Problem 2-1 at the end of this chapter. You will need to be familiar with the following steps to complete that problem. The instructions use the Setup Checklist. You can also enter beginning balances from the General Ledger Navigation Aid or by selecting *Chart of Accounts* from the **Maintain** menu. You can enter the balances for Problem 2-1 at this time or return to these steps when you are ready to complete that problem.

Step 1 From the Maintain menu, choose *Setup Checklist.*

Step 2 Click on *Account Beginning Balances* in the General Ledger section of the checklist. The Select Period window will open. (see Figure 2–13)

Step 3 Select the period for which you want to enter beginning balances. Because Anderson Consulting Company will begin entering accounting data in January 2001, you will enter the balances as of January 1, 2001.

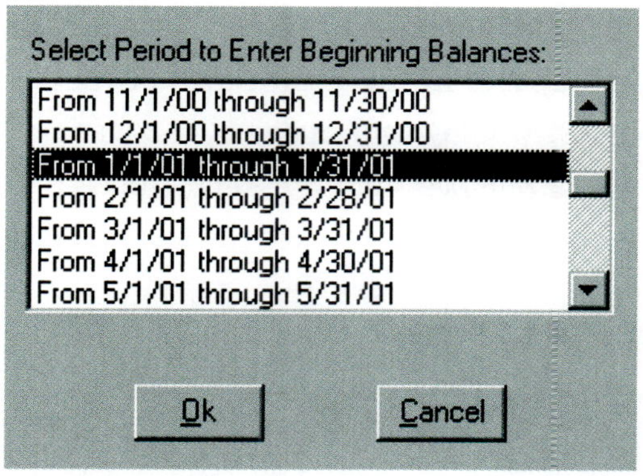

Figure 2–13 Select period for beginning balances

Step 4 Select **OK.** The Chart of Accounts Beginning Balances window will open.

Step 5 Click in the white cells of the grid to enter a balance. Asset and expense accounts have debit balances. Liability, equity, and income accounts have credit balances. If you scroll through the Chart of Accounts, you will see that the white cell is always in the appropriate column.

Step 6 Enter the amount of each account's balance.

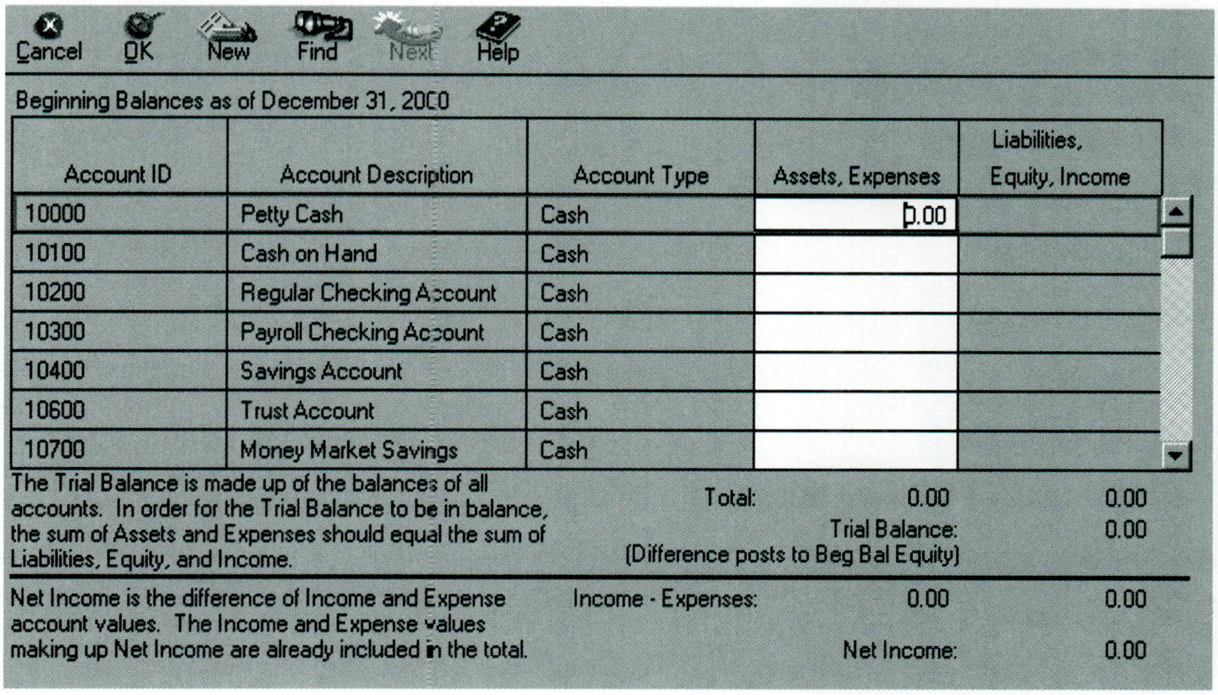

Figure 2–14 Enter beginning balances

Note

A running beginning balance is kept as you enter the account balances. If the beginning balances are not equal, Peachtree will create an equity account where the difference will be posted.

Step 7 Scroll down the list to be sure the amounts are correct.

Step 8 Select the **OK** button when you have entered all beginning balances. Peachtree will tell you that the journal entries for the beginning balances are being created.

Step 9 Check to see that *Beginning Account Balances* is now checked on the Setup Checklist.

PRINT A TRIAL BALANCE

A trial balance is proof that the debits and credits in the general ledger are equal. To print the trial balance,

Step 1 Open the General Ledger Navigation Aid.

Step 2 Select **General Ledger Reports** in the Report area of the folder. The Select a Report window will open.

Step 3 Select *General Ledger Trial Balance* from the Report list.

Step 4 Click the **Preview** icon on the toolbar to view the trial balance on the screen. The filter window will open.

Step 5 In the *As of Date* field, select Current Period.

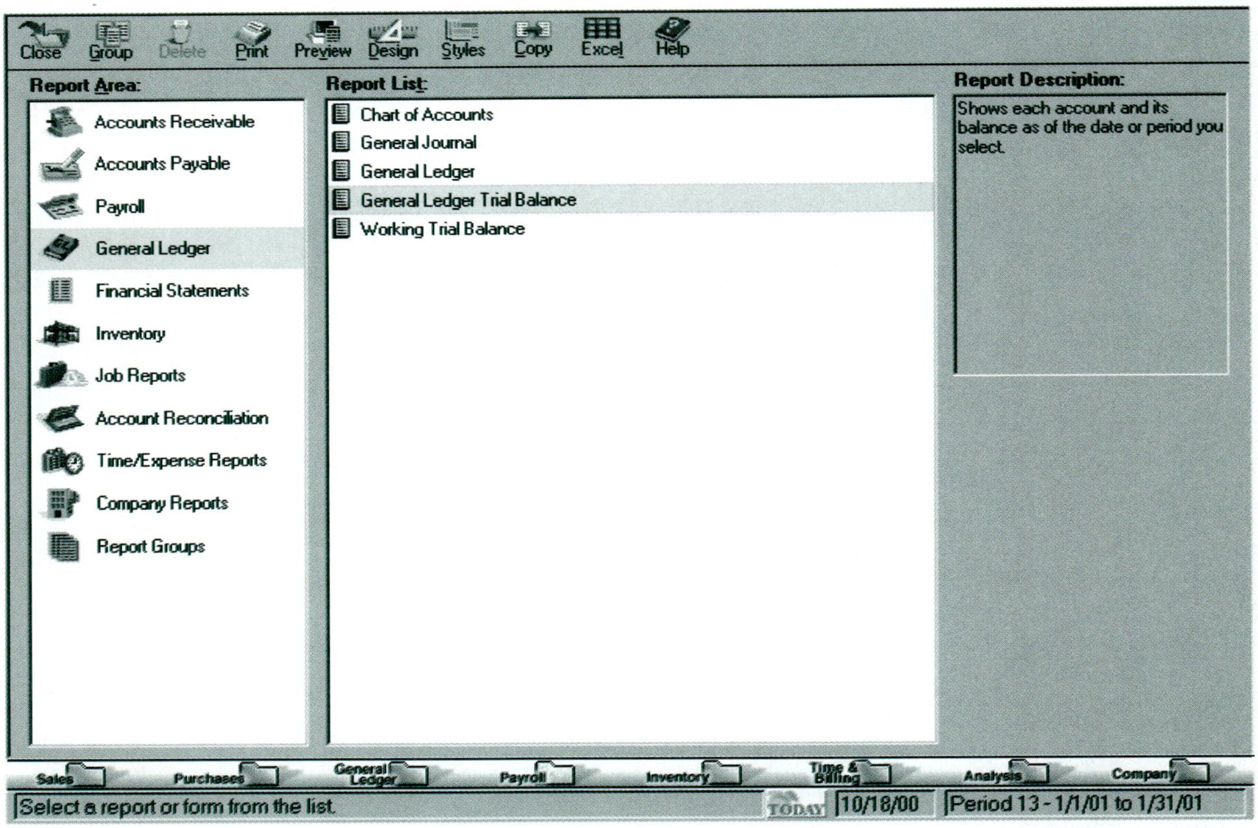

Figure 2–15 Select a report

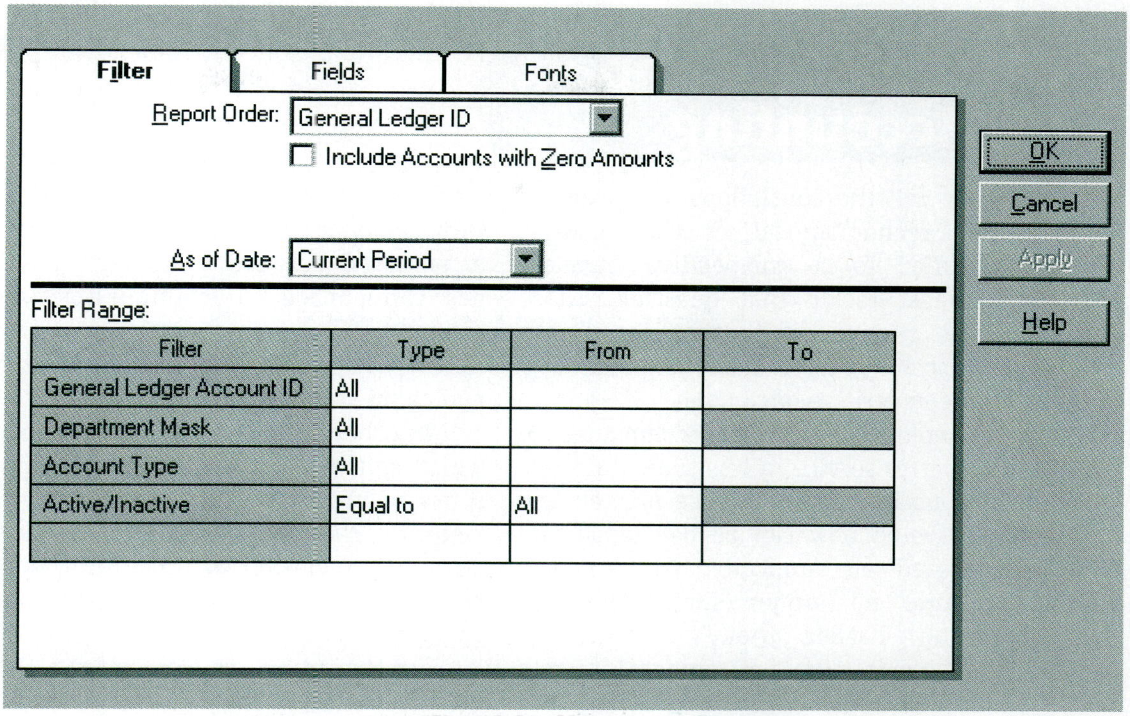

Figure 2–16 Select the date for the report

Step 6 Click **OK.**

Step 7 With the trial balance on the screen, click **Print.** Peachtree uses the last date of the current accounting period as the date for the trial balance.

Step 8 Close the Trial Balance window.

Step 9 Close the Select a Report window.

Technology's Impact On Accounting

How will the continuous advancement of technology affect the business world? To be competitive, business owners must tackle that question. Those firms that survive will be those having an ongoing strategy to leverage new technology for a competitive advantage.

Technology can enable companies to provide better service in less time. Accounting information that was once printed and hand delivered now can be developed and disseminated electronically. As a result, accountants no longer simply just do accounting. Rather, today's accountants provide a wide range of services to help businesses compete in a global economy.

One of the most notable technological advances has been distributive computing. Distributive computing means dividing the computation chores required to execute an application among several locations. For example, an accounting department can manage desktop systems from a location and turn personal computers (PCs) into centrally managed network computers. The business can manage and maintain a network of computers from a single location, a strategy that reduces the cost and complexity of managing stand-alone PCs.

Another notable advance is the speed at which software programs run. For example, software programs run approximately 30% faster on Windows 98 than on Windows 95. As each generation of accounting application software is developed, it becomes easier to use and requires less hard-drive space.

For the future, we can expect technology to impact both personal finance and accounting. People will contiue to use elecctonic tax filing and receive "next-day" refunds. There will be unprecedented continued growth in E-commerce, online banking, and investing.

SUMMARY OF KEY POINTS

1. The Peachtree Accounting New Company Setup wizard will guide you through each step of the setup procedure.
2. You can use either the Enter key or the Tab key to move to the next field on any Peachtree data entry window.
3. Peachtree provides sample Charts of Accounts for many types of businesses that you can use in setting up your company files.
4. The accrual method of accounting is used by most businesses.
5. Peachtree allows you to use either batch or real-time posting.
6. You can return to the Setup Checklist after the initial setup has been completed.
7. Accounting data should be backed up at the end of each work session.
8. A running balance is maintained as you enter beginning balances.

*inter*NET CONNECTION

Technology and software developments for business progress daily. Keep current with the lastest news courtesy of AccountingNet. They offer accounting students an up-to-date news and research digest, study help, job leads, and professional contacts. You can look them up at **http://www.accountingstudents.com/**. Keeping current on *Peachtree* is easy, too, by news sent to you through **http://www.peachtree.com**.

Name ______________________________ Date ______________

CHAPTER REVIEW AND APPLICATIONS

Completion

In the space provided, write the word or words that best complete each statement.

1. Entering them in the appropriate column of the Beginning Balances window will enter asset and expense account balances as ____________ balances.
2. Income is recorded when the cash is actually received in the ____________ method of accounting.
3. Transactions are posted to the ledger when you save the entry in the ____________ posting method.
4. Peachtree Accounting divides the fiscal year into ______ accounting periods.
5. You can access the Maintain Chart of Accounts window from the ____________ menu or the ____________ Navigation Aid.
6. When you enter information in a data entry window, use the ____________ or ____________ key to move to the next field.
7. If you record income when you invoice your customer, you are using the ____________ method of accounting.
8. All of the information that you enter in New Company Setup can be changed later ***except*** the ____________.
9. If you choose to have Peachtree add the company name to your backup file, it will also add the ____________ ____________ following the company name.
10. The file extension for a Peachtree backup file is ____________.

Problem 2-1

Applying Your Knowledge

Instructions

Step 1 Start Peachtree Accounting if it is not already running.

Step 2 Change the system date to January 31, 2001.

- From the **Options** menu, choose *Change System Date.*
- Use the drop-down calendar or key in the system date.
- Select **OK.**

Step 3 Use the Setup Checklist to enter the beginning balances for the following accounts for Anderson Consulting Company.

Name ______________________ Date ______________

Account ID	Account Description	Amount
10000	Petty Cash	100.00
10200	Regular Checking Account	2,500.00
10300	Payroll Checking Account	4,500.00
10400	Savings Account	15,000.00
10800	Certificates of Deposit	25,000.00
11000	Client Fees Receivable	1,200.00
15000	Furniture and Fixtures	10,000.00
15100	Equipment	17,000.00
15200	Automobiles	5,200.00
15500	Building	125,000.00
20000	Accounts Payable	35,000.00
39005	Retained Earnings	170,500.00

Step 4 Mark the Beginning Balances as complete on the checklist.

Step 5 Print a General Ledger Trial Balance. Peachtree dates the trial balance the last day of the current accounting period.

Step 6 Back up your files for use in Chapter 3.

OPTIONAL PROBLEM 2–2

Instructions

Set up the accounting system for a business that you own or would like to own.

Chapter 3

Maintaining Accounts

OBJECTIVES

When you have completed Chapter 3, you should be able to:

1. Restore a backup file.
2. Edit the Chart of Accounts.
3. Add and edit customer records.
4. Add and edit vendor records.
5. Print a Chart of Accounts, Customer List, and Vendor List.

When you created the files for Anderson Consulting Company in Chapter 2, you chose to use *Peachtree Complete Accounting's* sample Chart of Accounts for a consulting company. When you choose this option, it is unlikely that the Chart of Accounts will exactly fit your needs. You will want to edit the Chart of Accounts and delete those that your company will not use. You may also need to add some additional general ledger accounts and create accounts for your customers and vendors. You will complete those tasks in Chapter 3.

As noted in Chapter 2, it is important to back up your accounting data on a regular basis. In actual practice, the backup file is used only if the data on the hard drive is accidentally deleted or corrupted. However, when you are working in a computer lab, you will need to restore the data from your last work session to ensure that you are actually working from your files and that no one has made changes since your last work session.

RESTORE COMPANY FILES

To restore a backup file, you will complete the following steps.

Step 1 Insert the disk containing the backup file in the computer's floppy drive (usually drive A).

Step 2 Open the **File** menu.

Step 3 Choose *Restore*. The Open Backup File screen will open.

Step 4 Select the file location (floppy drive A) and highlight the file you want to restore.

Step 5 Select **Open**.

Step 6 You will be warned that restoring a file will overwrite the existing data for that company.

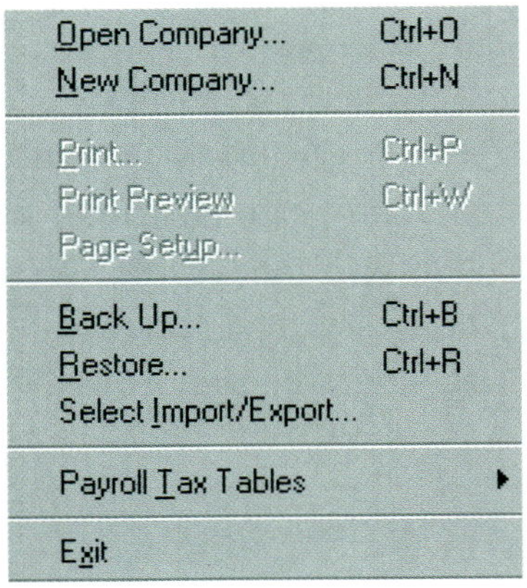

Figure 3–1 Restore a backup file

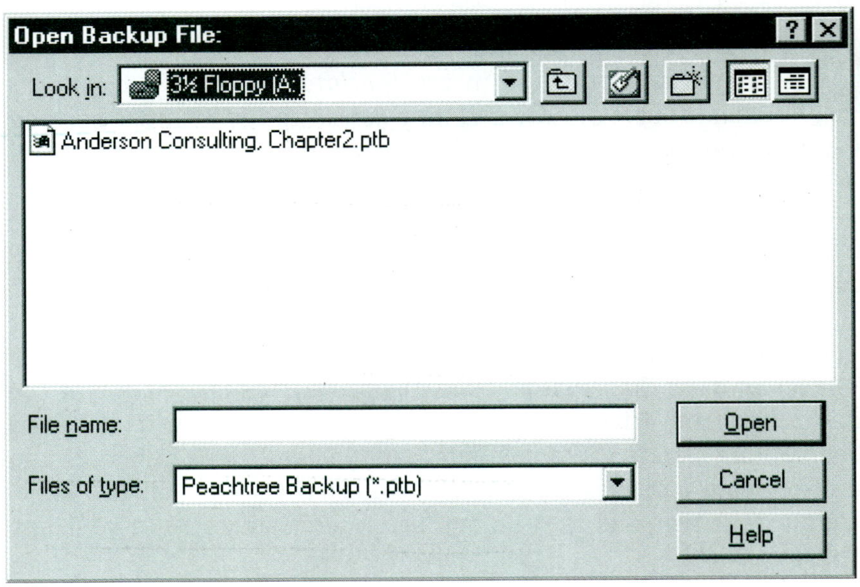

Figure 3–2 Restore a backup file

Note
You are instructed to backup your data at the end of each chapter, and before restoring a new file. If you omit that step, your data may be lost.

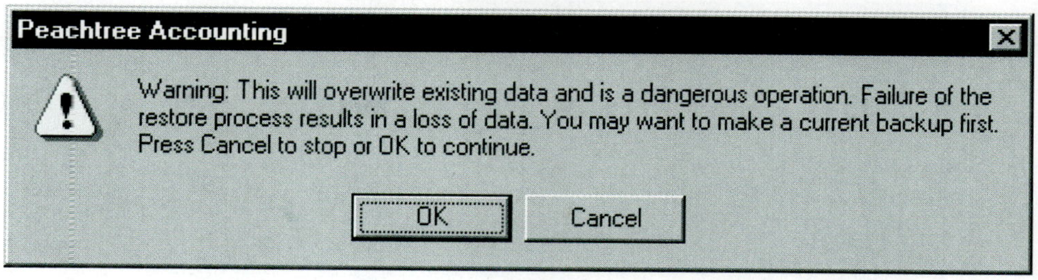

Figure 3–3 Overwrite warning

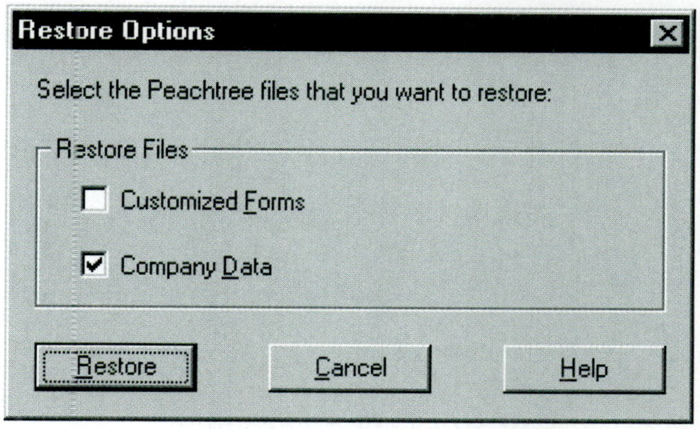

Figure 3–4 Choose files to restore

Step 7 Choose **OK.** You will be prompted to select the file you want to restore.

Step 8 Verify that the *Company Data* field is checked.

Step 9 Click **Restore.**

Step 10 The restore process will be tracked on your screen and the file will open.

MAINTAIN CHART OF ACCOUNTS

The Chart of Accounts is nothing more than a list of places to enter accounting transactions. It contains an *Account ID,* sometimes called an account number; a *Description* for each account; and an *Account Type* code. *Peachtree* Accounting allows a great deal of flexibility in designing the chart. However, using a sample, as you did for Anderson Consulting Company, saves a great deal of time.

The following instructions will help you modify the Chart of Accounts for Anderson Consulting Company. You will practice editing an existing account, deleting an existing account, and adding a new account to the sample Chart of Accounts you chose during the setup procedures. You will further edit the chart in Problem 3–1 at the end of this chapter.

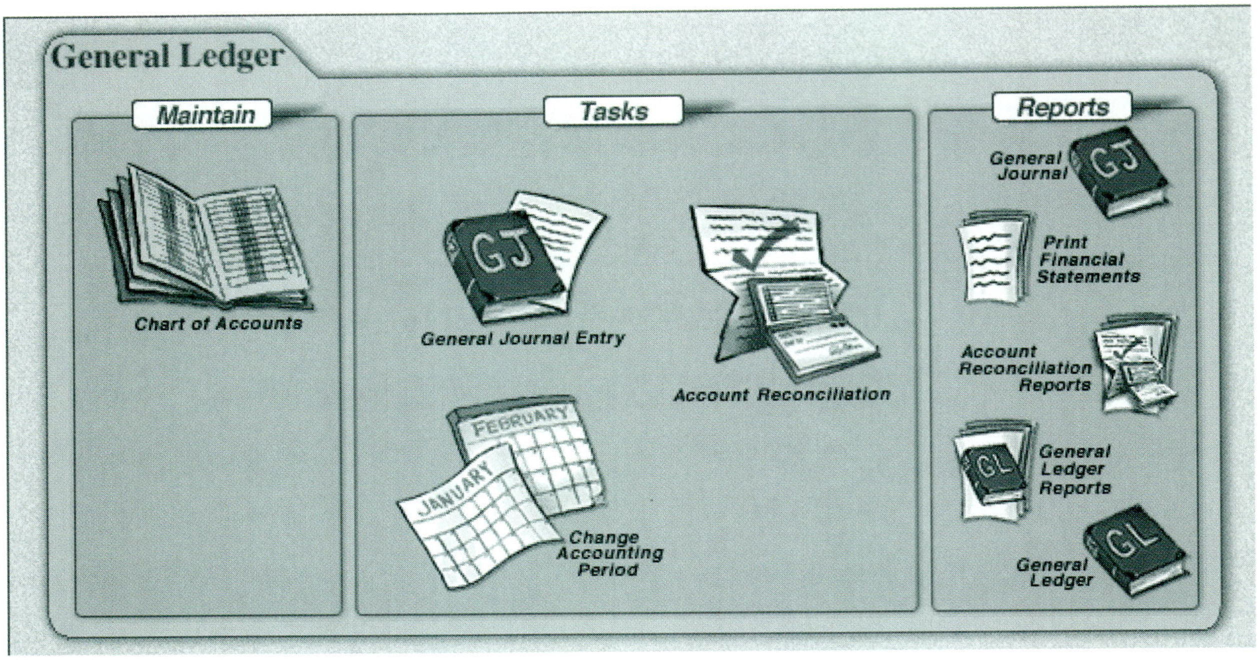

Figure 3–5 General Ledger Navigation Aid

Edit an Existing Account

Step 1 Open the General Ledger Navigation Aid.

Step 2 Select *Chart of Accounts* from the **Maintain** section of the Navigation Aid. The Maintain Chart of Accounts window will open.

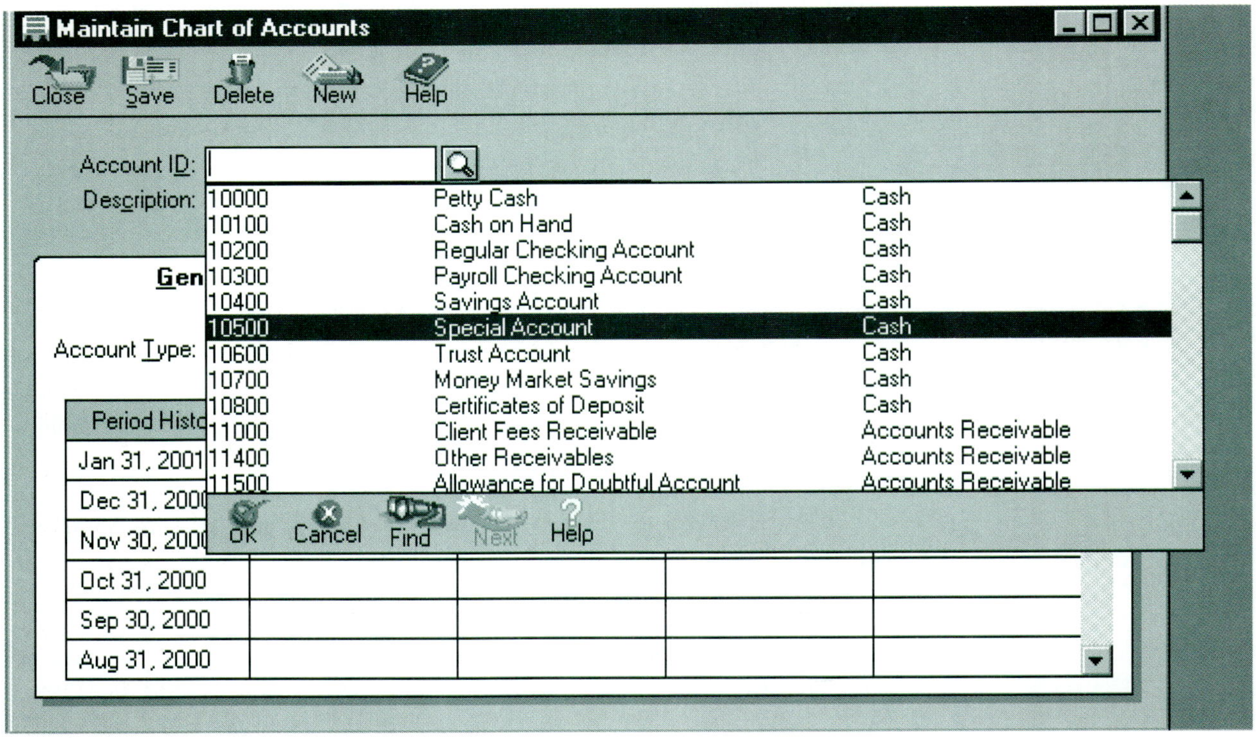

Figure 3–6 Select the account to edit

Step 3 Use the lookup button to view the Chart of Accounts.

Step 4 Scroll down to the account you want to edit.

Step 5 Press the Enter or Tab key.

Step 6 Make the desired change in the account information.

Step 7 Click the **Save** icon to record the change.

Change the account description for Account 10500 to Special Savings Account.

Delete an Account

In order to delete an account from the Chart of Accounts, there must be no transactions posted to the account.

Step 1 Open the Maintain Chart of Accounts window.

Step 2 Enter the *Account ID* or use the lookup box to select the account that will be deleted.

Step 3 Press Enter or Tab to access the account information.

Step 4 Click the **Delete** toolbar button.

Step 5 Answer **Yes** when asked if you are sure that you want to delete the account.

Delete 65000 Employee Benefit Programs Expense.

Make an Account Inactive

If an account has transactions posted from a previous period and you want to delete the account, you will make an account inactive to ensure that no further transactions are posted. After two year-end closings, the account will be deleted.

Step 1 Open the Maintain Chart of Accounts window.

Step 2 Select the account you want to make inactive.

Step 3 Select the *Inactive* check box to the right of the description.

Step 4 An X in the check box marks it as inactive.

Add an Account

You can set up an account by using the General Ledger Navigation Aid, by selecting *Chart of Accounts* from the **Maintain** menu, or by using the *Accounts* fields on most windows accessed from the Tasks menu. The account ID determines how the account is identified and sorted in the Chart of Accounts list, lookup lists, transactions, and reports. Most charts of accounts are set up with specific account types grouped together.

The *Description* field can contain up to 15 alphanumeric characters to name the account. Once you enter an ID and select the **Save** button, you cannot change or edit the ID; however, you can change the description. The names you give to accounts are important. You want to use names that are easily understood by everybody who uses the system.

The selection that you make in the *Account Type* field defines how the account will be grouped in reports and financial statements. They also control whether the account is closed at the end of the fiscal year.

Note

The *Account Type* field contains more choices for account classification than what you may have used in manual accounting. Scroll through the list to be sure that you select the type that most accurately identifies the information that will be entered in the account you are adding to the chart.

Step 1 Open the General Ledger Navigation Aid.

Step 2 Select the *Chart of Accounts* icon.

Step 3 Key in the account number in the *Account ID* field.

Step 4 Enter the account name in the *Description* field.

Step 5 Select an account classification from the drop-down list in the *Account Type* field.

Step 6 Click the **New** icon on the toolbar to add another account, or click the **Save** icon.

Add 65000 Educational Expense to the Chart of Accounts.

Chart of Accounts Report

The Chart of Accounts lists all the accounts you have set up for your company. A printed listing of the accounts may be helpful in analyzing transactions that you will enter in Peachtree Accounting. You can generate a Chart of Accounts listing from the **Reports** menu or from the Reports section of the General Ledger Navigation Aid.

When the Select a Report window opens (see Figure 2-15), there are two methods of displaying the Chart of Accounts. If you double-click *Chart of Accounts* in the Report List, the chart will be displayed. You can also select the **Preview** toolbar button. With this approach, a dialog box will open (Figure 2-16) that allows you to filter the information included in the report and/or change the order of the accounts. You will practice filtering report information in Chapter 10.

Display the Chart of Accounts for Anderson Consulting Company.

MAINTAIN CUSTOMER ACCOUNTS

Use the Maintain Customers/Prospects window to enter, change, and store information about companies and people to whom you sell goods and services. You can also enter information about companies and people with whom you would like to do business (prospects). You can maintain a great deal of information about each customer. The more data you enter when you set up the customer account, the more efficient it will be when you enter accounting transactions for the customer.

Since you are still setting up the records for Anderson Consulting, use the Setup Checklist to open accounts for customers.

Step 1 From the **Maintain** menu, select *Setup Checklist.*

Step 2 Under the Accounts Receivable heading, click the Customer Records setup option. The Maintain Customers/Prospects window will open. This window is slightly different from the one that opens from the **Maintain** menu or the Sales Navigation Aid.

Header

The header fields are located above the folder tabs of the Maintain Customers/Prospects window. This is where you enter lookup information about the customer—the Customer ID, name, and status.

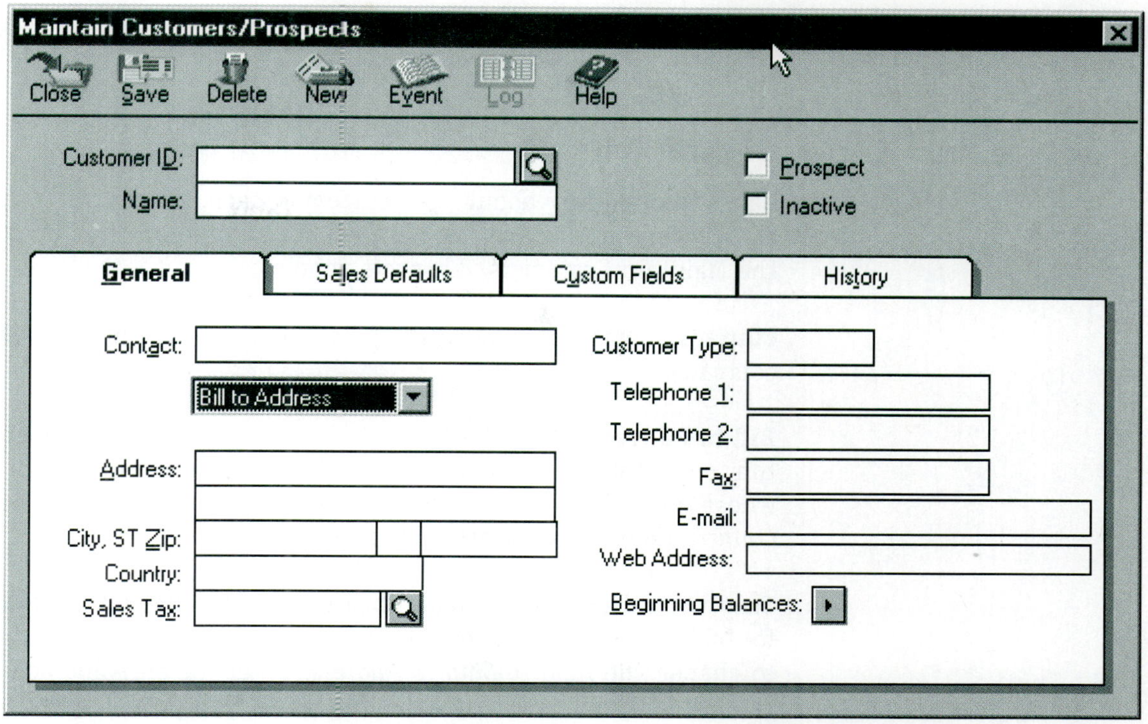

Figure 3–7 Maintain Customers/Prospects window, General tab

> **Note**
> You can also open the Maintain Customers/Prospects window from the Sales Navigation Aid. Open the folder and click the **Customers** icon.

Customer ID: By assigning each customer a unique identification number, you can quickly access the customer's record when you enter accounting information. You can enter up to 20 alphanumeric characters for a Customer ID. It is important to use a consistent and logical coding system.

An example of a coding system might be the first three letters of the company name or an individual's last name. In case of duplicates, a sequential number can be added. Thus, Trent Manufacturing Company would be assigned ***Tre*** or ***tre*** as the Customer ID. The code is case sensitive, so that codes Tre and tre are seen as two different Customer IDs. In the customer listing, numbers sort before letters, and capital letters sort before lowercase letters. You may find it easier to work with lowercase codes. For existing customers, you can use the lookup button to select the customer you want.

Name: The *Name* field will accept up to 30 alphanumeric characters for a customer's name.

Prospect: Potential customers are called prospects. If you check this box, this company or person is not included on any Accounts Receivable reports. However, if you generate an invoice for the prospect or clear the check box, the prospect will be considered a regular customer.

Inactive: If a customer's account is checked as inactive, Peachtree will display a warning if you try to make a sale to that customer. Inactive customers will be deleted when you close the fiscal year.

Complete the header information for a new customer:

- *ID* (Ste)
- *Name* Stephens Office Supply

General Tab

Basic information about the customer such as contact, customer's address, and phone and fax numbers are entered on the General tab in the Maintain Customers/Prospects window.

Contact: Enter the name of the person you most often deal with in the company.

Bill to Address: With the *Bill to Address* showing next to the arrow button, enter the name of the individual or department in the company to whose attention the bill is directed as well as the address. Complete the *Country* field for international customers.

Ship to Address: If the individual or company has different addresses for billing and shipping, use the drop-down arrow next to *Bill to Address* to change the field to *Ship to Address*. Enter the shipping address. You can enter up to nine ship to addresses. If you do not enter a ship to address, the bill to address will be the default shipping address.

Sales Tax: Enter the sales tax code that applies to the customer. You can use the lookup button to display tax codes that have been set up. You have not yet set up tax codes for Anderson Consulting Company.

Customer Type: This field can be used to group customers. For example, you may want to track sales to customers by region. You do not have to enter information in this field. It can be used as a filter, however, for Accounts Receivable reports.

Telephone 1, Telephone 2, Fax: Enter the telephone number or numbers, including extensions. Enter the fax number.

E-mail: You can enter up to 64 characters in the *E-mail* field. If you open the Maintain Customers/Prospects window from the Sales Navigation Aid or the menu rather than from the Setup Checklist, an E-mail icon will appear to the right of this field. Clicking on the E-mail icon will open a new message window with this address.

Web Address: Enter the customer's Web site address (up to 64 characters). Clicking the Web icon on subsequent Maintain Customers/Prospects windows will launch your default Internet browser and take you directly to the customer's Web site.

Beginning Balances: To enter beginning balances for customer records, select the arrow button. The customer's beginning balance consists of outstanding invoices. You can enter the numbers of the actual invoices you sent to the customer. You will need to be sure that the total amount of the Customer Beginning Balances is equal to the amount you entered as a beginning balance in Chapter 2.

Enter the following General tab information for Stephens Office Supply.

- *Contact* James Stephens
- *Bill to Address* 1588 East Clinton Avenue, Indianapolis, IN 46235
- *Telephone* 318-555-9852
- *Fax* 318-555-9898
- *E-mail* jstephens@prodigy.net
- *Web Address* www.stephensoffice.com
- *Beginning Balance* Invoice 00-965, dated 12/15/00; P.O. 98525; Amount $249; Account 11000 Client Fees Receivable

Sales Defaults

Use the Sales Defaults tab to establish sales transaction defaults for each customer record. You can change any information that you enter on this tab when you enter transactions, if necessary.

Sales Rep: If a particular sales representative is responsible for contacting this customer, enter the representative's name here.

G/L Sales Acct: Enter the General Ledger account for the default sales account for this customer. This is normally an income account.

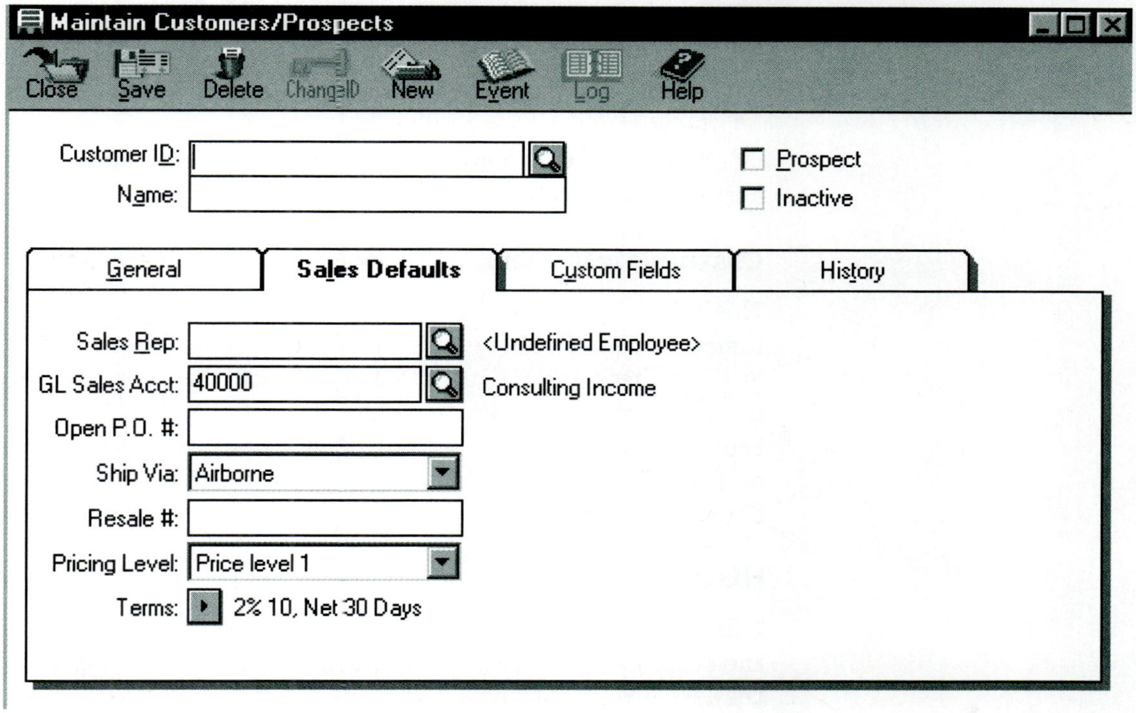

Figure 3–8 Sales Default tab

Open P.O. #: You can enter a standing purchase order number you can use for this customer. This will be the default on *Sales Orders* and *Sales/Invoicing* windows.

Ship Via: You can select the primary shipping carrier you want to use to ship items to this customer. Whatever you select here will default for sales transactions you enter for this customer.

Resale #: If this customer purchases items for resale, enter the resale number here. Resale numbers are required by most states for businesses that sell taxable goods. It enables the business to sell goods to other businesses for resale without charging a tax, or to buy goods from other businesses for resale without paying a tax. If a customer intends to resell your goods, enter the customer's resale number (also called seller's permit) here.

Note

Any of the defaults that you enter in this window can be changed later or changed for a specific sales transaction when you enter the transaction.

Pricing Level: You can have multiple sales price levels for inventory items and for service items. This field would be used if the company offered a lower price if a customer purchases in larger quantity.

Terms: You can choose to use the standard default payment terms (2/10, n/30) that were accepted during the company setup (Figure 2–9), or set up a unique set of terms for this customer. To change the payment terms for this customer, select the *Terms* button and uncheck the *Use Standard Terms* field. Fill in the appropriate terms. The *Credit Limit* field is on the Customer Terms window.

Enter the following Sales Default tab information for Stephens Office Supply.

- *GL Sales Acct* 40000 Consulting Income
- *Ship Via* US Mail
- *Terms* Net 30 days
- *Credit Limit* $3,000

When you have finished filling in the information, select the **Save** button on the toolbar.

Custom Fields Tab

This tab contains five custom fields that you can set up for each customer. Custom fields are used to track specific information that your business needs about its customers. Peachtree already provides fields to record most common business data, but you may want to maintain information that does not fit in any of the fields on the General or Sales Defaults tabs. Custom fields let you set up and store that data.

History Tab

This tab is for display purposes only. Based on transactions posted to the customer's account, this tab will tell you such things as the date of the last invoice, statement, and payment received as well as the year-to-date and period-to-date sales history for the customer.

Note

You can type + or double-click inside the Customer ID field of any task (transaction) window and the Maintain Customers/Prospects window will open.

Customer List Report

The Customer List identifies all the customers that you have set up for your company. A printed listing of the customers with their ID may be helpful in analyzing transactions that you will enter in Peachtree Accounting. You can generate a Customer List from the **Reports** menu or from the Reports section of the Sales Navigation Aid.

From the **Reports** menu, select *Accounts Receivable.* When the Select a Report window opens, double-click *Customer List* in the Report List. The chart will be displayed.

Display the Customer List for Anderson Consulting Company.

MAINTAIN VENDORS

You will use the Maintain Vendors window to enter, change, and store information about the companies and people from whom you purchase goods and services. The Maintain Vendors window can be accessed from the Vendors Records section of the Setup checklist, by choosing *Vendors* from the **Maintain** menu, or by clicking the **Vendors** icon in the Purchases Navigation Aid.

Many of the fields in the Maintain Vendors window are similar to those in the Maintain Customers window. The following discussion focuses on those that differ from the Maintain Customers window.

General Tab

Account #: This is the code the vendors use to identify your account with them. Since many vendors request that you include this number on your checks or any correspondence to them, it is important that you have the number readily available.

Vendor Type: You can use this field to group vendors. For example, if you use some vendors for service and some for products, you could enter *Service* or *Product* in this field. The field is case sensitive and is limited to eight characters.

1099 Type: Use the drop-down arrow to select the type. If the vendor is an independent contractor to whom you pay more than $600 a year, you are required to issue a Form 1099 to the vendor at the end of the fiscal year. If you pay more than $10 in interest to the vendor, you must issue a 1099.

Enter the following vendor information.

• *Vendor ID*	Tho
• *Name*	Thomas & Bernard, Inc.
• *Contact*	Brian Bernard
• *Account #*	An6546
• *Address*	587 South Hamilton Avenue, Indianapolis, IN 46225
• *1099 Type*	Independent Contractor
• *Telephone*	318-555-7471
• *Fax*	318-555-6521
• *Beginning Balance*	Invoice 00-4588; dated 12/28/00; $4565.00

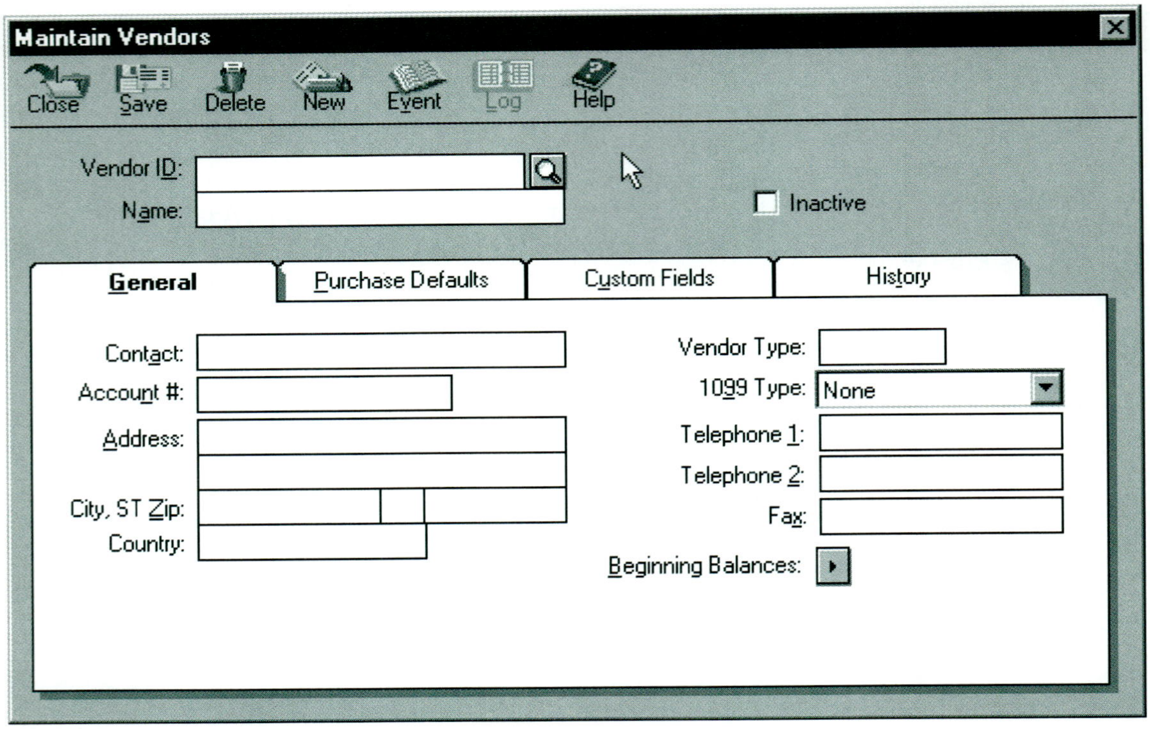

Figure 3–9 Maintain Vendors window

Purchase Defaults Tab

Purchase Acct: Enter the account number to which most purchases from this vendor are posted.

Tax ID#: If the vendor receives a 1099, you must enter the vendor's tax ID number in this field.

Note

The History tab will show that the company has been a vendor as of the date that you enter the beginning balance. If you want to enter a different date on the History tab, it must be entered prior to entering the beginning balance.

Enter the following for Thomas & Bernard, Inc.

- *Purchase Acct* 68500 Legal and Professional Expense
- *Tax ID* 31-4567441
- *Ship Via* Courier
- *Terms* Net 30 days

Vendor List Report

The Vendor List shows all vendor records that you have entered for your company. A printed listing of the vendors can be sorted by Vendor ID or by name. Sorting by ID is the default. You will use other sorting options in Chapter 10. You can generate a Vendor List from the Reports menu or from the **Reports** section of the Purchases Navigation Aid.

Display the Vendor List for Anderson Consulting Company.

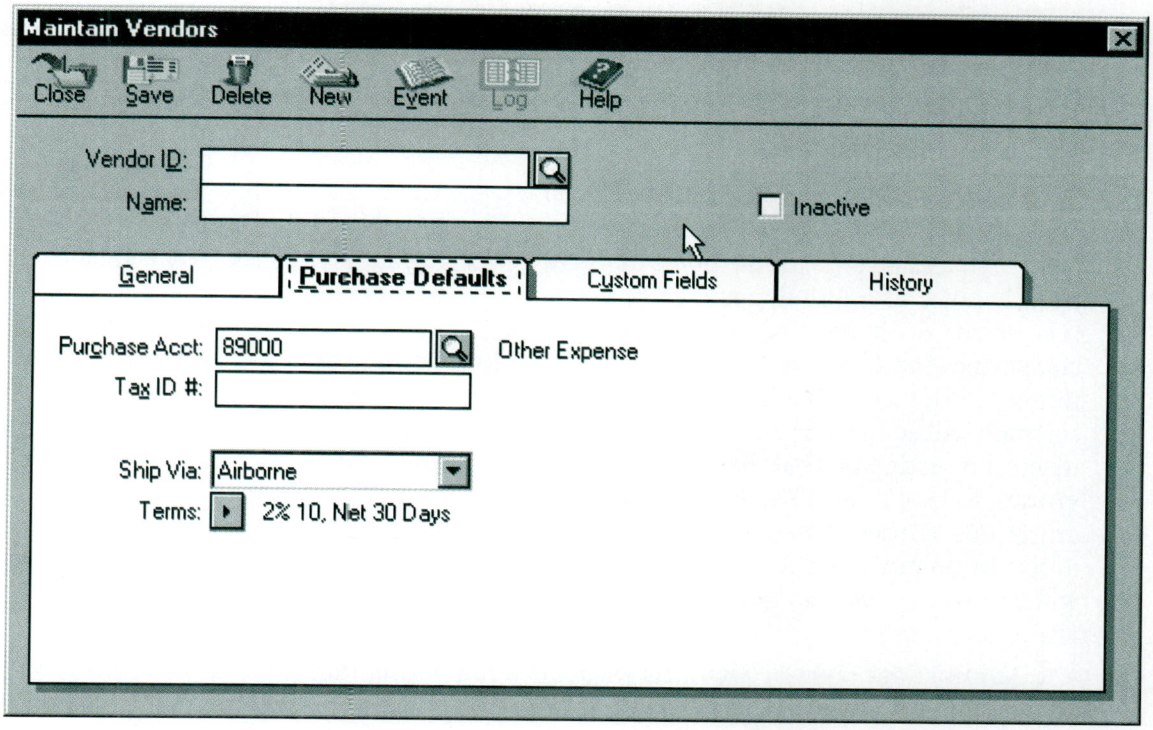

Figure 3–10 Purchase Defaults tab

Practice Safe Computing

You are extremely fortunate if you have never experienced the utter helplessness of losing hours of hard work because of a lost floppy disk or a system crash. So beware of the first rule of computing—back up your data at regular intervals. The second rule is: use antivirus software. Although antivirus software manufacturers estimate that data loss due to viruses is less than 10%, know that there are 15,000 viruses or variants. Installing an antivirus program and following a few rules will insure that you do not become part of the unlucky 10%!

1. Never accept disks or programs without checking them with an antivirus program.
2. Know the origin of any software you use, especially shareware and demos.
3. If you lend a disk to someone, check it when you get it back, before you use it again.
4. Do not leave a floppy disk in the disk drive longer than necessary.
5. Scan any program or document that you download before you open or read it. Beware of forwarded e-mail messages with attached files.
6. Keep your antivirus software up-to-date.

Remember that when you practice safe computing, you protect yourself as well as other users to whom you may send data.

SUMMARY OF KEY POINTS

1. Restoring a Peachtree Accounting backup file ensures that you are working with the appropriate accounting records.
2. You can easily modify a chart of accounts by editing, deleting, or adding accounts.
3. An account can be deleted only if it does not contain accounting entries.
4. An account with entries can be made inactive. The account will remain in the accounting records until two year-end closings have occurred.
5. Accounts are sorted in the Chart of Accounts according to the account type classification.
6. The information you enter in the Maintain Customers/Prospects window appears as default information in the Sales/Invoicing window (Chapter 5). This speeds up the data entry process.
7. Customer and Vendor IDs are case sensitive.
8. The beginning balances that you enter for customers and vendors must total the respective balances that you entered for Accounts Receivable and Accounts Payable.

*inter*NET CONNECTION

Do you have a question about setting up *Peachtree*? To troubleshoot that topic and others, locate **http://www.peachtree.com/support/peachfacts**.There you will find answers to frequently asked questions (FAQs) about accounts payable, accounts receivable, conversion, error messages, general ledger, import, installation and setup, network, payroll and year end, reports and printing, system, and other topics. The site also offers a search function to the FAQ.

Name ______________________________ Date ______________

CHAPTER REVIEW AND APPLICATIONS

Completion

In the space provided, write the word or words that best complete each statement.

1. Use the ____________ menu to restore backup files.
2. The Maintain Chart of Accounts window can be opened from the ____________ Navigation Aid, from the ____________ menu, or from the ____________ Checklist.
3. An inactive account will remain in the accounting records through ____________ fiscal year closings.
4. The order of accounts in the lookup list is determined by the ________field in the Maintain Chart of Accounts window.
5. You can generate a Chart of Accounts report from the ____________ menu or from the ____________ Navigation Aid.
6. An individual or company that you would like to do business with is called a ____________.
7. Peachtree allows you to maintain as many as ____________ *Ship to Address* choices.
8. If you want to group customers according to the region of the state, for example, you would enter a group category in the ____________ field of the Maintain Customers/Prospects window.
9. To enter the credit limit for a customer, open the ____________ window from the Maintain Customers/Prospects window.
10. The Vendor List report can be accessed from the ____________ Navigation Aid.
11. The total of the beginning balances you enter for all vendors must be equal to the amount you entered as the beginning balance of the ____________ account in the General Ledger.
12. The dates that appear on the information in the ____________ tab of the Maintain Vendors window cannot be changed after you enter the beginning balance.

Name ______________________ Date ______________

Problem 3-1

Applying Your Knowledge

Instructions

1. Delete the following accounts from the Anderson Consulting Company Chart of Accounts.

Account Number	Account Description
10500	Special Savings Account
11400	Other Receivables
14100	Employee Advances
15300	Other Depreciable Property
15400	Leasehold Improvements
17300	Accum. Depreciation-Other
17400	Accum. Depreciation-Leasehold Improvements
19100	Organization Costs
19150	Accum. Amortiz.-Org. Costs
24400	Client Escrow Funds
24900	Suspense-Clearing Account
39006	Owner's Contribution
60000	Default Purchase Expense
65500	Freight Expense
72500	Penalty and Fines Expense

2. Change the Account Description for the following accounts.

Account Number	Account Description
39005	Richard Anderson, Capital
39007	Richard Anderson, Withdrawals

3. Print a Chart of Accounts.
4. Back up your file or continue working with Problem 3-2.

Problem 3–2

1. Set up accounts for the following customers.
   - Accept the defaults for any fields not listed.
   - Use the first three letters as the Customer ID.

   Digital Solutions
   1489 South Main Street
   Marion, IN 46789

Telephone	318-555-8791
Fax	318-555-6352
Beginning Balance	Invoice 00-966, dated 12/16/00, $425
Credit Limit	$1,000

   Stacy's Creations
   892 Artists Circle
   Indianapolis, IN 46203
   318-555-2554

Beginning Balance	Invoice 00-968, dated 12/18/00, $326
Terms	Net 15 Days
Credit Limit	$1,000

   Flowers Family Practice
   965 South Broadway
   Indianapolis, IN 46209

Telephone	318-555-8741
Fax	318-555-5255
Beginning Balance	Invoice 00-967, dated 12/18/00, $200
Terms	3/10, Net 30
Credit Limit	$5,000

2. Print a Customer List.
3. Back up your company file or continue working with Problem 3-3.

Name ______________________________ Date ________________

Problem 3-3

1. Set up accounts for the following vendors.
   - Accept the defaults for any fields not listed.
   - Use the first three letters of the vendor's name as the ID.

Business Financial Solutions
485 West Broad Street
Columbus, OH 43215
614-555-8975

Beginning Balance	$19,335; Invoice 9858, dated 12/23/00
Purchase Account	64500 Dues and Subscriptions
Terms	Net 30
Credit Limit	$30,000

American Electric Power
550 East Main Street
Indianapolis, IN 46220

Purchase Account	78000 Utilities Expense
Terms	Due at end of month

WSXY Television
965 West Front Street
Indianapolis, IN 46225

Beginning Balance	$8,500; Invoice 1287, dated 12/28/00
Purchase Account	60100 Advertising Expense
Terms	Net 30

Lenox Conference Center
1589 Lenox Circle
Indianapolis, IN 46210

Beginning Balance	$2,600; Invoice 988, dated 12/15/00
Purchase Account	68500 Legal and Professional Expense
Terms	Net 30

2. Print a Vendor List.
3. Back up your accounting file.

Chapter 4

General Ledger

OBJECTIVES

When you have completed Chapter 4, you should be able to:

1. Describe the purpose of the General Ledger.
2. Recognize and be able to use the components of the General Ledger Navigation Aid.
3. Enter transactions in the General Journal.
4. Edit a General Journal transaction.
5. Delete a transaction.
6. Print General Journal and Trial Balance reports.
7. Reconcile an account.
8. Define terms used in the chapter.

The General Ledger is the heart of any accounting program. It contains the complete collection of accounts, transactions associated with these accounts, and the account balances for a specified period of time.

For Chapters 4 through 14 of this tutorial, you will enter accounting transactions for Premier Fitness Club, Inc. The backup file for the company is located on the CD that is packaged with the textbook. Follow the instructions given in Chapter 3 to restore the file.

Because *Peachtree Complete Accounting 8.0*'s General Ledger is integrated with other modules such as Accounts Payable and Accounts Receivable, you will record fewer transactions in the General Ledger than you would in a manual accounting system. You will enter all transactions involving the vendors in the Accounts Payable module. You will enter all transactions involving customers in the Accounts Receivable module. Regardless of where transactions are entered, *Peachtree* will automatically update the General Ledger when you post transactions in any module.

Figure 4–1 The Navigation Aid for General Ledger

> **Note**
> You used the **Maintain Chart of Accounts** icon earlier, when you set up the Chart of Accounts for this business.

In this chapter, you will enter and edit transactions in the General Journal, reconcile accounts, and generate General Ledger reports. You can use the General Ledger Navigation Aid or the **Tasks** menu to complete these tasks.

GENERAL JOURNAL ENTRY

When you select the General Journal Entry task icon shown in Figure 4–1, the General Journal Entry window will open (Figure 4–2). The General Journal is used to enter transactions that are not readily categorized in the Tasks menu. Depreciation would be an example of something that would be entered into the General Journal. You can also edit adjustments made in account reconciliation.

> **Note**
> Use the **Delete** icon to delete an entire transaction.

Unlike other transaction entry screens in Peachtree, you must provide the complete accounting entry (debit and credit distributions) in the General Journal. In other components, Peachtree automatically posts to certain accounts, based on the default General Ledger accounts you set up in the Maintain windows.

In the General Journal, you enter both debits and credits, and when the amounts balance, you can post the General Journal by selecting the **Post** button if you are using the real-time posting method. If you are using the batch-posting method, you would select the **Save** button and post at a later time.

Each Peachtree data entry window contains a toolbar at the top of the screen. The toolbar has icons that represent tasks that are available from that data entry window.

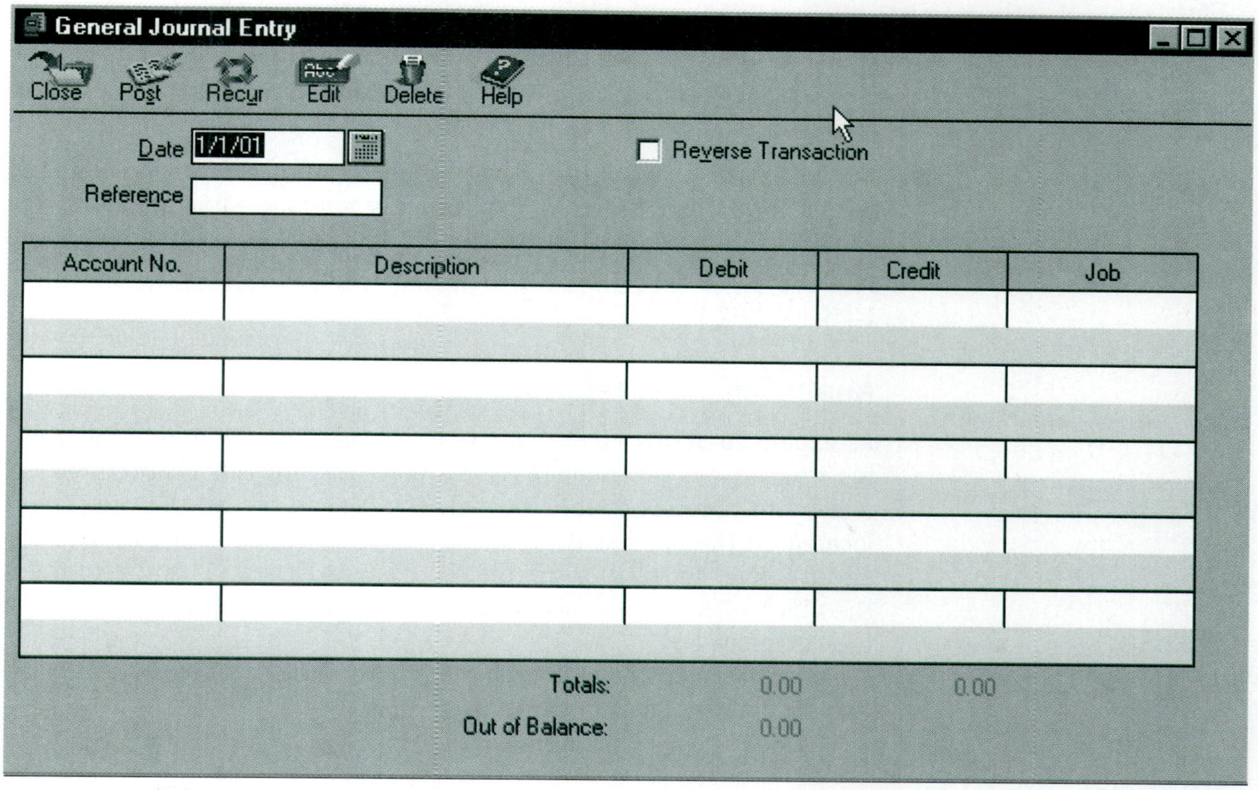

Figure 4–2 General Journal Entry window

Below is a description of the data entry fields on the General Journal Entry window.

Date: The first day of the current accounting period is the default date when the window opens, You can key in the transaction date, or you can use the drop-down calendar to select the date.

Reference: You can enter up to 20 alphanumeric characters. If you use a numeric reference, Peachtree will automatically add 1 to the reference number of each subsequent entry. You can leave the *Reference* field blank.

Account No.: Enter or select the number for the account you want to debit or credit for the transaction. While standard accounting practices dictate that the debit part of each transaction is entered before the credit, *Peachtree* allows you to enter either the debit or credit first.

Description: Add a description explaining the journal entry.

Debit: Enter the debit amount for the transaction.

Credit: Enter the credit amount for the transaction.

Job: The Job lookup field will be used when you need to track information by job. This field will be discussed in Chapter 9.

Reverse Transaction: Activate the *Reverse Transaction* field when you want to reverse a journal entry at the beginning of the next accounting period. Enabling this field will cause the system to automatically post an entry with the same accounts and amounts, where the debits become credits (and vice versa). Some end-of-period adjusting entries will be marked as transactions to be reversed.

Out of Balance: *Peachtree* calculates any difference between debits and credits for each transaction. For correctly journalized transactions, the value shown in this field will be zero. *Peachtree* will not allow you to post an out-of-balance entry. Therefore, any difference must be corrected before you can post the transaction.

Analyzing Transactions

As explained at the beginning of this chapter, you will enter accounting transactions for Premier Fitness Club, Inc. for this chapter and the remaining chapters of this tutorial. The backup file for the company is located on the CD that is packaged with the textbook. If you have not already done so, restore the file for Premier Fitness. This file contains the Chart of Accounts, customers, vendors, and beginning balances for the company.

Analyze the following transaction to gain practice in using the General Journal Entry task.

Transaction

On January 2, 2001, you discovered that a $300 purchase of supplies was incorrectly posted to the Prepaid Insurance account. Record the correcting entry.

COMPUTER PRACTICE

Enter a Transaction

Step 1 Open the General Ledger Navigation Aid.

Step 2 Select the **General Journal Entry** task icon.

Step 3 In the *Date* field, key 01/02/01 and press Tab.

Step 4 In the *Reference* field, key Correction and press Tab.

Step 5 In the *Account No.* field, key 14300 and press Tab.

Step 6 In the *Description* field, key Correcting Entry and press Tab.

Step 7 In the *Debit* field, key 300.00 and press Tab until the cursor moves to the next line.

Step 8 In the *Account No.* field, key 14000 and press Tab.

Step 9 In the *Description* field, press Tab to accept the information shown.

Step 10 Tab to the *Credit* field, key 300.00, and press Enter.

Step 11 Select **Post.**

Note

The totals shown for the Debit and Credit columns should be 300.00. The *Out of Balance* field should be 0.00, which indicates that the transaction is in balance and can be posted.

Edit a Transaction

If you need to edit a journal entry, you would complete the following steps.

Step 1 Open the General Ledger Navigation Aid.
Step 2 Select the **Task** icon for General Journal Entry.
Step 3 Select the **Edit** button on the toolbar.
Step 4 The *Show* field should display Period 1.
Step 5 Select the transaction you previously entered.
Step 6 Select **OK.** The entry will appear.
Step 7 Tab to the *Reference* field, key Memo 1, and press Enter.
Step 8 Select **Post.**

> **Note**
> The transaction for truck maintenance should appear on the screen.

Delete a Transaction

On rare occasions, you might need to delete a journal entry. To do so, you would follow these steps.

Step 1 Open the General Journal Entry window.
Step 2 Select the **Edit** button.
Step 3 Select the transaction you previously entered and edited.
Step 4 Select **OK.** The entry will appear.
Step 5 Click the **Delete** button.
Step 6 Answer *No* when asked if you want to delete the record.
Step 7 Select **Close.**

> **Note**
> A dialog window will appear asking, "Are you sure you want to delete this Record?"

GENERAL JOURNAL REPORT

The General Journal report lists all General Journal entries in debit and credit format. To display the report, select **General Journal** in the Reports section of the General Ledger Navigation Aid. The report format window will open.

Filter Tab

The Filter tab allows you to determine the data criteria for the reports you want to see or print. For the General Journal report, Peachtree displays several filter options. The *Report Order* field enables you to sort by transaction date, transaction reference, or account ID. Checking *Include Accounts with Zero Amounts* will not affect the General Journal report, but will be a factor in other reports; for example, the Trial Balance. Checking the *Truncate Transaction Description* field will shorten the description to the width of the column. *Print Report in Summary Format* will show only the transaction date, the transaction reference, the transaction credit, and the transaction debit.

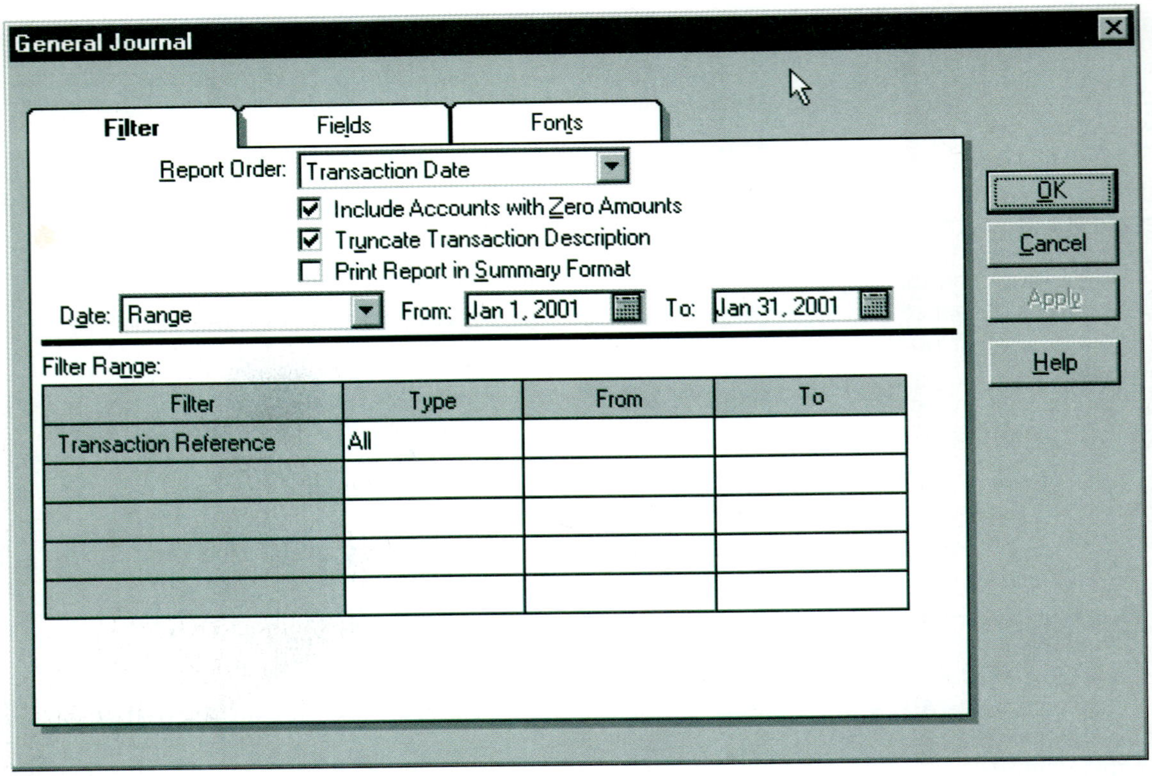

Figure 4–3 General Journal Report

In the *Date* field, you have the choice of All, Range, Today, This Period, This Quarter, This Year, and Week, Month, Period, Quarter, and Year to Date. If you select Range, you can enter a beginning and ending date in the next two fields.

The *Filter Range* fields allow you to include all data records or a range of data records in the report. In the table, the *Filter* column defines the specific data records you want to include in the report. Accepting the default will list all transactions in the date period. When you place the cursor in the *Type* column, you can change the type from All to Range. You would then enter the beginning record and the ending record in the *From* and *To* fields. If you want just one record, enter the same beginning and ending record.

Fields and Fonts Tabs

The report design features that are available on the Fields and Fonts tabs allow you to change the appearance of reports. You can select a different font for printed reports or you can add or eliminate a column of information from a report. For the reports that you generate in this chapter, accept the defaults.

GENERAL LEDGER REPORTS

Peachtree provides several General Ledger reports you can use to track the accounting entries you enter.

Open the General Ledger Navigation Aid. From the Reports column, select **General Ledger Reports.**

Five reports can be generated.

1. Chart of Accounts—a complete listing of all General Ledger accounts.
2. Working Trial Balance—used to determine needed adjustments to the account balances.
3. General Ledger Trial Balance—a listing of the current balance for each account.
4. General Journal—a listing of General Journal transactions; used to verify the GL postings.
5. General Ledger—a list of all General Ledger accounts, beginning balances, and all account activity for the current period.

The Select a Report window (Figure 4–4) allows you to choose the type of report you want to display or print. When you open this window from the General Ledger Navigation Aid, General Ledger will be selected in the Report Area. Select a report from the Report List (right column). Once you select the report, you can choose to display the report on the screen (**Preview** icon) or print a hard copy (**Print** icon) by using the toolbar at the top of the window.

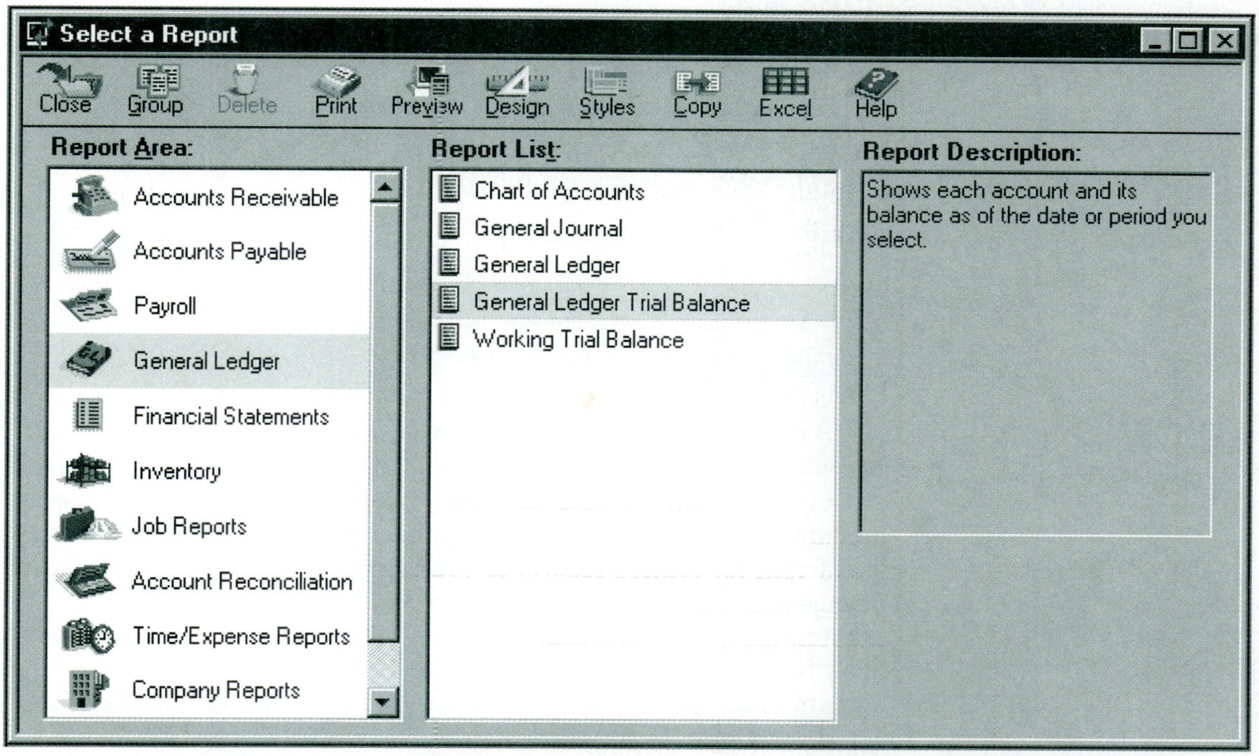

Figure 4–4 Select a General Ledger report

To generate a report, the software analyzes the information you entered and places it in the proper predesigned reports. All you have to do is select the report you want and indicate whether you want to display the report on the screen or print a copy.

Preview the General Ledger Trial Balance report and the General Journal report.

COMPUTER PRACTICE

Preview the Trial Balance Report

The General Ledger Trial Balance lists the balance for each General Ledger account and proves that the General Ledger is in balance.

Step 1 Open the General Ledger Navigation Aid.

Step 2 Select **General Ledger Reports** (Figure 4-1).

Step 3 Select General Ledger Trial Balance from the Report List (Figure 4-4).

> **Note**
> The General Ledger Trial Balance window will ask if you want to post all the journals at this time.

Step 4 The Trial Balance will be displayed.

Step 5 Select **Close.**

> **Note**
> The Print window will appear, showing the number of copies being printed (1) and all range selected (ALL).

Preview the General Journal Report

As noted previously, the General Journal Report lists all General Journal entries in debit and credit format.

Step 1 Open the General Ledger Navigation Aid.

Step 2 Select **General Journal** in the Reports section.

> **Note**
> The General Journal window (with the Filter tab) will be displayed.

Step 3 Verify that the Filter tab displays the correct period.

Step 4 Select **Ok.**

Step 5 The report will be displayed.

Step 6 Select **Close.**

RECONCILING ACCOUNTS

Peachtree allows you to reconcile any account in your Chart of Accounts. Typically bank accounts, credit card accounts, and cash accounts (such as petty cash) are reconciled. You can reconcile an account only once per accounting period. You can, however, return to the Account Reconciliation window anytime during the period to make changes or adjustments.

Instructions for reconciling the cash account with the bank statement follow. However, there will not be a practice session for reconciling accounts since you have not entered a sufficient number of transactions.

> **Note**
> The first cash account (in the Chart of Accounts) will be the default account displayed when you choose to reconcile an account.

Step 1 Select *Account Reconciliation* from the Tasks section of the General Ledger Navigation Aid.

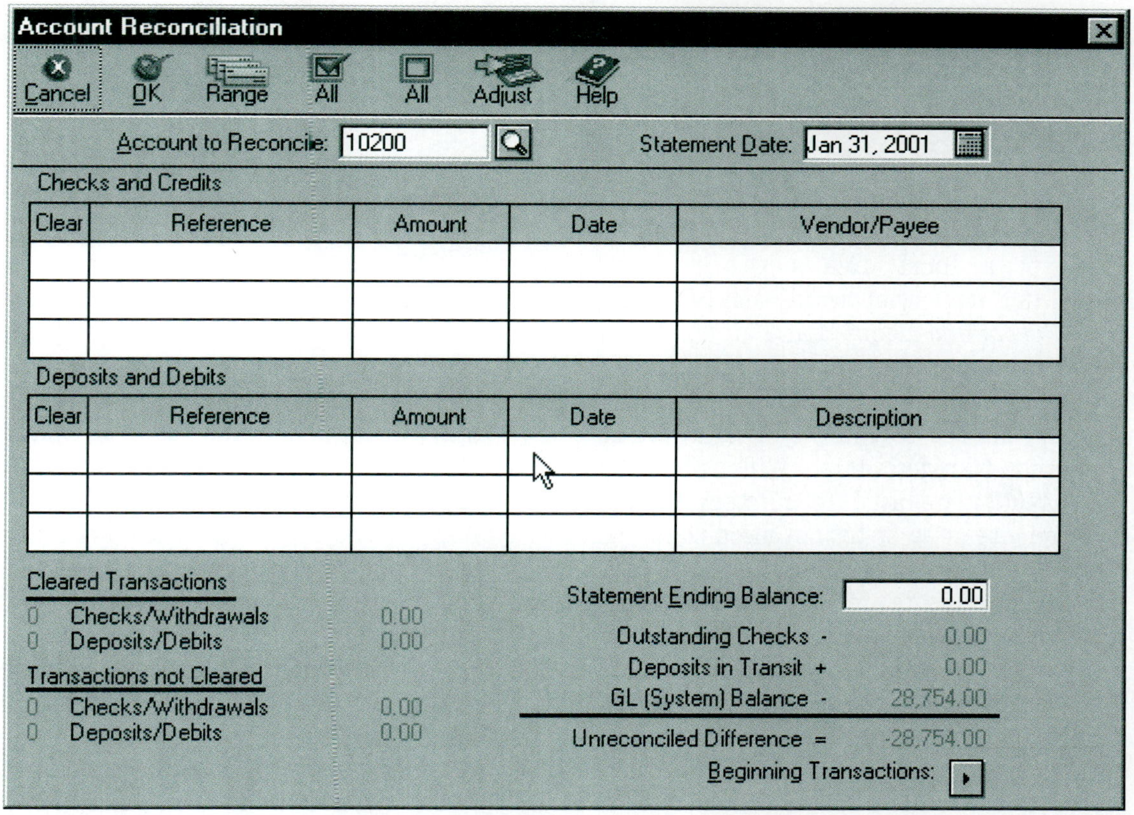

Figure 4–5 Account Reconciliation window

> **Note**
> The statement date must be in the current accounting period.

Step 2 Select the account that you want to reconcile (Regular Checking Account).

Step 3 Enter the closing date from the bank statement (in the *Statement Date* field).

Step 4 Enter the Statement Ending Balance.

Step 5 Mark each check that has cleared by selecting the Clear box. If all transactions have cleared, select **Check All** from the toolbar.

Step 6 Mark each deposit included on the statement.

Step 7 Select the **Adjust** icon to enter additional transactions, such as service charges. Entries you make here will appear in the General Journal.

Step 8 Select **OK** when all charges have been recorded.

Step 9 When all the cleared transactions for an account have been marked and additional charges recorded, the *Statement Ending Balance* should match the ending balance of the Regular Checking Account in the General Ledger. The *Unreconciled Difference* should be zero.

> **Note**
> If you are interrupted in the middle of reconciling, select **Ok** and exit the window. You will be able to pick up where you left off at a later time.

Networks

The computers in the computer lab at your school are most likely part of a local area network (LAN). But what does that word—*networking*—mean? *Networking* means that a group of computers at a particular site are interconnected so that all of the computer users can access specialized software and hardware to share and transfer data. Wide area networks (WANs) are used to connect computers at remote sites or to join more than one LAN.

In many businesses, both large and small projects are completed collaboratively. The complexity of business projects, from the space shuttle to the production of this textbook, require the skills of many individuals. For example, within a textbook company's network, shared files can be placed in a location where all team members—editors, artists, and printers—have access to the latest edition of any book. Whether the participants are located within the same building, across town, or several continents away, networks allow teams to work together more easily.

To illustrate the benefits of networking technology in a computer lab, assume that, rather than working separately on an accounting application, several students are linked together via a network. A continuously updated data file would be available to all members of the team. Each student working with the software would be able to perform specialized tasks—accounts receivable, accounts payable, analysis—thus allowing the team to accomplish a specific task more effectively.

No longer is it necessary for individual computers to be physically connected in order for data to be shared. The Internet connects every stand-alone computer to a WAN. Regardless of the geographical distance between project members, data files can be exchanged in a matter of minutes by simply attaching a file to an e-mail message.

SUMMARY OF KEY POINTS

1. The General Ledger contains a complete collection of accounts and the transactions associated with each account.
2. *Peachtree* is an integrated accounting system. Entries made in any module will automatically be posted to the affected accounts in the General Ledger as well as the subsidiary ledgers.
3. Use the **General Journal Entry** window to enter, edit, or delete transactions in the General Ledger.
4. The General Journal report lists entries in debit and credit format.
5. The Filter, Fields, and Fonts tabs of the report window are used to filter information and determine how it is presented on financial reports.
6. General Ledger reports include the Chart of Accounts, Working Trial Balance, General Ledger Trial Balance, General Journal, and General Ledger.
7. The Account Reconciliation feature enables you to adjust accounts (such as credit card and cash accounts) to bring them into balance with another document (bank or credit card statement).

*inter*NET CONNECTION

Help in understanding General Ledger beginning balances is located at **http://www.peachtree.com/support/peachfacts/html/32233.cfm**.

Name ______________________________ Date ______________

CHAPTER REVIEW AND APPLICATIONS

Completion

In the space provided, write the word or words that best completes each statement.

1. The ____________________ field can be used to enter a source document number.
2. Printing a ____________________ shows that the General Ledger is in balance.
3. To delete a journal transaction, select the ____________________ from the **General Journal Entry** window.
4. To print a General Journal report, open the ____________________ Navigation Aid and then select ____________________.
5. When entering General Journal transactions, the amount in the Out of Balance section must be ____________________ before you can post the transaction.
6. Accepting the defaults on the Filter tab of the General Journal report window will include ____________________ transactions in the current accounting period.
7. To print a General Journal report with one specific transaction, key the ____________________ transaction reference in the *From* and *To* fields.
8. The ____________________ report is usually printed to determine the amount of adjusting entries.
9. An account can be reconciled ____________________ time(s) during an accounting period.
10. Adjustments that are entered during the account reconciliation process will be recorded as ____________________ Journal entries.

Name ______________________ Date ______________

Problem 4

The General Ledger for Premier Fitness Club, Inc. now contains the beginning accounting balances and the correcting entry that you recorded in this chapter. Print the following General Ledger Reports and then answer the Analyzing Your Work questions that follow. All reports will be for the current accounting period, January 1–January 31, 2001.

Note

The Student Template Disk has been created so that it is not necessary to enter the decimal and the zeros for even-dollar amounts. This feature is turned "on" or "off" in the **Options/*Global*** menu.

Instructions

Step 1 Start *Peachtree*.

Step 2 If you have not recorded the correcting entry in the Computer Practice activity in this chapter, record that entry before proceeding.

Step 3 Display and then print the Chart of Accounts report.

Step 4 Display and then print the General Journal report for January.

Step 5 Display and print the General Ledger Trial Balance report.

Step 6 Display the General Ledger report.

Step 7 Close all display windows.

Step 8 Back up your file for use in Chapter 5.

Analyzing Your Work

Answer each question in the space provided.

1. List the total debit/credit balance shown on the General Ledger Trial Balance report dated January 31.

   ____

2. What is the Regular Checking Account balance?

   ____

3. What is the Prepaid Insurance account balance?

   ____

4. What is the balance in Common Stock?

   ____

5. What is the balance of the Inventory Account?

   ____

Chapter 5

Sales and Accounts Receivable

OBJECTIVES

When you have completed Chapter 5, you should be able to:

1. Verify the Accounts Receivable setup.
2. Enter a sales invoice transaction.
3. Enter a Sales Order.
4. Enter a Sales Quote.
5. Enter a credit memo.
6. Print invoices.
7. Print the Invoice Register and Sales Journal.
8. Define terms used in the chapter.

In Chapter 4, you learned to use the tasks and reports of the General Ledger Navigation Aid. In this chapter, you will use the Accounts Receivable tasks in the Sales Navigation Aid for activities such as entering and verifying an invoice, printing customer invoices and statements, and creating a credit memo.

When a business sells a product or service for cash, the transaction is straightforward. However, if a business sells products or services on credit and maintains its own customer accounts, the transaction process becomes more complex. In accounting terms, credit sales are referred to as *sales on account*. In manual accounting, a sales journal is used to record such transactions. In *Peachtree Complete Accounting 8.0*, sales journal entries are automatically created when you enter sales invoices using the **Sales/Invoicing** task option.

An important part of managing a business is to collect amounts due as quickly as possible. *Peachtree* can provide an aging report for Accounts Receivable that lists outstanding receivables according to the length of time they are past due. *Peachtree*'s Accounts Receivable reports track these items (and a variety of others). In this chapter you will use various Accounts Receivable tasks windows to record transactions that affect Accounts Receivable.

VERIFYING THE ACCOUNTS RECEIVABLE MODULE SETUP

Before you begin entering Accounts Receivable transactions, verify that the default information has been set up properly. The default information is automatically used for each new customer you add to the system. The default information will display in various fields when you enter Accounts Receivable transactions. You can change the default information when you add a new customer to the system.

COMPUTER PRACTICE

Accomplish the following steps to verify that the Accounts Receivable defaults have been set up properly for Premier Fitness Club.

Step 1 Select the **Maintain** menu.

Step 2 Select Setup Checklist.

Step 3 Select Customer Defaults from the Accounts Receivable section.

Payment Terms Tab

Note

If you select *C.O.D.* or *Prepaid* as the type of payment, you cannot access the other terms' fields.

You will use the tabs illustrated in Figure 5-1 to verify and/or change the default information that has been set up. The Payment Terms tab will be displayed when the Customer Defaults window opens.

The standard payment terms are verified on this tab. The information shown in Figure 5-1 should match the defaults on your screen.

Step 4 Verify that Premier has increased its credit limit for charge customers to $5,000.

If you offer a discount for prompt payment of invoices, enter the number of days in the discount period, and the discount percentage. You will also enter the General Ledger links by entering the appropriate account number for the *GL Sales Account* and the *Discount GL Account*. Remember that this is default information that is applied to each customer and will print on the invoice. You can override this information for an individual customer if the default information is not appropriate.

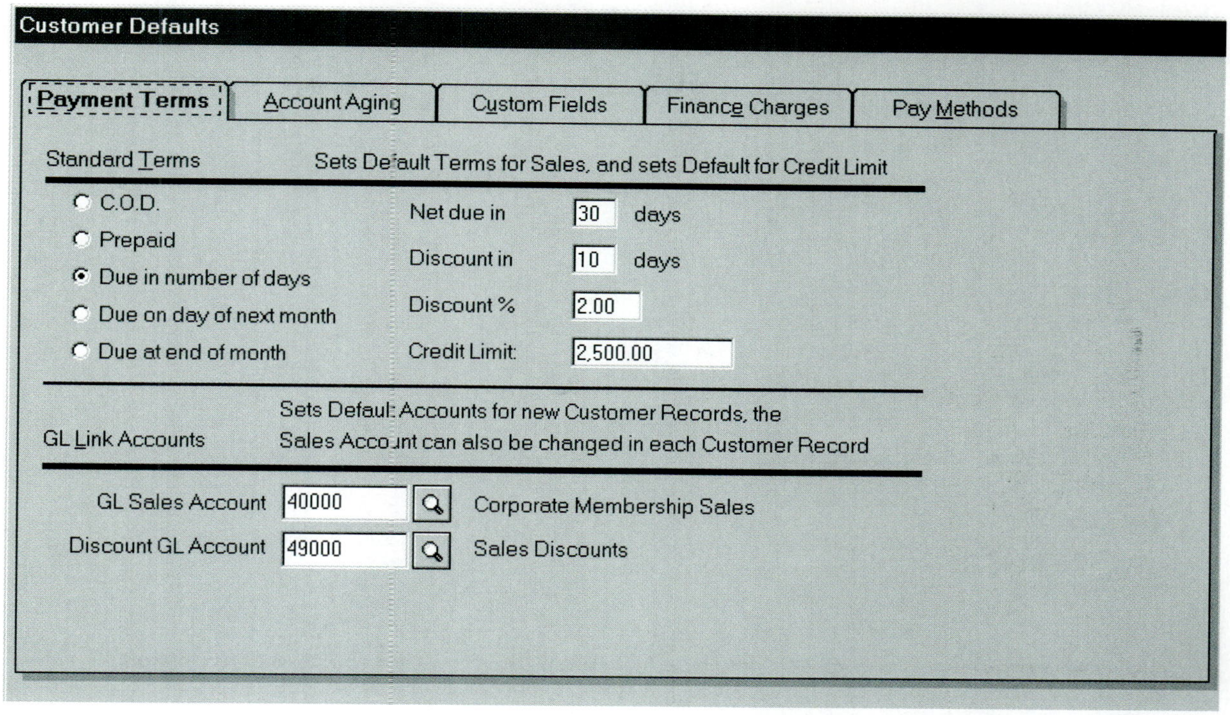

Figure 5–1 Tabs used in verifying default information

Account Aging Tab

To set up how sales invoices are aged and what aging brackets will be used for Accounts Receivable reports, select the Account Aging tab in the Customer Defaults window. Choose either Invoice Date or Due Date in the *Age Invoices by* fields. If you age by Invoice Date, Accounts Receivable reports will show how old each customer invoice and balance is. If you age by Due Date, the reports will show how overdue each customer invoice is. Because the same terms are normally applied to the majority of customers, most companies choose to age customers by Invoice Date.

The Aging Categories determine the range of days and the column headings for the Aged Receivables report and the Collection Manager in Analysis (Chapter 14). The # of days box can be the number of days beyond the Invoice Date if that is how invoices are aged. For example, entering 0 for the first column would display all current invoices. In Figure 5–2, however, the first column will display all invoices that are not current and are up to 30 days overdue. The fourth column will show all invoices that are more than 90 days overdue.

Step 5 Select the Account Aging tab. The information shown in Figure 5–2 should match your screen. The default has been set for 30 days from the due date.

Custom Fields Tab

You will not be using the Custom Fields tab. This tab could be used to track additional information about each customer.

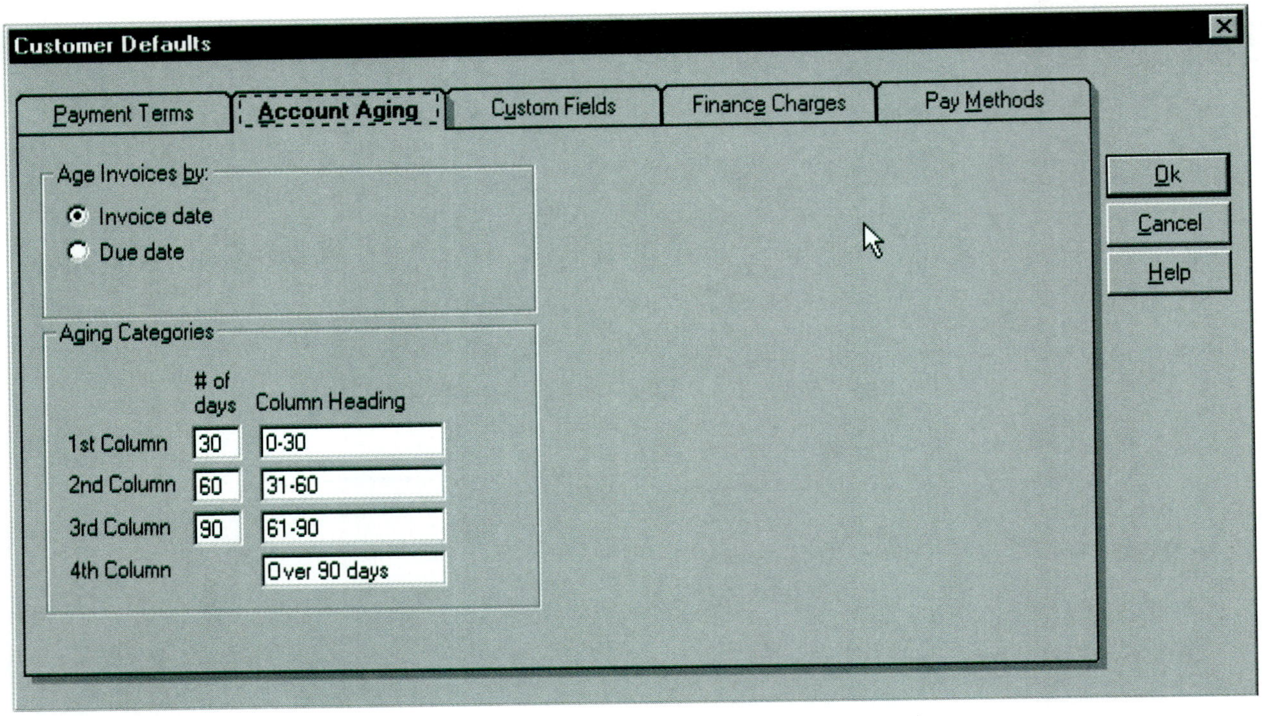

Figure 5–2 Establish aging categories for Accounts Receivable reports

Finance Charges Tab

Peachtree will calculate a finance charge if a customer does not pay within the payment terms. The percentage to be applied is entered on the Finance Charges tab. The defaults can be overridden when you enter an individual customer's information. At the present time, Premier Fitness does not add finance charges.

Step 6 Select the Finance Charges tab (Figure 5–3). If your screen matches the one shown in Figure 5–3, no finance charges will be applied. If you want to set up a finance charge, activate (check) the *Charge finance charges* box. To set the defaults for Finance Charges, you would complete the following steps:

Step 7 In the *On invoices* field, enter the number of days past the due date of an invoice when finance charges will be added.

Step 8 In the *days overdue up to: $* field, enter the maximum amount to which the base (or first) interest rate will apply.

Step 9 In the *Annual interest rate* field, enter the first percentage rate.

Step 10 In the *On balances above that* field, enter the percentage rate that will be charged for amounts above the base amount.

Step 11 The *Minimum finance charge: $* field sets a fixed amount that a customer will be charged when the calculated percentage of the outstanding balance is less than the minimum.

Step 12 Activate the *Charge interest on finance charges* box if you want to compound late charges.

Note

You will be using various task windows to enter transactions throughout this chapter. The task windows contain many of the same fields; for example, the Sales Quote and Sales/Invoicing windows contain nearly identical fields.

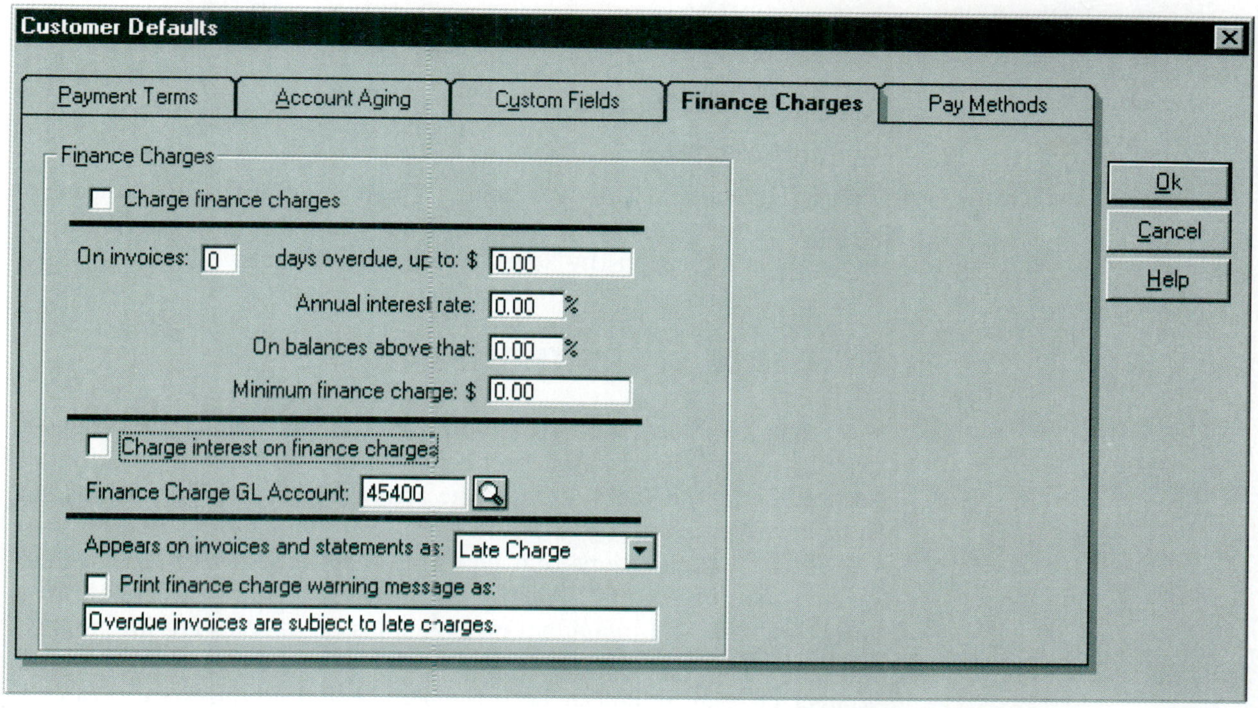

Figure 5–3 Enter default information about finance charges

Step 13 Select the appropriate *Finance Charge GL Account* from the Lookup Box (for example, Interest Income).

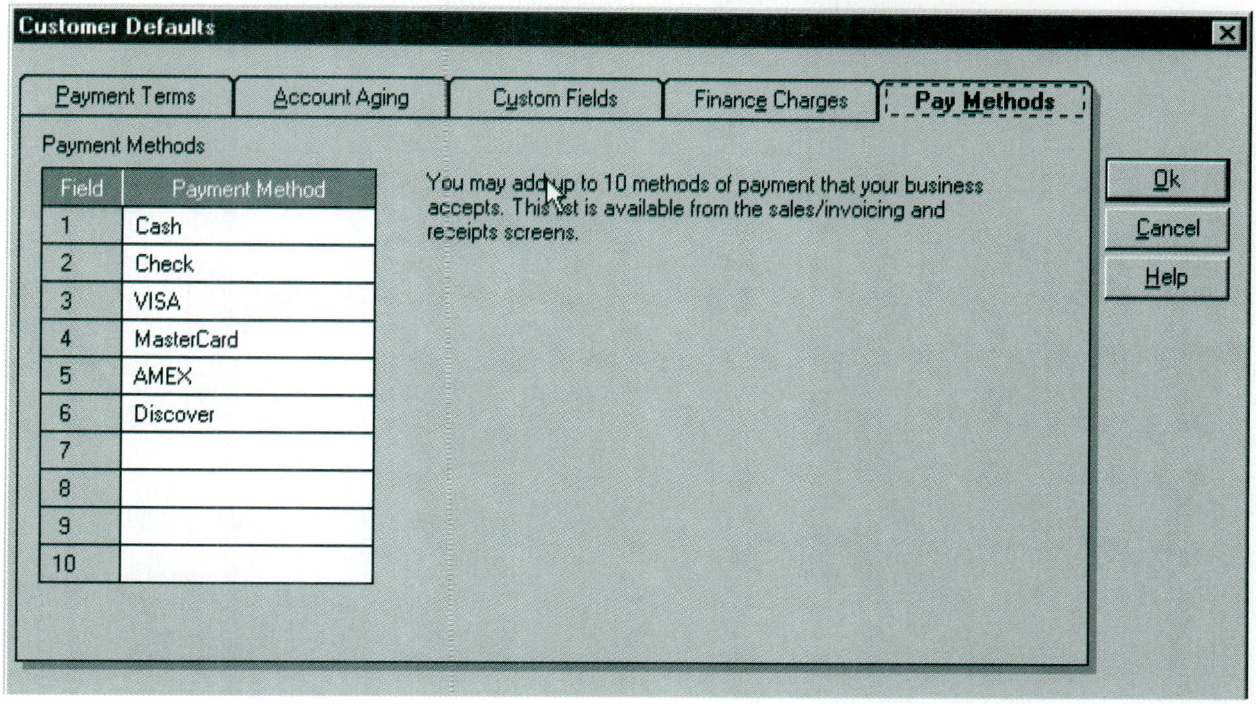

Figure 5–4 Enter payments you accept

Note

You will use the Tasks section of the Sales Navigation Aid to enter Accounts Receivable transactions.

Step 14 Be sure that you have not changed any of the defaults in this window.

Step 15 Select **Ok.**

Pay Methods Tab

The Pay Methods tab provides fields for you to enter the methods of payment you accept from customers. What you enter here will be the choices that appear in the Receipts windows (Chapter 7).

ENTERING SALES TRANSACTIONS

From the Sales Navigation Aid you can perform maintenance of records, open Task windows, and generate reports that affect Accounts Receivable. In the Tasks section, the arrows illustrate relationships and workflow of tasks that you would most likely follow.

The first transactions that you will record for Premier Fitness Club, Inc. are sales on account. Premier is a physical fitness center that offers both corporate and individual memberships. Most sales are for monthly memberships. In addition to membership sales, Premier sells a limited number of retail products. Both the service and products are taxable.

You will use the Sales/Invoicing task to enter sales of products or services on account and to create an invoice for the customer. The basic entry generated is a debit to Accounts Receivable and a credit to the revenue account. The entries you record here are posted to the General Ledger, customer records, and possibly inventory and job records. If a customer wants to buy a product that is not in stock, the Sales Orders feature will be used (explained later in this chapter).

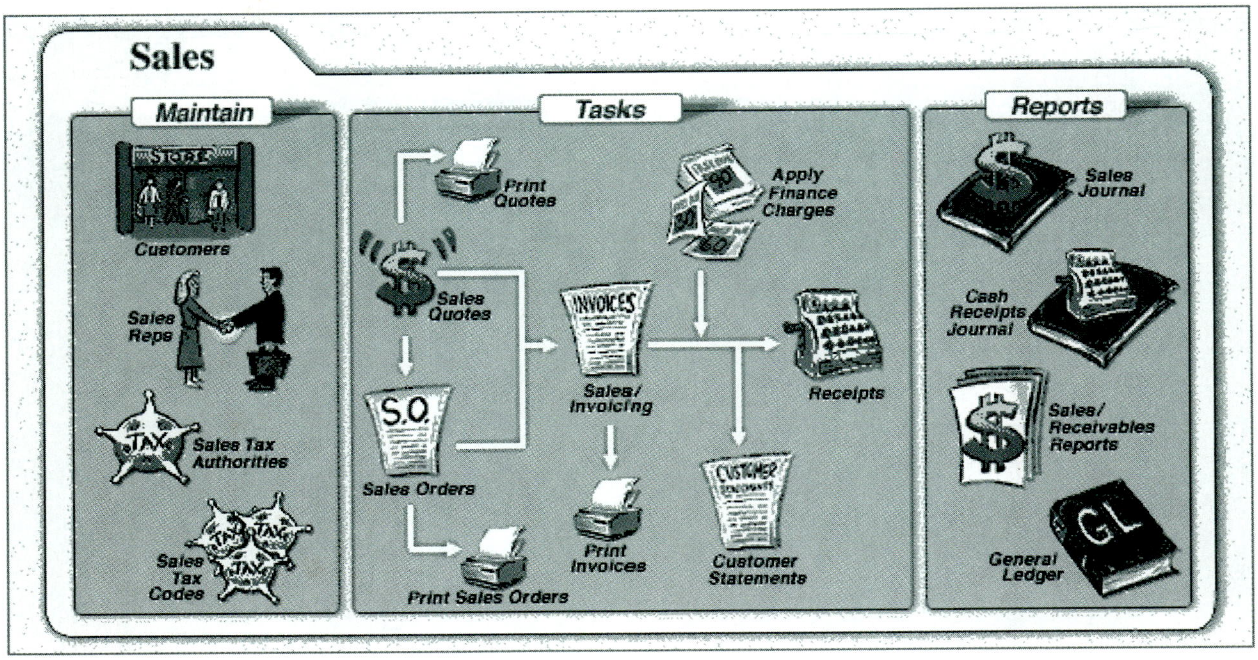

Figure 5–5 Sales Navigation Aid

> **Note**
> The **Delete** icon deletes the transaction after it is displayed in the Sales/Invoicing window.

> **Note**
> You read about how to add, edit, and delete customers in Chapter 3, "Maintaining Accounts." If you need to review the process, go back and look over the section pertaining to those activities.

Explore the Sales/Invoicing window as the various fields are explained. From the Sales Navigation Aid, click **Sales/Invoicing.**

To change the display format of the Sales/Invoicing task window, select the **Template** toolbar button. You can choose the Product or Service predefined template. Figure 5–6 illustrates the product template. You can also design your own template or use the Customize Templates option to change a template you have created. You cannot alter the predefined templates. Because Premier sells both products and service, you will use the product invoice.

Notice that on the product template, there are fields for *Quantity, Item,* and *Description,* while the service template has only a *Description.*

Customer ID: Enter or select the Customer ID. To display a list of existing customers, type ? in this field or select the Lookup button. To add a new customer, you can click **New** at the bottom of the customer list window, type +, or double-click in the field to open the Maintain Customers/Prospects window. When you select a customer, Peachtree supplies the customer default information, including billing and shipping addresses, sales account, shipping method, payment terms, and sales tax code.

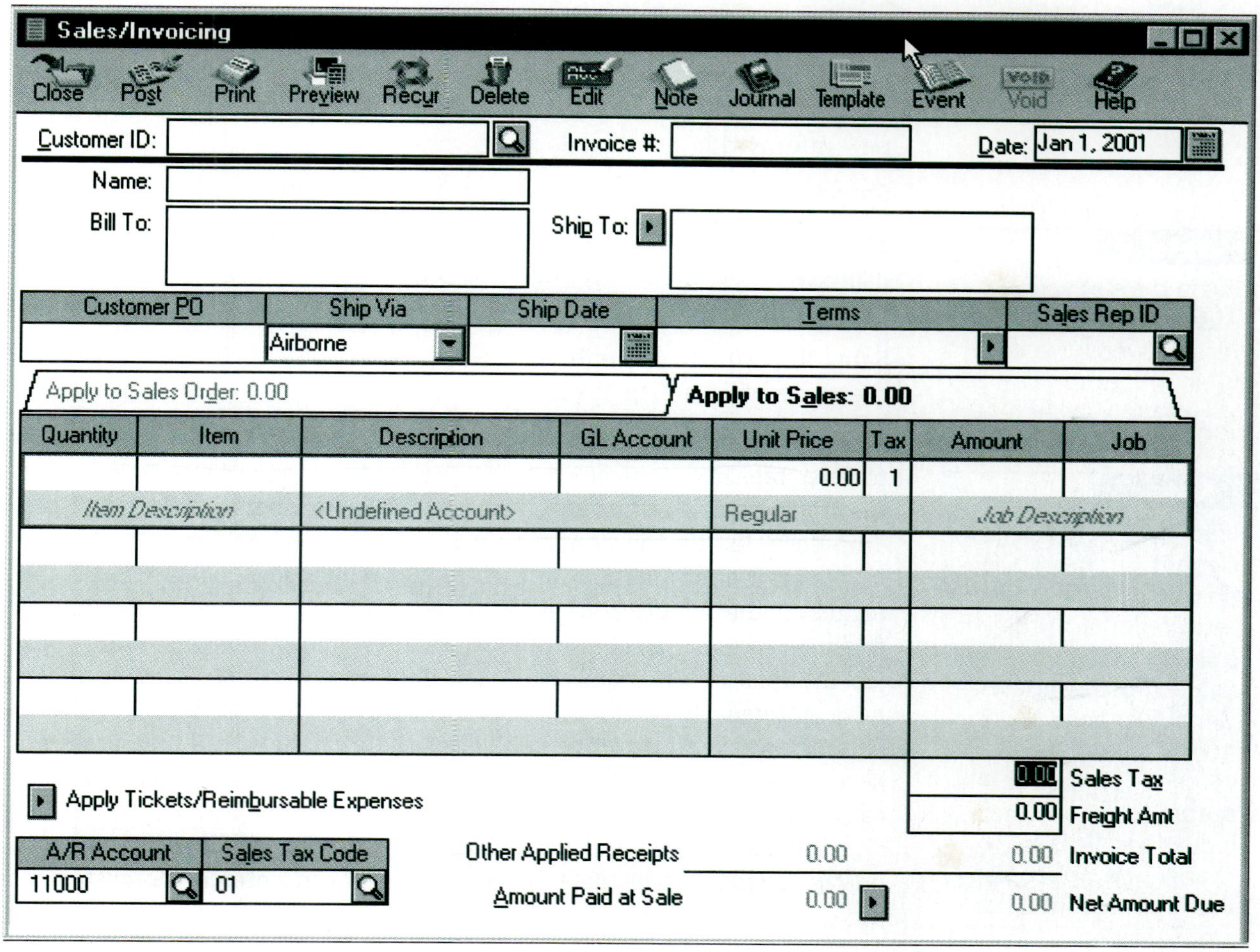

Figure 5–6 Sales/Invoicing window

Invoice #: Leave the *Invoice #* field blank if you want *Peachtree* to print the invoice. *Peachtree* will assign sequential numbers when the invoices are printed. If you print an invoice number with a number assigned or print it again at a later time, *Peachtree* will print DUPLICATE on the invoice.

Note

Default information for the *Name* and *Bill To* fields is displayed when you select a Customer ID.

Date: Enter the date of the Sales Invoice if it is different from the displayed date. You can simply enter the day (i.e., 25) and *Peachtree* will convert it to the standard format. You can also use the pop-up calendar to select the date.

Ship To: If you entered a default shipping address in the customer's record, the first *Ship To* address will be displayed. If the customer wants the order shipped to a different address, use the drop-down list (arrow) to select another recorded address or create a new *Ship To* address for this order.

Customer PO: If you entered a default open purchase order number in the customer record, it will appear on the invoice. You can leave the *Customer PO* field blank, enter the number from the customer's current order, or enter any other information that will identify the invoice for the customer. The information you enter in this field will appear on the invoice and on the customer's statement.

Ship Via: If you entered a default shipping method in the customer record, that information will be displayed. You can change the shipping method for this order by selecting from the drop-down list and entering new information.

Ship Date: Identify the date when the order will be shipped.

Note

If you have to void an existing invoice for any reason, select the **Void** toolbar button.

Terms: The default payment terms you entered for the customer are displayed. You can select the *Terms* button to enter different terms for this order.

Sales Rep ID: If you entered a Sales Representative for this customer, the name will be displayed.

Note

If you have the *Hide General Ledger Accounts* global option activated, Peachtree will not display *G/L Account* fields in this window. If General Ledger Accounts are hidden, you can use the Journal button to modify the ledger accounts or change the option so that the account fields are displayed.

Apply to Sales Tab: To enter new items on the invoice, select the Apply to Sales tab. If the invoice is to be applied to an open Sales Order, select the Apply to Sales Order tab. The Sales Order numbers will be listed in a drop-down list on the right side of the Sales Order tab.

Enter the information for each item on the invoice on a separate line, including the quantity, item ID, description, unit price (the number of decimal places is selected in Global/*Options* menu), sales tax status, and job information (if applicable). Continue entering line items until you have entered them all. Since the items that Premier sells have been entered as inventory, when you select the item code, the unit price will be entered automatically. When you enter the quantity, Peachtree will calculate the total amount for the item.

The default G/L sales account that appears for each line item is based on the customer sales default you set when you entered the customer's account or the item ID. Use the Lookup button or enter a different account number if necessary.

Note
The A/R account will display because you entered it as a default.

A/R Account: In the Customer Setup (Chapter 4), you entered the GL Accounts for sales, sales discounts, and Accounts Receivable. The Accounts Receivable account for this invoice is identified in the *A/R Account* field.

Sales Tax Code: The default sales tax code for the customer will be based on the shipping address. You can select another tax code from the choices available. Defaults can be changed in the Maintain menu.

Freight Amount: If freight is charged to the customer, enter the amount.

Invoice Total: Peachtree will compute the *invoice total.*

Amount Paid: A partial or full payment for the invoice is entered in the *Amount Paid at Sale* field. Entering an amount in this field will display *Reference* and *GL Account* fields. You must enter a reference, such as the customer's check number. Then enter the General Ledger Account to which the payment is applied.

Net Amount Due: *Peachtree* will compute this amount automatically.

After all appropriate fields have been completed, select **Post.** Posting an invoice closes that one and opens a new invoice window.

Note
If you check the ***Assign Invoice Numbers*** box, you are prompted to enter a beginning invoice number. Sequential numbers will be assigned, and they will be as many as the *Number of Times* field shows.

CREATING RECURRING JOURNAL ENTRIES

The **Recur** icon on the *Sales/Invoicing* window toolbar allows you to enter a journal entry *one time* and have that entry *automatically* re-created in future months or accounting periods. You can change or delete a recurring entry at any time. To create a recurring journal entry:

Step 1 Complete the steps to create an invoice.

Step 2 Select the **Recur** icon.

Step 3 In the *Number of Times* field, enter the appropriate number. (For example, enter 12 if the transaction is to occur monthly for one year.)

Step 4 Activate the appropriate field for *When to Recur* (e.g., *Monthly*).

Step 5 Select **OK.**

ENTER A SALES ORDER

Sales Orders let you enter items a customer wants to buy and have shipped at a later date. You will invoice the customer when you ship the items.

Product template is the default sales template for Sales Orders, and it displays the invoice data-entry fields that you saw on the Sales/Invoicing window. Peachtree Accounting provides two predefined

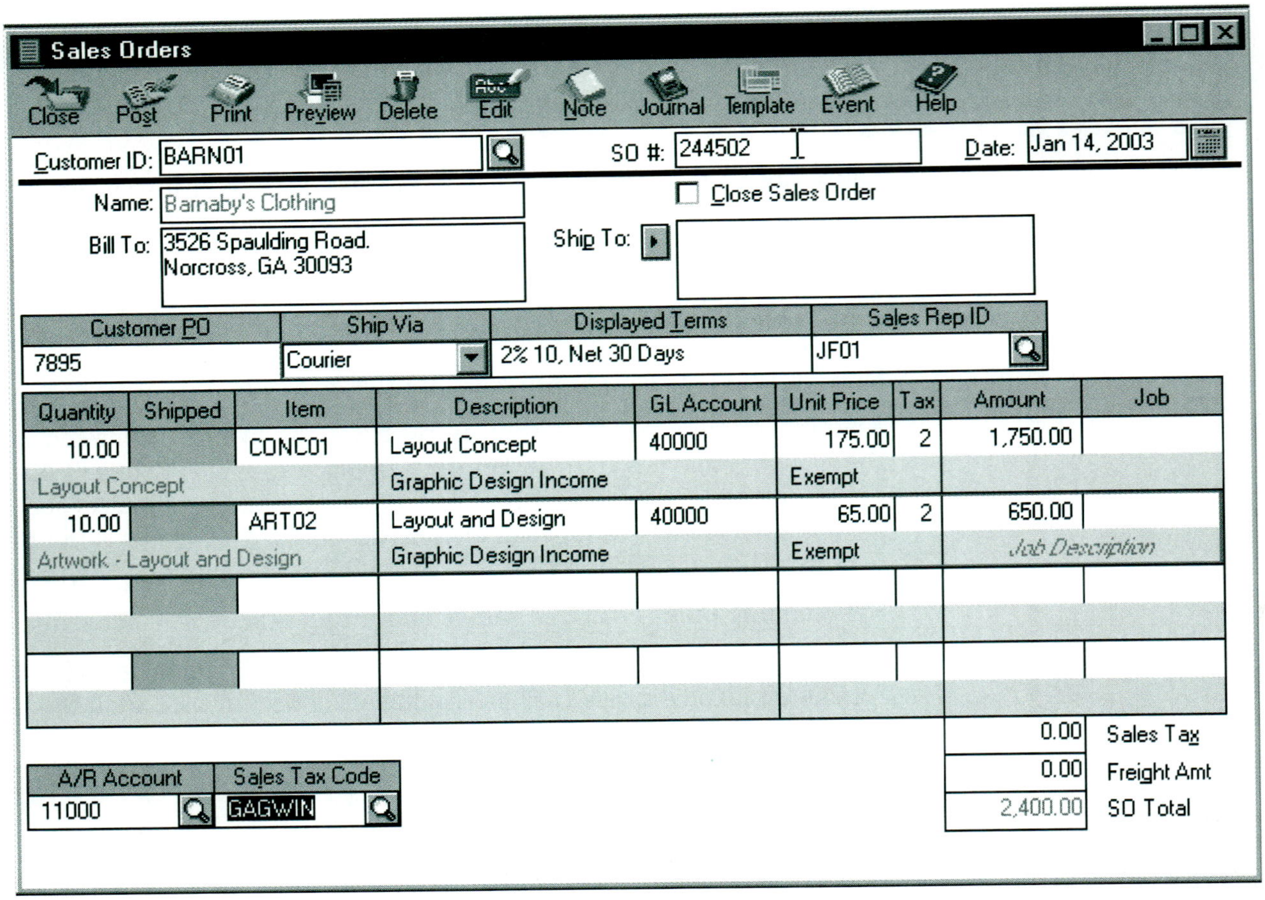

Figure 5–7 Sales Order window

> **Note**
> The *Description GL Account, Unit Price,* and *Amount* fields are automatically filled in because item information was entered in the template file.

templates for entering quotes and sales invoices; however, in the Sales Order window, only the Product predefined template is provided.

To enter sales orders, select **Sales Orders** from the Sales Navigation Aid. The Sales Order illustrated in Figure 5–7 is for one of Peachtree's sample companies.

The most important difference between entries made in the Sales Order window and those made in the Sales/Invoicing window is that a sales order is not posted to the customer's account or the General Ledger until the customer has been invoiced.

When you select a *Customer ID,* default information will be displayed in many of the fields. You can, of course, change any default information that does not apply to the Sales Order you are entering. Enter a Sales Order number (*SO #*) if you want to change the one Peachtree will automatically enter. If you have not previously entered a Sales Order, this field will be blank. Once you enter the first one, Peachtree automatically increases subsequent numbers by one.

Notice that the *Shipped* field is darkened on the Sales Order, indicating that the field is not accessible. Contrast the appearance of this field in Figure 5–7 with Figure 5–8 when you invoice and ship the items on the Sales Order.

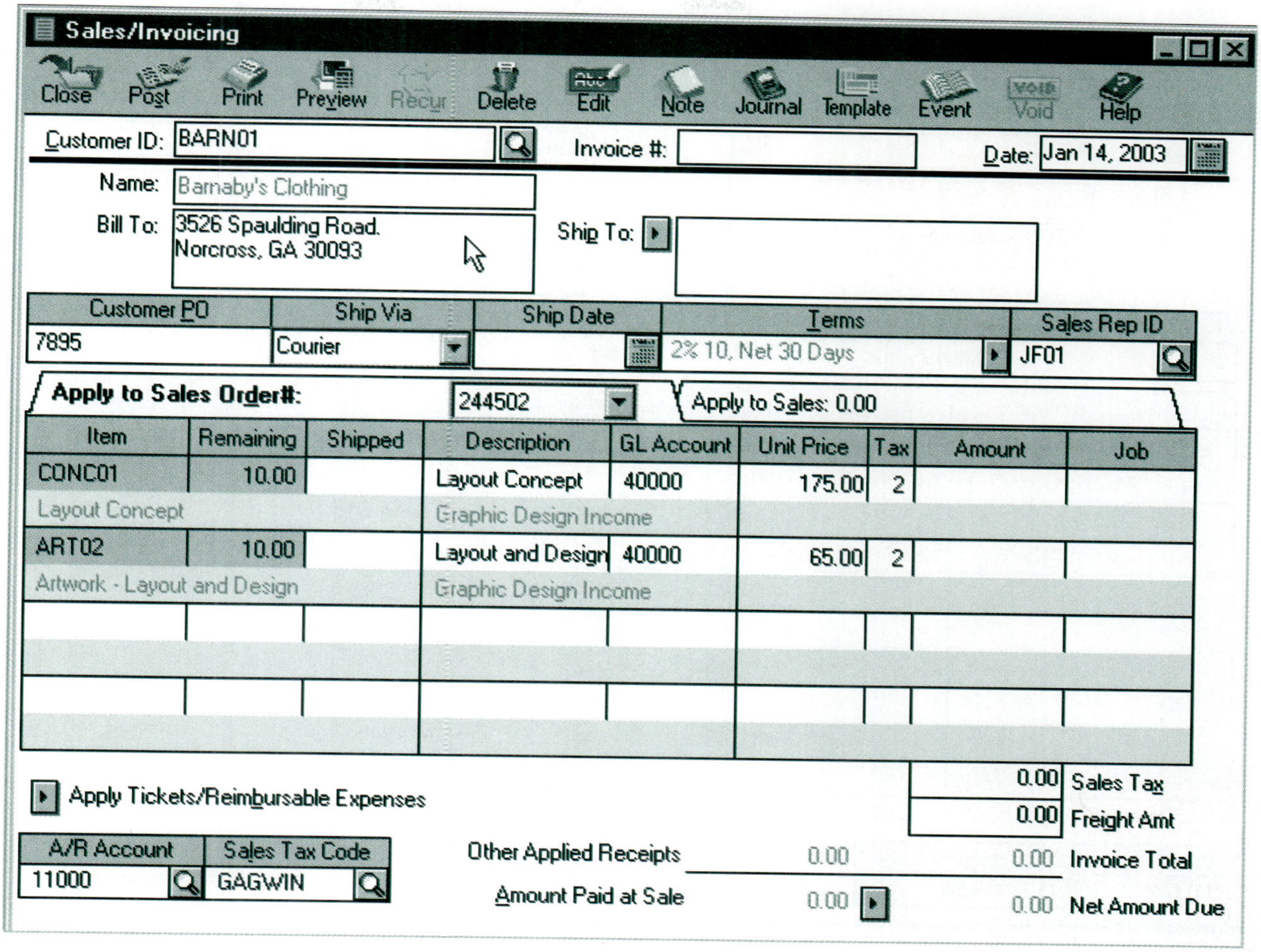

Figure 5–8 Invoicing and shipping a sales order

Ship and Invoice Items from a Sales Order

> **Note**
> A warning message may be displayed on the screen asking, "This invoice will cause the Customer Balance to go over the Credit limits by $xxx. Is this OK?" Select **OK.**

When you ship the items from a Sales Order, you will open the Sales/Invoicing window. When you select a customer who has an open Sales Order, the Apply to Sales Order tab will be active. You will select the Sales Order that is being invoiced from the drop-down list on the right side of the Apply to Sales Order tab.

Notice that the *Shipped* field is now active and the *Item* and *Remaining* fields are not accessible. To invoice the customer, simply enter the number of each item that is being shipped. If a partial order is being shipped, Peachtree will subtract the number being shipped and show only those that are backordered in the *Remaining* field. When you print invoices (explained later in this chapter), this invoice will print with those that you entered directly in the Sales/Invoicing window.

Enter a Sales Quote

A customer may request a price quotation before deciding to submit a Sales Order. You will notice that the Quotes window contains the same fields as the Sales/Invoicing and Sales Order windows. The following illustration is from one of Peachtree's sample companies.

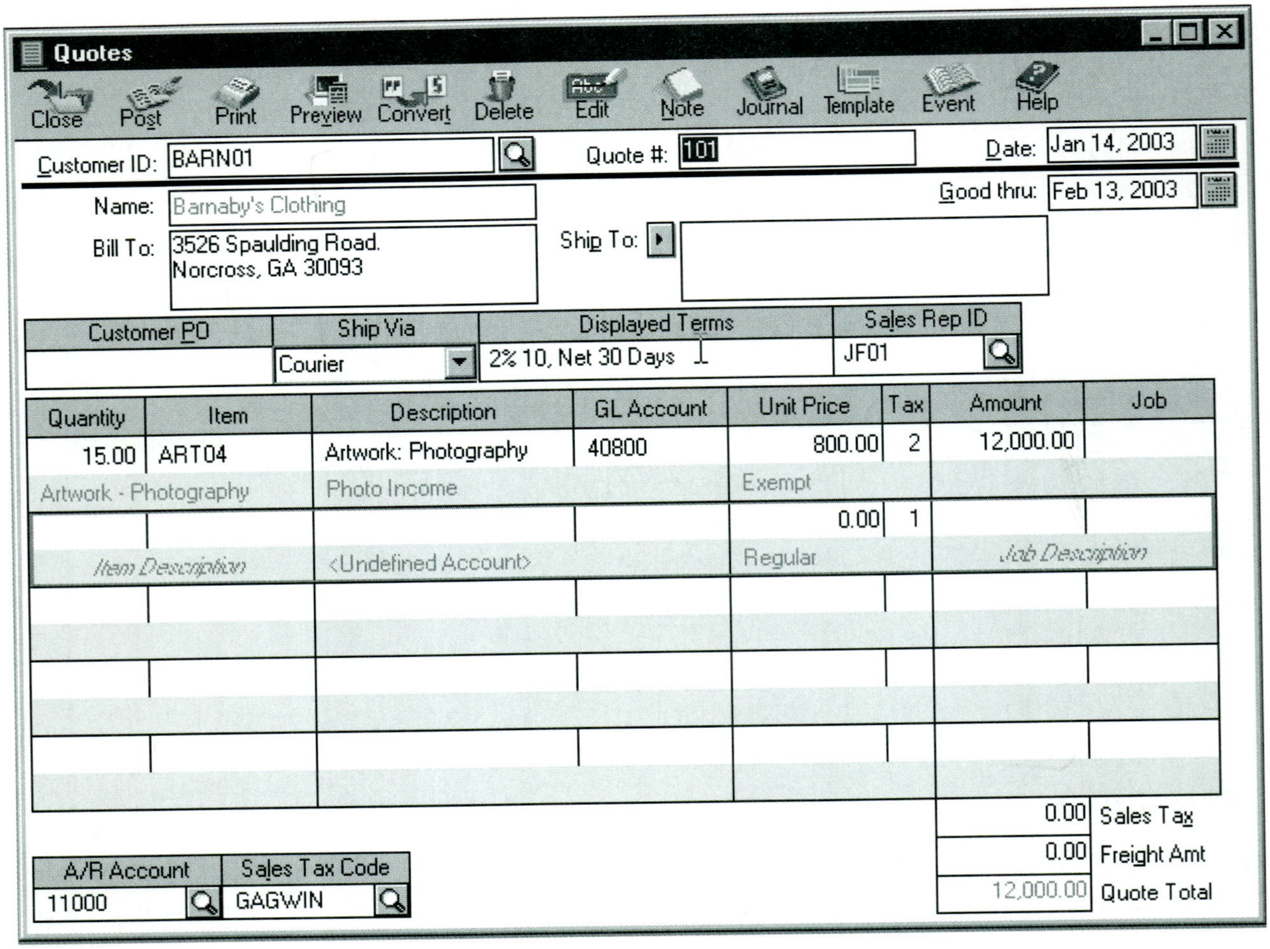

Figure 5–9 Sales Quote window

> **Note**
>
> You can set your preference for how you enter and display numbers in *Peachtree*. From the Options menu, select *Global*. If you do not want to type in the decimal point each time for whole numbers, then set the Decimal Entry option to *Manual* and set the *Number of decimal places:* at 2.

Step 1 From the Sales Navigation Aid, select **Sales Quotes.**

Step 2 Enter or select the Customer ID. The default information for shipping address, shipping method, terms, and Sales Rep will be displayed.

Step 3 Leave the *Quote #* field blank if you want Peachtree to print the quote. If you print the quote with a quote number assigned or print it again later, the invoice will have the word DUPLICATE on it.

Step 4 Enter the date of the quote if it is different from the displayed date. Then enter the date that the quote will expire.

Step 5 Enter the customer's purchase order number now.

Step 6 Enter the information for each item included on the quote on a separate line. The default G/L sales account that appears for each line item is based on the default for the Item ID selected.

Step 7 Select the sales tax code for this sale.

Step 8 If you intend to charge freight for shipping this order, include an amount in the *Freight* field.

Step 9 Select **Save.**

Note

Quotes are not posted to the General Ledger. When you convert the quote to an invoice, the sale will be posted to the General Ledger. Quotes can also be converted to Sales Orders, but again you must invoice the customer to actually post the sale.

Convert a Quote to an Invoice

When a customer decides to accept a quotation, you will convert the quote to an invoice or a Sales Order, so that the General Ledger accounts and the customer's account reflect the sale. When you convert a quote, the quote number is retained for reference. However, you cannot edit the quote in the Quotes window.

Step 1 Open the Navigation Aid for Sales.

Step 2 Select **Sales Quotes.**

Step 3 Select the **Edit** button on the toolbar.

Step 4 Select the quote to be converted.

Step 5 Enter any additional information supplied with the quote acceptance (e.g., purchase-order number).

Step 6 Select the **Convert** icon. The Convert Quote window will display.

Step 7 Activate the *Sales/Invoice* or the *Sales Order* field.

Step 8 Select **OK.**

Step 9 Select the **Close** icon when you are finished.

Enter a Credit Memo

Note

Selecting the **Print** icon will automatically save and post the credit memo. If you do not print at this time, you will save the memo, to be posted when all journals are posted.

Businesses expect that there will be times when a customer will not be completely satisfied with a product or service. If the customer returns the merchandise for a full refund or credit, that is called a *sales return*. If the product that a customer received is damaged but still useable, the business may give the customer a price reduction or a sales allowance.

A credit memo is entered basically the same way as an invoice, with two exceptions.

1. For a Service Invoice, enter non-inventory items with a minus sign (-) in front of the amount. *Peachtree* will automatically credit Accounts Receivable and debit the income account.
2. For a Product Invoice, enter returned inventory items as a negative quantity.

To create a credit memo:

Step 1 Open the Sales Navigation Aid.

Step 2 Select the **Sales/Invoicing** task and select the Customer ID.

Step 3 Enter the information as a negative invoice; enter a minus sign (before *Quantity*, for inventory items; or before *Amount*, when there is no item listing).

Step 4 Enter a credit memo number in the *Invoice #* field.

Step 5 To print the credit memo, select the **Print** icon. It is recommended that you print credit memos from the Sales/Invoicing menu rather than from the File menu when you print invoices. You will learn to apply credit memos in Chapter 7.

ACCOUNTS RECEIVABLE REPORTS

Accounts Receivable reports detail transactions and other information for all your sales—both sales on account and cash sales (Chapter 7). Some of the standard Accounts Receivable reports are described below.

Print Customer Invoices

When you enter customer invoices, you can leave the *Invoice #* field blank and have *Peachtree* automatically assign numbers to invoices when they are printed. You can print invoices one at a time from the Sales/Invoicing window by simply selecting the **Print** button, or you can print a batch of invoices from the Select a Report window. Printing from the Sales/Invoicing window both prints and posts the invoice.

To print invoices, scroll down the list of Accounts Receivable reports on the Select a Report window to the Invoices/Credit Memos/Packing Slips folder. This folder contains several types of predefined invoice forms from which to choose. Select the desired form. You can print invoices on plain paper or on preprinted forms.

When you print invoices, you can choose to print invoices that have not been printed (those without an Invoice #), or you can choose to reprint previously printed invoices.

Print the Invoice Register

The Invoice Register lists all invoices that have been printed by the system or were entered with an invoice number. The filter options allow you to specify how you want the register to print, such as by range of invoice numbers, range of Customer IDs, range or match for customer type, or unprinted invoices. You can also limit the report to current-period invoices.

The following instructions explain the steps for printing the Invoice Register and the Sales Journal. You will use these instructions to print the reports in the end-of-chapter applications.

Step 1 Open the Sales Navigation Aid.

Step 2 Select **Sales/Receivables** from the Reports menu.

Step 3 Select *Invoice Register* in the Report List.

Step 4 Select the Preview button to filter the report or double-click to display the current period report.

Step 5 With the Invoice Register displayed on the screen, select the **Print** button on the toolbar.

Step 6 Select **OK** when the Printer window appears.

Step 7 After the Invoice Register is printed, select **Close.**

Print the Sales Journal

The Sales Journal displays all of the sales transactions in a typical journal format. This display will allow you to see which General Ledger accounts will be affected when the transactions are posted. To view the Sales Journal on the screen, or print a hard copy:

> **Note**
> If you receive an error message, you must be already printing another application. Close the other application, or restart Windows.

Step 1 Open the Sales Navigation Aid.

Step 2 Select the **Sales Journal** report icon.

Step 3 Verify that Range is selected in the *Date* field, and that the *From* and *To* fields contain the appropriate dates.

Step 4 Select **OK.**

Step 5 Select **Print.**

Step 6 **Close** the report window.

When Sales/Invoicing transactions that involve inventory items are posted to the General Ledger, Peachtree automatically includes in the entry a debit to the appropriate Cost of Goods Sold account and a credit to the Inventory account. With this approach, it is not necessary to adjust the Inventory at the end of the accounting period. To view an entry, select the **Journal** button on the toolbar of the Sales/Invoicing window. You will see the additional debit and credit. Looking behind the scenes on the Sales/Invoicing window will help you to understand the entries on the Sales Journal report. For the services it provides (membership fees), Premier charges the cost portion of the sale to Salary Expense.

Print the Customer Ledgers Report

Customer Ledgers lists detailed transaction information as well as outstanding balances per customer. This report is helpful when you want to know the total activity for a particular customer. You can also access a customer's ledger account from the Maintain Customers/Prospects window by selecting the **Current Balance** button at the bottom of the window. When Peachtree posts a Sales/Invoicing transaction, Accounts Receivable is debited and a revenue account is credited in the General Ledger. In addition, the customer's account is debited in the Customer Ledgers (or Accounts Receivable subsidiary ledger).

Regulating the Online World

Software publishers naturally guard their products against piracy and copyright violations. This diligence is sometimes in conflict with educational institutions, libraries, and researchers whose goal is to access and disburse information.

The Digital Millennium Copyright Act, enacted by Congress in 1998, provides copyright protection to publishers, but it also addresses access to and fair use of information. Some of the provisions of the Act include:

- It is a crime to circumvent the anti-piracy measures built into the software.
- It is a crime to manufacture, sell, or distribute code-cracking devices designed to copy software.
- It is legal to crack copyright protection devices to test computer security systems, to determine product interoperability, and to conduct encryption research.
- There are exemptions from anti-circumvention provisions for libraries, archives, and educational institutions.
- Internet service providers cannot be charged with copyright infringement liability for simply transmitting information over the Internet.
- Educational institutions are not liable for copyright infringement by faculty and graduate students.

With the digital revolution continuing unabated and the Internet becoming more popular every day, regulation of cyberspace (and enforcement of cyberspace law) is sure to be a future topic of academic and legislative debate.

SUMMARY OF KEY POINTS

1. The Accounts Receivable default settings determine the information displayed in the Sales data-entry windows as well as on Accounts Receivable reports.
2. The Sales/Invoicing window is used to invoice customers for credit sales of products or services. Entries are posted to customers' accounts and to the General Ledger accounts.
3. Sales Orders are created when products have been ordered but not yet shipped to the customer. Sales Orders are not posted to the ledger accounts until the items are shipped and an invoice is entered.
4. A Sales Quote can be converted to either an invoice or an order.
5. A credit memo is created when a customer returns merchandise or is granted a sales allowance. Enter a negative quantity for a product invoice or a negative amount for a service invoice.
6. The Invoice Register lists each invoice number with the date, quote number, customer name, and invoice amount. You can also include invoices without numbers by selecting unprinted status.
7. The Sales Journal lists sales transactions in journal format.

*inter*NET CONNECTION

Have a question about an accounting issue? Try posting to a discussion group. Examples of some groups are located at **http://www.electronicaccountant.com/#search**. Even if you don't have a question, you can read what others have asked and how their questions were answered.

Name ______________________ Date ______________

CHAPTER REVIEW AND APPLICATIONS

Building Your Vocabulary

In the space provided, write the letter of the item that best matches the description. *(Obj. 8)*

a. Sales
b. A/R Account
c. Sales on account
d. Invoice Register
e. Product Invoice
f. Credit Memo
g. Report filter
h. Sales Allowance
i. *Terms*
j. Service Invoice

______ **1.** When a customer buys a product or service but does not pay until a later date.

______ **2.** This field will take into account any discounts, the number of days for which a discount is offered, and the date payment is due.

______ **3.** This Navigation Aid is used to enter customer's invoices.

______ **4.** A reduction in the price charged to a customer for damaged goods.

______ **5.** A printed list of invoice transactions.

______ **6.** The General Ledger account, to which a charge sale will be posted, is identified in this field.

______ **7.** A type of invoice that does not have *Item* or *Quantity* columns.

______ **8.** Type of invoice that tracks a company's inventory.

______ **9.** This entry will be posted as a negative invoice.

______ **10.** The options on this window allow you to print invoices that were entered without invoice numbers or those for which you entered an invoice number.

Name ______________________________ Date ________________

Problem 5

Complete the following transactions for Premier Fitness Club, Inc. Premier sells two types of monthly memberships: corporate and individual. The club also sells three inventory products: pants, shirts, and workout tapes. The appropriate sales and cost accounts for the product sales have been entered in the template file. The balances have been entered in the template file on your Student Template Disk. The following prices are currently in effect.

Individual Memberships	$30.00 per month
Corporate Memberships	$25.00 per month
Products:	
Pants	$15.00
Shirts	$20.00
Workout Tapes	$30.00

All sales are subject to sales tax at the rate applicable for Chicago, Illinois.

Instructions

Step 1 Restore the backup file for Premier Fitness Club, Inc. that you created in Chapter 4.

Step 2 Enter the following Sales Order and Sales Quote transactions.

Jan 3 The Fitness Store ordered 75 shirts to be shipped on or before January 25. (Delivery dates are for reference only; they are not entered on the Sales Order.) The PO number is 7541. Assign 101 as the first Sales Order number.

Jan 8 Gibbons Gym ordered 50 workout tapes for delivery on or before January 30; PO 6254; Sales Order 102.

Jan 12 Sigmachi Industries requested a sales quotation (with a reduced price) for 100 shirts and 100 pants. Prepare a Sales Quote (No. 25) with a price of $18 for shirts and $12 for pants. The quote is good for 30 days. Print the quote.

Jan 15 Alpha Insurance ordered 15 shirts and 15 pants for delivery on or before January 28; PO 7550; Sales Order 103.

Step 3 Open the Sales Navigation Aid and print the Sales Orders (Plain Sales Order w/Totals).

Step 4 Enter the following Sales/Invoicing transactions. Add new customers as needed. Use 101 as the first invoice number.

Transactions

Jan. 2 Bailey Automotive, a new customer, has opened an account with Premier. Set up Bailey in the Accounts Receivable module, using the following information:

Customer ID	Bai
Customer Name	Bailey Automotive, Inc.
Contact Person	George Johnson
Address	7892 Orange Avenue, Chicago, IL 80021
Telephone	312-555-0909
G/L Account Number	40000
Terms	Net 30 days
Sales Tax	01 Chicago Sales Tax

Jan. 2 Bailey Automotive purchased 5 corporate memberships, on account, for $25.00 each. Bailey's PO is 3452.

Jan. 2 Sigmachi Industries purchased 20 monthly corporate memberships for $25.00 each. Sigmachi's purchase order number is PO 8456.

Jan. 3 Alpha Insurance purchased 30 corporate memberships for $25.00 each. In addition, Alpha purchased five workout tapes for $30.00 each. Alpha's purchase order number is PO 7563.

Jan. 6 A new individual customer purchased a one-year membership for $30.00 per month. The customer is George Allen of 1475 Chester Avenue, Chicago, IL 80009. His telephone number is 312-555-0101. Apply 01-Chicago Sales Tax to sales for this customer. Assign "Ale" as the Customer ID. Create a recurring entry to bill the customer monthly. Terms are 30. Do not assign invoice numbers for future transactions

Jan. 8 The Fitness Store purchased 10 corporate memberships for $25.00 each. The purchase order number is 1527.

Jan. 9 Sigmachi Industries purchased 20 corporate memberships, on account, for $25.00 each; PO 8525.

Jan. 10 Alpha Insurance purchased 20 shirts at $20.00 each; PO 7590.

Jan. 10 The Fitness Store purchased 10 workout tapes for $30.00; PO 1590.

Jan. 11 Christy's Golf House purchased 15 corporate memberships for $25.00; PO 6586.

Jan. 13 Sigmachi Industries purchased 20 pairs of pants and 20 shirts for $15.00 and $20.00 each, respectively; purchase order number is 8895.

Jan. 14 Christy's Golf House purchased 20 shirts for $20.00 each;

Name ______________________________ Date ______________

PO 6758.

Jan. 16	Premier sold 20 corporate memberships to Bailey Automotive for $25.00 each; PO 3470.
Jan. 17	Premier sold two pairs of pants to George Allen for $15.00 each; George Allen does not have a PO number.
Jan. 17	Sigmachi Industries purchased 150 additional monthly memberships; PO 8920.
Jan. 20	The Fitness Store purchased, on account, 20 shirts for $20.00 each; PO 1835.
Jan. 23	Premier sold 10 corporate memberships to The Fitness Store for $25.00 each; PO 4512.
Jan. 24	Premier sold 5 workout tapes to Alpha Insurance for $30.00 each; PO 1284.
Jan. 24	Alpha Insurance purchased 30 pants for $15.00 each. Their purchase order number is 7580.
Jan. 24	Invoiced and shipped Sales Order 101 to The Fitness Store.
Jan. 25	Premier sold 5 corporate memberships to Gibbons Gym for $25.00 each; PO 5648.
Jan. 27	Christy's Golf House purchased 20 pairs of pants for $15.00 each; PO 6585.
Jan. 27	Shipped and invoiced Sales Order 103 to Alpha Insurance
Jan. 28	Sigmachi Industries informed you that a clerical error was made on their Jan. 17 purchase. Their original order should have been 125 memberships, not 150. Please edit the Sales Invoice for Sigmachi Industries.
Jan. 28	Shipped and invoiced Sales Order 102 to Gibbons Gym.
Jan. 30	Received PO 8935 from Sigmachi Industries accepting Sales Quote 25. Convert the quote to a Sales Order (Sales Order 104).
Jan. 31	Issued a credit memo to Alpha Insurance for $50 as an allowance for shipping incorrectly sized shirts on Invoice 122. Use CM 122 as the invoice number for the credit memo.

Note
Allow any of the customers to exceed their credit limit, if necessary.

Step 5 Print the Invoices. Select *Invoice Plain* from the list of forms.

Step 6 Print the Invoice Register report for January.

Step 7 Print the Customer Ledgers report for January.

Step 8 Print the Sales Journal report for January.

Step 9 Preview the General Ledger report. Use your printed reports and the General Ledger to answer the Analyzing Your Work questions that follow.

Step 10 Close all open windows and back up your Premier Fitness Club file. Identify the file as Chapter 5.

Analyzing Your Work

Answer the following questions in the space provided.

1. What is the balance of the Corporate Membership account on January 31?

2. What is the account balance for Sigmachi Industries on January 31?

3. What is the account balance for Accounts Receivable as of January 31?

4. What is the balance of Cost of Goods Sold—Shirts on January 31?

5. What is the total of all sales (products and service) for January?

6. Which customer has the highest outstanding balance?

Chapter 6

Purchasing and Accounts Payable

OBJECTIVES

When you have completed Chapter 6, you should be able to:

1. Verify the defaults for Accounts Payable.
2. Change the accounting period and the system date.
3. Enter a purchase order.
4. Receive items from a Purchase Order.
5. Enter a Purchase Invoice.
6. Print Accounts Payable reports.
7. Define terms used in the chapter.

Businesses not only sell on credit, but also use credit to purchase merchandise for resale, supplies, equipment, and services. Vendors who extend credit normally allow companies a period of 30 days from the date of purchase before payments are due. Many vendors, as part of their credit policy, offer cash discounts for prompt payment for goods purchased on account. Just as customers may return merchandise, a business may also return damaged merchandise to vendors.

A business must, in order to remain successful, have timely and accurate information about purchases and accounts payable. Such businesses acquire needed goods on time, keep track of the amounts owed to vendors, and pay invoices promptly so that the firm maintains a good credit rating.

Thus far you have used the General Ledger and Sales Navigation Aids to record transactions. In this chapter, you will use the tasks in the Purchases Navigation Aid to enter purchase orders and record the receipt of merchandise with and without a purchase order.

VERIFY THE DEFAULTS FOR ACCOUNTS PAYABLE

Peachtree Complete Accounting 8.0 allows you to set up default (common) information for vendors. Use this feature to build all your vendor records. Enter basic setup information that applies to most of your vendors and purchase transactions in the Vendor Defaults window. When you set up new vendors and enter transactions, the default information is automatically included. This can save a great deal of time during data entry.

When setting up specific vendors, the default information will automatically appear in the specified fields. Remember that if the default information is not relevant to a particular vendor, it can be changed for that vendor in the Maintain Vendor window.

Defaults for vendors are entered during New Company Setup. You can use the Maintain menu or the Setup Checklist to verify the defaults that were established at that time. Please verify that the following default information has been entered for Premier Fitness Club.

Step 1 From the menu bar, select Maintain.

Step 2 Select the *Default Information* submenu, then *Vendors.*

Step 3 Select the Payment Terms tab.

Payment Terms Tab

The standard payment terms entered (Figure 6–1) will be used for all vendors. Select terms that are appropriate for most of your vendors. You can then change the standard terms for *individual* vendors who offer different terms.

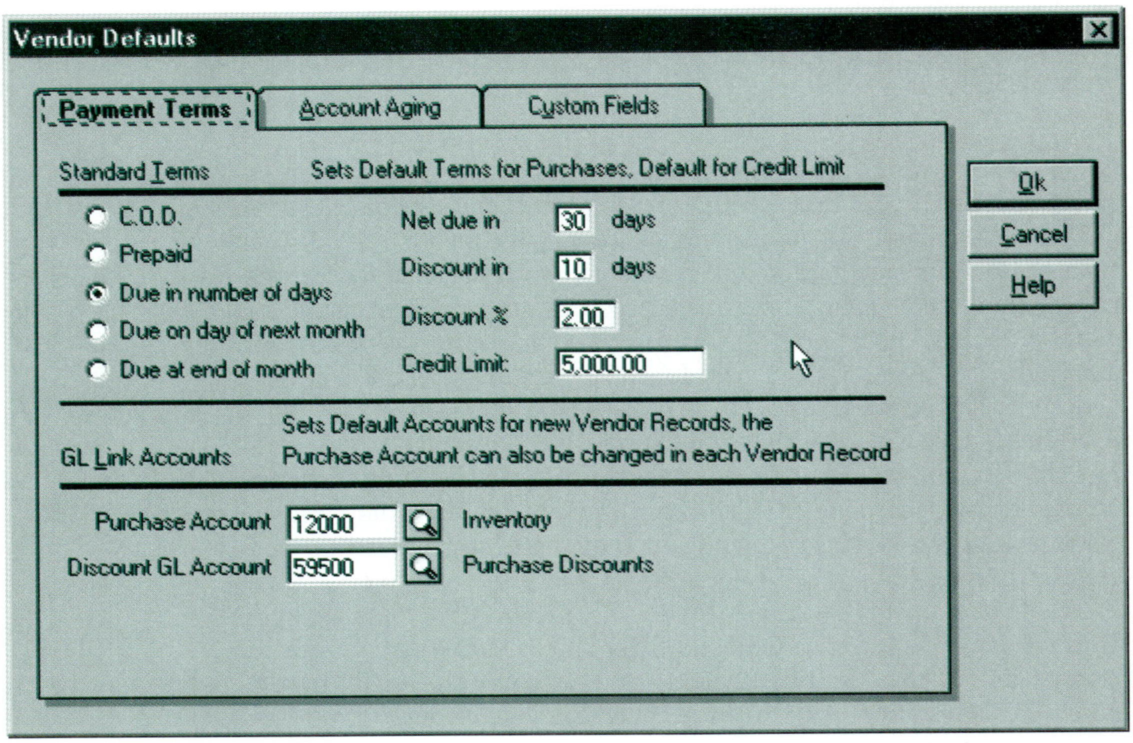

Figure 6–1 Payment Terms tab of Vendor Defaults

Note

If you select *C.O.D.* or *Prepaid* as the Standard Terms, you cannot access the fields on the right side of the screen, because they will no longer be applicable.

Your screen should match Figure 6–1. If a change is needed, select the area you need to change and enter the appropriate information. For example, if you select the *Due in number of days* field, you will be able to enter the number of days in the discount period and the percent of discount offered. You can also change the General Ledger accounts used for Purchases and Discounts. When you enter a vendor payment, *Peachtree* will determine whether a discount is to be applied and will calculate the discount and net amount of the payment.

Account Aging Tab

Step 4 Select the Account Aging tab (Figure 6–2).

Note

You must use the Inventory account for purchases in order for *Peachtree* to update the Cost of Sales accounts when items are sold.

The *Age Invoices by* option allows you to set up the Accounts Payable Aging report by the invoice date or by the due date. Your default settings should match Figure 6–2. The default for *Age Invoices by* should be set for *Due date*. For the Aging Categories, the *1st Column, # of days* field should be set at 30 days. To change any of this information, select the field and enter the aging categories to meet your company's requirements.

If you set up Account Aging by *Due date,* the Aged Payables reports will list how overdue each invoice and each vendor balance is (compared to the date the payment was due). If you age by invoice date, the report will show how old each invoice and each vendor balance is (compared to the date of the invoice). A company's management decides which option should be used. Most companies age Accounts Payable by due date and age Accounts Receivable by invoice date.

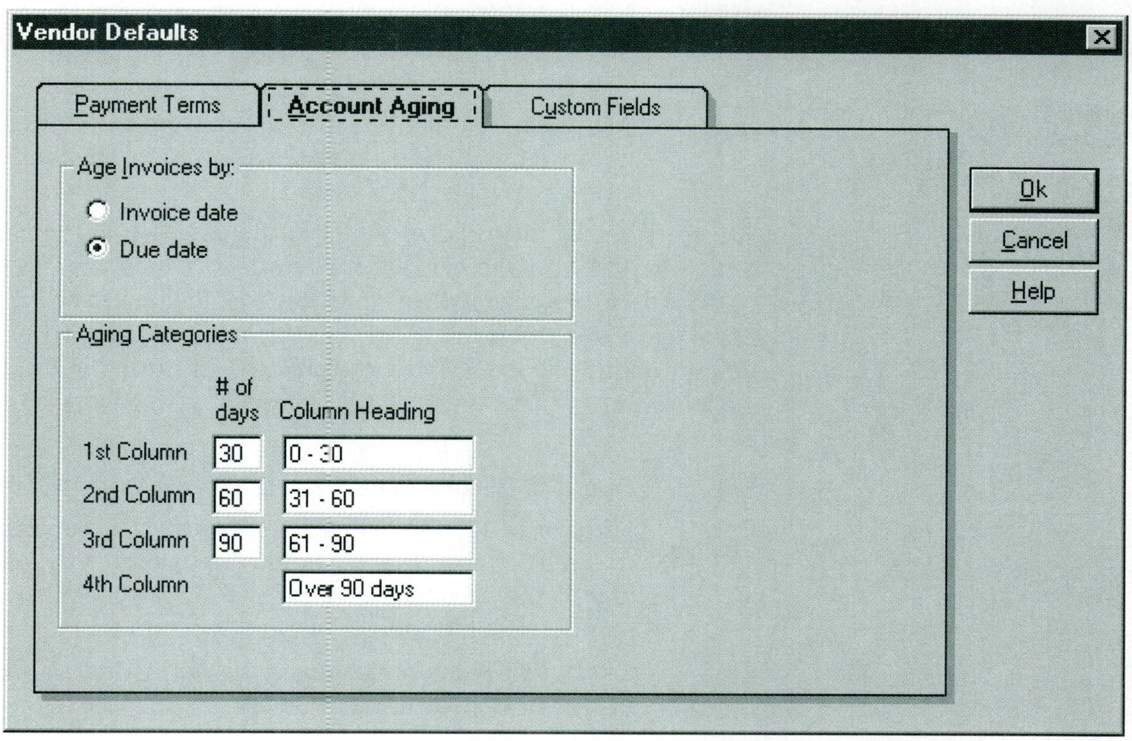

Figure 6–2 Accounting Aging tab; Step 4

Custom Fields

Custom fields offer you a way to keep track of specific information about the people who supply you with goods and services. *Peachtree* provides fields for most common business data. Custom fields let you set up and store the data that does not fit in the predefined fields. For example, you can label vendors by location (in state, out of state, international). You would enter the label as Location. Then, when you enter a vendor, you would enter the vendor's location under the Custom Fields tab.

On the Custom Fields tab, select the Enabled check box to enter or change the field label. If you decide not to use a field, simply clear the Enabled check.

Step 5 Select **Ok** if you changed any default settings or **Cancel** if all settings were correct.

CHANGE THE ACCOUNTING PERIOD AND SYSTEM DATE

In *Peachtree* it is necessary to change the accounting period at the end of each month. For both batch and real-time posting methods, you should print invoices and/or checks before you change the accounting period.

Step 1 Open the **Tasks** menu.

Step 2 Select *System* and then *Change Accounting Period* from the submenus.

Step 3 Select the period from the drop-down list box.

Step 4 Select **Ok.** You will be asked if you want to print reports, etc. If you have printed reports when you were instructed to do so, you can select **No** when the message appears.

Note

This changes the date for transactions you enter in *Peachtree.* It does not affect your computer date or the dates in any other applications you are running.

The system date in *Peachtree* refers to the date you enter transactions. Since the dates in the tutorial for this text do not correspond to the current date, it is a good idea to set the system date to correspond with the date in the problem you are completing. If you want to change the default date used when entering transactions during the current period following the procedure below, you must change the *Peachtree* system date.

Step 1 From the **Options** menu, select *Change System Date.*

Step 2 Enter or select the default date of the transactions you want to enter for the current period. For this tutorial, use the first day of the accounting period. In actual practice, the system date and computer date will likely be the same.

Step 3 Select **OK.** *Peachtree* changes the system date, which is displayed in the status bar.

ENTER PURCHASE TRANSACTIONS

Enter a Purchase Order

Note

The vendor must already be entered in Maintain Vendors before you can enter a purchase order. To enter a one-time purchase from a vendor you do not want to keep in your files, use the Payments or Write Checks window and leave the Vendor ID blank.

A purchase order is a purchase request for items from a vendor. When you post a purchase order, you actually do not update any accounting information. The accounts are updated when you actually receive the items on the purchase order and record the receipt through the Purchases/Receive Inventory window.

The Purchases Navigation Aid displays maintenance records, tasks, and reports that affect Accounts Payable. The Tasks section arrows illustrate relationships and workflow of tasks.

Step 1 Select **Purchase Orders** from the Tasks section of the folder.

The toolbar of the Purchase Orders window contains many of the same buttons that you used in the task windows for entering Sales transactions. A complete list of toolbar buttons, with their functions, is in the Appendix.

The Purchase Orders window has a number of fields in which you will enter information or accept the default information.

Practice entering the purchase order as it is illustrated and explained. **Do not post the order, however.** Figure 6–4 shows a purchase order that Premier created during the previous year.

Vendor ID: You can key the Vendor ID or select the vendor from the lookup box next to the *Vendor ID* field. When you select a vendor,

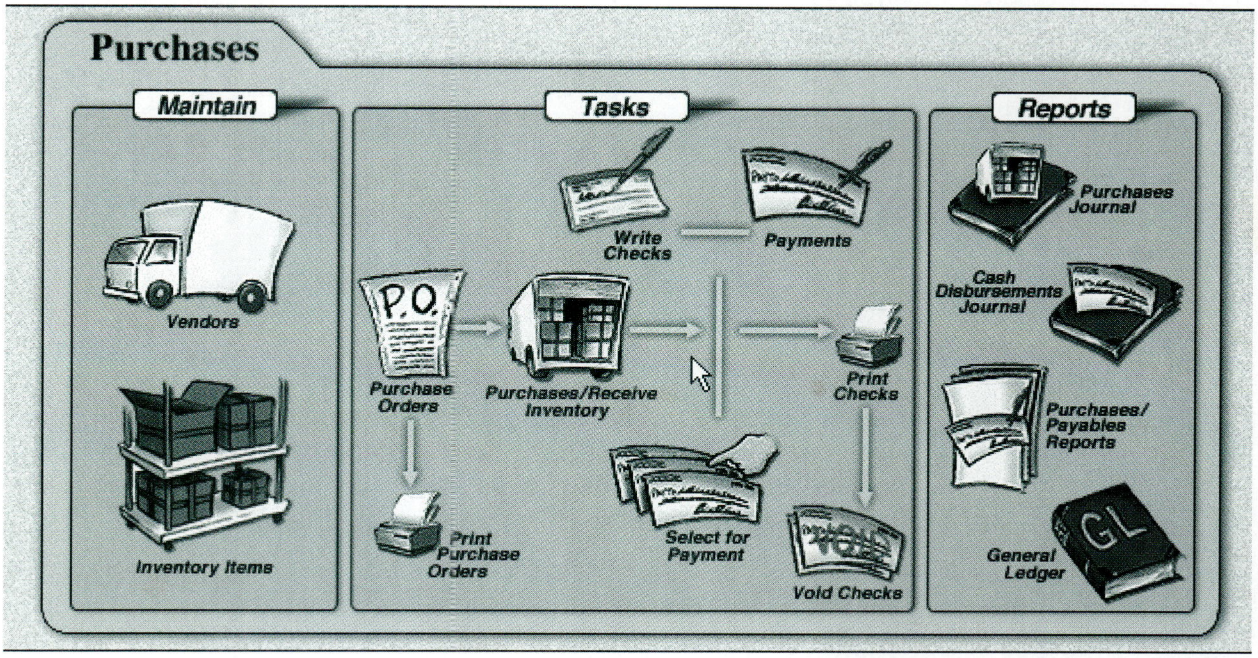

Figure 6–3 Purchases Navigation Aid

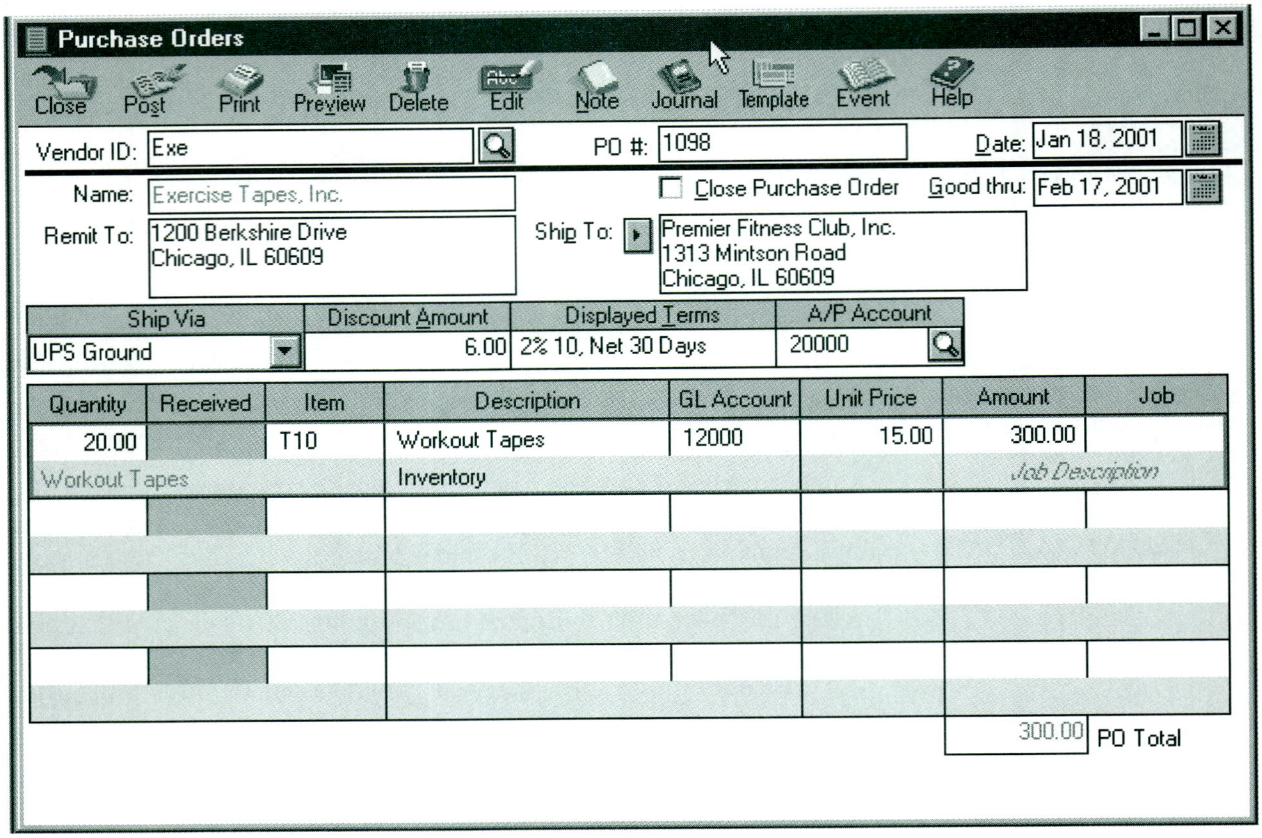

Figure 6–4 Enter a Purchase Order

Peachtree will supply the information for the *Name, Remit To,* and *Ship To* fields.

P.O. #: If you print purchase orders and leave the *P.O. #* field blank, *Peachtree* will assign consecutive numbers to this order and future ones. You can enter a P.O. number and still print the purchase order.

Date: Enter the order date if it differs from the default date displayed in the *Date* field.

Name: The name field is automatically filled in when you select the Vendor ID.

Good Thru: The default is 30 days from the purchase order date.

Close Purchase Order: The *close purchase order* field indicates whether the purchase order is open or closed. If a purchase order is open, the *Close Purchase Order* box is blank. When you record the receipt of the order, *Peachtree* will close the purchase order automatically.

Remit To: The *Remit To* field is filled in automatically, according to the default information you entered for the selected vendor.

Ship To: If shipping address information was entered when the vendor was added to the system, the first *Ship To* address will appear as the default. You can use the drop-down menu to select an alternate address from those entered previously. You could also enter a new address for this order only.

Ship Via: If you entered the default *Ship Via* information during new company setup, *Peachtree* will display the default when you complete the *Vendor ID* field. You can also change the default in the *Ship Via* field when you enter a purchase-order transaction.

Discount Amount: Vendors often offer a discount to encourage prompt payment of invoices. The *Discount Amount* will be calculated based on the terms for this order. You can also enter a specific amount as a discount for an order.

Displayed Terms: The default terms are entered when you set up the company. If different terms apply for this purchase order, enter this now.

A/P Account: The number for the Accounts Payable account in the General Ledger will appear by default. This field is filled in when you select the *Vendor ID*.

Quantity: Each item will be entered on a separate line. Enter the number of items being purchased in the *Quantity* field.

Item: Enter the item to be purchased from this vendor. The item numbers for Premier's merchandise are entered in the template file. Select the item code from the drop-down list.

Received: This field is darkened on the Purchase Orders window, indicating that it is unavailable for entering data.

Description: The *Description* field will display the description for the code selected. You can also enter a different description that you want to appear on reports and purchase orders.

G/L Account: Each item purchased will be charged in the General Ledger to a purchases, asset, or expense account. Enter a *G/L Account* number for each item. The General Ledger account(s) will be updated when the journals are posted.

Note

Purchase orders do not affect the Vendor Ledger or the General Ledger until the ordered items are received from the vendor. You can print or view the purchase order the same as you can an invoice.

Unit Price: Enter the vendor's price per unit in the *Unit Price* field or accept the price from the inventory item default. *Peachtree* will calculate the extension for the item.

Amount: If a unit price has been entered, the extension for it will be calculated and the amount will display in the *Amount* field. You can also enter the amount in this field.

Job: Purchases can be tracked for specific jobs. Use of the Jobs Navigation Aid will be discussed in detail in Chapter 9.

PO Total: The PO Total field represents the total line-items on the purchase order. The total is recalculated after each line is entered.

After you have entered all of the information for a purchase order, select **Post** or **Print**. Selecting **Print** both posts *and* prints the purchase order. If you select **Save**, you can continue to create additional purchase orders and print all the purchase orders later.

Accounting Behind the Screens

When you select the **Journal** button in the Purchase Orders window, *Peachtree* displays the Accounting Behind the Screens window. The Purchase Order Journal tab displays the purchase order transaction in traditional journal format. You can modify the transaction by changing account IDs of journal distributions listed. However, notice the reminder above the journal entry that nothing will be posted until the items have been received.

Print Purchase Orders

There are several ways to print purchase orders. You can print an individual purchase order immediately after you enter it. You can print purchase orders from the Purchases Navigation Aid or print P.O.'s that do not have P.O.'s from the Accounts Payable Report List.

To print a purchase order when you enter it, simply click the **Print** toolbar button on the Purchase Order window. To print a purchase order at any other time,

Step 1 Open the Purchase Order window.

Step 2 Select the **Edit** toolbar button. The Select Purchase Order window will open.

Step 3 From the displayed list, select the purchase order you want to print.

Step 4 Select **OK.** *Peachtree* displays the purchase order.

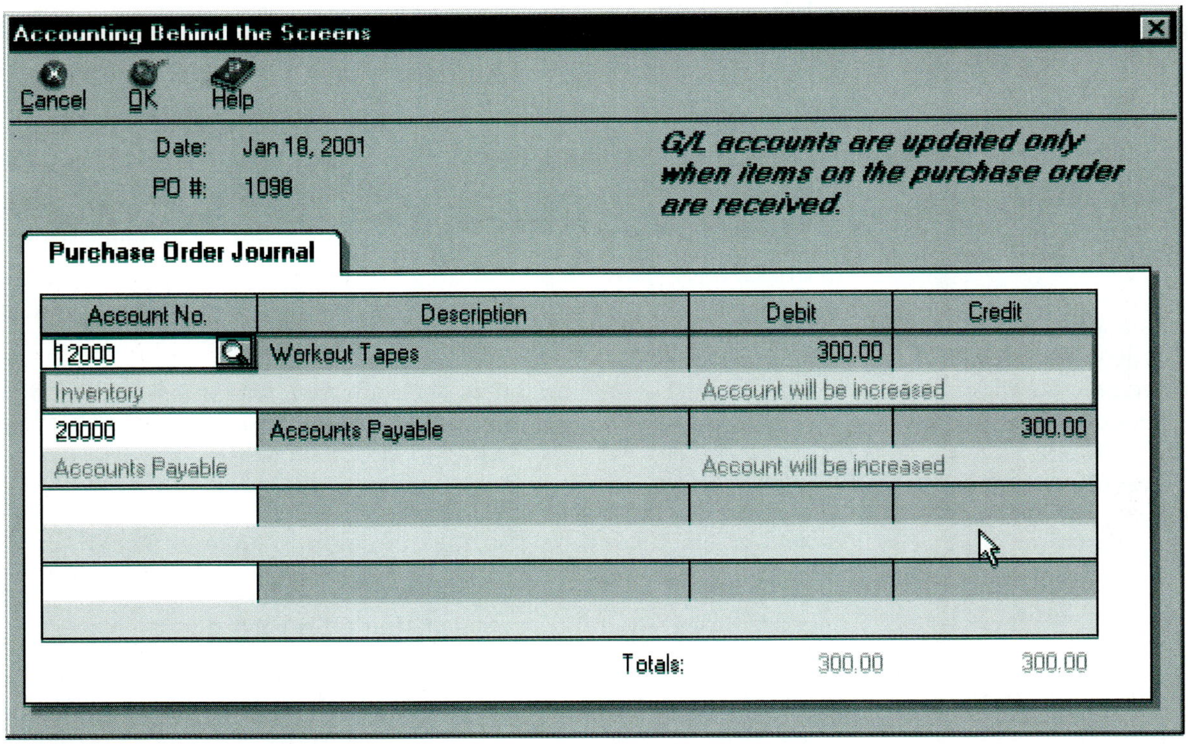

Figure 6–5 Traditional journal format

Step 5 Select the **Print** toolbar button. A dialog box will ask whether you want to print a plain purchase order or use a preprinted form.

Step 6 Select **P.O. Plain.** You will be asked whether you want to print a real or practice form. Select **Real.**

Step 7 If the purchase order has a number assigned, the form will be printed. If you left the *P.O. #* field blank, the About to Print Purchase Order dialog box will appear. Enter or accept *First purchase order number.*

Step 8 Select **OK** to accept this as the purchase order you want to print.

To print a purchase order from the Purchases Navigation Aid,

Step 1 Select the **Print Purchase Orders** button.

Step 2 The Print Forms: Purchase Orders window will open. Select the form you want to print.

Step 3 Select **Real.**

Step 4 Select **OK.** All purchase orders that do not have purchase order numbers assigned will print.

Receiving Inventory on a Purchase Order

After you have entered a purchase order with a vendor, the next step is to receive the inventory for that purchase order as it arrives. You may receive all of the items on the purchase order, less than a complete order, or even more than you ordered. When the order arrives, you will enter the receipt of the order.

Note

If you have received inventory from a vendor by entering a purchase using the *Waiting on Bill* option, *Peachtree* will warn you when you select this vendor so you don't enter the invoice for this vendor's order twice by mistake.

Step 1 From the Purchases Navigation Aid, select Purchases/Receive Inventory. The Purchases/Receive Inventory window will open.

Step 2 Enter or select the Vendor ID. If there are open purchase orders with this vendor, the Apply to Purchase Order # tab displays in front.

Step 3 Enter the vendor's invoice number in the *Invoice #* field. This is a required field. If you have not yet received a vendor invoice (bill) for this shipment, check the *Waiting on Bill from Vendor* box. When the vendor sends you the bill, edit this invoice; clear the *Waiting on Bill from Vendor* box; and enter the invoice number.

Note

If you have the *Hide General Ledger Accounts* global option activated, *Peachtree* will not display the A/P Account field in the Purchases/Receive Inventory swindow.

Step 4 Enter the date of the transaction if it is different from the displayed date.

Step 5 Make any necessary changes to the shipping information, discount, or terms.

Step 6 From the drop-down list on the Apply to Purchase Order # tab, select the purchase order number that you want to receive inventory against. The line-item list will appear. The first two columns on the line-item list, *Item ID* and *Remaining,* are gray, meaning you cannot edit them. If you need to edit the

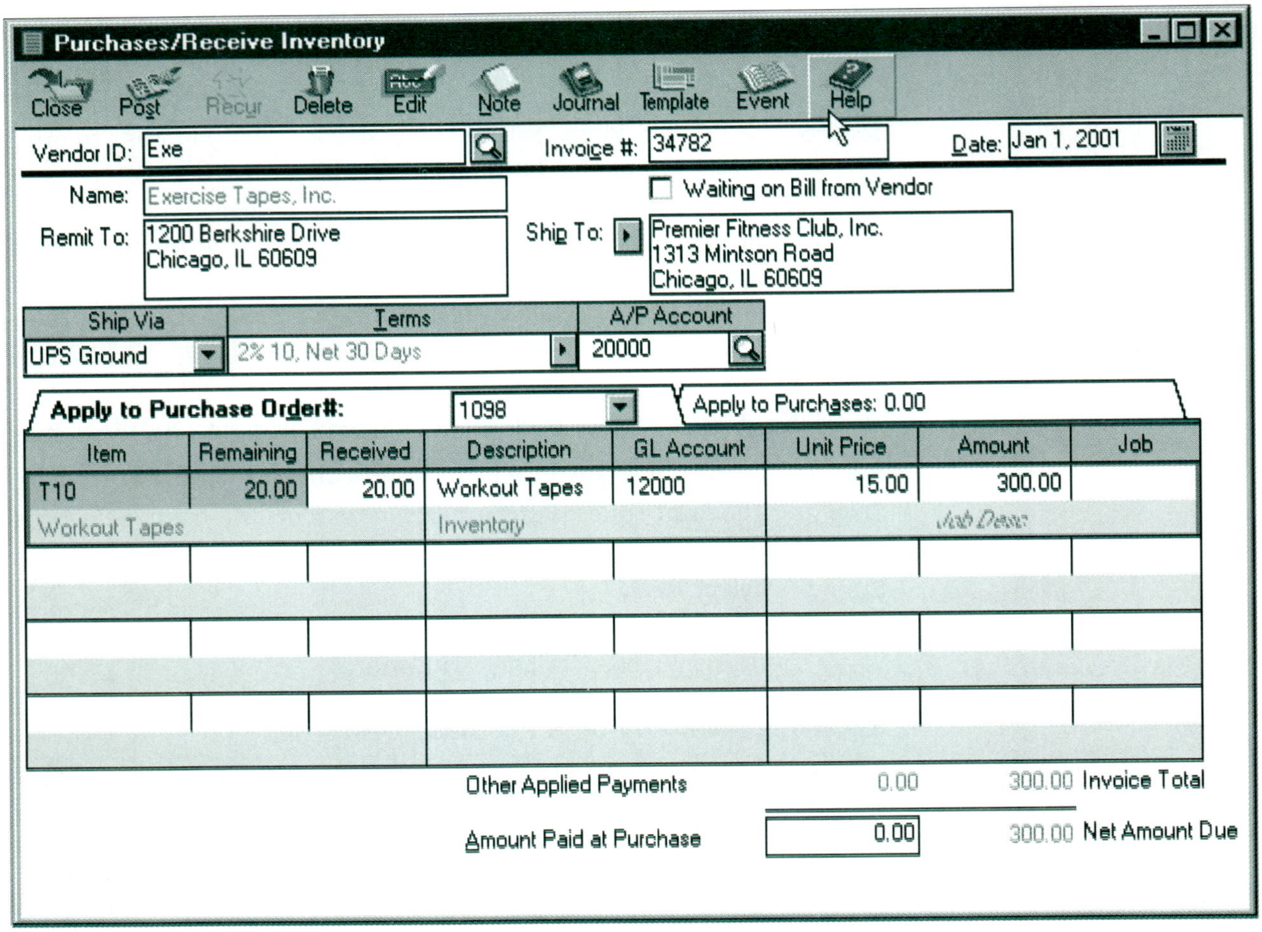

Figure 6–6 Receive items from a purchase order

purchase order, you would have to open the Purchase Order task window.

Step 7 In the *Received* field, enter the quantity of an item received. The *Remaining* column shows the number of items left to be shipped to complete the purchase order. For example, if there were 50 items on a purchase order and you were shipped 30 of them, the next time you display the Purchases/Receive Inventory window for this order, the *Remaining* column will show that 20 items still need to be shipped.

Step 8 The default *G/L Account* that appears for each line item is based on the vendor purchase account default or the item ID selected. You can change the account ID.

Step 9 Continue entering items until you have completed receiving the items in this shipment. The Net Amount Due displays what you currently owe for the purchase.

Step 10 When finished, select the **Post** button to record the purchase.

Note

If there are multiple lines of items on the P.O., and you received all of the items, you can select *Receive All* from the **Edit** menu. Selecting *Receive None* removes all entries from the *Received* field.

Entering a Purchase Invoice Without a Purchase Order

Businesses often make purchases on account without going through the purchase order process. The Purchases/Receive Inventory window allows you to either receive inventory (explained previously) or enter vendor invoices. If you select a vendor with no open purchase orders, the Apply to Purchases tab will display. Follow these steps to enter purchases that did not originate with a purchase order.

The illustration is a transaction from Problem 6 at the end of the chapter. If you enter the transaction as a practice here, do not repeat it at the end of the chapter.

Step 1 Open the Purchase folder.

Step 2 Select the **Purchases/Receive Inventory** Navigation Aid.

Step 3 Select the *Vendor ID* code.

Step 4 Enter the vendor's invoice number in the *Invoice #* field. This field is mandatory in *Peachtree*. If no number appears on the vendor's invoice, assign a number.

Step 5 Tab to the *Date* field. Enter the date from the vendor's invoice.

Step 6 If the vendor default information is correct, tab to the *Quantity* field.

Step 7 Enter the quantity and item code.

Step 8 Enter a description or use the default one.

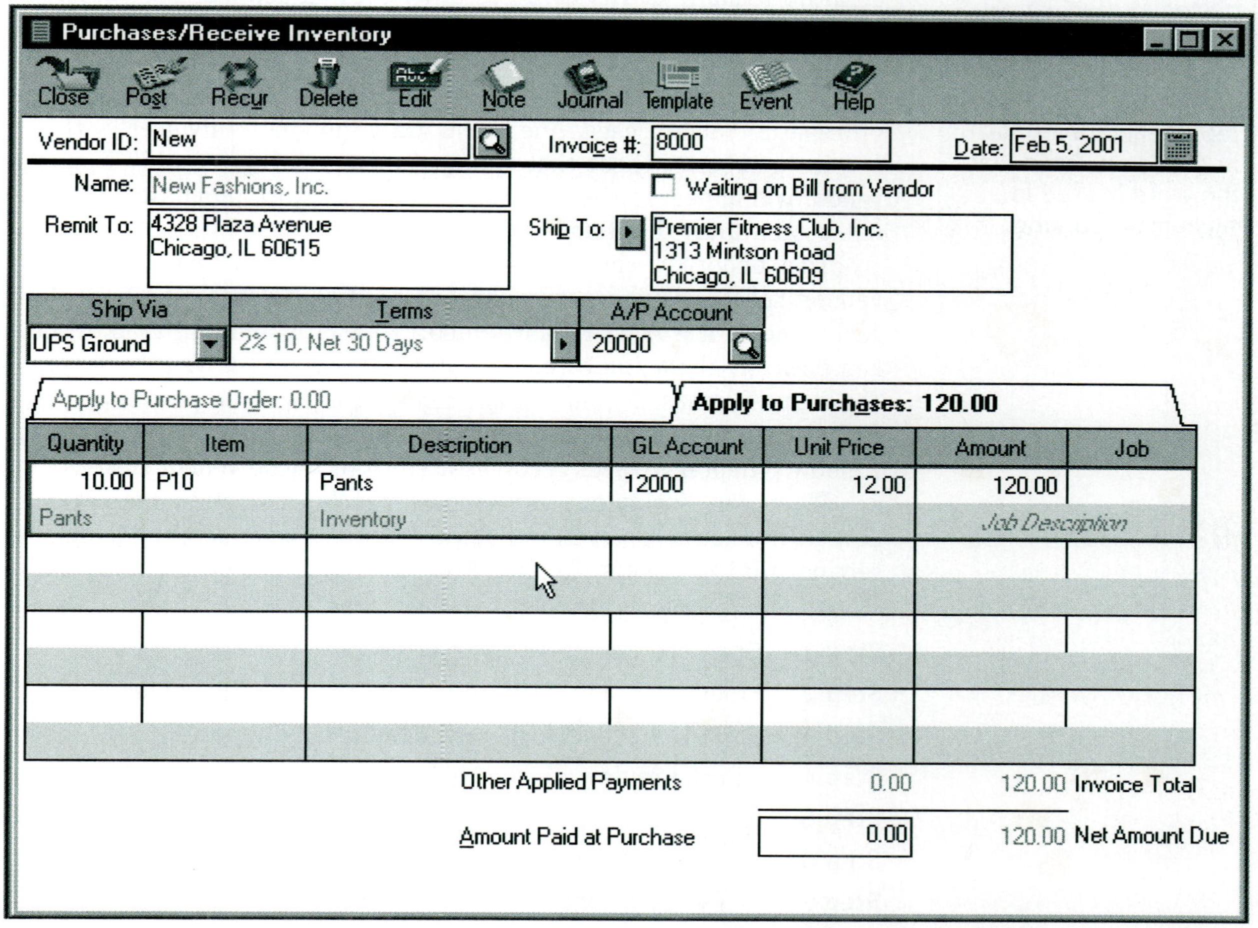

Figure 6–7 Enter a vendor invoice without a purchase order

Step 9 Select the *GL Account* number. Accept the default or enter a different account number.

Step 10 Enter the cost per item in the *Unit Price* field. The *Amount Field* will be calculated.

Step 11 When you have entered all items, select the **Post** icon.

ACCOUNTS PAYABLE REPORTS

Accounts Payable reports detail transactions and other information for the purchases that you make. While a number of the reports may contain similar information, each has a unique purpose. You will print some of the Accounts Payable reports in Problem 6 at the end of this chapter. You may want to explore other reports after you have completed the end-of-chapter problem when the reports will contain more purchase transactions.

Information about purchase orders can be found in three reports. The Purchase Order Register lists the purchase orders (by number) for a selected date range. The Purchase Order Report lists purchase orders with line-item detail including quantity ordered, quantity received, and quantity remaining. The Purchase Order Journal lists purchase orders in journal format. You would use this report to verify all P.O.'s for a specific date range (usually the current accounting period).

Note

Remember that purchase orders are not posted to the General Ledger until the items have been received. The Purchase Order Journal report is not a journal in the same sense that the word is used in manual accounting.

The Purchase Journal is a record of purchases and includes detailed information about each line item. Only purchase invoices with an invoice number or those that you marked as waiting for a bill from the vendor will appear in the Purchases Journal because purchase orders are not posted until the items have been received.

The Vendor List shows all vendor records that you have entered. The Vendor Ledgers report shows the outstanding balance you have with each vendor. The Aged Payables report lists outstanding payables, broken down by the aging categories that were set in the Vendor Defaults. The Items Purchased from Vendors report is a list of all purchases made from vendors. This includes purchases made for cash in the Payments window (Chapter 8). This report is used to reconcile vendor statements.

When you display or print a report, *Peachtree* displays a report window with three tabs. In this chapter you will simply accept the default settings for the reports. To print Accounts Payable Reports, follow these steps.

Step 1 Open the Purchases Navigation Aid.

Step 2 From the Reports section, select **Purchases/Payables Reports.**

Step 3 From the Report List, select the desired report.

Step 4 Select **Preview** on the toolbar.

Step 5 Accept the default settings on the Filter tab. Click **Ok.**

Step 6 Select the **Print** toolbar button.

Step 7 Close the report window.

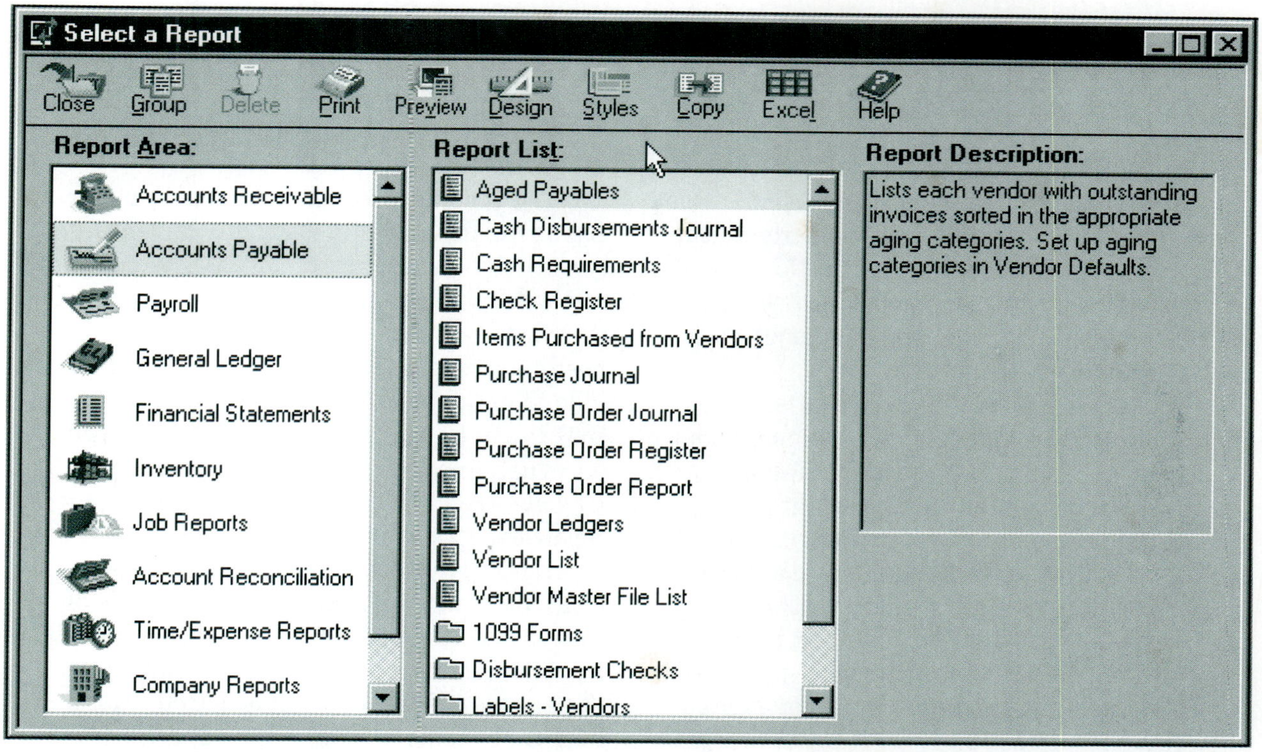

Figure 6–8 Select an Accounts Payable report

Accidents Will Happen

Everyone makes mistakes; but if you do not back up your data, the mistake can be extremely costly. No computer system can be completely protected from catastrophes such as power outages or computer viruses.

Although more than half of all computer users have lost data or files, only about a third of them back up their files regularly. According to data-recovery experts, although almost 50 percent of business users value their data at more than $2,000, most users do not back up their files every week. Of course, depending on what business you're in, those lost files might be worth much, much more.

There are two easy ways to protect yourself from a data disaster. First, always make multiple copies of important files. Keep the copies in a separate place away from the original. If you save your backup files on your PC's hard drive, for example, you'll be out of luck if your PC breaks down or gets infected by a virulent computer virus. Thus, save the file to your office's network, if it has one, or even on a good, old-fashioned floppy disk.

The second essential data-saving strategy is to occasionally back up the entire contents of your computer's hard drive. This method helps protect not only your important data but also those programs that you need to access it. Because most applications hide files all over the system, you'll find that it can be almost impossible to find the one that is causing a specific problem. It may be even harder to replace the file or repair the damage.

Again, you *could* back up the data to disks or a network. But the sheer size of today's software applications—and the capacity of most new hard drives—would make that process long and excruciating. For a long time, experts have recommended backing up PC files to magnetic tape (in fact, the files of most office networks are backed up this way). The necessary hardware, software, and the tape itself can be expensive, but it's worth it—especially if you are trying to run a business off a single, stand-alone PC or a few non-networked ones.

SUMMARY OF KEY POINTS

1. When products or services are received but payment will be made later, it is referred to as a purchase on account.
2. Entering basic setup information that applies to most of your vendors and purchase transactions in the Vendor Defaults window will save time during data entry.
3. A purchase order is a purchase request; posting a purchase order does not actually update any accounting information.
4. The Accounting Behind the Screens feature displays purchases transactions in traditional journal format.
5. The Purchases/Receive Inventory window is used to record vendor invoices when items are received from a purchase order and when items are purchased that did not originate with a purchase order.
6. Purchase orders can be printed as they are created or in a group from the Accounts Payable report window.
7. Accounts Payable reports include the Purchase Order Register, Purchase Journal, and Vendor Ledgers.

*inter*NET CONNECTION

As a professional, you can benefit greatly from connecting with others in your field. Here's a list of some U.S. associations. (International resources can be found at

http://raw.rutgers.edu/raw/aaa/links/intassoc.htm .)

American Accounting Association

http://raw.rutgers.edu/raw/aaa/index.html

American Institute of Certified Public Accountants (has a student section)

http://www.aicpa.org

American Society of Women Accountants

http://www.aswa.org

Association of Government Accountants

http://www.agacgfm.org

Financial Executives Institute

http://www.fei.org

Institute of Management Accountants

http://www.rutgers.edu/Accounting/raw/ima

National Association of Enrolled Agents

http://www.naea.org

National Association of Black Accountants

http://www.nabainc.org

Name ______________________________ Date ______________

CHAPTER REVIEW AND APPLICATIONS

1. Payment terms that are common to most vendors should be set in the ____________________ .
2. If you want to track specific information about your vendors and *Peachtree* does not provide a field for it on the Accounts Payable task windows, you can set up ____________________ in the vendor defaults to record the information.
3. To change the date for transactions you enter in *Peachtree*, change the ____________________ date.
4. To change the accounting period, use the ____________________ menu and select the ____________________ and ____________________ submenus.
5. Entering a purchase order does not update General Ledger or Vendor Ledger accounts. Those accounts will be updated when ____________________.
6. To record the receipt of a purchase order, use the ____________________ task window.
7. The *Peachtree* feature that lets you see purchase transactions in traditional journal format is called ____________________.
8. To print a single purchase order after it has been posted, use the ____________________ toolbar button on the Purchase Order window to display the order.
9. If you want to know the total amount owed to each vendor, print a ____________________ report.
10. Line-item details about purchase orders can be found in the ____________________ report.

Name ______________________________ Date ______________

Problem 6

Record purchase transactions for Premier Fitness Club

Instructions

Step 1 Restore the backup file for Premier Fitness Club, Inc., from Chapter 5.

Step 2 Change the Accounting Period to February 1–February 28, 2001.

Step 3 Change the System Date to February 1, 2001.

Step 4 Enter the following purchase transactions. If you want to print the purchase orders after all have been entered, you must leave the *P.O.#* field blank and assign the beginning number (2001) when you are ready to print.

Step 5 Print the purchase orders.

Step 6 Print the Purchase Order Register.

Step 7 Print the Purchase Journal.

Step 8 Print the Vendor Ledgers report.

Step 9 Display the General Ledger.

Transactions

Feb. 1 Premier ordered 50 shirts for $12.00 each, and 50 pants for $8.00 each, both on Purchase Order 2001, from Sports World. Ship via UPS Ground. Terms 2/10, n/30.

Feb. 5 Premier purchased 10 pants from a new vendor, New Fashions, Inc., without a purchase order. Invoice 8000. New Fashions, Inc. is located at 4328 Plaza Avenue, Chicago, IL 60615. Telephone, 312-555-0985. Contact is Donald Thompson. Vendor Type: Product. Ship: UPS Ground. Terms 2/10, n/30.

Feb. 9 Premier purchased office supplies from Frank's Office Supplies for $160.50. Frank's Office Supplies is located at 1876 Michigan Avenue, Chicago, IL 60617. The telephone number is 312-555-4884. Vendor Type: Supplies. Charge the purchase account to Office Expense (71000), invoice 258. Terms n/30. Ship: UPS Ground. Enter 100 in the *Quantity* field.

Feb. 10 The company ordered 20 workout tapes from Exercise Tapes, Inc. for $15.00 each, on Purchase Order 2002.

Feb. 11 Premier received a shipment of 50 shirts and 50 pants ordered from Sports World from Purchase Order 2001. Invoice 7248 accompanied the shipment.

Feb. 12	You ordered one case of cleaning materials from Smiling Cleaners for $107.00, Purchase Order 2003. Charge this item to 68000 Laundry and Cleaning Expense.
Feb. 14	The company ordered 120 shirts, for $12.00 each, on Purchase Order 2004 from Sports World.
Feb. 15	You received invoice 753 and a shipment of 20 workout tapes from Exercise Tapes, Inc. (P.O. 2002).
Feb. 16	You ordered office supplies from R&R Supplies for $214.00 on Purchase Order number 2005. R&R Supplies is located at 3425 Westchester Drive, Chicago, IL 60611. The telephone number is 312-555-1199. Charge the supplies to account 71000 Office Expense. Terms n/30. Ship via Airborne. Vendor Type: Supplies.
Feb. 17	You received shipment and Invoice 9238 from Smiling Cleaners for $107, for P.O. 2003.
Feb. 18	You received Invoice 7275 and a shipment of P.O. 2004 from Sports World.
Feb. 19	Premier ordered 5 gifts for several top corporate clients, for a total of $535.00, on Purchase Order 2006. The purchase order was issued to R&R Supplies. The purchase should be charged to 66000 Gifts Expense.
Feb. 21	Premier ordered additional cleaning materials (Qty. 1) from Smiling Cleaners for $321.00, Purchase Order 2007.
Feb. 27	The company ordered 40 workout tapes from Exercise Tapes, Inc., for $15.00 each, on Purchase Order number 2008.
Feb. 28	You ordered 30 pants from Sports World on Purchase Order 2009.

Note

Enter 1 as the quantity if one is not specified.

Name ______________________________ Date ______________

Analyzing Your Work

Use the printed Accounts Payable reports to answer the following questions.

1. What was the value of all the purchase orders issued during February?

   ____

2. By what amount did Inventory (12000) increase during February?

   ____

3. What was the total of the Purchase Journal for February? Why is this amount different from the increase in the inventory account (Question 2)?

   ____

4. To which vendor does Premier owe the highest amount?

   ____

5. What was the total increase in Accounts Payable during February?

   ____

6. Challenge Question: What is the amount of open purchase orders as of February 28? Where can this information be found?

   ____

Chapter 7

Cash Receipts

OBJECTIVES

When you have completed Chapter 7, you should be able to:

1. Apply a cash receipt to a sales invoice.
2. Enter a cash-sale transaction.
3. Recalculate the account balance after a receipt transaction.
4. Calculate sales discounts.
5. Enter prepayments or deposits.
6. Print Accounts Receivable reports.
7. Apply finance charges.
8. Print customer statements.
9. Define terms used in the chapter.

In earlier chapters, you read about how a business needs good records that show where its money comes from, where it goes, and how the organization is performing. This chapter deals with cash received at the time of the sale or receipts from customers on account. Businesses must record each cash transaction.

Note

A credit card charge is to be treated as a check.

Checks and bank credit card charges are usually considered as cash. When a customer pays cash, a receipt is often prepared. A receipt includes information, such as the date the cash was received, the amount, a brief description of the product or services sold, and the name of the customer. A cash register receipt is often used as the receipt.

Peachtree Complete Accounting 8.0's Receipts task window allows you to enter all checks, cash, and credit card slips you receive and deposit them in your checking account. When you receive cash from customers on account, the accounting entry is a debit to Cash and a credit to Accounts Receivable. If the customer takes a cash discount, there is also a debit to Sales Discount.

When you record cash sales, the entry is a debit to Cash and a credit to a sales revenue account. If you use a cash register, it probably provides the data you need to make the entry in the Cash Sales Journal (using the Receipts window). You will most likely make this entry whenever you remove cash from the cash register and deposit it in the bank. You can also use the Cash Receipts Journal for other cash receipts. The entry would debit Cash and credit another account, according to the source of the receipt. An example would be the sale of used office equipment.

RECEIVE PAYMENT FROM A CUSTOMER

When a customer pays an invoice, enter the amount in the Receipts window. If you sent an invoice to a customer, you must apply the receipt to the invoice. Invoices entered through Sales/Invoicing appear as distribution lines when you enter the Customer ID. You can check the Pay column beside each invoice being paid in full by the receipt.

To apply a receipt to a customer's invoice, complete the following steps. Open the windows as you follow the illustration, but do not post the receipt at this time. You will have an opportunity to practice these steps in Problem 7 at the end of the chapter.

Step 1 Open the Sales Navigation Aid.

Step 2 Select **Receipts.** The Select a Cash Account window will open.

Step 3 Select the cash account from the drop-down list (i.e., Regular Checking Account). The Receipts window will open.

Step 4 The Receipts window will display.

Step 5 Enter a *Deposit ticket ID* that will easily identify the source of the receipt.

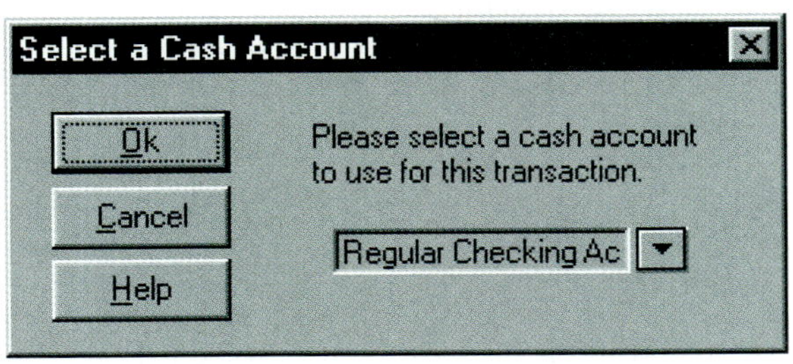

Figure 7–1 Select the cash account for receipts

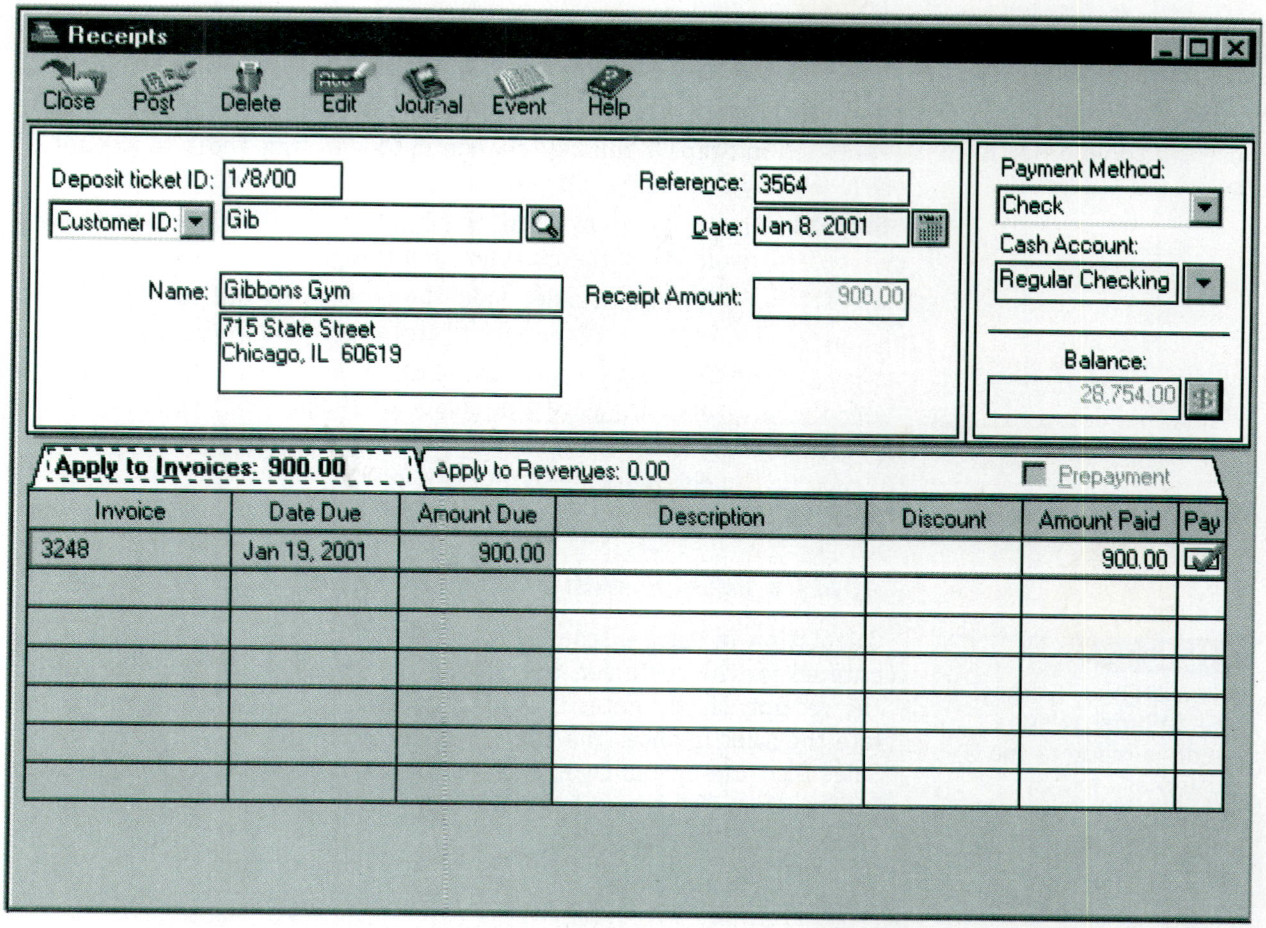

Figure 7–2 Apply customer receipt to a sales invoice

The *Deposit ticket ID* field is correlated with the Account Reconciliation process. *Peachtree* automatically enters the deposit ticket ID as a numeric representation of the accounting system date. All receipts that use the same *Deposit ticket ID* will appear as one lump sum in Account Reconciliation. For example, if you make daily deposits, all receipts with the date of 1/8/01 will be combined in the Account Reconciliation window. This should be the same as the amount that appears on your bank statement for that date. If you want each receipt transaction to be reconciled as a separate item, enter a unique *Deposit ticket ID* for each one.

> **Note**
> If you have the *Hide General Ledger Accounts* global option activated, the Cash Account lookup list displays only names of cash accounts currently set up in the Chart of Accounts. If you want to apply an alternate G/L account (an account that uses an account type other than Cash) for this payment receipt, you must select the **Journal** button.

Step 6 Enter or select the *Customer ID*. *Peachtree* will supply the customer's name and address.

Step 7 When you select a customer who has unpaid invoices, *Peachtree* lists them on the Apply to Invoices tab. If there are no unpaid invoices, *Peachtree* displays the Apply to Revenue tab.

Step 8 Enter a *Reference* number that will help identify the receipt (for example, the customer's check number). You must enter a reference number in order to post the receipt.

> **Note**
> You can key the Customer ID. You can use the Lookup Box to select the customer.

Step 9 Select the *Payment Method* (for example, Cash or Check). Payment methods were set up in Customer Defaults (Chapter 3).

Step 10 The *Cash Account* field will display the account you selected in Step 3. You can change it by entering another account or by selecting a different one from the drop-down list.

Step 11 On the Apply to Invoices tab, check the *Pay* box next to each invoice that the customer is paying.

- If the customer paid the invoice in full, check the *Pay* box. *Peachtree* will fill in the *Amount Paid* field.
- If the customer made only a partial payment on the invoice, place the cursor in the Amount column for the invoice and enter the amount paid. *Peachtree* will automatically check the *Pay* box.

Step 12 Select *Post* to record the receipt.

Apply a Receipt with a Sales Discount

> **Note**
> If a customer overpays the amount owed, a credit is made to the customer's ledger account. If less than the total invoice amount is paid, the payment amount is applied to the invoice balance.

Calculation of sales discounts is based on three factors: the terms you entered for the customer, the date of the sales invoice, and the date of the receipt. If you enter these factors accurately, *Peachtree* will calculate the sales invoice. The amount of the discount will be posted to the Sales Discount account you selected in the Accounts Receivable Default Information. The amount that *Peachtree* calculates and displays can be overridden if necessary.

Edit or Delete an Invoice with a Receipt

If you would like to edit or delete an invoice for a customer and you have already entered a receipt, you will need to first delete the receipt before you can edit or delete the invoice. You need to delete the receipt if you want to change the invoice number or the customer on an invoice or if you want to delete the entire invoice.

> **Note**
> In cases where maintaining an audit trail is important, you will want to void rather than delete an invoice.

Step 1 From the Receipts window, select the *Edit* toolbar button.

Step 2 From the list, select the receipt and then *OK* to display the receipt.

Step 3 Once the receipt is displayed, select the **Delete** toolbar button.

Step 4 Open the Sales/Invoicing window.

Step 5 Select the *Edit* toolbar button so you can edit the original invoice.

Step 6 From the list, select the invoice you want to edit, and click *OK*.

Once *Peachtree* displays the original invoice, make any necessary changes. If this invoice is for items ordered on a sales order, you cannot change the Customer ID. If you want to remove the invoicing transaction, select the **Delete** toolbar button. If you were editing the invoice, select the **Post** button. You will need to enter the receipt for the payment again if you edited the invoice.

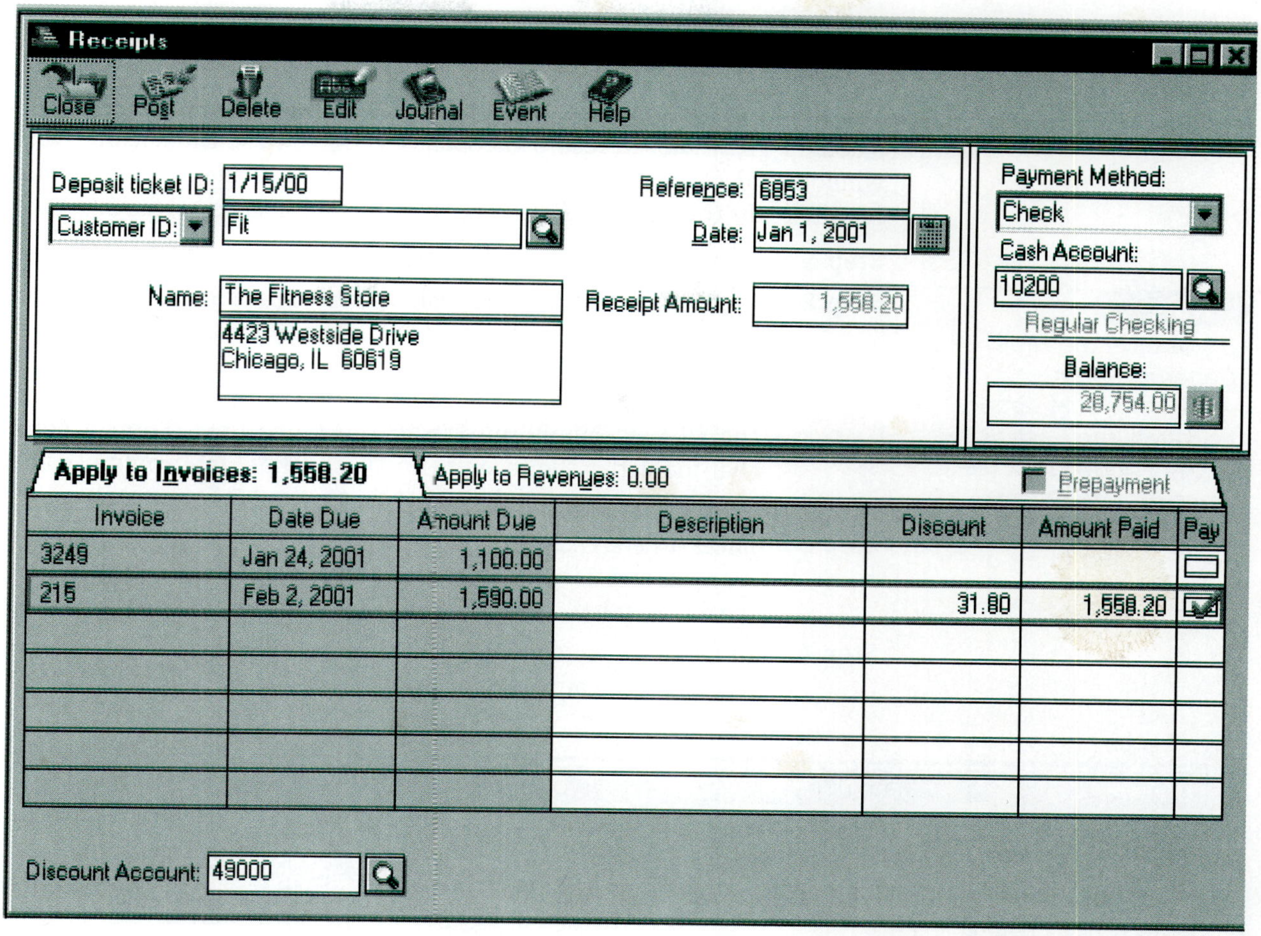

Figure 7–3 Apply a receipt with a discount

Apply a Credit Memo to an Invoice

You entered a credit memo for Alpha Insurance in Chapter 5. Once you have entered and posted a credit memo, follow these steps to apply it to an invoice.

Step 1 From the Sales Navigation Aid, select *Receipts*.

Step 2 On the Receipts window, select the Customer ID (Alp). The credit memo appears (a negative amount) in the line-item list.

Step 3 Enter or accept the system date for the transaction.

Step 4 Select the *Pay* check box for the credit memo. This will post the credit memo (refund). If a discount has been calculated, delete it.

Step 5 Now, find the invoice you want to apply it to, and pay it for the same amount, only positive. The amount of the receipt will display zero (0.00).

Step 6 Enter a receipt reference number (use the credit memo number).

Step 7 Select **Save.** This will clear both transactions from the Customer Ledger.

ENTER RECEIPTS FOR CASH SALES

If you made a direct sale that did not require an invoice, it is considered a cash sale. To record the transaction, you use the Receipts task window and enter the transaction on the Apply to Revenues tab. This requires you to specify a *Reference* number and a sales account.

Note

If you have the *Hide General Ledger Accounts* global option activated, the Cash Account lookup list displays only names of cash accounts currently set up in the Chart of Accounts.

Step 1 From the Sales Navigation Aid, select **Receipts.**

Step 2 If you want to track the cash sale to a specific customer, enter the *Customer ID*. Entering a *Customer ID* for a cash-sale transaction will not affect Accounts Receivable. You are merely tracking the total sales made to the customer. You can leave the *ID* field blank and tab to the *Name* field. Enter a name that identifies the receipt (i.e., Cash Sale). You would use this method to record cash register receipts, for example.

Step 3 Enter a *Reference* for this transaction. This must be a unique number and is generally the customer's check number or a receipt number. "CASH" should not be used as the reference.

Step 4 In the *Cash Account* list, enter or select the bank account in which the receipt is deposited.

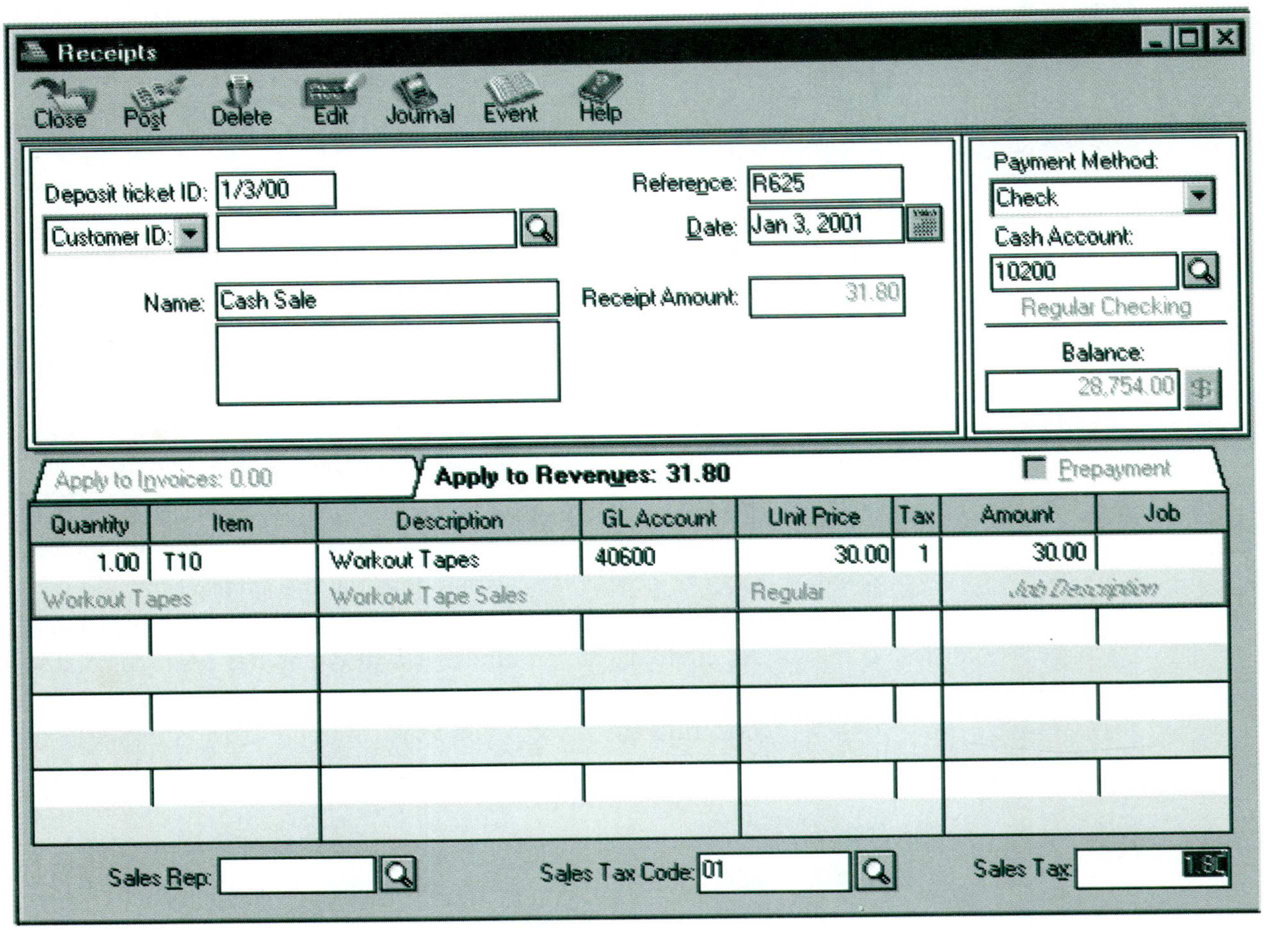

Figure 7–4 Enter a cash sale

Step 5 On the Apply to Revenues tab, enter the line items on the receipt the same way you did in the Sales/Invoicing window.

Step 6 Select the *Sales Tax Code* at the bottom of the window. The *Sales Tax* field will be calculated. If you chose a Customer ID for a cash sale, the tax will calculate automatically. You must select the tax code for cash sales without an ID.

Step 7 Select *Post*.

Recalculate Cash Balance Automatically

As discussed in an earlier chapter, you can choose to turn off certain options on the Accounting tab of the Maintain Global Options window. One such option is recalculating the cash balance each time you open Receipts, Payments, or Payroll Entry windows, or when you post a receipt, payment, or paycheck.

If *Peachtree* displays the word *Uncalculated* in the *Balance* field, the *Recalculate cash balance automatically in Receipts and Payments* global option is currently not selected. Turning off the recalculate feature can speed up data entry. For this tutorial, the recalculate feature is active for Premier Fitness Club's accounting system.

If the recalculation option is not active, you can change the global option or manually update the cash balance after each entry or when you need to know the account balance. To recalculate the balance manually, click the *$* next to the *Balance* field. The balance will appear as of the date in the Receipts window.

ENTER A PREPAYMENT OR DEPOSIT

Sometimes a customer will make a deposit against or prepay for an order. If you check the *Prepayment* box on the Apply to Revenues tab, you cannot apply the receipt to an existing invoice.

To enter a receipt as a prepayment, perform the following steps. The steps are for illustration only; you will not enter a prepayment.

Step 1 Open the Sales Navigation Aid.

Step 2 Select the **Receipts** icon.

Step 3 Enter the date of the deposit in the *Deposit ticket ID* field.

Step 4 Enter or select the Customer ID. This is a required field for a prepayment.

Step 5 Enter the customer's check number in the *Reference* field.

Step 6 Enter the date on which the deposit or prepayment was received.

Step 7 Select the Payment Method.

Step 8 On the Apply to Revenues tab, check the *Prepayment* box. Only the *Description, G/L Account,* and *Amount* fields are active on the distribution lines.

Step 9 Enter a description.

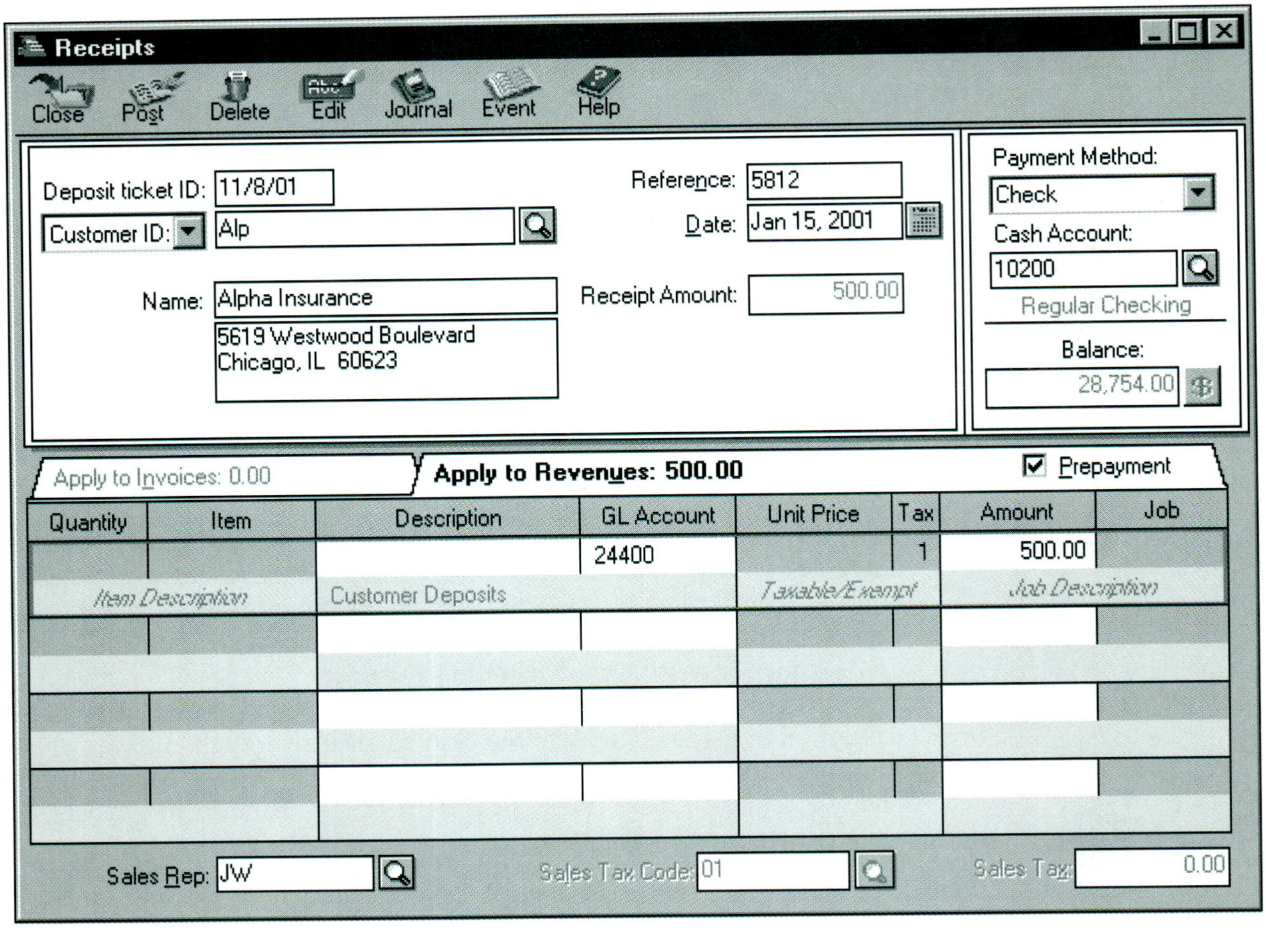

Figure 7–5 Prepayment or deposit by a customer

> **Note**
> When a field on a screen is grayed out, it is unavailable for editing or entering information.

Step 10 In the *G/L Account* field, select the account for prepaid income or customer deposits.

Step 11 Select **Post.**

After you have posted the prepayment, it will display as a credit invoice for the customer. You can apply the credit to the appropriate invoice when you access the Receipts window again and enter the Customer ID.

PRINTING ACCOUNTS RECEIVABLE REPORTS

If your company has a large number of charge customers, management will want to review the status of accounts on a regular basis. Accounts receivable reports detail transactions and other information for all your sales—both invoiced and cash sales. The Accounts Receivable module provides several summary reports giving information about customers—from a record of how much each customer has purchased in the year to date, to credit terms and credit limit for the customer, to the amount of current and past due bills.

In addition to the Accounts Receivable reports you prepared in Chapter 5, you can prepare customer statements, including collection notices to customers whose accounts are past due. You can also calculate and add a finance charge, which is a penalty levied on customers who do not pay their bills on time. Figure 7–6 illustrates a partial list of available reports. Scroll through the list and briefly select each report. A short description of the selected report will appear on the right side of the window.

You will print several reports for Premier Fitness Club in the problem at the end of this chapter. The Cash Receipts Journal prints a list of your customer receipts in journal format. You can use this report to verify the General Ledger posting of receipt transactions. The Aged Receivables report shows the status of receivables, aged by invoice date or due date, depending on what you set up in Customer Defaults.

The Customer Ledgers report lists customers with detail transaction information as well as outstanding balances per customer. The Customer Sales History report lists sales totals for each of your customers. Sale amounts are derived from recorded invoices in the Sales/Invoicing window as well as cash sales entered in the Receipts window.

In addition to printed reports, you can look up the Current Payment Status of any Sales Invoice. Use the following procedure to determine if payments have been applied to an invoice.

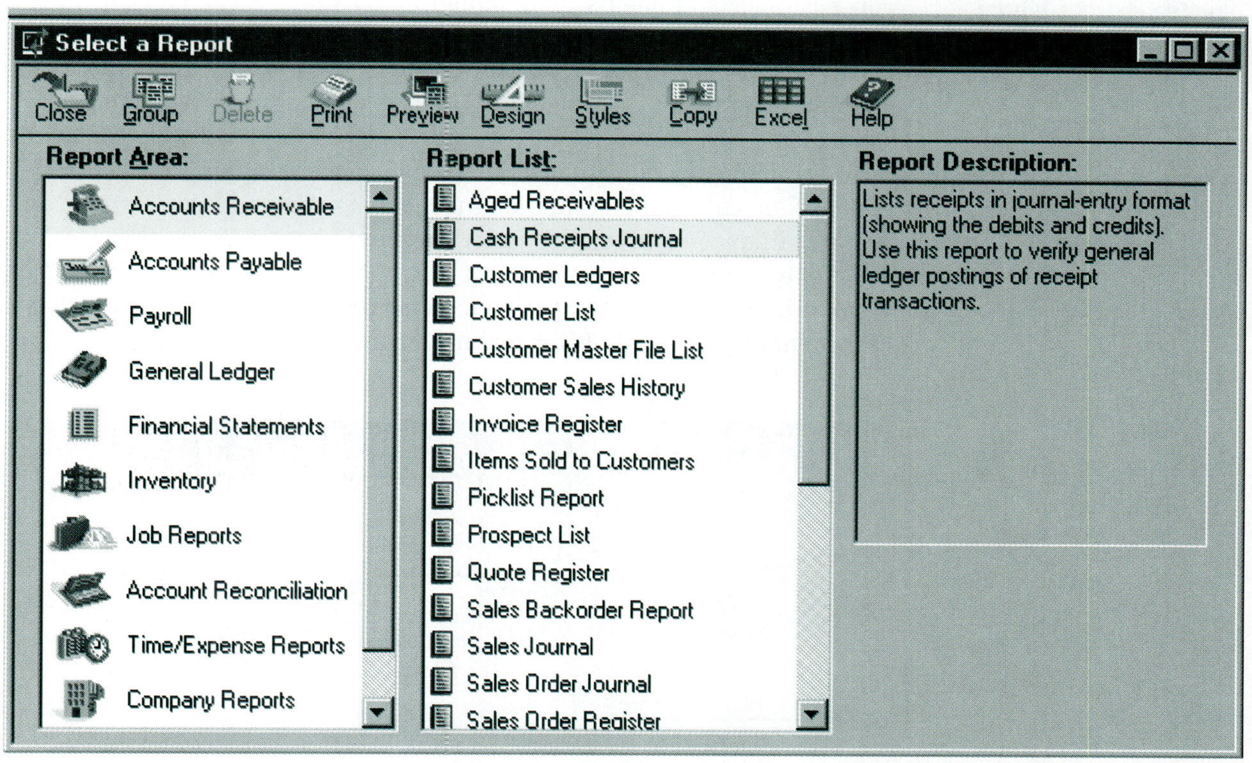

Figure 7–6 Select an Accounts Receivable Report

Step 1 Open the Sales/Invoicing window.

Step 2 Select the *Edit* toolbar button to display the Select Transaction Lookup List. The payment status appears in this list as Unpaid, Partially Paid, or Paid in Full.

Step 3 Select an existing sales invoice transaction to display.

Step 4 The Payment Status appears just below the *Date* field.

APPLYING FINANCE CHARGES

> **Note**
> Because *Peachtree* knows "FC" as *finance charge*, never use FC as a reference for a customer's invoice or any journal entry. *Peachtree* will treat this code as a finance charge and recalculate the customer's charges!

Most customers pay on time. Some pay early to take advantage of discounts offered for prompt payment. For example, for an invoice that has terms of 2/10, n 30, you would find that a few customers will pay in 10 days to get a discount. You would find that most customers will pay the full amount by thirty days. There will be a few customers who do not pay when the net amount is due. Those customers are the ones to whom finance charges must be applied.

Premier Fitness Club does not assess finance charges. The following information is given for your knowledge of this function. You will not apply this in the end-of-chapter problem.

> **Note**
> You should apply finance charges before printing your statements.

The Finance Charges Journal details how charges were calculated. The journal entries are identified with the prefix "FC" (Finance Charge). *Peachtree* tracks charges daily, but it calculates charges only when you print the Finance Charges Report. Because finance charges should show on customer statements, you should apply finance charges before you print the statements.

Select the **Apply Finance Charges** task icon from the Sales Navigation folder. The Calculate Finance Charges window (Figure 7–7) will appear. In this window you will identify the customers for whom you want to calculate finance charges. Select the appropriate customer ID for *Starting Customer* and *Ending Customer* fields. If you want to calculate finance charges for one customer only, select the *Starting Customer Only* button and select **Ok**. (Figure 7–8 will appear.) This screen allows you to apply finance charges, print a calculation sheet, and generate a report. After making your choices, select **Ok**.

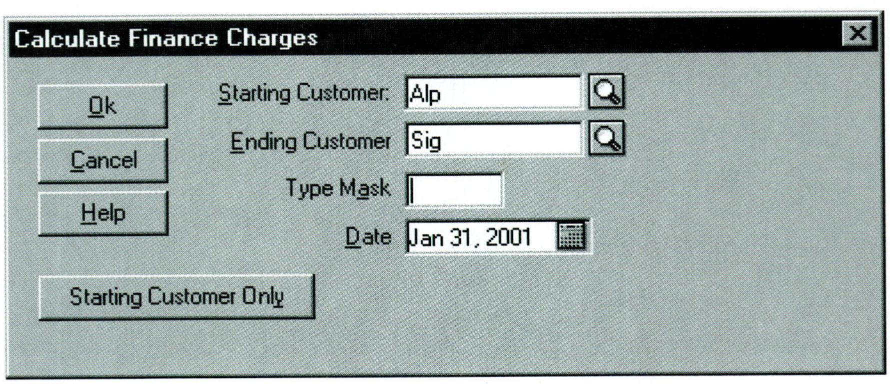

Figure 7–7 Calculate finance charges

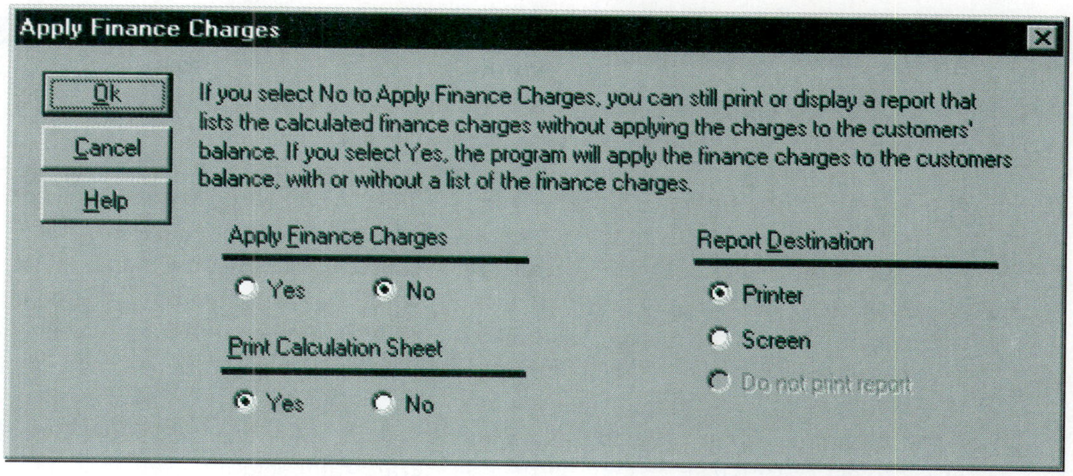

Figure 7–8 Apply charges and print reports

> **Note**
> When the statement finishes printing, a message box displays, asking if the statements printed are okay and if it is okay to update the customer file. Select **Yes** to continue.

CUSTOMER STATEMENTS

Periodically you will send statements to customers, usually on a monthly basis. Your statements will note invoices that are currently due (or past due). Statements also reflect payments received during the period. From the Reports section of the Sales Navigation Aid, select **Sales/Receivables Reports**. Scroll through the Reports List (Figure 7–6) until you find the Customer Statements folder. Select the desired form from those listed.

> **Note**
> To keep Balance Forward amounts correct, enter, print, and post all invoices and receipts prior to preparing customer statements.

COLLECTION LETTERS

You may send collection letters to customers whose accounts are past due. The five letters vary in tone and severity depending upon the lateness of the payment, from a friendly reminder for the first letter to a much firmer tone for accounts more than 90 days overdue. All of the letters can be customized to reflect your company's preferences.

Scroll through the Report List for Accounts Receivable until you find the Collection Letters folder. Select Collection Letters. Select Preview to see one or more of the collection letters.

> **Note**
> Collection letters only print for the amount overdue *in the aging bracket specified in the Oldest Outstanding invoice filter.*

The Permanent Record

Avoiding catastrophe isn't the only good reason to keep extra copies of your work. Many files are constantly being worked on and changed. Files often pass through many hands before they reach their final state. But everyone else's hard work shouldn't go to waste, and the previous versions shouldn't simply be erased. Even after a project is finished, it may be necessary to call up a file, months or even years later.

It's hard to quantify exactly how much time, money, and trouble you'll save by permanently archiving your files. In many cases, the most compelling reason is a legal one. Anyone who works for or with the government, for example, is required to keep meticulous books. CPA firms have to record not only all their clients' current tax information, but also all changes that have been made to it. Of course whenever the IRS audits someone, they are allowed to ask for tax records for the past several years. It'll be hard to meet that requirement if you threw them out with that old PC.

Consider a company that performs the same service for a clients once a year, every year. (Let's say they cater, in addition to other events, many local office Christmas parties.) If the company did not have the last year's files archived (what food the clients ordered, how much of it they ate, what the total cost was), the company probably wouldn't find themselves in any legal tangles by the loss of the orginal file of data. But to plan work for next Christmas will be a lot harder because they'll have to start from scratch.

Eventually even the heftiest hard drive will run out of room. Networks, too, may perform much more slowly when they're bogged down with years of files. Traditional disks suffice for archiving small files, but recordable CD-ROMs and Zip disks have now replaced them in many offices. The benefit of these devices is that you can put a large number of files on a single disk, and you can keep all the data and correspondence from the project together. (Label it "Christmas Party 2001" and file it away until next December.) There are even software applications available to help you keep track of all that archived data.

At the very least, before you delete an important document to make room on your hard drive, print it so that you will have a hard copy.

SUMMARY OF KEY POINTS

1. You will use the Receipts window for receipts that are applied to an invoice and for receipts from cash sales.
2. The source document for cash sales is usually a cash register receipt or a written receipt.
3. The *Deposit ticket ID* field should contain the same identifier for all receipts that are included in a single bank deposit.
4. Using the Apply to Invoices tab of the Receipts window speeds up the recording process.
5. Sales discounts are calculated automatically based on the invoice date, receipt date, and the terms applied to the invoice.
6. If you need to edit an invoice after a receipt has been applied, you will need to delete the receipt, edit the invoice, and then reapply the receipt.
7. You can track cash sales to individual customers by following the procedure for cash sales. Such an entry will be posted as a debit to the checking account (cash) and a credit to a sales revenue account.
8. *Peachtree's* Recalculate Cash Balance feature displays a new cash balance after each receipt or payment is posted.
9. The Cash Receipts Journal report displays receipt transactions in traditional journal format.
10. You can use the edit function of the Sales/Invoicing window to determine the payment status of any invoice that has been entered.
11. You can use the Apply Finance Charges feature to calculate finance charges and print a report even if the charges are not applied to the customer's account.
12. Customer statements and collection letters can be automatically generated from the accounting records.

*inter*NET CONNECTION

Even if you're already employed, you will find this job site useful: **http://www.accountingjobs.com/**. It contains not only a place to post a resume and look at job openings, but it also has numerous links such as employer evaluations, finance and accounting resources, a searchable CPA directory, chat forums, audio interviews, news and research, and how to get incorporation and trademark protection.

Name ______________________________ Date ______________

CHAPTER REVIEW AND APPLICATIONS

1. For accounting purposes, bank credit card receipts and checks are considered to be the same as ____________________.
2. To delete a cash receipt transaction, display the receipts by using the ____________________ toolbar button.
3. When a customer pays for an invoice that you posted previously, use the ____________________ tab in the Receipts window.
4. When you record a receipt from a customer that does not apply to an invoice, enter the information on the ____________________ tab of the Receipts window.
5. Matching deposits with those on the bank statement will be necessary when you complete the ____________________ process.
6. You must enter a ____________________ in order to post a receipt transaction.
7. To review all receipts in a traditional debit and credit format, print a ____________________ report.
8. If a customer makes a payment or deposit before a sales order or an invoice has been entered, it is entered as a ____________________.
9. To display the outstanding balance for each customer, print a ____________________ report.
10. To learn the total sold to each customer on account, as well as cash sales, generate a ____________________ report.
11. To learn the payment status of an invoice, display the invoice on the screen. The payment status will display as *Unpaid,* ____________________, or ____________________ in the Select Transaction Lookup List after you click the **Edit** toolbar button.
12. To edit an invoice after a receipt has been applied, you must ____________________ the receipt before you can change the invoice.

Name ______________________________ Date ______________

Problem 7

Instructions

Step 1 Analyze each transaction.

Step 2 Restore your Premier Fitness Club, Inc. file from Chapter 6.

Step 3 Enter the transactions. Apply sales discounts as appropriate.

The Regular Checking Account will be used for all receipts from customers. Use consecutive receipt numbers, beginning with CR 01-04 for cash sales. Use the date as the Deposit Ticket ID.

Step 4 Print the Cash Receipts Journal.

Step 5 Print the Customer Ledgers report.

Step 6 Print an Aged Receivables report.

Step 7 Display the General Ledger.

Step 8 Back up the file.

Transactions

Feb. 1	Received CK 4501 from Bailey Automotive for Invoice 101.
Feb. 3	You received cash for 50 individual memberships, at $30.00 each, plus sales tax. Reference CR 01-04.
Feb. 6	Received check number 1252 from George Allen for Jan. and Feb. memberships.
Feb. 6	Received check number 4624 for $1,029.85 from Gibbons Gym for Invoice 3248 and Invoice 120.
Feb. 7	Premier sold 20 workout tapes for $30.00 each, plus sales tax; CR 01-05.
Feb. 10	You received cash for 20 corporate memberships for Gibbons Gym, at $25.00 each, plus sales tax; CR 01-06.
Feb. 14	Premier sold 10 shirts for $20.00 each, plus sales tax; CR 01-07.
Feb. 15	Received cash for 40 individual memberships at $30.00 each, plus sales tax; CR 01-08.
Feb. 16	You received check number 459 for $1,530 from Sigmachi Industries, in full payment of invoice numbers 3247 and 102.
Feb. 18	You received check number 765 for $1,636.00 from Alpha Insurance, in full payment of invoice numbers 3250, 103, and 107.
Feb. 20	You received check number 8905 for $1,624.70 from The Fitness Store, in full payment of invoice numbers 105, 3249, and 116.

Feb. 21	You received check number 480 for $1,272.00 from Sigmachi Industries, in full payment of invoice numbers 106 and 110.
Feb. 25	You received check number 1275 for $821.50 from Christy's Golf House, in full payment of invoices 109 and 111.
Feb. 28	You received check number 1542 from Christy's Golf House in full payment of invoice 121.

Analyzing Your Work

Answer the following questions in the space provided.

1. What is the balance of the Regular Checking Account on February 28?

2. What is the balance for Accounts Receivable on February 28?

3. What is the total of the Cash Receipts Journal for February? Is this the amount of cash received? Explain.

4. What is the outstanding balance for The Fitness Store as of February 28?

5. What is the oldest outstanding invoice on February 28?

Chapter 8

Cash Disbursements

OBJECTIVES

When you have completed Chapter 8, you should be able to:

1. Use Payments task to pay vendor invoices.
2. Use Write Checks task to pay expenses.
3. Select multiple vendors and invoices for payment.
4. Void a check.
5. Enter a prepayment to be applied to a purchase invoice.
6. Print checks.
7. Print Accounts Payable reports.
8. Define terms used in the chapter.

In Chapter 6, you purchased merchandise using a purchase order, recorded the receipt of the purchase order, and entered purchases using the Purchases/Receive Inventory window. Once you have received goods or services from a vendor, you need to pay the vendor's invoice. In *Peachtree Complete Accounting 8.0*, a *vendor* is any company or person you pay. Government agencies to which you pay taxes and other institutions are also considered vendors.

For a cash purchase transaction, the sales receipt is your record of payment. When you pay by check or credit card, the check stub and credit card receipt are source documents. When a business purchases merchandise, the cash disbursement record should list the date that the cash was paid; the amount of the invoice paid; a brief description of the product or service paid for; and of course, the name of the vendor.

ENTERING CASH DISBURSEMENTS

In *Peachtree*, cash disbursements, or payments, can be made from three different Tasks windows. These are illustrated in Figure 8–1, the Purchases Navigation Aid.

You will use the **Payments** task to pay invoices that you have entered in Purchases/Receive Inventory or to pay a vendor for a cash purchase. **Select for Payment** allows you to select multiple invoices and/or vendors to pay. You will use **Write Checks** to make payments for expenses that do not involve an invoice or include inventory items.

Payments Task Window

You will use the Payments task window for

- payments to vendors when invoices have been previously entered (Apply to Invoices tab).
- payments that do not have a vendor invoice (Apply to Expenses tab).
- prepayments to vendors using the Apply to Expense tab.
- writing a check to a customer for a sales return or allowance.

You can print the checks in *Peachtree* or enter the information for checks that you have written manually. The information fields for the Apply to Expenses tab are explained below.

Vendor: Enter or select the Vendor ID code. The address information is filled in automatically. Perhaps you want to write a check to a vendor without adding the vendor to your vendor list. If so, then skip the *Vendor ID* field.

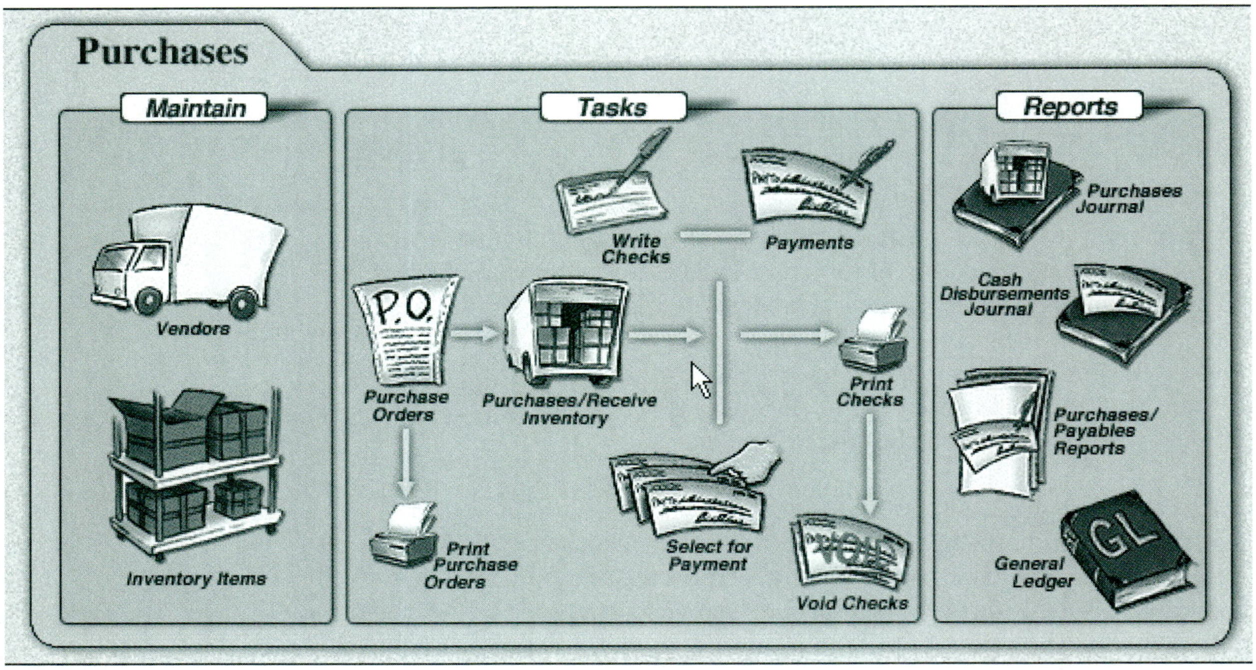

Figure 8–1 Purchases Navigation Aid

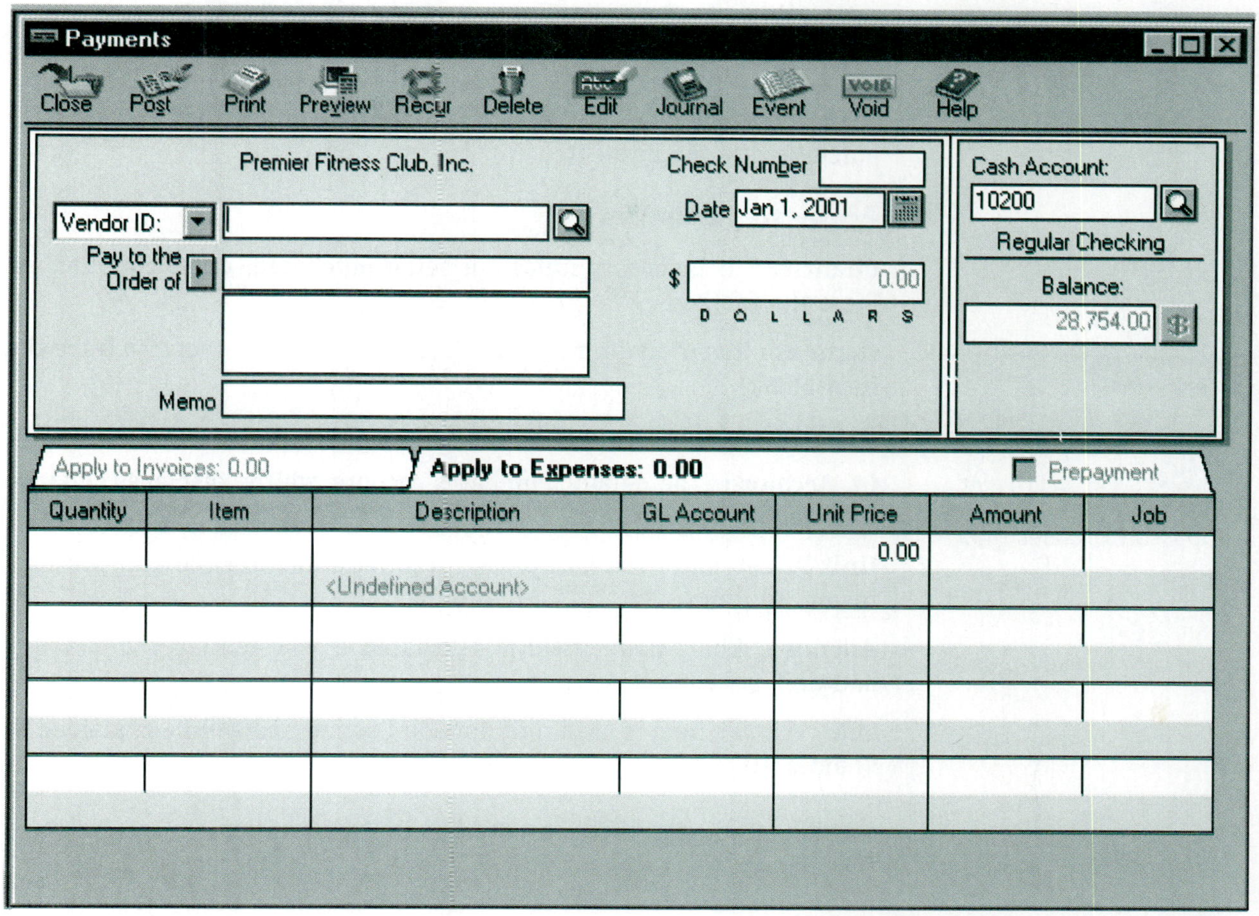

Figure 8–2 Enter cash purchases or a manually written check

Pay to the Order of: For a payment to a vendor who is not in the system, select the arrow button, *Pay to the Order of*. A Pay to Address window opens, where you can enter the name and address of the payee. The arrow button also can be used to modify an address for an existing vendor.

Check Number: If you are entering a handwritten check, enter the number in the *Check Number* field. If you want *Peachtree* to print the check, leave the number blank.

Date: Enter or select the actual date of the payment.

Memo: You can enter any description you want. The default is the vendor's account number for your company. This appears in the window only, not on the printed check.

Cash Account: The cash account you selected when the window opened is displayed.

The Payments window displays a check form at the top. In the check form, enter vendor information, the check number, and the date. The bottom half of the window is divided into two tabs: Apply to Expenses and Apply to Invoices. Which tab is active depends on whether the vendor selected has open invoices in the system. The Apply to Expenses tab will display if you left the *Vendor ID* blank, or if there are no open invoices for the selected vendor. You can select Apply to Expenses even where there are open invoices, if you are making a payment for a cash purchase or a prepayment.

Apply to Expenses

Quantity: If inventory items are being purchased, enter the number. Press the tab key.

Item: For inventory items, enter the item's ID code, otherwise leave the field blank.

> **Note**
> The *$* field on the check will be filled in based on the information you have entered on the Apply to Expenses tab.

Description: Enter a one-line description that will appear on reports.

GL Account: The default Purchases account will be displayed. Change the number if necessary.

Unit Price: Enter the unit price. *Peachtree* will enter the unit price for inventory items.

Amount: The *Amount* field is calculated if you entered the quantity and unit price.

Job: The *Job* field is used only for Job Costing and will be explained in Chapter 10.

When you are finished entering the information, select **Post** and then **Close.**

COMPUTER PRACTICE

Analyzing Transactions

You are ordering a 12-month *Health/Fitness* magazine subscription for $225.00. You plan to write a manual check to pay for the subscription. The check number will be 5001. Please enter this payment.

Entering a Manual Check

Step 1 Open the Purchases Navigation Aid.

Step 2 Select the **Payments** icon.

Step 3 Verify that the *Cash Account* field displays Regular Checking Account.

Step 4 Leave the *Vendor ID* field blank.

Step 5 In the *Pay to the Order of* field, enter Health/Fitness.

Step 6 Enter 5001 in the *Check Number* field.

Step 7 In the *Date* field, key the date 02/01/01; press Tab.

Step 8 On the Apply to Expenses tab, enter 1 as the *Quantity*.

Step 9 Leave the *Item* field blank.

Step 10 Enter One-Year Subscription in the *Description* field.

Step 11 Enter 64500 in the *G/L Account* field; press TAB.

Step 12 Enter 225.00 in the *Unit Price* or *Amount* field.

Step 13 Select **Post.**

Step 14 Select **Close.**

Analyzing Transactions

When reviewing the subscription information, you discover that a 24-month subscription is only $300.00. You decide to get the two-year subscription, so you will want to change the entry before you actually write the check.

Edit a Cash Disbursement Transaction

Note
This transaction should be displayed on the screen.

Step 1 Open the **Payments** window.

Step 2 Select the **Edit** toolbar button.

Step 3 In the *Show* field, select Period 2.

Step 4 Select the transaction for the subscription.

Step 5 Select **Ok.**

Step 6 In the *Description* field, enter 24-month Subscription.

Step 7 In the *Amount* field, enter the new amount, 300.00.

Step 8 Select **Post.**

Step 9 Select **Close.**

Analyzing Transactions

Prior to your writing a check for the magazine, the owner changes her mind about getting the magazine. You will thus delete the transaction.

Delete a Cash Disbursement Transaction

Step 1 Open the Purchases Navigation folder.

Step 2 Select the **Payments** icon.

Step 3 Select the **Edit** icon.

Step 4 In the *Show* field, select Period 2.

Step 5 Highlight the subscription transaction.

Step 6 Select **Ok.**

Step 7 Select the **Delete** icon. A dialog window will appear, asking "Are you sure you want to delete this Record?"

Step 8 Select **Yes.**

Step 9 Select **Close.**

Paying Vendor Invoices

When you select a vendor with open invoices, the Apply to Invoices tab will display by default. To apply a payment to an open invoice, you will complete the following steps.

Step 1 With the Payments window open (Figure 8–3), select the *Vendor ID*. If there are unpaid invoices for the vendor, *Peachtree* lists them on the *Apply to Invoices* tab.

Step 2 The *Description* field displays on the window only. It does not print on the check.

Step 3 If you are paying an invoice in full, choose the *Pay* box next to the invoice. The amount will be entered automatically, both in the *Amount Paid* field and in the $ amount on the check.

Step 4 Based on the date of payment and the terms, a discount amount will be calculated. You can change the calculated discount amount, if necessary.

Step 5 You can pay multiple invoices to a single vendor with one check. Just check the *Pay* box next to each invoice you want to pay.

Step 6 When you have completed paying invoices for a single check, select the **Post** or **Print** button.

The check displays the amount to be paid when you mark an invoice for payment. If you mark more than one invoice for payment, the *$* field displays a running total.

> **Note**
> If the word *Uncalculated* appears in the *Balance* field, the *Recalculate cash balance automatically in Receipts and Payments* global option is turned off. You can manually update the cash balance by clicking the *$* next to the field.

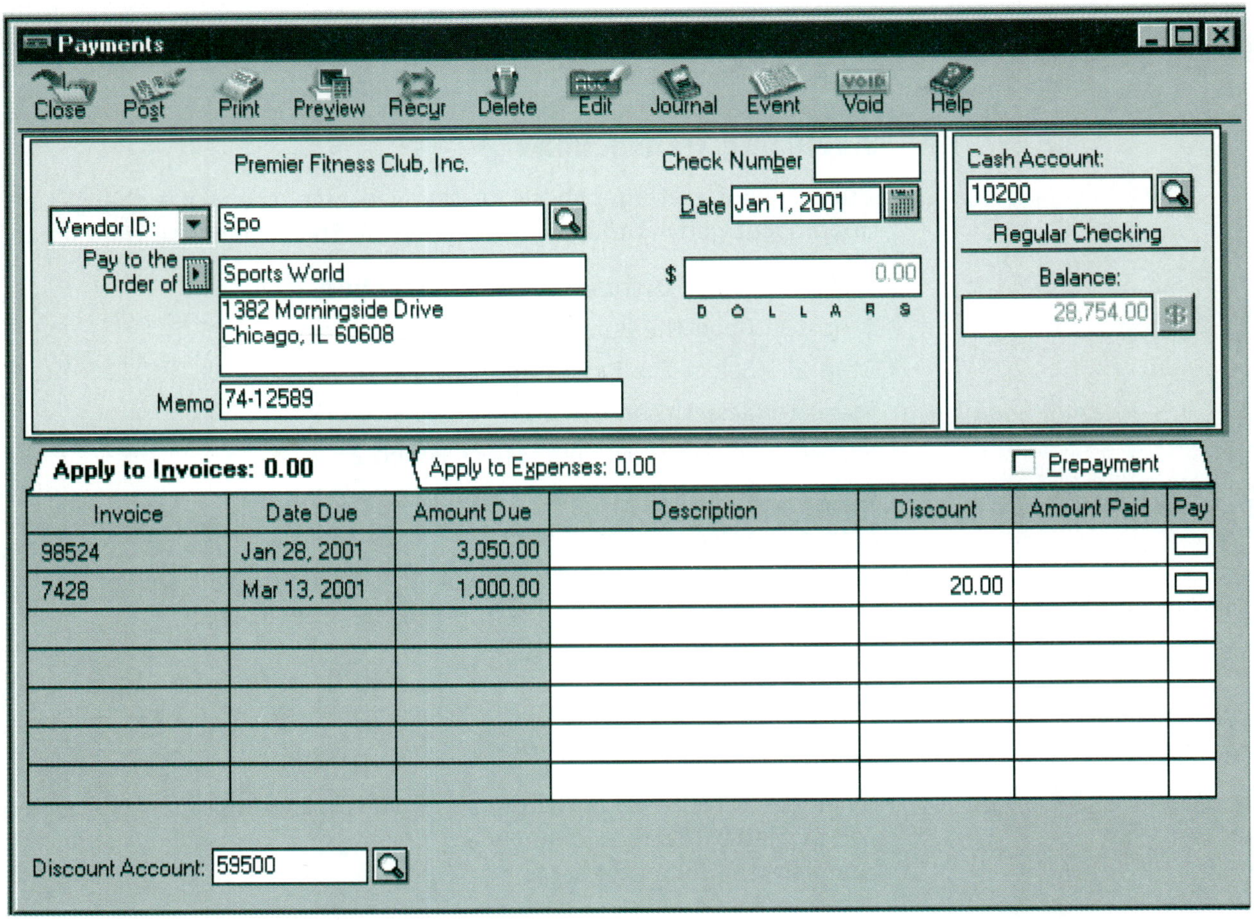

Figure 8–3 Select invoices to pay

Paying Multiple Vendors

The Select for Payment option in the Purchases folder allows you to select several vendors to pay at once. Select a number of invoices to pay and then print a large run of checks at a single time.

Selecting multiple vendors is a two-step process. You can filter the list of vendors so that only those that you select will display in the list.

Step 1 From the Purchases Navigation Aid, choose **Select for Payment.**

Step 2 At the Select for Payment Filter Selection window, you can enter a vendor *Type* to limit the number of vendors displayed or use a date filter.

Step 3 Enter the *Check Date* (the date you will print the checks). Be sure that the date is correct. The date will be displayed in the next window, but it cannot be changed after you leave the filter window.

Step 4 Select which invoices you want to display.

Step 5 When all selections are correct, select **Ok.** The Select for Payment window will open.

Step 6 Verify that the *Cash Acct.* and/or *Discount Acct.* is correct.

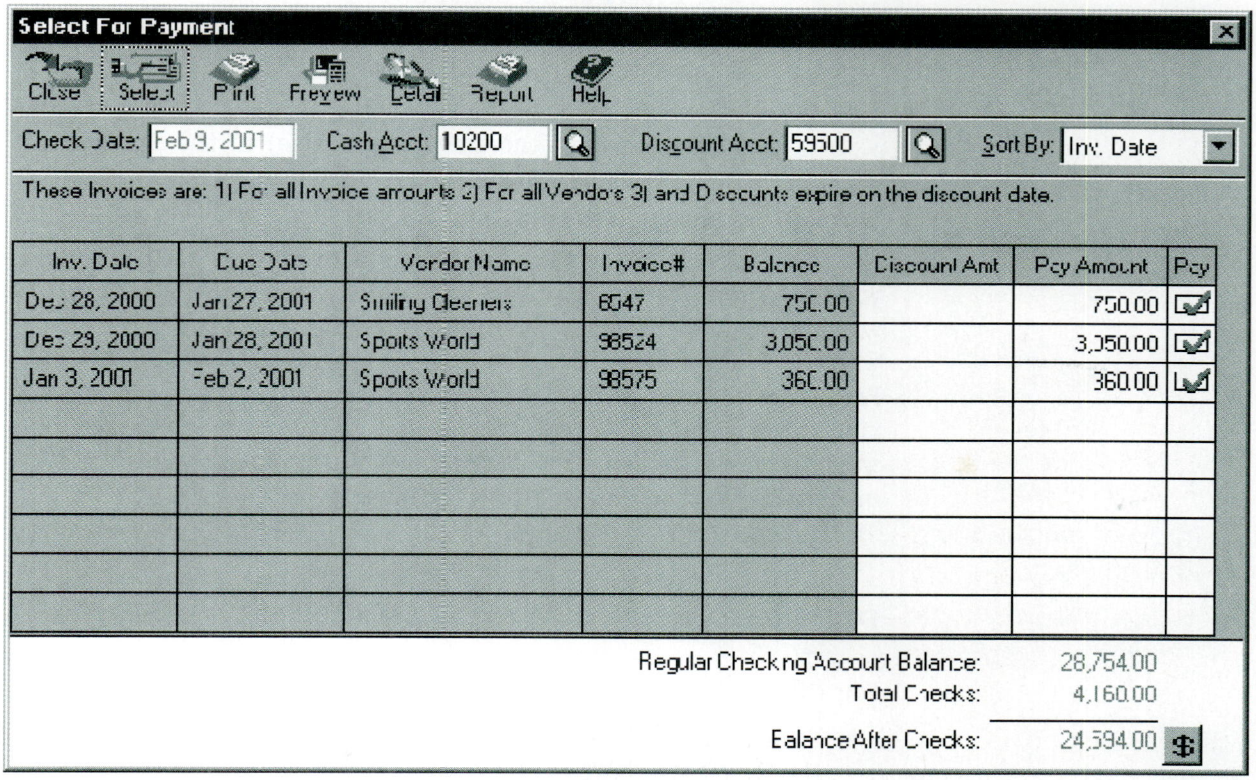

Figure 8–4 Select invoices for more than one vendor

Note

To display information about the invoice that you want to pay, select the **Detail** button.

Step 7 All open invoices within the filtered list will be checked automatically. Uncheck the *Pay* box for any invoice you do not want to pay at this time.

Step 8 Change the amount of discount taken on an invoice, if necessary.

Step 9 You can print checks from this window or print checks as a batch at a later time.

Entering and Applying a Deposit or Prepayment

You can only enter a prepayment to a vendor whose information has been saved in *Peachtree*.

Step 1 Open the **Payments** window.

Step 2 Select the *Vendor ID* from the lookup box.

Step 3 Select the Apply to Expenses tab.

Step 4 Mark the *Prepayment* box on the folder tab.

Step 5 Enter a *Description* and the *Amount*.

Step 6 **Post** the prepayment check.

Step 7 To apply the prepayment (after an invoice has been received), select the Apply to Invoices tab. The prepayment will display in the list of invoices.

Step 8 Select the *Pay* box for the prepayment. A negative amount will display in the *Check Amount* field.

Step 9 Select the invoice against which you want to apply the prepayment. Enter the amount (positive) in the *Amount Paid* field. The check amount should then be zero.

Step 10 **Save** the payment.

The Write Checks window is a simplified version of the Payment window. Write Checks allows you to quickly enter check information without making individual line-item distributions. Like the Payments window, Write Checks lets you write a check to a vendor. Unlike Payments, however, Write Checks doesn't let you pay vendor invoices or make prepayments. Write Checks should be your choice whenever you want to make payments for transactions, such as expenses, that don't involve invoices or the need to track inventory.

PRINTING CHECKS

You can print checks in a number of ways.

- Print an individual check by clicking the **Print** toolbar button on the Payments or Write Checks window.
- Print checks for multiple invoices by selecting **Print** from the Select for Payment window.
- Choose Print Checks from the Purchase Navigation Aid or the **Tasks** menu.
- From the Accounts Payable Report List, choose *Disbursement Checks*.

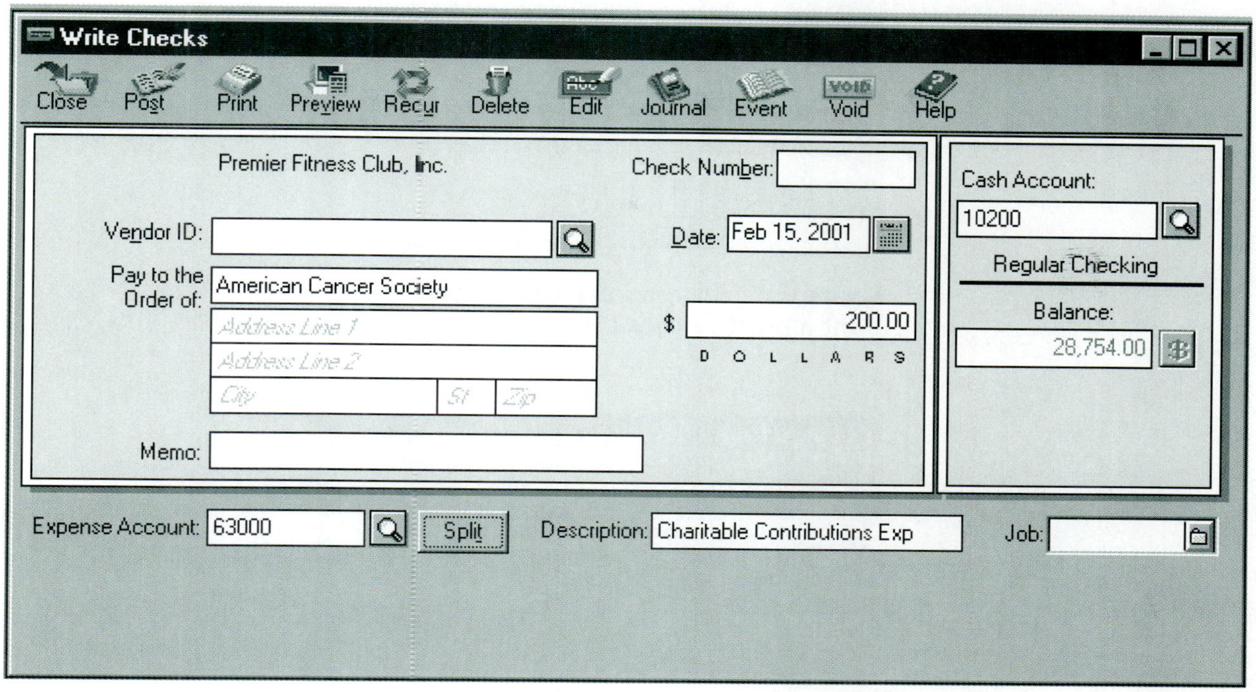

Figure 8–5 Write Checks task window

> **Note**
> All checks written in either the Payments or the Write Checks window are listed in the Cash Disbursements Journal.

Selecting *Print Checks* from the Purchases Navigation Aid will print checks from the information you have entered in any of the Payments windows. To print checks, leave the *Check Number* field blank. *Peachtree* will assign the next sequential check number. You can print a single check by selecting the **Print** button on the Payments window.

When you select **Print Checks** from the Purchases Navigation Aid, the screen shown in Figure 8–6 will appear. You will see various form options. The first one is highlighted AP Preprint 1 Stub; select **Ok** to accept the default. (Figure 8–7 will appear.) This screen allows you to print either a practice form or a real form. If you are using prepared checks, you would want to print a practice check to properly align the form. Select the *Real* button to print the batch of checks. (Figure 8–8 will appear.) Enter the first check number. Select **Ok** to print the checks. Select **Ok** when the checks have printed properly.

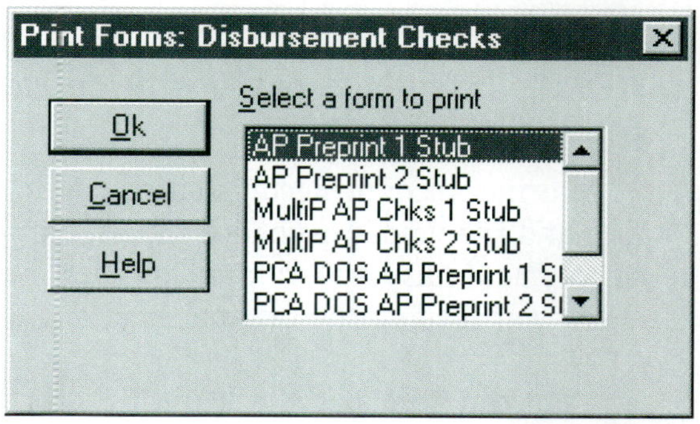

Figure 8–6 Selecting the appropriate check form.

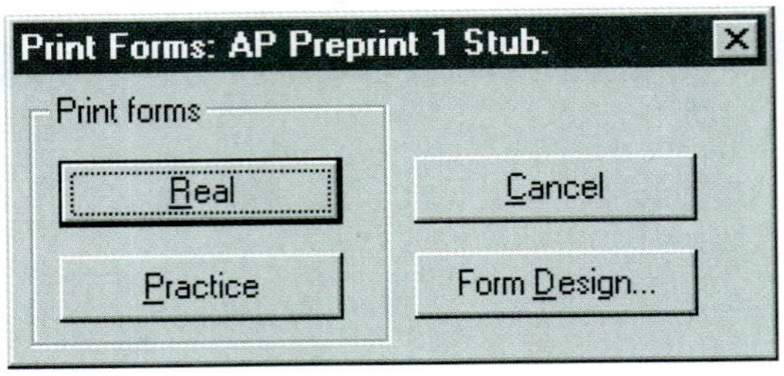

Figure 8–7 Determining whether to print a practice check

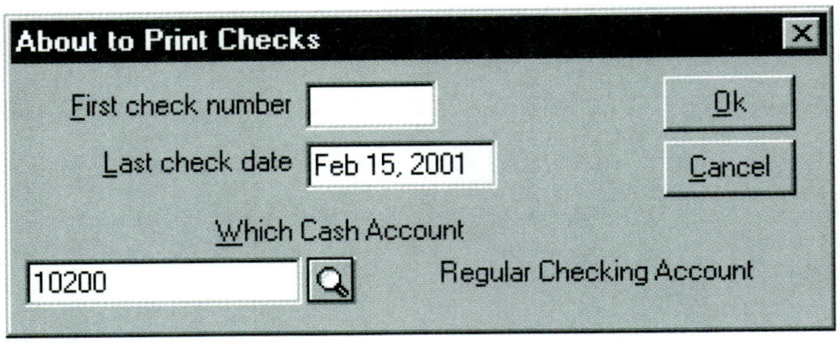

Figure 8–8 Enter the first check number

VOIDING CHECKS

You can void only checks that have a check number. This is because the check number is used to reference the transaction that reverses the payment. Thus, either manually written or printed checks can be voided. You can void checks from the payment windows or from the Navigation Aid or menu.

Step 1 From the Purchases Navigation folder, select **Void Checks.**

Step 2 The Void Existing Checks window will display a list of the checks you have written for the cash account you identify. The source column identifies Accounts Payable checks as "AP," and Payroll checks as "PR."

Step 3 From the list, select the check you want to void.

Step 4 Select the **Void** button. The check information will display.

Step 5 Verify that the correct check is displayed.

Step 6 Enter the date you want the check to be voided.

Step 7 Select **Ok.**

During Account Reconciliation, both the original-payment transaction and the voided-payment transaction clear automatically. The voided payment displays in the Deposits and Debits section. The voided check will display the original Payment Reference Number, followed by a "V."

You can edit any check until it has been printed. With the check displayed on the screen, select the **Edit** toolbar button.

THE CASH DISBURSEMENTS JOURNAL

The Cash Disbursements Journal report lists each payment in full detail, either in payment order or in date order. To print or display this report, open the Purchases Navigation Aid (Figure 8–9).

Click on the **Cash Disbursements Journal** icon. Enter or verify the *Cash Account ID*. Select the appropriate dates to include in the report. Then select **Ok** and the report will display. After reviewing the information, you can print it by selecting the **Print** button.

In addition to the Cash Disbursements Journal report, you will most likely want to print the Check Register. The report lists all checks, including payroll checks. If you accept the default printing, the report includes all the checks printed (and unprinted) for the current accounting period. You can limit the checks on the report by check number or invoice number.

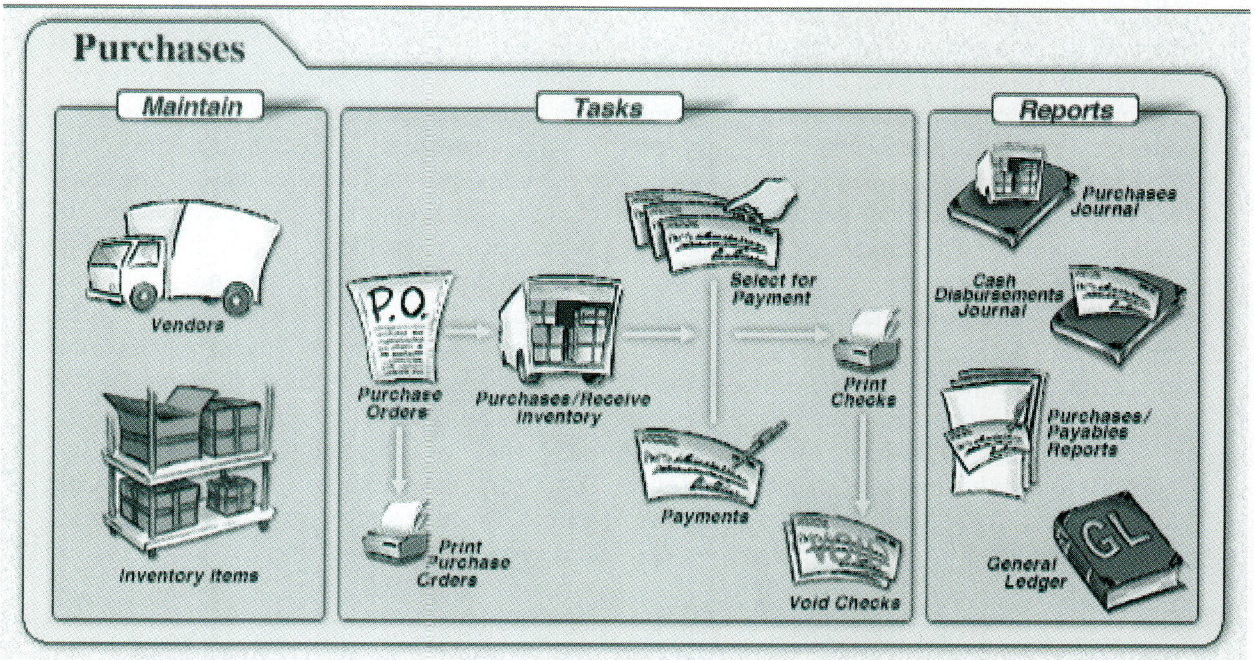

Figure 8–9 Open the purchase folder to print reports

Moving On Up

Not all businesses need the same accounting software. A young girl might keep track of her lemonade sales on a simple spreadsheet (or even a pad of paper); but a multinational corporation probably will use its own specialized software and hire a squad of programming experts to keep it working smoothly.

Of course most businesses fall somewhere in-between these two extremes! Their finances can be managed using off-the-shelf software.

Several companies make such financial management software for expanding companies; each package has its own benefits and drawbacks, but all systems share three general characteristics.

First, these systems are designed to help small or medium-sized companies that are rapidly increasing their business and hiring new employees. But when a company becomes very large, these systems may not fit the firm anymore. Processes like payroll, for instance, become impossibly complex in a large company. The frequency of incoming and outgoing transactions will overwhelm applications that were designed for smaller companies (not to mention the people who are using them). The software itself isn't bad, but it no longer fits the company.

Second, most mid-level financial packages try to give businesses flexibility by separating the software into separate modules. Each is designed to accomplish a specific task—Accounts Receivable, for example, or Payroll—and the modules interact with each other through a General Ledger module.

This design makes the software more efficient and allows businesses to buy only those modules that they will use. For example, companies that outsource their payroll don't have to bother with the software's available payroll functions. But for those firms that keep the payroll task inhouse, payroll is a full-time job. In that case, the employee in charge of payroll only deals with the Payroll module. That employee never has to worry about the modules of Accounts Payable or Receivable.

Finally, many applications include functions that let companies automate common processes and help them plan their finances in greater detail. Some software even includes modules for managing inventory or scheduling transactions.

For example, a distributor can customize its system in many ways. The distributor can set up the inventory system to automatically re-order a certain item from a supplier before the item runs out. The distributor might give its retail partners restricted access to its inventory records through a network or Internet connection, so that the retailers could select what they want and receive delivery automatically. Some software packages would make it easier for the distributor to sell merchandise and services on a Web site.

SUMMARY OF KEY POINTS

1. Cash disbursements can be made from the *Payments*, *Write Checks*, or *Select for Payment* windows.
2. You can enter checks one at a time. Or you can select multiple vendors and/or invoices for payment.
3. After a deposit or prepayment has been made, you must apply it to an open invoice.
4. Posting cash disbursement transactions updates the affected General Ledger accounts.
5. Checks can be voided if they have been assigned a number and have not been cleared.
6. The Cash Disbursements Journal lists all cash transactions in traditional journal format.
7. The Check Register lists all checks written in the current accounting period in numerical order.

interNET CONNECTION

The Institute of Management and Administration publishes a journal, *Managing Accounts Payable*. You can read sample articles at **http://www.ioma.com/nls/archives.shtml**, which normally covers topics such as improving operations, using technology, evaluating results from nation-wide company surveys, handling high-volume transactions, and dealing with change.

Name ______________________________ Date ______________

CHAPTER REVIEW AND APPLICATIONS

Completion

In the space provided, write the word or words that best complete each statement.

1. *Peachtree* provides three cash disbursement windows. They are ______________, ______________, and ______________.
2. Checks can be voided only if they ______________.
3. To pay invoices from several vendors at the same time, use the ______________ task option.
4. *Peachtree* calculates the discount you are entitled to based on the invoice date, the ______________, and the ______________.
5. If the *Balance* field in a Payments window has question marks rather than an amount, it means that ______________.
6. The Write Checks window cannot be used for ______________ or ______________.
7. You can print disbursement checks in four ways: ______________, ______________, ______________, and ______________,
8. The ______________ report will list all disbursements in debit and credit format.
9. The ______________ lists checks in numerical order.
10. In the Payments window, if you select a vendor with an open invoice, the ______________ tab will be active.

Name ______________________________ Date ______________

Problem 8

You read about processing purchase orders and receiving goods and services in Chapter 6. In this chapter, you read about how to pay for those purchases. Analyze each of the following transactions and enter the transactions using the Purchases Navigation Aid.

Instructions

Step 1 Restore the Premier Fitness Club, Inc. backup file from Chapter 7.

Step 2 Open the Purchases Navigation Aid.

Step 3 Use the **Purchases/Receive Inventory** icon to record the receipt of merchandise for a purchase order.

Step 4 Use the **Payments** icon to select invoices to be paid or to apply a purchase to an expense.

Transactions

Feb. 1	Issued a check to Thomas Realty for $1,000, for March's rent.
Feb. 5	Paid Invoice 8000 for New Fashions, Inc., less discount.
Feb. 7	Issued a check to Chicago Electricity for $450, for utilities.
Feb. 9	Paid Frank's Office Supplies for Invoice 258.
Feb. 15	Issued a check to WCKG Television for $500, for advertising.
Feb. 17	Received a shipment and Invoice 567 from R&R Supplies, for Purchase Order 2005. You can now pay the invoice.
Feb. 19	Enter a prepayment to R&R Supplies for $1,000 for custom-designed stationery. The prepayment will be applied at a later date.
Feb. 28	Received Shipment and Invoice 9335 from Smiling Cleaners for P.O. 2007.

Step 5 Print the checks (MultiPAP Chks 1 Stub). The first check number is 1220. Set the last check date as 2/28/01.

Step 6 Use the Select for Payment option to pay the following invoices. Set the due date and discount dates to March 30 so that all invoices are displayed. Check date will be February 28.

- Sports World, Invoice 98524
- Sports World, Invoice 7248
- Sports World, Invoice 7275
- Smiling Cleaners, Invoice 6547
- Exercise Tapes, Inc., Invoice 753

Step 7 Print the Select for Payment checks.

Step 8 Print the Check Register report.

Step 9 Print the Cash Disbursements Journal report.

Step 10 Print the Vendor Ledgers report.

Step 11 Display the General Ledger report.

Analyzing Your Work

Use your printouts and your *Peachtree* file to answer the following questions about Problem 8.

1. What is the balance of Accounts Payable on February 28? What is the significance of that balance?

____

____

2. Which vendor has the highest balance on February 28?

____

____

3. What is the total of all disbursements during February?

____

____

4. What was the net amount of change in Accounts Payable during February?

____

____

5. Are there open purchase orders at the end of February? If so, to whom?

____

____

Chapter 9 Job Costing

OBJECTIVES

When you have completed Chapter 9, you should be able to:

1. Verify default settings for Job Costing.
2. Track job costing for Purchases.
3. Track job costing for Sales.
4. Generate a Job Ledger report.
5. Generate a Job Profitability report.
6. Define terms used in the chapter.

Job costing, although an optional feature, is a useful one. It calculates the profitability of a particular job and helps management set estimates and budgets. For example, through the Accounts Payable and Payroll windows, you can track invoices for materials and services used to complete a project. To track expenses and revenue, you can assign salary (or hours) of employees, payments, inventory adjustments, and sales and purchases transactions to a specific job or project. To use job costing, simply identify the project for which you want to track expenses and income.

JOB COSTING DEFAULTS

To use job costing, first set up some default information to be automatically displayed in job windows or to be automatically used by *Peachtree Complete Accounting 8.0*. Use the **Maintain** menu and select *Default Information, Jobs.*

You can customize job windows by adding fields to store additional information about your jobs. If you use the field labels on the Custom Fields tab of the Maintain Jobs window, those labels will be available to you for all the jobs in the system. *Peachtree* allows you to add up to five fields on the Custom Fields tab. You can customize some reports to include these fields.

Step 1 From the Maintain menu, select Default Information.

Step 2 From the submenu, select Jobs (Figure 9–1).

Step 3 Check the *Enabled* box to change a Field Label for any of the five fields. In order to key information in the Field Label, you *must* enable a field. If you clear the *Enabled* box for any label, that field will be *inaccessible* from the Maintain Jobs window.

Step 4 Select **Ok** to accept the default labels. You will return to the main menu.

Setting Up Job Costs

The first step in setting up job costing is to determine how detailed you want the job information that you track to be. There are three

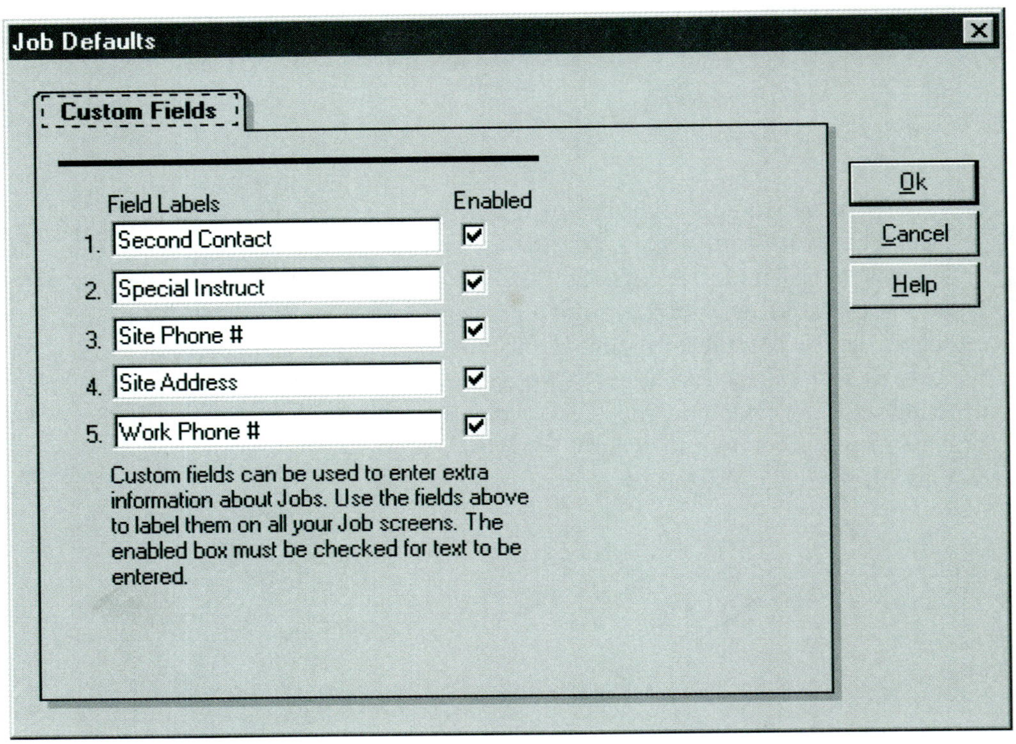

Figure 9–1 Select Jobs from the Default Information option

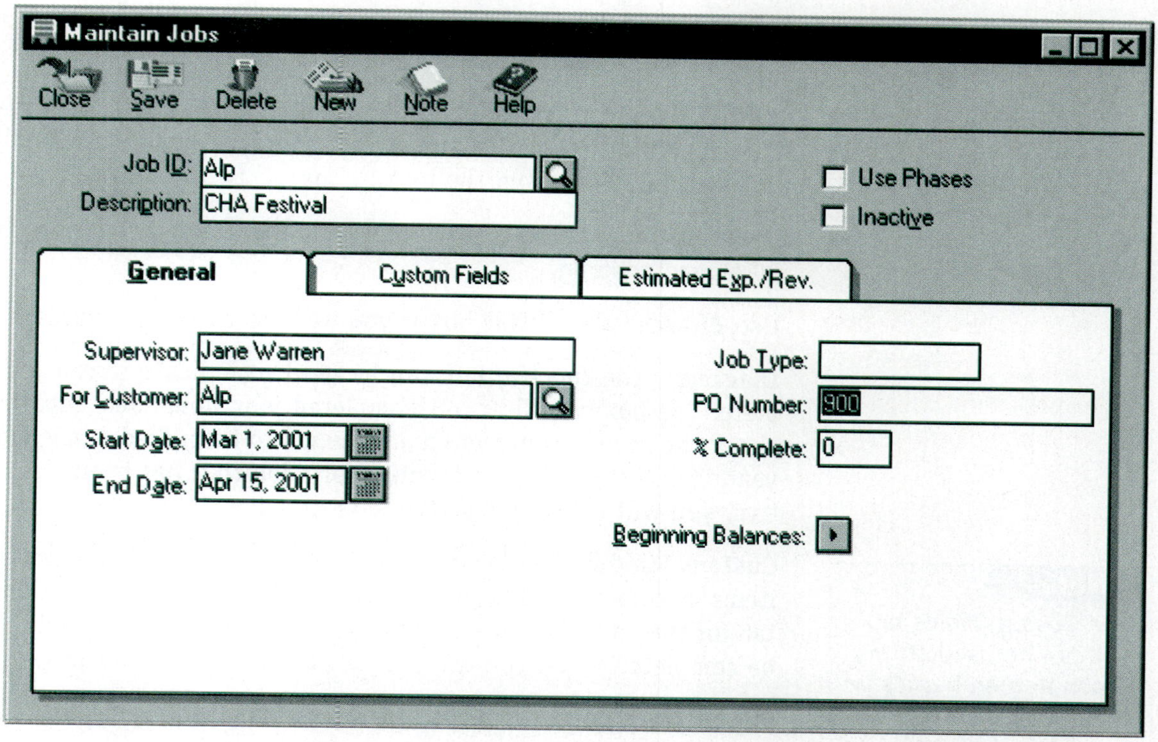

Figure 9–2 Set up jobs

options in the *Job Costs* choice on the **Maintain** menu. If you want to track only the total cost incurred or total profit earned from a job, use the *Jobs* option. If you want to track income and expense in different stages of a job, use the *Phases* option. You can use phases for any job in the Maintain Jobs window. You can also set up and apply cost codes (categories of expense) to any phase of any job. This chapter will deal with setting up Job IDs only.

Use this procedure to set up a new job record.

Step 1 Do one of the following to display the Maintain Jobs window.

- From the **Maintain** menu, select *Job Costs,* and then choose Jobs.
- From the **Maintain** menu, select *Setup Checklist.* Under the Jobs heading, click the Job Records setup option.
- Click the **Jobs** icon on the Company Administration Navigation Aid.

Step 2 Enter a new job ID and complete the necessary job information. Explanation of the various fields is explained below.

Step 3 Check the *Use Phases* box if you want to use phases for this job. You can access this option later, if you are undecided when you set up the job.

Step 4 When you finish filling in the window, select **Save.**

You can enter four types of information: General, Custom Fields, Estimated Expense/Revenue, and Beginning Balances. Use this window to add a new job, change existing job information, or delete a job.

Header information always displays, regardless of which tab you have selected. Header information includes

Job ID: You can enter a code (up to 20 characters) to identify a job. This field is case sensitive and cannot contain commas. You could select an existing *Job ID* from the lookup box.

Description: The descriptive name for the job or project can be up to 30 characters long.

Use Phases: Check this box if you want to establish Phases.

Inactive: The *Inactive* box can be used to indicate that a job is complete. The box can filter out completed jobs from some reports. If you check the *Inactive* box, you mark the job to be purged at the end of the year. If you try to enter activities for a job that has been marked inactive, you will be warned of the job's inactive status.

Note
The Custom Fields tab will not be used at this time. Remember it's there, when you want to identify unique information that you want to print on job reports.

Custom Fields: The Custom Fields tab can be used to track non-cost items associated with a project. You will not enter information on this tab for the end-of-chapter problem. The fields on the General tab should be completed when you use the job ID for a new job or project.

Supervisor: Enter the name of the individual who is responsible for the job or project. You can enter up to 30 characters.

For Customer: Select the customer to whom the job is assigned. You could use the lookup box to choose a customer from your files.

Start Date: Enter the start date for the job. The starting and ending dates appear only on reports.

End Date: Enter the date the job was completed.

Job Type: You can group jobs into categories in this field. Some reports can be filtered by *Job Type*. You can enter a unique code of up to eight characters. This field can be used to identify a sales region, for example. This field is case sensitive.

PO Number: Enter the customer's *Purchase Order Number* for the job.

% Complete: You can use this field to update progress of the job.

Beginning Balances: To enter beginning balances that exist when the job is set up, select the *Beginning Balances* arrow button. This field will not be used in the end-of-chapter problem.

The Estimated Exp./Rev. tab contains two information fields.

Estimated Revenues: Enter an estimate of the revenue expected from the job.

Estimated Expenses: Estimate what expenses the job might entail.

CREATING A JOB COSTING ENTRY FOR SALES

Entering job costs for sales will review the concepts presented in Chapters 5 and 7. Use the Sales Orders and Sales/Invoicing windows to enter sales related to job costing. Open the Sales Navigation Aid. (Figure 9–3 will appear).

Select the **Sales/Invoicing** icon (Figure 9–4 will appear).

The fields on the Sales Orders and Sales/Invoicing screens, other than the *Job* field, were identified in Chapter 5.

Complete the following steps to assign job costs to a sales order.

Step 1 Open the Sales Navigation Aid folder.

Step 2 Select the **Sales Order** icon.

Step 3 Select the *Customer ID* for the client that you want to invoice for the job.

Step 4 In the *Quantity* field, enter the number of units that you want to charge the customer. You can also use this field to enter the number of labor-hours you want to bill.

Step 5 You can select an inventory *Item* or just enter a *Description*. You can use the *Item* and *Description* fields for entering job details.

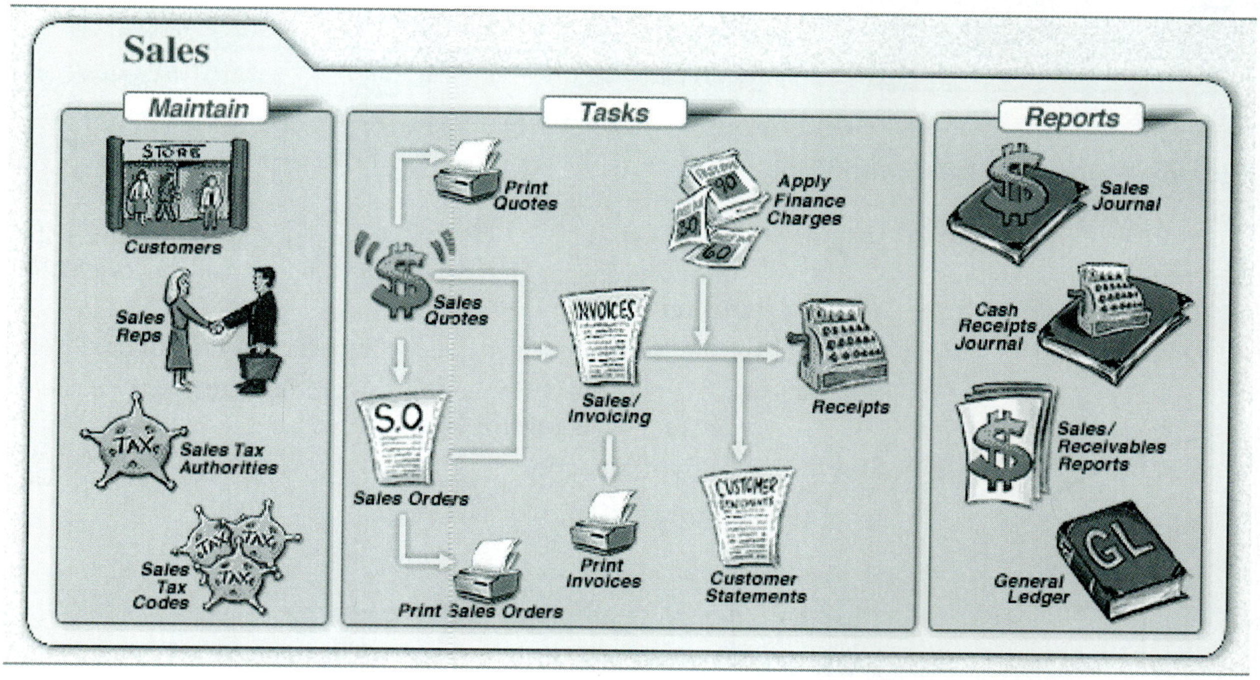

Figure 9–3 Sales Navigation Aid folder

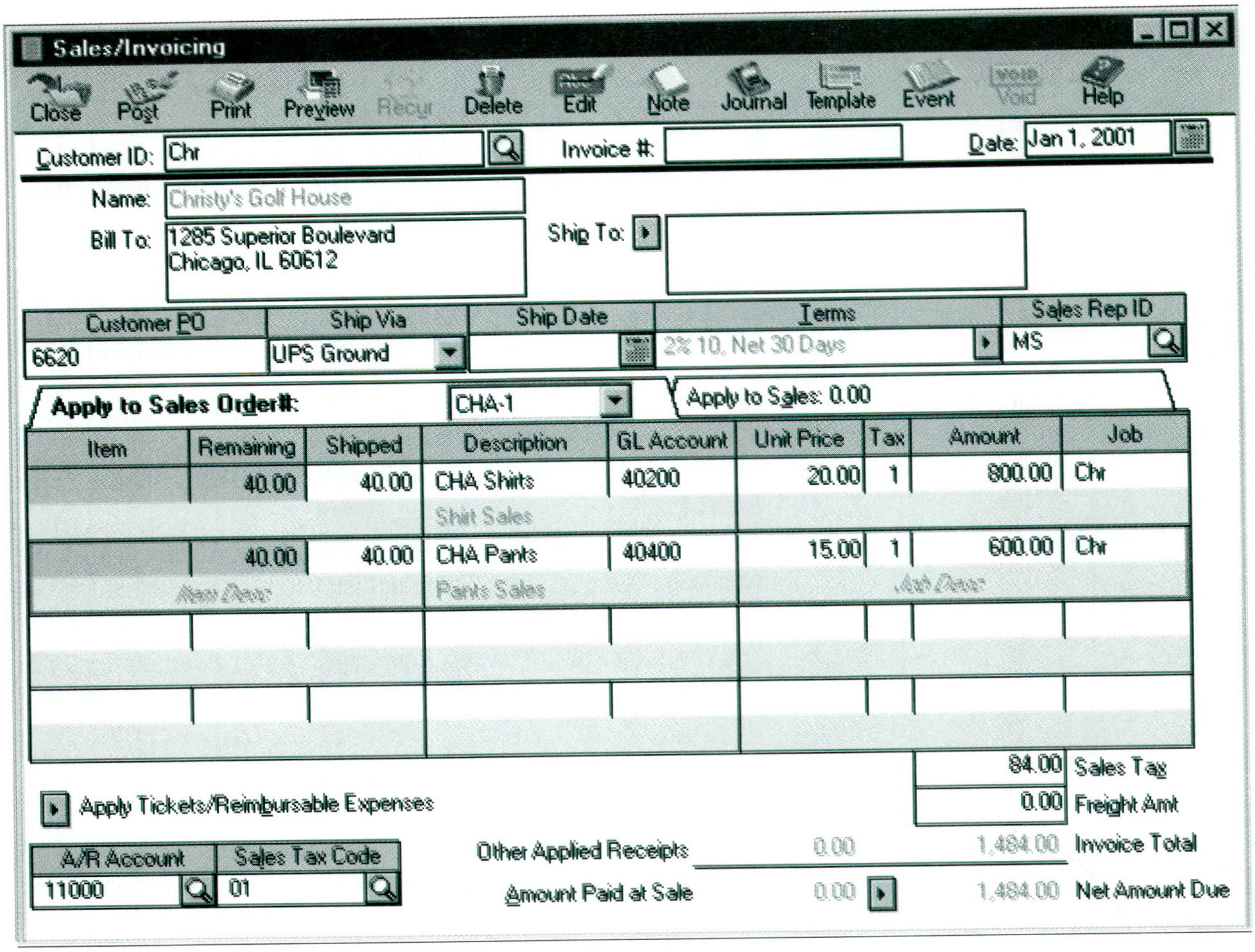

Figure 9–4 Invoicing for a specific job

Step 6 Enter the Unit Price (or total Amount) and Tax. If you enter a *Quantity* and a *Unit Price,* the *Amount* will be calculated (Chapter 5).

Step 7 In the *Job* field, select the *Job ID* from the lookup box.

Step 8 When the order is shipped to the customer, convert the *Sales Order* to a *Sales Invoice* (see Chapter 5).

Step 9 Post the transaction.

CREATING A JOB COSTING ENTRY FOR PURCHASES

Entering job information for inventory items is more complicated than non-inventory items, such as the special order items that you will create in Problem 9 at the end of this chapter. Using the Inventory

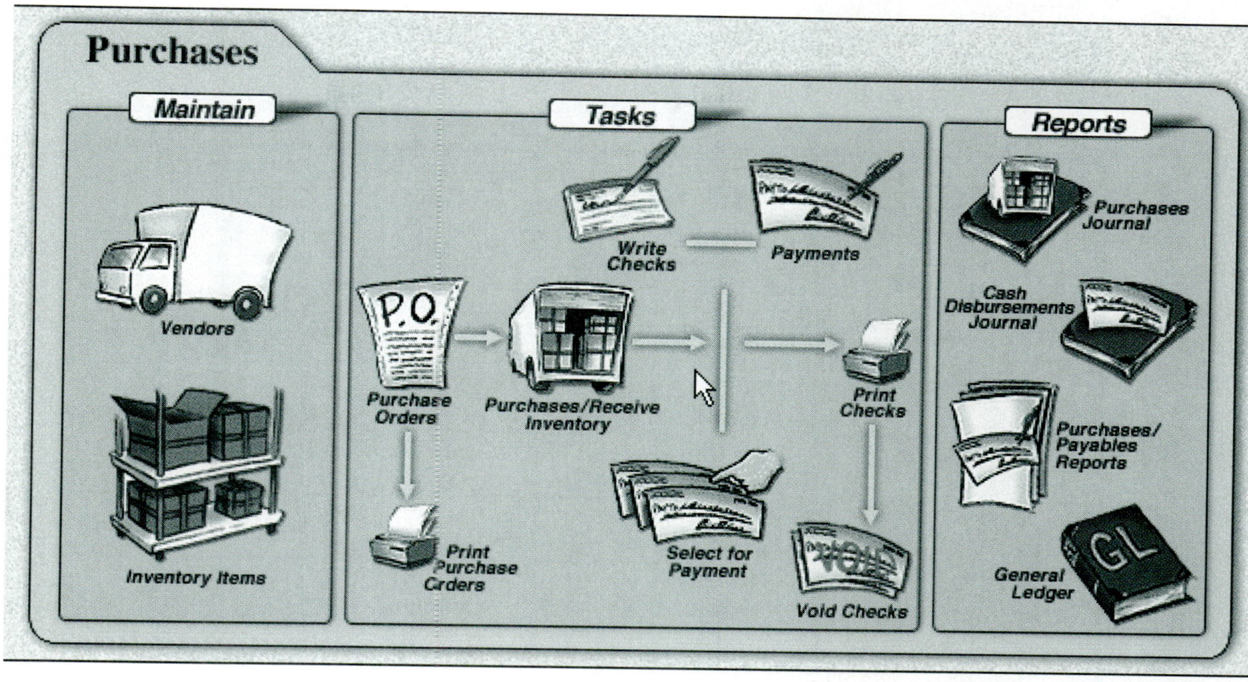

Figure 9–5 Purchases Navigation Aid

> **Note**
> The cost applied to the job is determined by the cost assigned to the item when you set up the inventory record.

Adjustments window is explained, but you will not use this function in the tutorial activities.

If you have already purchased and entered a stock item that you want to use for a job or you have the item in stock, you must use the Inventory Adjustments window for recording the usage of that item. You can specify the job costing information in that window. If you apply the stock item directly to the customer's invoice, the cost of sales entry will be posted at the time of the sale and an inventory adjustment is not necessary. If you do not enter the stock item on the invoice, you will have to make an inventory adjustment for the stock item. This removes the item from inventory and posts the cost of sales to the job.

Except for the *Job* field, the Purchase Orders and Purchases/Receive Inventory screens were presented in Chapter 6.

Use the following steps to apply purchase transactions directly to Job Costing. (See also Problem 9 at the end of this chapter.)

Step 1 Open the Purchases Navigation folder.

Step 2 Select the **Purchase Order** icon.

Step 3 Complete the fields on the Purchase Order window, including the *Job* field.

Step 4 When the order is received, select the **Purchases/Receive Inventory** icon.

Step 5 Apply the receipt to the purchase order.

Step 6 Select the *Job* ID from the drop-down menu.

Step 7 Post the entry.

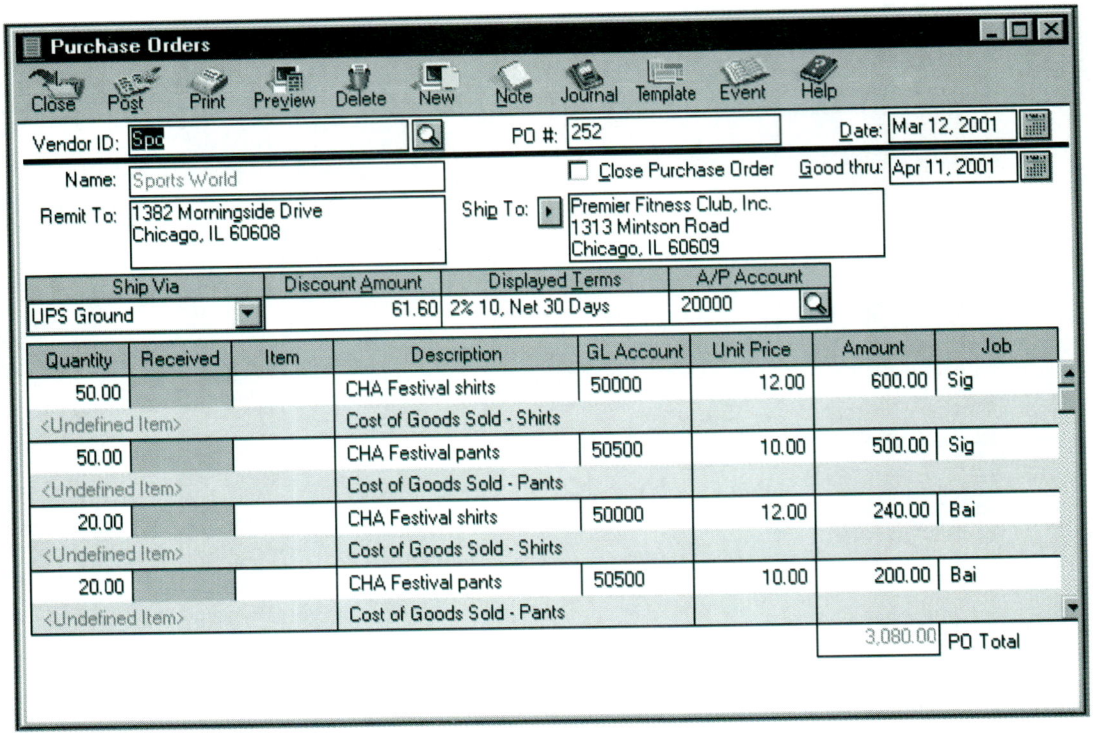

Figure 9–6 Purchase order with Jobs identified

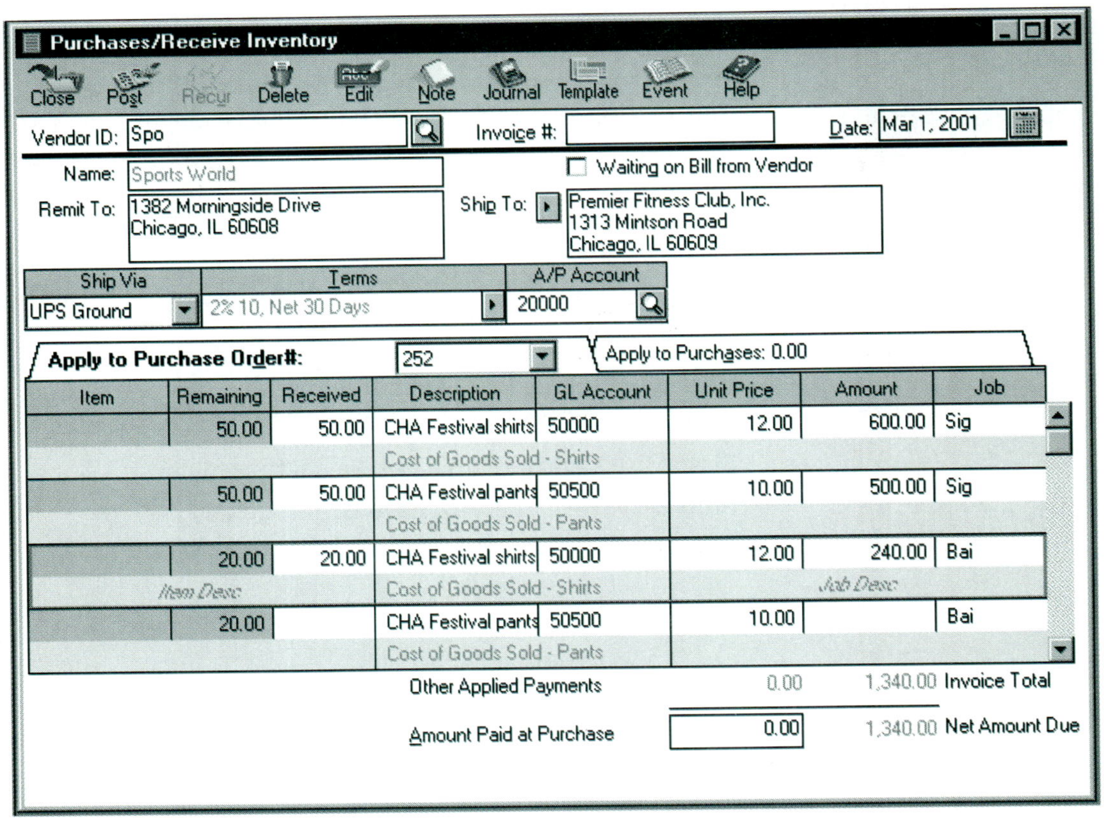

Figure 9–7 Receiving purchase order for jobs

JOB REPORTS

You can generate a variety of job reports during the time a job is underway or at the completion of the job. The amount of data reflected in job reports will depend, of course, upon how much detail you have maintained on the job. In *Peachtree*, you can choose to include a range of data in any of the reports. That same flexible functionality applies to job reports.

Note

Refer to the *Peachtree* manual for information on setting up job costing and payroll interfaces in order to apply hours and wages for employees to a job ID.

Figure 9-9 illustrates the number of job reports available in *Peachtree*. The Job List report provides a one-line view of each job with starting and ending dates. It includes completion status. It can be generated when you want a quick list of all your jobs. The Job Master File List report is a more detailed version of the Job List.

You will generate a Job Ledger and/or Job Profitability report when you work the Chapter 9 end-of-chapter problem.

The Job Ledger report lists all the transactions that have been assigned to a job. It includes information about the actual transaction. You can summarize a transaction by Job or by General Ledger account. The Job Register report is a simpler version of the Job Ledger report because it includes only the amount of the transactions for a specified period. It is an overview of job activity.

The Job Profitability report lists actual expenses and revenue for given jobs. The profits are displayed both in actual dollar amounts and in percentages. Transactions shown on this report can also be summarized by Job, General Ledger account, or Phase or Cost Code. By excluding active jobs, you can see how profitable completed jobs have been.

To print Job Reports, follow these steps.

Step 1 Open the Company Navigation Aid (Figure 9-8).

Step 2 Select the **Job Reports** icon (Figure 9-9 will appear).

Step 3 Highlight the needed report.

Step 4 Select the **Preview** icon.

Step 5 Use the Filter tab to select a range of items to include in the report. The Fields and Format tabs offer additional options for customizing the report. Online help provides help on using these tabs.

Step 6 Select **Ok** to generate the report.

Step 7 To print the report, select **Print.**

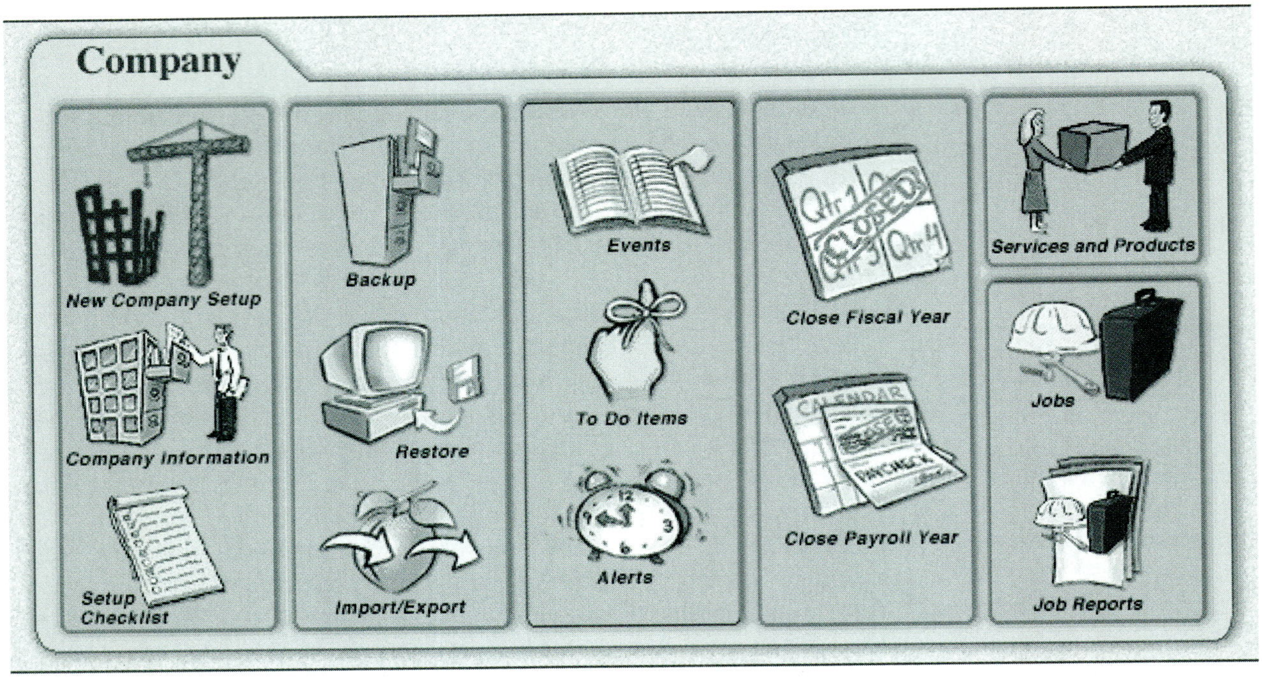

Figure 9–8 Use the Company Navigation Aid folder to print job reports

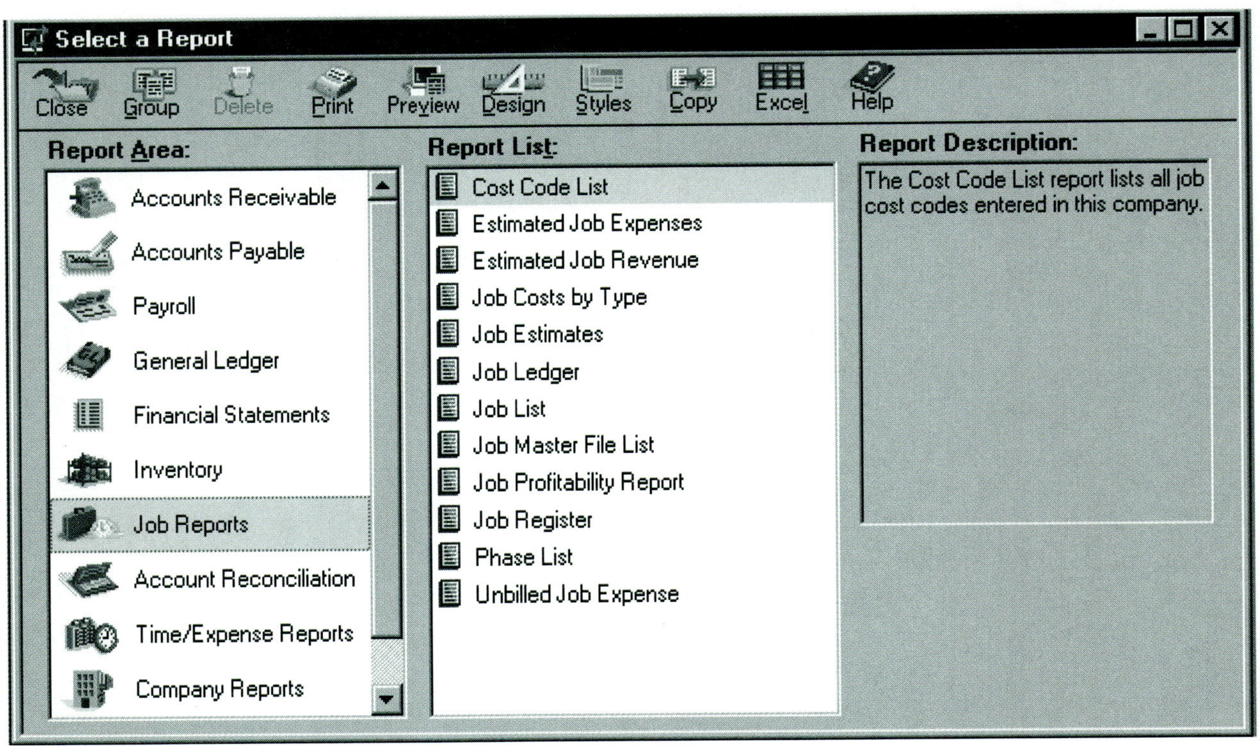

Figure 9–9 Select Job reports

The Global Economy

The business world is a far different place than it was just a few years ago. Most businesses now compete in a much bigger marketplace with very high stakes—whether they like it or not.

This situation is especially true for businesses in the United States, where a decade of high-flying economic performance and technological innovation encouraged foreign trade and investment.

Globally, political and economic borders have melted down and merged. The breakup of the Soviet Union opened formerly closed Communist countries; treaties knocked down barriers between Canada, the United States, and Mexico; and much of Europe began the process of fusing into a single economic entity. Once you go global, you can't ever go back.

But the new global economy does not just affect large corporations and deep-pocketed financiers. These days, even the owner of a small-town five-and-dime needs to pay attention to what is happening in the rest of the world. The goods she sells on her shelves may come from any number of countries, through any number of any other countries, before she ever puts them on sale. Manufacturers and suppliers in all industries now have to compete with companies all over the world.

Technology has done a great deal to drive the changes in this new economy, and it will continue to do so in the future. For example, computer email now makes it much easier to stay in touch across long distances. The total number of email messages sent each year far exceeds that of postal mail.

This technologically tightened chain of communication has had its greatest effect on the service industries, and the United States economy is increasingly a service-driven one. For instance, there is little reason anymore for a business's lawyer or accountant to be located in the same city, or even the same state. Companies have the freedom to search out the best person for the job.

Finally, technology has allowed some businesses to sell their product in new ways. A company can put up a site on the World Wide Web to sell products. A company can start a branch in a foreign country—or even incorporate their business there.

Of course, competing in a global economy puts new burdens on a business, because each country has its own customs, currencies, and—unfortunately—tax regulations. But these days your business's bottom-line may have everything to do with the price of tea in China.

SUMMARY OF KEY POINTS

1. When you analyze the costs associated with a specific job or project, you allow management to determine how each factor affects the cost.
2. Default settings for Job Costing allow you to set up fields unique to a specific job or project.
3. Use the Maintain Jobs option to set up the amount of data that will be maintained for each job.
4. Sales and purchases can be tracked for each job.
5. The Job Ledger lists all transactions that have been assigned to a job: the *Job ID*, the customer, customer activity, and the balance and status of the job.
6. The Job Profitability report provides actual dollar amounts and percentages for expenses and revenues.

*inter*NET CONNECTION

AccountingNet offers a searchable file of controversial and intriguing ideas. Here's an editorial about an alternative to a work-in-progress system of private companies' production cost accounts. How does this method allocate maintenance and repair expenses? (Search for keyword "functional," date "any," "private business, general accounting" for a 1/11/99 essay, "Accounts Related to Functional Activities," by Dr. Emanuel Schwarz.) **http://www.accountingnet.com/research/solutions/index.html**

Name ______________________ Date ______________

CHAPTER REVIEW AND APPLICATIONS

Completion

In the space provided, write the word or words that best complete each statement.

1. From the **Maintain** menu, you would choose ____________ to establish custom fields for Jobs.
2. You can open the Maintain Jobs window from the ____________ Navigation Aid or by choosing ____________ or ____________ from the **Maintain** menu.
3. The ____________ field on the Maintain Jobs window should be entered when a job is finished.
4. The ____________ report provides an overview of job activity.
5. The ____________ field is used to group or sort jobs for reports and analysis.
6. The ____________ report lists jobs with complete detail.
7. The ____________ report is a simplified version of the Master File List.
8. The ____________ lists all transactions that have been assigned to a job.
9. The ____________ report lists actual expenses, revenues, and gross job profit.
10. The profitability of completed jobs can be calculated by excluding ____________ from the Job Profitability Report.

Problem 9

In this chapter, you read about how to track specific costs associated with a job or project. Premier needs you to track the customer orders for the Chicago Health Association's upcoming festival by using the Jobs function.

Several of your customers are participating in the festival and have ordered specially designed items for their employees to wear at the festival. Enter each of the transactions below after you set up the appropriate job numbers. Include the following information for all job numbers: Jane Warren as supervisor; Job beginning date, 3/1/01. Use CHA Festival as the description for each job.

Instructions:

Follow this procedure.

Step 1 Restore your backup from Chapter 8.

Step 2 Change the system date to 3/31/01.

Step 3 Change the accounting period to March 1–31, 2001 (no need to print checks or reports).

Step 4 Set up a job file for each of the four customers identified in the transactions.

Step 5 Enter the order from each customer as a sales order. Since these are special orders rather than inventory items, ***do not*** use item designations. Enter a description only. Use CHA-1 as the first sales order number since you will not print the sales orders. Allocate sales to the appropriate income account.

Step 6 Place the festival orders with orders with Premier's vendor. Identify each job on the distribution list of the Purchase Order window. Since the inventory items are not being used, charge the purchases to the appropriate cost of sales account.

Step 7 When the orders are received from the vendor, enter receipt of the purchase order.

Step 8 Convert the Sales Orders to Sales Invoices by indicating shipment to each customer. Allow Peachtree to assign the invoice numbers. The customers will be allowed to exceed their credit limit if necessary.

Step 9 Print the designated Jobs reports.

Step 10 Enter ending date for the CHA Jobs.

Step 11 Back up your file for use in Chapter 10.

Name ______________________ Date ______________

Transactions

Mar. 2	Sigmachi Industries ordered 50 shirts (at $20.00 each) and 50 pairs of pants (at $15.00 each) for the festival. Their purchase order number is 9000. Use Sig as the Job ID.
Mar. 5	Bailey Automotive ordered 20 shirts (at $20.00 each) and 20 pairs of pants (at $15.00 each) for the festival. Bailey's purchase order number is 3510. Use Bai as the Job ID.
Mar. 9	Alpha Insurance ordered 30 shirts (at $20.00 each) and 30 pairs of pants (at $15.00 each) for the festival. Alpha's purchase order number is 7610. Use Alp as the Job ID.
Mar. 10	Christy's Golf House ordered 40 shirts (at $20.00 each) and 40 pairs of pants (at $15.00 each) for the festival. Christy's purchase order number is 6620. Use Chr as the Job ID.
Mar. 12	Placed Purchase Order 252 with Sports World for the special orders for the festival. Cost of shirts is $12.00; pants, $10.00.
Mar. 25	Premier received shipment from Sports World for all the festival orders. Invoice 9574.
Mar. 26	Shipped the special orders and invoiced Premier customers for the festival merchandise.
Mar. 31	Print a Job Ledger Report.
Mar. 31	Print a Job Profitability Report.
Mar. 31	Print a Job Register Report.
Mar. 31	Enter 4/01/01 as the ending date for the CHA Jobs.

Analyzing Your Work

Answer each question in the space provided.

1. What is the total profit on job activity for the period of March?

____

2. What percentage profit was earned on Jobs?

____

Chapter 10

Reports

OBJECTIVES

When you have completed Chapter 10, you should be able to:

1. Print the Balance Sheet.
2. Print the Income Statement.
3. Print the Cash Flow report.
4. Print the Statement of Changes in Financial Position.
5. Create a Report Group.
6. Define terms used in the chapter.

Business reports provide a summary of the company's financial position and are the basis for making management decisions. *Peachtree Complete Accounting 8.0* provides you with a versatile reporting program. While the software comes with predefined statements, each report has selection criteria that allow you to customize the appearance of and determine what information appears on the report. You can preview reports on the screen or print them. You can also group several reports together for more efficient printing.

PRINTING FINANCIAL STATEMENTS

A financial statement gives a picture of how your business is doing. In essence, the whole point of an accounting system is to produce accurate financial statements. You need annual financial reports for income tax purposes, official financial statements, and most other reports. You can, however, have your computer print a Balance Sheet and an Income Statement every month.

BALANCE SHEET

The Balance Sheet shows the assets, liabilities, and equity accounts of a business as of a specific date.

Note
If a message appears asking, "All the journals needed to be posted. Post them all now?" then answer yes.

You can generate financial reports from the **Reports** menu or from the General Ledger Navigation Aid. From the Navigation Aid, select **Print Financial Statements.**

When you preview or print a financial statement, Peachtree displays the following options:

Time Frame: You have the choice of a range of periods, current period, or current three periods. If you select a range, use the *From* and *To* list boxes.

Print Page Numbers: If you check this box, page numbers will print on the top right corner of the page. Both the page number and the number of pages are indicated. For example, if you are looking at page 2 of a 13-page document, it will display on the report as "Page: 2 of 13."

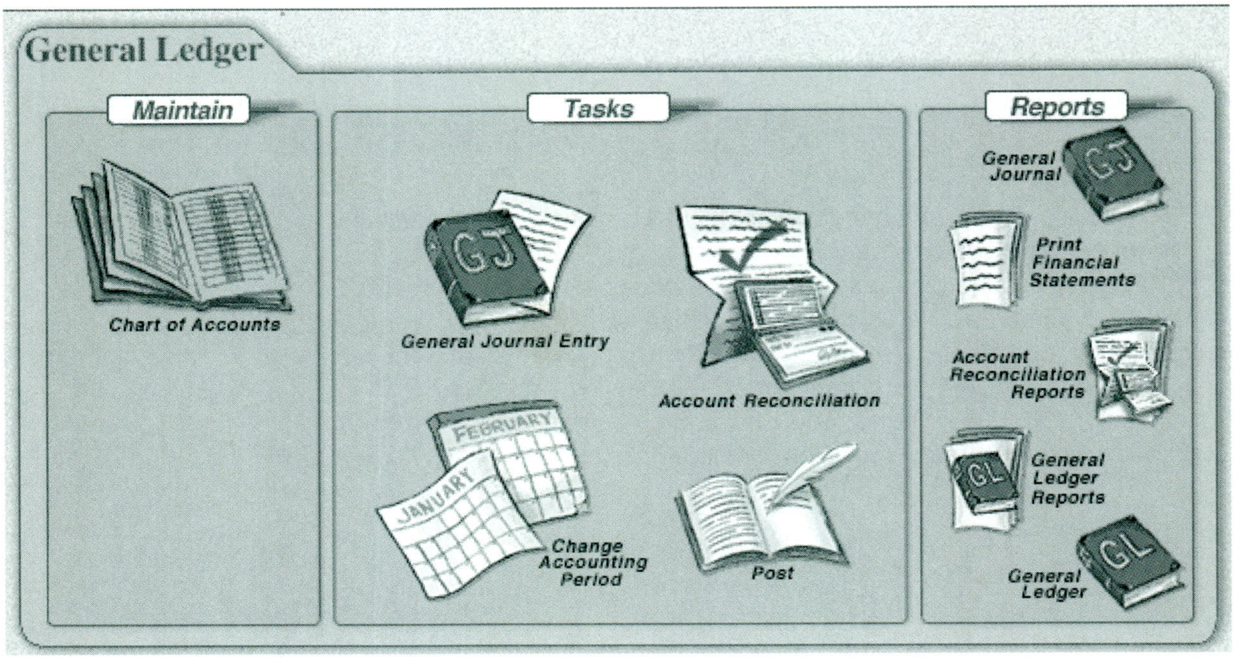

Figure 10–1 Open the General Ledger folder to print financial statements such as an Income Statement or a Statement of Cash Flow

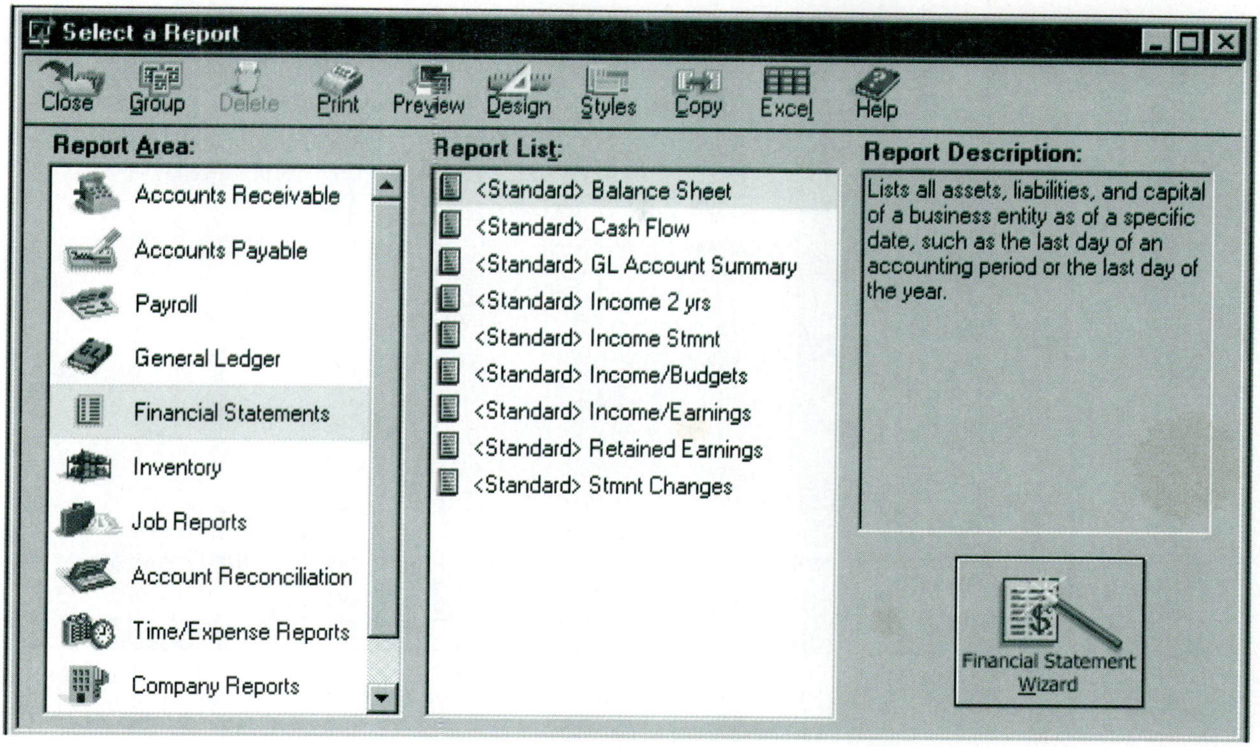

Figure 10-2 Select Financial Statement to print

Show Zero Amounts: Select this check box to show accounts with zero amounts.

Print All Words Capitalized: Select this check box if you want the report to print in all capitals.

Right Margin/Left Margin: Enter the size of the margins you want, in inches.

Center on Page: Select this check box if you want each page of the report to be centered on the page instead of left justified when it is printed.

Number of Copies: Enter the number of copies you want to print. You can enter any number from 1 to 99.

When you have made your selections on the options window, select **OK.** When the report is displayed, it's easy to use shortcut keys to view the entire report.

Home: Moves you to the top of the report.

Esc: Closes the report.

Page Up: Moves you back one "page." If the data on the report is not grouped in categories, then a "page" is the amount of information that fits on one screen. If the data on the report is grouped, then a "page" is one group.

Page Down: Moves you forward one page (or screen).

End: Moves you to the last line in the report.

Note

On long reports, *Peachtree* sometimes displays the first screen while the rest of the report is being assembled. When that happens, if you try to use "Page Down," the screen may go blank. Wait a moment and then scroll down.

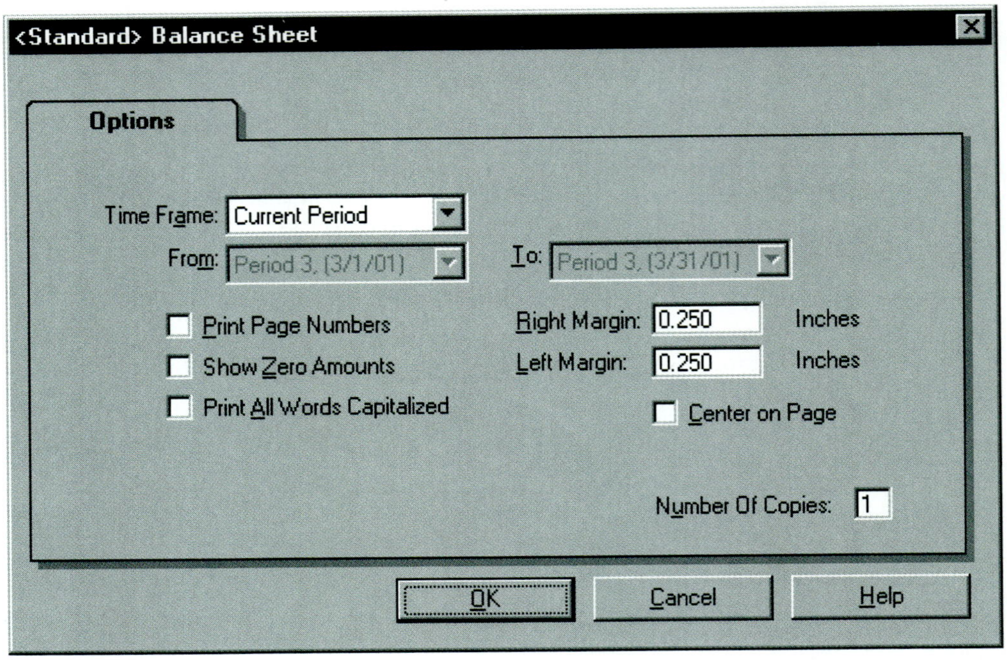

Figure 10–3 **Filter information for financial statements**

If you want to view more of the report on the screen, select the **Hide** icon. The report moves up the screen until the header is no longer visible. Select the **Show** icon to bring back the header. The Show/Hide option affects only your screen view of the report, not your printed report.

INCOME STATEMENT

An Income Statement shows the financial performance in terms of revenue and expense activity for a specified period of time. Its accounts are grouped in categories according to the account type you assigned when the Chart of Accounts was set up. Premier's statement includes totals for revenues, cost of sales, gross profit, expenses and net income. Data for the current month and for year-to-date are displayed, including a percentage of revenue analysis for both sets of figures.

When you choose the Standard Income Statement from the Report List (Figure 10–2), the Report Options window opens (Figure 10–3).

STATEMENT OF CASH FLOW

The Statement of Cash Flow report provides you with relevant information about changes in the company's cash receipts and cash payments during a specified period. (The term *cash* here means both cash and cash equivalents.) To qualify an asset as a cash equivalent, it must be readily convertible to a known cash amount. For a short-term investment to qualify as a cash equivalent, it must fall due within three months of when the company acquired it.

In the Statement of Cash Flow, cash receipts and cash disbursements are classified as Cash Flows from operating, investing, or financing. At the end of the report is a summary that contrasts beginning and ending balances and calculates the net increase or decrease in cash. The statement shows data for the current month and year-to-date.

To view or print the Statement of Cash Flow, select Cash Flow from the Report List. The Options tab contains the same filtering fields you saw for Balance Sheets and Income Statements.

Once you have made your selections, select **OK**; the report will be displayed on the screen. Because this statement contains categorized information, using the shortcut key, Page Down, would display for you the remainder of the Cash Flows from operating activities—not necessarily another full screen of data.

STATEMENT OF CHANGES IN FINANCIAL POSITION

A Statement of Changes describes changes in the company's financial position that may not be apparent from the Balance Sheet or Income Statement. This report identifies the changes that have affected the company's working capital, assets, and liabilities for a given period of time. The net income (or loss) is the most common reason for changes in working capital. Working capital is the starting point for the analysis that results in the Statement of Changes in Financial Position.

VIEWING AND EDITING REPORTS

When some reports are displayed on the screen, as you scroll through you will notice that some areas are outlined in a blue box. A blue box indicates a link that will take you to the Task window, where you can view or modify the transaction, post it, and return to the report. This feature is referred to as *drilling-down*. When your cursor passes over a transaction line, it changes into a magnifying glass. Double-click in the detail box to open the task window. When you save or post the change and close the task window, the report will reflect the change you just made. The drill-down feature is not available in financial reports because the information contained in them comes from multiple sources, rather than from a single transaction.

Grouping Reports

Perhaps you need several reports for the same meeting. To save time, you can group reports so that you can print them all at once. Instead of having to select each individual report for printing, you can simply select the report group.

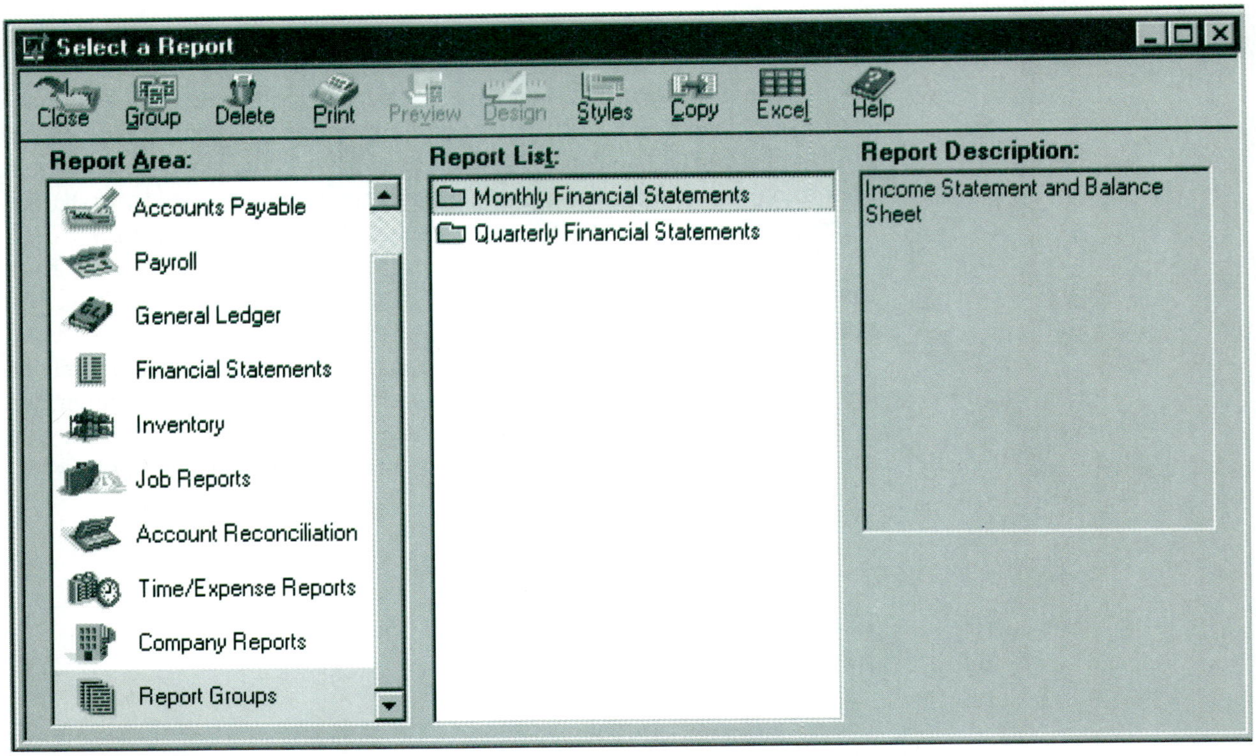

Figure 10–4 Create Report Groups

Grouping the Balance Sheet and Income Statement is an excellent application of this feature. The two statements are normally generated for the same time period. Here's how to create a "group" that will print the Balance Sheet and Income Statement at the same time.

Step 1 Select **Print Financial Reports** from the General Ledger Navigation folder.

Step 2 With the Select a Report window displayed (Figure 10–4), scroll down and click the **Group** icon.

Step 3 In the Report Index of the Report Group window, highlight Balance Sheet.

Step 4 Click the **Add** icon in the center of the screen.

Step 5 Highlight Income Statement in the Report Index.

Step 6 Click the **Add** icon.

Step 7 Select **Save** on the toolbar when you have finished adding reports to the group.

Step 8 In the Save As window, enter the name of the report group in the *Name* field. (If you have created other report groups previously, those groups would be listed below the *Name* field.)

Step 9 Enter a description of the report group in the *Description* box (i.e., Monthly Financial Statements).

Step 10 Select **Ok** to save the group. The Report Group will be displayed.

When you have saved the group, the Group Report window will display the name and description of the group you created. You can then add other reports to the group, remove a report, or create a new group.

When you choose to print statements from a Report Group (rather than printing each statement separately), you cannot preview the statements before you print. If you need to filter the information for any of the reports in the group, you should print the statements separately. For example, in Problem 10 you are instructed to print an Income Statement and a Balance Sheet for the month of February. You must print these as separate statements rather than using the Report Group for monthly financial statements. Choosing to print the Monthly Financial Statements group will print statements for March, the current accounting period.

Us versus the Machine

Was the human body designed to sit in front of a computer all day? You may have had the pleasure yourself and know that it's not very comfortable.

Repetitive strain injuries ("RSI"—also known as Cumulative Trauma Disorder) are caused by the repetitive activities people do every day, such as typing, talking on the telephone, using a mouse, and even writing with a ballpoint pen. Over time, the repeated strain can cause damage to tendons, cartilage, and other soft tissue.

It's becoming more of a problem. In the last 20 years PCs have become a mainstay in most workplaces; there are now more than ten times as many RSIs reported every year than there were in 1980. In fact, the Federal Occupational Safety and Health Administration estimates that in 1995 (the last year for which data was available) more workdays were lost due to RSIs than all other illness combined.

The most well known RSI is Carpal Tunnel Syndrome, a painful and dangerous condition suffered by workers whose jobs involve a great deal of typing.

Although it is well-known, Carpal Tunnel is not the most common RSI, however, nor the only typing-related one. RSIs can also develop when a PC user manipulates a mouse by merely pivoting the wrist, rather then moving the entire arm. Also, many injuries are caused by the very common practice of pinching a telephone receiver between one's shoulder and ear.

Can you believe that typing (keyboarding) is the most dangerous activity most people do each day? It is. But by instituting a few simple ergonomic practices you can reduce your risk.

First, the best way to prevent permanent damage is to rest often—and before your hands start hurting. Stretch your wrists frequently by pressing your palms together.

Second, when you type, always make sure that your wrists are elevated above the keyboard, as if you were playing a piano.

Third, avoid misusing your "wrist-rest." It's okay to rest your wrists there when you aren't typing; but you should not rest them when you are typing.

Finally, make sure your workspace is set up so that you can easily maintain the correct posture and form for typing. Experiment with raising or lowering the level of the keyboard, tilting the front of the keyboard so that it is a little higher than the back, or simply trying out a more supportive model of chair.

SUMMARY OF KEY POINTS

1. Financial reports reflect the financial position of the company and are crucial to the management who must make decisions.
2. The Balance Sheet lists, for a specific date, the balances of the asset, liability, and equity accounts.
3. The Income Statement reflects revenue and expense activity both for the current period and for the year-to-date.
4. The Statement of Cash Flow report categorizes the receipts and expenditures of cash and reports changes in cash.
5. The Statement of Changes report reflects changes in the company's working capital for the current month and the year-to-date.

*inter*NET CONNECTION

What do you think of the end-of-report qualifications made by this company? Why would the author of the annual report include these notes? **http://www.3com.com/annual/1996/results14.html** This site **http://www.gannett.com/annual/ar98/ar98toc.htm** is by the management of Gannett Co., Inc. Who might find this report useful?

Name ______________________________ Date ______________

CHAPTER REVIEW AND APPLICATIONS

Building Your Vocabulary

In the space provided, write the letter of the item that best matches the description.

a. Statement of Changes
b. Report Groups
c. Home
d. Esc
e. Cash Flow Report
f. Income Statement
g. Drilling-down
h. Balance Sheet
i. Range
j. Page down
k. End

______ **1.** A statement that identifies the financial status of a company by showing the ending balances of the asset, liability, and equity accounts.

______ **2.** To close a report, press this key.

______ **3.** A financial statement that lists all revenue and expenses. It also indicates a profit (or loss) for the period.

______ **4.** To go to the next page in a report, use this feature.

______ **5.** A financial statement that shows all of the cash used in the business both for the current month and the year-to-date.

______ **6.** A financial statement that identifies changes in working capital and provides an analysis of each component.

______ **7.** Shortcut to go to the last line of a report.

______ **8.** A time-saving way to print multiple reports.

______ **9.** Use this key to return to the beginning of a report.

______ **10.** The feature that allows you to open the task window from the displayed report.

Name ______________________________ Date ______________

Problem 10

Beginning with Chapter 4 of this tutorial, you have entered selected transactions for Premier Fitness Club, Inc. Even though the transactions do not provide a complete picture of operations, you will now generate reports that will be used for decision making. Premier prints a Balance Sheet and an Income Statement at the end of each month. At the end of each quarter, they print those two statements as well as a Statement of Cash Flow and a Statement of Changes in Financial Position.

Complete the following activities for Premier Fitness Club, Inc. on March 31, 2001.

1. Restore the backup file from Chapter 9.
2. Create a Report Group named Monthly Financial Statements. The group will include the Balance Sheet and Income Statement.
3. Create a report group named Quarterly Financial Statements. The group will include the Balance Sheet, Income Statement, Statement of Cash Flow, and Statement of Changes in Financial Position.
4. Print an Income Statement for February 1–February 28, 2001. You will need to enter appropriate dates since the dates are for a previous accounting period.
5. Print a Balance Sheet for February 1–February 28, 2001.
6. Print the Quarterly Financial Statements group.
7. Back up your file for use in Chapter 11.

Analyzing Your Work

Answer the following questions in the space provided.

1. What was the net income for the month of February 2001?

___

2. What is the significance of the balance for Accounts Payable on the February 28, 2001 Balance Sheet?

___

3. What is the balance of Accounts Payable for March 31, 2001?

___

4. What is the total revenue for the first quarter of 2001?

___

5. What is the gross profit for the first quarter of 2001?

___

6. What is the net income for March 2001?

___

7. What is the net income for the first quarter of 2001?

___

Chapter 11

Payroll Setup

OBJECTIVES

When you have completed Chapter 11, you should be able to:

1. Verify the Payroll default settings.
2. Set up or verify employee defaults.
3. Enter general pay-level information for employees.
4. Add employees to the company payroll.
5. Print an Employee List.
6. Define terms used in the chapter.

Peachtree Complete Accounting 8.0 automates payroll. After you set up default information and create records for your employees. *Peachtree* automatically calculates the paychecks. You can print a batch of payroll checks for all employees or you can print a single paycheck.

There are four stages in processing Payroll information.

1. The Default Information level is where you will set up Premier for all its employees. You will set up General Ledger accounts, pay levels, custom fields, and payroll fields.
2. The Employee Information level is where you will set up employee name, address, social security number, tax filing status, and pay levels. You will also indicate whether the employee is using company defaults for the payroll fields.
3. Payroll Journal entries is the level at which you actually process payroll checks (Payroll Entry).
4. In the Payroll Reports level, you will analyze payroll data.

You will verify default information and enter employee information in this chapter and pay employees and print reports in Chapter 12.

Note

If you have not installed the sample tax table, complete the installation before you begin Chapter 11. See page 3 of this text for step-by-step instructions.

The Payroll Navigation Aid displays maintenance records, tasks, and reports that affect Employees and Payroll Entry areas of *Peachtree*. In the Tasks section, arrows illustrate relationships and workflow of tasks that you would most likely follow. You can access the Payroll Setup Wizard from the **Maintain** menu or from the Setup Checklist, as well as from the Payroll Navigation Aid.

PAYROLL SETUP WIZARD

The Payroll Setup Wizard walks you through setting up most employee defaults and standard payroll fields. As you answer the prompts in the wizard, *Peachtree* will create most of the common payroll fields used in calculating deductions and taxes. For example, you are asked what the unemployment percentage for your company is. Based on the percentage you enter, *Peachtree* creates the State Unemployment Insurance (SUI) employer tax field and calculation formula that applies to it.

It is important to understand that when you install *Peachtree,* federal, state, and local payroll taxes will not calculate automatically unless you subscribe to the *Peachtree* Payroll Tax Service. A subscription entitles you to install the latest Tax Service updates as they become available. Otherwise you must manually set up formulas to calculate the taxes. Therefore, as you complete this tutorial, the percentages calculated in your solutions will not necessarily match the current tax rates.

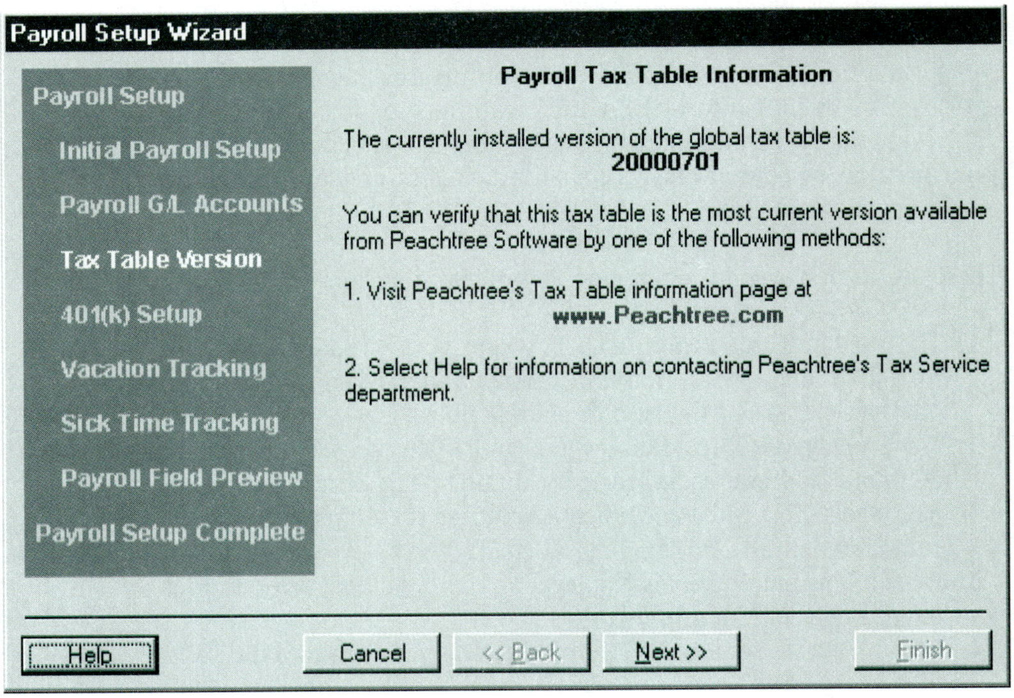

Figure 11–1 Payroll Setup Wizard

> **Note**
> If employee defaults have not been established for your company, *Peachtree* automatically displays the Payroll Setup Wizard the first time you choose *Default Information/Employees* from the **Maintain** menu or choose *Employee Defaults* from the Setup Checklist.

The *Peachtree* Payroll Setup Wizard establishes the following:

- State and locality defaults.
- State unemployment percentage and limit.
- Common federal and state payroll fields for employee-paid and company-paid taxes.
- General Ledger account defaults for payroll fields.
- Optional payroll fields for employee tips and meals.
- Optional payroll fields for employee and employer 401(k) contributions.
- Optional payroll fields for employee vacation and sick time.

Verify the payroll default information and work through each step as it is explained.

Step 1 Start *Peachtree*, if it is not already running.

Step 2 From the **Maintain** menu, choose *Default Information* and then *Payroll Setup Wizard.*

Step 3 If employee defaults had not been established for Premier, *Peachtree* would display the Payroll Setup Wizard the first time you chose *Default Information* and *Employees.* Because employee defaults were established in your template file, you will need to open the Payroll Setup Wizard (Figure 11-1).

Step 4 The payroll year displayed identifies the tax table being used in the template file.

Step 5 Click the **Next** button to move through the Payroll Setup Wizard. The defaults have been established and you should not change any of them.

Step 5 From the **Maintain** menu, choose *Default Information* and then *Employees.*

EMPLOYEE DEFAULT INFORMATION

> **Note**
> The defaults in Payroll setup will be used when you process payroll in the next chapter.

You can set up initial payroll fields from either the Checklist or the Maintain menu. Here are the steps to verify that employee defaults have been set up properly.

Step 1 From the Maintain menu, select Default Information.

Step 2 Select Employees from the submenu (Figure 11-2 will appear).

General Tab

The General tab (Figure 11-3) is active when the Employee Defaults window opens. Verify the information in each field.

State/Locality: *Peachtree* automatically fills in state and locality fields, based on the company information you entered in the new company setup procedure. Please verify (or enter) IL for the state. Also, verify or enter Chicago for the locality.

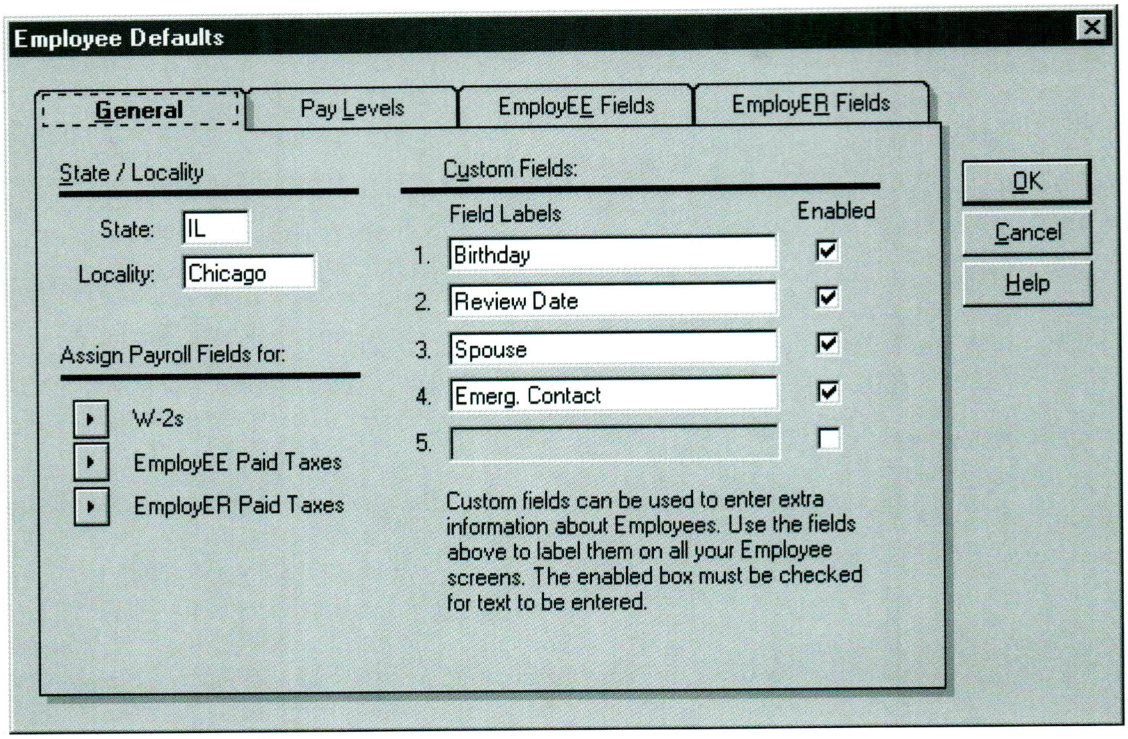

Figure 11–2 Verify employee defaults

Custom Fields: The custom fields are optional. (For this session, do not change the defaults.) *Birthday, Review Date, Spouse,* and *Emergency Contact* have been enabled so that this information can be entered for each employee.

Assign Payroll Fields for: Selecting the arrow button in any of the four fields will open a *second* window where defaults can be set. These fields can help you to calculate and then to post employee deductions, allowances, and employer taxes. Check out these fields in the following computer practice.

COMPUTER PRACTICE

Step 1 Select the **W-2s** arrow button on the General tab of the Employee Defaults window (Figure 11–3 will appear).

These fields are required data for a W-2 withholding form. Each field has a drop-down list from which you can make choices.

Step 2 Verify that your screen matches Figure 11–3. Select **OK** to save the information and to return to the Employee Defaults window (Figure 11–2).

Step 3 Select the **Employee Paid Taxes** arrow on the Employee Defaults window (Figure 11–4 will appear).

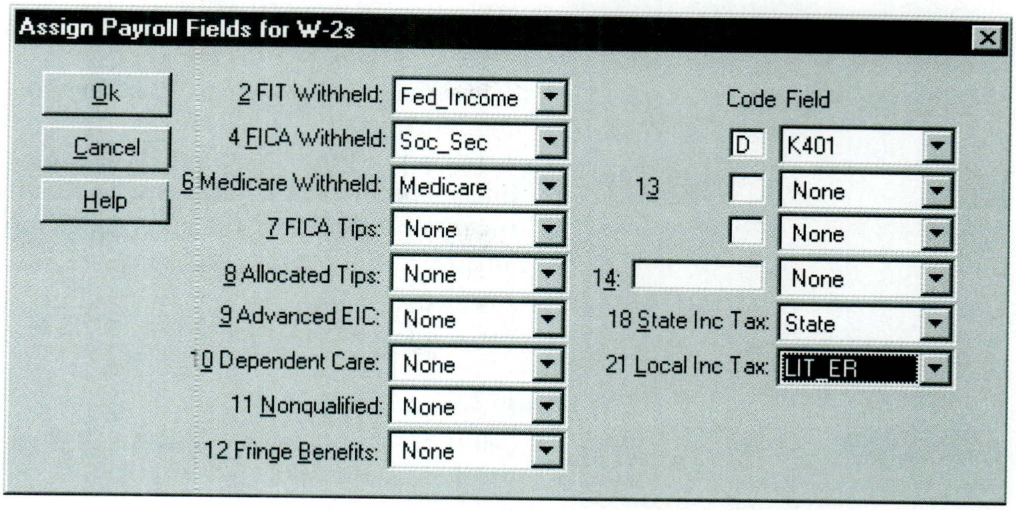

Figure 11–3 Fields for W-2 forms

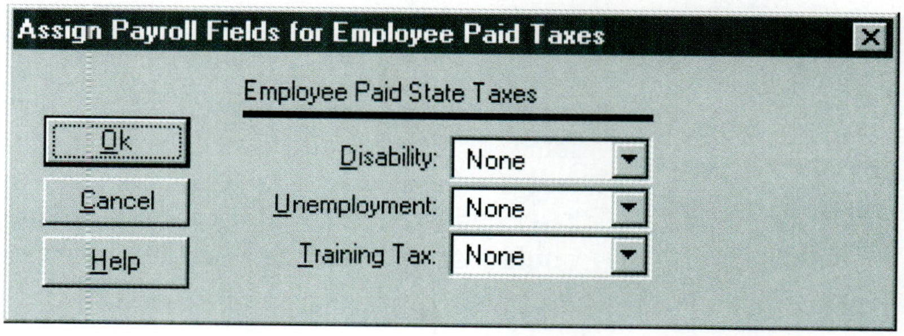

Figure 11–4 Step 3; select the Employee Paid Taxes

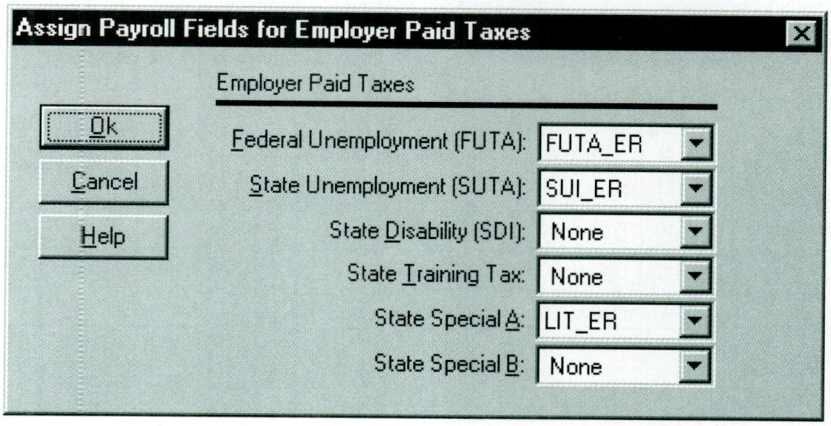

Figure 11–5 Establish company-paid taxes

On this screen you would identify taxes that would be paid by employees: *Disability, Unemployment,* and *Training*. In Illinois, the company pays these taxes for the employees. Therefore, the three fields should remain as None.

Step 4 Select **OK** to save the information and to return to the Employee Defaults window.

Note

Sometimes fields must be assigned more than once. For example, in California the employee portion of the state disability must be assigned on the *Local Income Tax* box, and on *Employee Paid Taxes,* under *Disability*.

Step 5 Select the **Employer Paid Taxes** arrow (Figure 11–5 will appear).

Step 6 Verify that your screen matches Figure 11–5. It shows data about taxes that the employer must pay. It has accounts associated with those required by Illinois. The FUTA (Federal Unemployment Tax Assessment) will be reported by you on a Federal 940 form, and the other taxes will be reported by you on a quarterly payroll tax form.

Step 7 Select **OK** to save the information entered and to return to the Employee Defaults window.

Pay Levels Tab

Note

The accounts entered here will be debited when you post the payroll entries.

Step 1 Select the Pay Levels tab (Figure 11–6 will appear).

Step 2 Your screen should match the defaults shown in Figure 11–6. Within these fields, you can assign account numbers to record payroll expenses for hourly and salaried employees. Verify for Premier that the account numbers for Wages Expense and Salaries Expense correspond with those in the Chart of Accounts.

Businesses have to keep records about payroll. Tax laws mandate some of these deductions; other deductions are voluntary. Payroll records detail wages and salaries paid, as well as amounts that have been deducted from the employees' compensation. Typical deductions would include taxes, health care, charity, and pension plans.

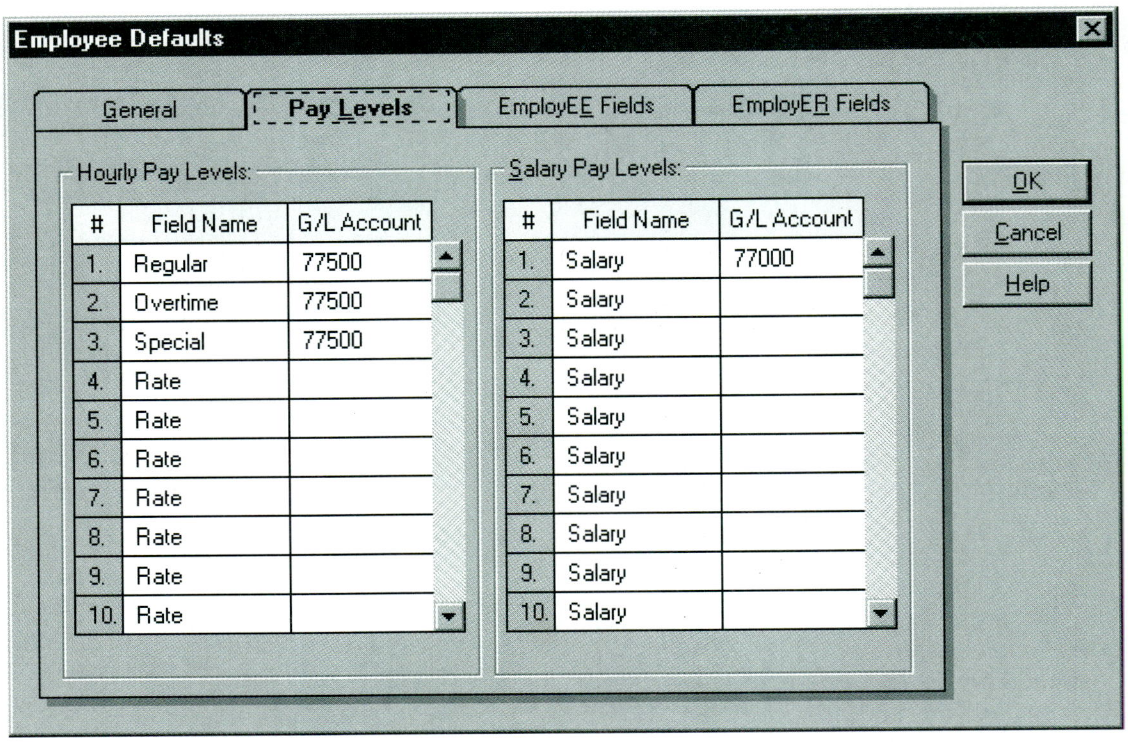

Figure 11–6 Pay levels tab

The law requires employers to withhold three types of taxes: federal and state income tax, social security, and Medicare taxes.

1. The amount of federal and state income tax is determined by the employee's marital status, number of exemptions claimed, and the employee's gross earnings.
2. The Federal Insurance Contributions Act of 1935 is more widely called the *Social Security Act*. The tax benefits employees and their families. It is paid for equally by the employee and the employer. The tax rates (and the earnings base to which they apply) are subject to change by Congress. *Peachtree's* tax tables reflect the rates in effect on the publication date for this text.
3. Medicare tax is like the social security tax. Prior to 1992, it was *part* of the social security tax. This tax is levied equally on the employee and employer. It provides some medical care for the employee and his/her spouse after each has reached age 65. Medicare taxes are levied on all earnings.

Note
Because these are crucial fields, be careful when you make a change to any of these fields.

Employee Fields Tab

Step 1 Select the Employee Fields tab of the Employee Defaults window (Figure 11–7 will appear).

Note
Scroll down the *Employee* fields to be sure that the 401(k) field is enabled.

Data in these fields helps you in three ways. First, it identifies payroll deductions and allowances that will be subtracted from gross pay. Second, it tracks memo amounts, such as vacation and personal leave hours, to help you in making reports and in calculating taxes. (Memos are not posted to the General Ledger.) Third, it tracks tax amounts to generate the employee's W-2 form at the end of the year.

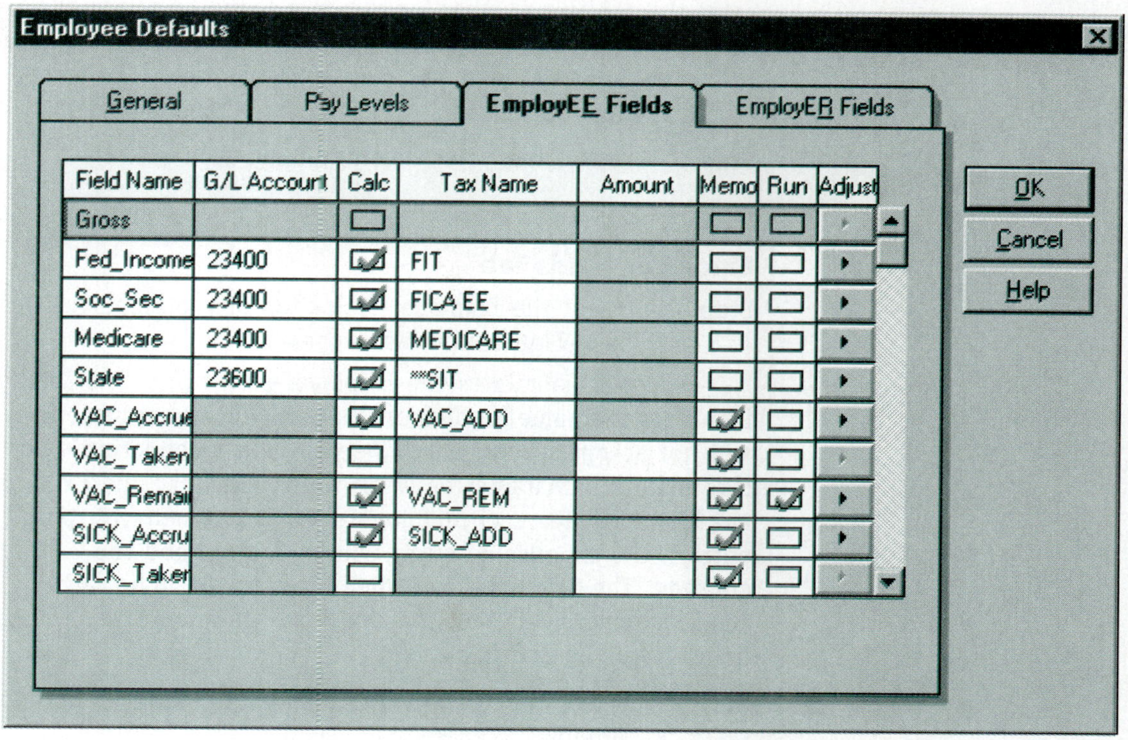

Figure 11–7 Enabling the taxes to be deducted from an employee's check

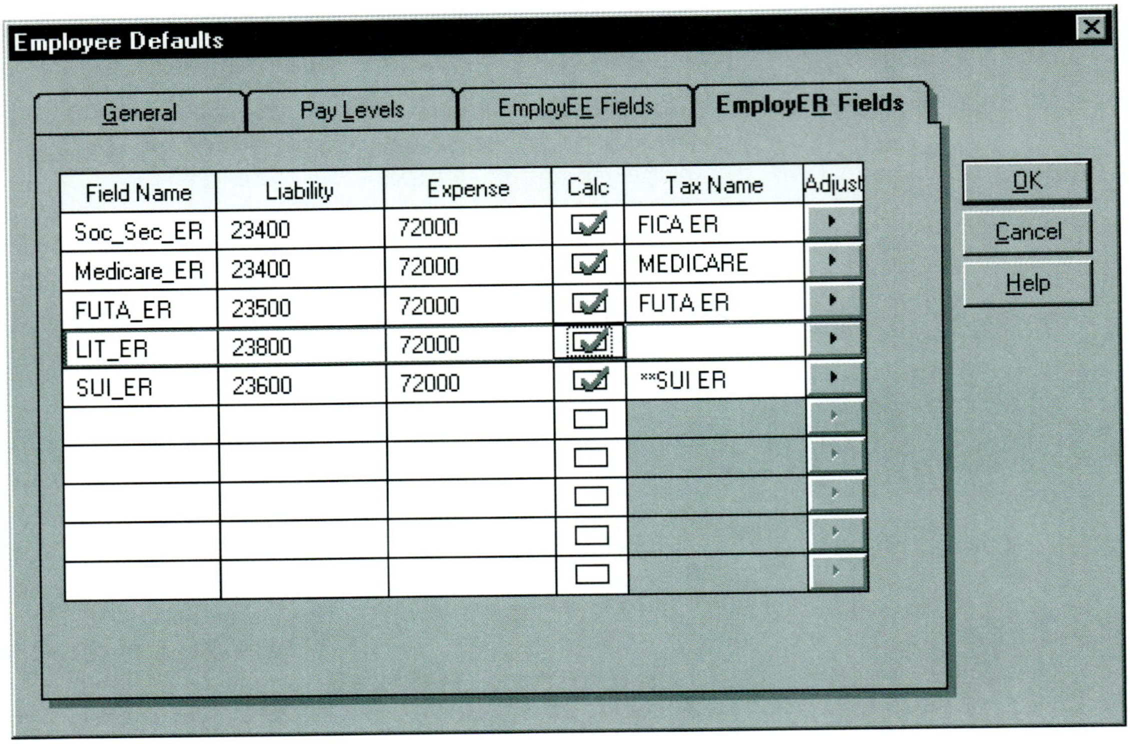

Figure 11–8 Employer-paid taxes

Peachtree automatically sets up some employee payroll fields during new company setup. The *Description* field identifies the deductions that will be applied to the employer's paycheck. The *G/L Account* field indicates the account number for the corresponding salary expense liability account. The *Calc* field indicates whether taxes are to be calculated. The formulas are stored in the *Calculation Name* field. The software will calculate the amount for each item that you have checked.

Step 2 Verify that your screen matches Figure 11–7.

Employer Fields Tab

Step 1 Select the Employer Fields tab of the Employee Defaults window (Figure 11–8 will appear).

Peachtree calculates the Employer-paid taxes. The *Description* field identifies the name for deductions as it will appear on reports. This field will not accept spaces; if you need to add a deduction, you would use the underline character between words. Liability and Expense accounts are identified for each employer-paid tax. When you post the payroll entries, the expense accounts will be debited and the liability accounts credited. The *Calc* field is enabled for each tax to be calculated. As with the Employee Fields tab, the *Tax Name* field identifies the tax table to be used for the tax deduction.

Step 2 Select the **OK** button to save any changes and to close the window.

MAINTAIN EMPLOYEE INFORMATION

The employees do the work of a business. The company pays them for doing so. You probably are working at or have worked at a job in which you earned a fixed rate per hour, called an *hourly wage*. Laws require that overtime (work in excess of 40 hours each week) be paid at least 1.5 times the regular rate.

In contrast, an employee who is paid a salary receives a fixed amount each pay period. In some states salaried employees are paid overtime for time beyond 40 hours each week. In other states, no overtime is paid regardless of the number of hours worked.

Most sales representatives receive a commission (a percentage of sales generated). In some instances, a salesperson may be paid a salary plus commission.

What information you will need about employees and sales representatives (and representatives who are employees) can be entered and edited through the **Maintain** menu or through the Payroll Navigation Aid. To set up employee data, you would follow these steps.

To enter or edit employee information, open the Payroll Navigation folder and select **Maintain Employees**. The screen shown in Figure 11–9 will appear. The header includes the following fields.

Employee ID: The *Employee ID* code can be up to 20 characters long. The ID helps sort and process payroll information. After you have

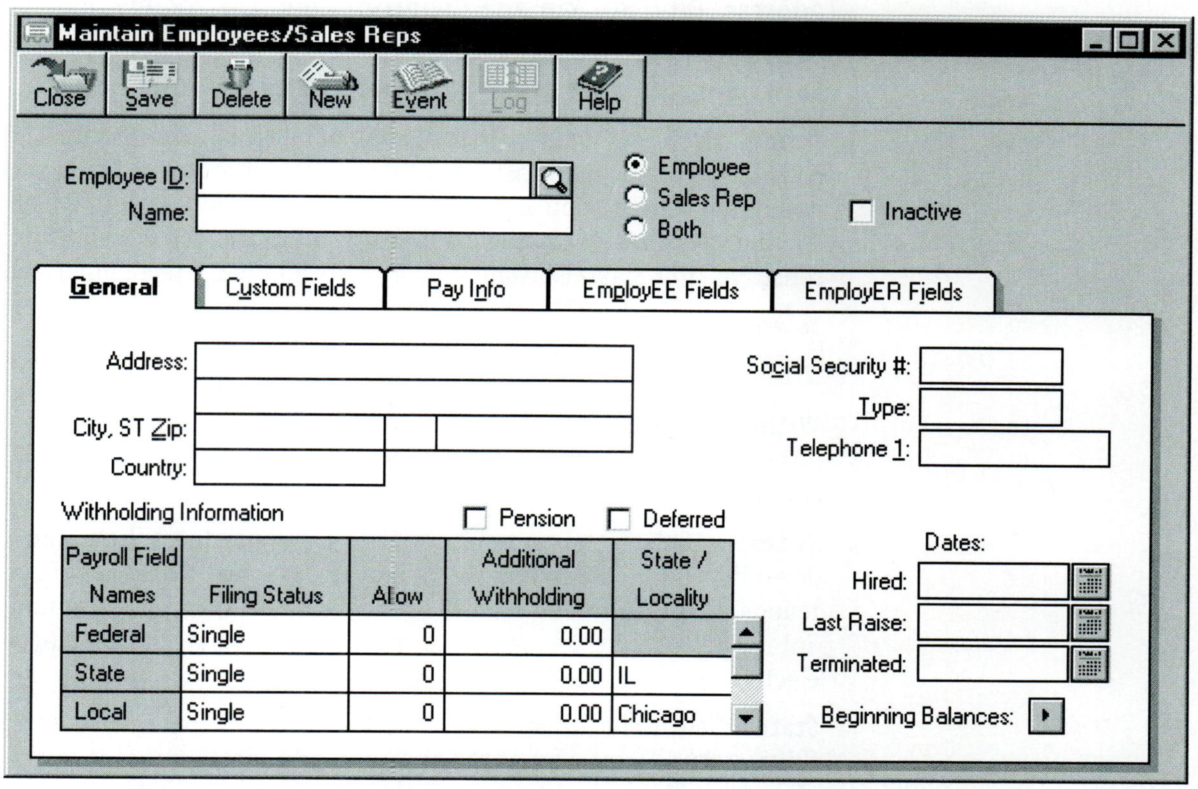

Figure 11–9 Maintain Employees screen

entered employees, you can select an existing employee ID from the lookup box. Premier uses the employee's initials as the ID. If there are duplicates, a number will be added after the initials.

Name: Employee names can be up to 30 characters long. When you select an existing employee ID, the information is automatically filled in. The name, as you enter it here, will print on payroll checks and reports.

Employee: The Employee option turns on all employee-specific fields.

Sales Rep: When *Sales Rep* is enabled, that person will be included in all reports about sales representatives. This option turns off tax filing, pay rate, and deduction information.

Both: Enable the *Both* field to identify an employee who is also a sales representative. Since all of Premier's employees are also sales representatives, you will use this classification.

Inactive: If you check the *Inactive* box, the employee is marked for deletion at the end of the year. If you attempt to enter a transaction for this employee, you will be warned of the inactive status.

General Tab

For each employee that you add to the system, you will be completing the following fields on the General tab.

Address, City, St., Zip and Country: Enter the address information. Enter a country only if you have employees outside the United States.

Social Security #: Enter the employee's Social Security number.

Type: Use *Type* to group (or sort) employees. For example, if an employee or sales rep is assigned to a particular group or team, you can enter that designation in this field. Thus you could enter "South" for all sales reps assigned to a southern sales territory. This field is case sensitive. You may also want to sort full- and part-time employees.

Telephone: Enter the employee's home telephone number.

Hired, Last Raise, Terminated: Enter the appropriate dates.

Withholding Information: The Tax Information block appears when either the *Both* or *Employee option buttons* is enabled in the Header section.

Federal: Select the appropriate federal filing status from the drop-down list. Enter the number of allowances claimed by this employee for federal taxes. Enter 99 if this employee is exempt from withholding. Enter the amount of additional withholdings that the employee has elected.

State: Select the filing status for state taxes. Enter only your state's filing status. Remember that the state and federal status is not always the same. Enter the number of *Allowances* and *Additional Withholding* for state taxes. Select the state ID that will print on the W-2 form. This ID also tells *Peachtree* which state tax table to use. Enter

99 if an employee is exempt from state withholding taxes. You must select the state from the drop-down list; do not key it in.

Local: Enter the local filing status and allowance information. Select Chicago from the drop-down list.

Note

To review default information for an employee, select Employee/Sales Rep from the Maintain menu. To review an employee's earnings history, select Payroll from the Reports menu. Then select Current Earnings Report, Quarterly Earnings Report, or Yearly Earnings Report. Select **Preview** or **Print.**

Pension and Deferred Boxes: Check off the *Pension option box* if you want pension to display on the W-2 form. Check the *Deferred* box if the employee participates in a deferred compensation plan. For example, if your company makes matching contributions to an employee's 401K. When you finish entering information on the General tab, select **Save.** Premier's plan is for employee contributions only.

Pay Info Tab

Select the Pay Info tab (Figure 11–10 will appear). Enter the type and frequency of pay for each employee or sales rep.

Pay Method: Select the employee *Pay Method* from the drop-down list in order to specify whether the employee is paid an hourly wage or a salary.

Frequency: For the frequency of your payroll, you can choose weekly, bi-weekly (every two weeks), monthly, semi-monthly (twice a month), or annually. What if you do not want to use the standard *G/L Accounts* for this individual?

Hours per Pay Period: If you selected Hourly—Hours per Pay Period in the *Pay Method* field, the total hours for the selected pay *Frequency*

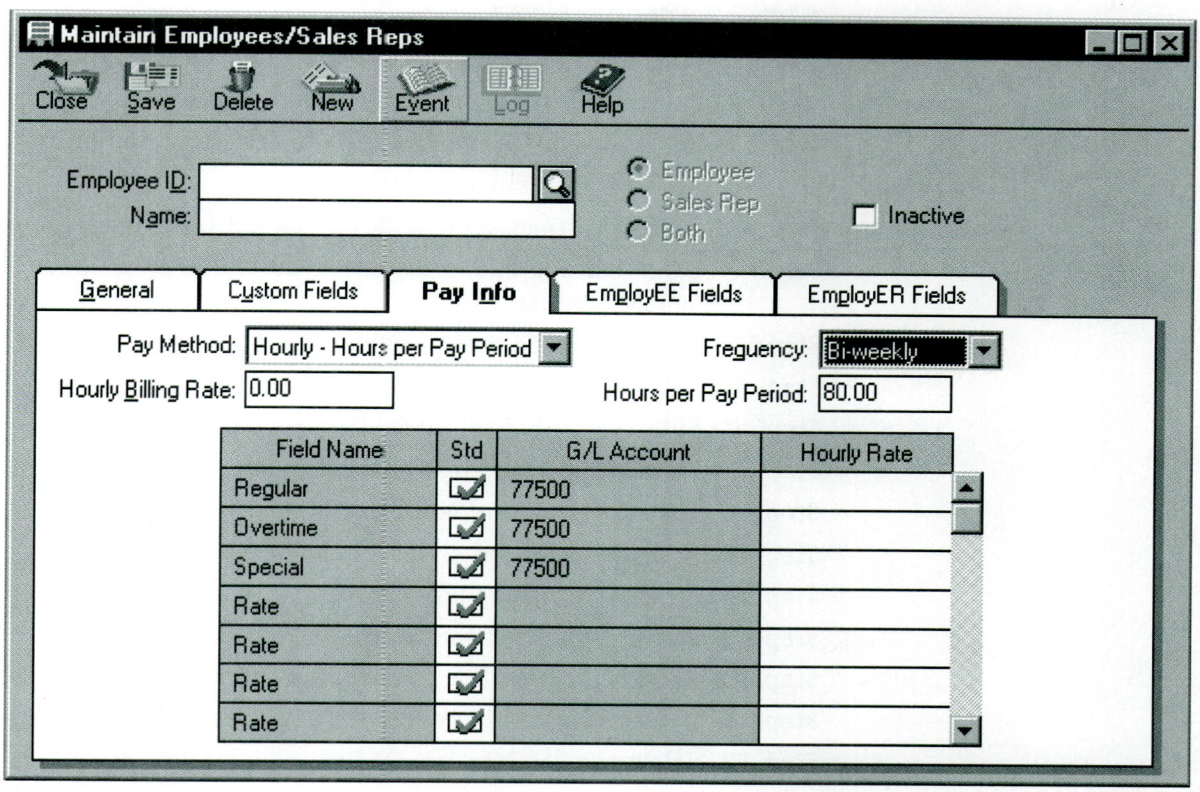

Figure 11–10 Pay Information fields

will be entered automatically. This field will not appear if you chose Salary in the *Pay Method* field.

Hourly Billing Rate: Enter a standard rate to bill customers for hours on employee time sheets.

Hourly Rate: If you selected Hourly—Hours per Period in the *Pay Method* field, an Hourly Rate column is displayed. Enter the individual's hourly rate of pay for regular, overtime, and special hours worked. If you selected Salary in the *Pay Method* field, this column will change to *Salary Rate*. For salaried employees, you will enter the salary for the pay frequency chosen.

Select the **Save** icon when you have completed all the fields. Select **Close** to return to the Main menu.

COMPUTER PRACTICE

Transactions

Premier hired Wally Jefferson as an employee on February 10, 2001. He lives at 801 Maywood Lane, Chicago, IL 60615. His home telephone number is (312) 555-6000, and his Social Security number is 300-50-1234. Use the employee's initials as the Employee ID. Wally is paid bi-weekly; he is an hourly employee receiving $10.00 per hour and receiving overtime at time-and-a-half after 40 hours during any week.

Adding an Employee

Step 1 Open the Payroll Navigation folder and select **Employees**.

Step 2 Enter WJ in the *Employee ID* field; press Enter.

Step 3 Enter the employee's name, Wally Jefferson, and press Enter.

Step 4 Activate the *Employee* button.

Step 5 Enter the street address, 801 Maywood Lane; press Enter.

Step 6 Enter Chicago and press Enter. Enter IL; press Enter. Enter 60615; press Enter.

Step 7 In the *Social Security #* field, enter 300-50-1234. Press Enter.

Step 8 Enter Sales in the *Type* field. Press Enter.

Step 9 Enter 312-555-6000 in the *Telephone* field. Press Enter.

Step 10 Press Enter to accept Single for *Federal* taxes.

Step 11 Enter 1 for *Allow*. Press Enter.

Step 12 Accept Single as the *State* filing status.

Step 13 Enter 1 for *Allow*.; press Enter.

Step 14 Verify the *State/Locality* is IL.

Step 15 Accept Single as the *Local* filing status and enter 1 for *Allow*.

Step 16 In the *Hired* field, enter 2/10/01; press Enter.

Step 17 Select the Pay Info tab.

Step 18 Select Hourly as the *Pay Method* and press Tab.

Step 19 In the *Hourly Billing Rate* field, enter 10.00; press Enter.

Step 20 Select Biweekly in the *Frequency* field.

Step 21 Verify that the *G/L Account* is 77500 for Regular, Overtime, and Special.

Step 22 Verify that 80 appears in the field *Hours per Pay Period.*

Step 23 Enter $10.00 in the Hourly Rate column of the table.

Step 24 Enter 15.00 as the *Overtime Hourly Rate*. Press Enter.

Step 25 Select the **Save** icon.

Editing an Employee

Subsequently, Wally Jefferson married. Please change his filing status and increase his allowances to 2 exemptions.

Step 1 Open the Payroll Navigation folder.

Step 2 Select the **Employees** icon.

Step 3 In the *Employee ID* field, select WJ. Press the tab key (or select the **Ok** icon at the bottom of the Employee list).

Step 4 In the *Federal* field, use the drop-down list to select Married as the filing status. Press Enter.

Step 5 Enter 2 in the *Allow* field; press Enter.

Step 6 From the *State* field, use the drop-down list to select Married as the filing status; press Enter.

Step 7 Enter 2 in the *State Allow* field; press Enter.

Step 8 In the *Local* field, select Married. Enter 2 in the *Allow* field.

Step 9 Select **Save.**

Step 10 Select **Close.**

For Your Eyes Only

Information is the lifeblood of today's businesses. A company generates all kinds of financial information—plans, reports, projections, and estimates. It is important to make sure this information doesn't fall into the wrong hands.

Companies must protect two types of information: internal information about its own finances and operations; and private information that it exchanges with customers or clients.

The first category includes trade secrets, strategic plans, and even the salary, benefit, and performance histories of specific employees. Failure to properly secure this sort of data can directly affect a company's survival. While most companies aren't betting all their chips on a single hot new product and don't feel a pressing need to seal up their projections and financial status reports, every company needs to keep close tabs on the information it amasses about its employees. Many companies draft strict, specific confidentiality agreements that must be signed by anyone who works for or with them in certain capacities.

More and more, however, companies are being forced to deal with the second category of secured data—and the subsequent problem of keeping others' information confidential. Partly this situation is because many businesses are now consulting firms. But even traditional retail and manufacturing companies have a collection of confidential information—whether they like it or not—when they start developing detailed client or customer mailing lists or sell their products and services through the World Wide Web.

Is it possible to protect your company from loss of either type of information?

First, clearly mark all confidential information as confidential.

Of course, marking data "confidential" isn't enough to protect your company from lawsuits. If your business is sued, your lawyers may be asked by the court to prove your company actually tried to restrict access in some way.

To do that on your office's computer network, you can place the files in areas that can only be accessed by an authorized group of users. On a stand-alone PC, you can, to some degree, protect confidential files by password-protecting each individual file and folder.

SUMMARY OF KEY POINTS

1. Federal and state laws require that employers withhold federal and state taxes from the earnings of employees.
2. Many payroll deductions are mandated by federal and state law; others are voluntary deductions, made at the employee's request.
3. *Peachtree*'s Payroll tracks earnings and deductions for employees, thus simplifying payroll processing.
4. *Peachtree* automatically tracks an employer's payroll obligations. It also generates tax reports.
5. It is crucial to achieve accuracy in establishing payroll defaults and in entering employee information.

*inter*NET CONNECTION

Networking can help give you added information about problem-solving options. At this site, you can find business and finance public message boards, live chat rooms and conferences, and hosted message boards: **http://www.onlinewbc.org/cgi-bin/webx.cgi?onlinewbc**

Name ______________________________ Date ________________

CHAPTER REVIEW AND APPLICATIONS

Completion

In the space provided, write the word or words that best complete each statement.

1. The ____________ walks you through setting up most employee defaults and standard payroll fields.
2. Optional fields that accommodate information such as birthday, performance review date, etc. are called ____________.
3. FUTA and SUTA are examples of ____________ paid taxes.
4. Taxes that will be deducted from employees' checks will be identified on the ____________ tab in the Employee Defaults window.
5. Three required federal taxes are ____________, ____________, and ____________.

Problem 11

Before you begin Problem 11, complete the Computer Practice activities contained in the chapter.

When you have verified the default settings for the payroll feature, enter the following employees into the system. Finally, answer the Analyzing Your Work questions. The filing status and allowances information is to be used for Federal, State, and Local taxes. Premier pays its employees biweekly.

Instructions

Step 1 Restore the Premier Fitness Club, Inc. backup file from Chapter 10.

Step 2 Employee records have been created for the employees listed below. Enter the additional information for each employee.

Step 3 Print an employee list.

Step 4 Back up the file to use in Chapter 10.

Step 5 Exit the program.

Name ______________________________ Date ______________

Transactions

1. Jane Warren, General Manager
   SSN# 285-61-1234
   3214 Latimer Drive
   Chicago, IL 60612
   Phone: 312-555-9837
   Bi-weekly Salary = $3,000.00
   Married; Allowances = 4
   Hire Date = 1/3/99

2. Tim Richards, Office Manager
   SSN# 241-75-1564
   8971 Monte Sane Drive
   Chicago, IL 60625
   Phone: 312-555-6710
   Bi-weekly Salary = $2,200.00
   Married; Allowances = 2
   Hire Date = 1/5/99

3. John Thompson, Exercise Instructor
   SSN# 425-43-8321
   3290 Lake Shore Boulevard
   Chicago, IL 60602
   Phone: 312-555-0098
   Hourly Rate = $15.00
   Overtime Rate = $22.50
   Single; Allowances = 1
   Hire Date = 1/10/99

4. Carolyn Speer, Exercise Instructor
   SSN# 785-71-1127
   7825 West Gate Street
   Chicago, IL 60622
   Phone: 312-555-0425
   Hourly Rate = $15.00
   Overtime Rate = $22.50
   Single; Allowances = 1
   Hire Date = 1/10/99

5. Mary Steward
   SSN# 581-56-1457
   5403 Orange Lake Boulevard
   Chicago, IL 60602
   Phone: 312-555-7250
   Hourly Rate = $12.00
   Overtime Rate = $18.00
   Single; Allowances = 1
   Hire Date = 1/10/99

Analyzing Your Work

Answer the following questions in the space provided.

1. How many people does Premier employ?

   ____

2. What is Jane Warren's employee ID?

   ____

3. What is the hourly overtime rate for Mary Steward?

   ____

4. What is the weekly salary of Tim Richards?

   ____

5. How many allowances has Jane Warren claimed?

   ____

Chapter 12

Payroll Processing

OBJECTIVES

When you have completed Chapter 12, you should be able to:

1. Pay employees.
2. Print payroll checks.
3. Void a payroll check.
4. Print a Payroll Check Register.
5. Print a Payroll Journal report.
6. Print a Payroll Register report.

Peachtree Complete Accounting 8.0 uses the employee files and default information that you created in the last chapter to calculate, process, and post the payroll. Once you have set up payroll properly, you have automated much of the subsequent work. All entries that you make in Payroll are posted both to the General Ledger and to the employees' files.

You can process payroll weekly, bi-weekly, semimonthly, monthly, or annually. If you have entered an employee ID, then the rest of the dialog box is filled in automatically, based on the information you entered as defaults in Chapter 11.

ENTERING A PAYROLL CHECK

The payroll check amount (net pay) is automatically credited to the cash account that you specify when you open the Payroll Entry window. When you open the Payroll Navigation Aid and select **Payroll Entry,** you will be reminded to sign up for *Peachtree* Tax Service. Simply click **Ok** to bypass this message. You will be then prompted to "select a cash account." Select the "Payroll Checking Account"; then select **Ok** to continue. The screen shown in Figure 12–1 will appear.

The following fields require information from you in order to process a payroll check.

Employee ID: Enter or select the employee ID code. If you select an hourly employee, the *Salary Amounts* fields will change to *Hours Worked*.

Check Number: If you want *Peachtree* to print the check, allow the *Check Number* field to remain blank. You will enter a beginning check number when checks are printed.

Date: Enter the check date for this payroll.

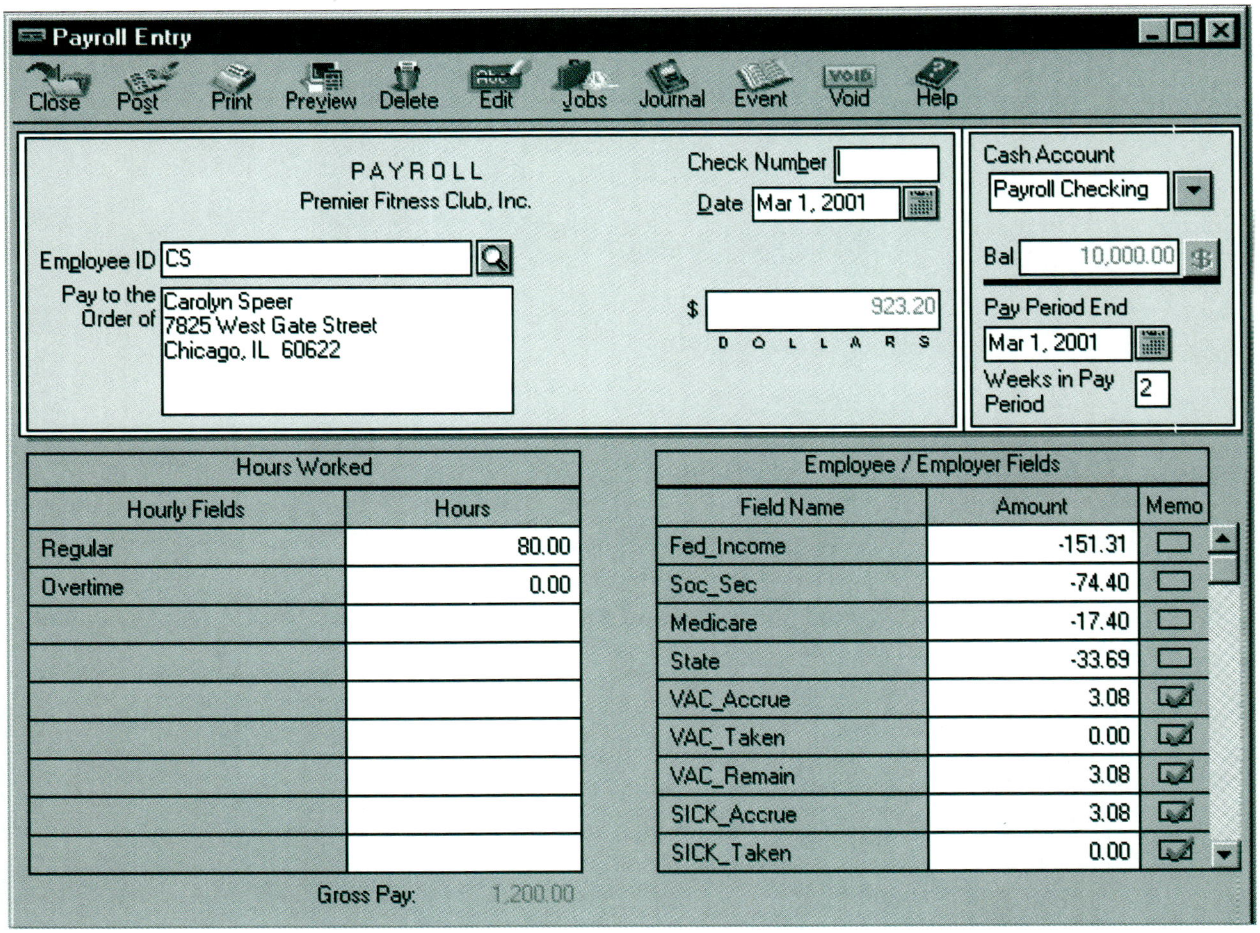

Figure 12–1 Enter a payroll check

Cash Account: The *Cash Account* field will display the account you selected when you opened the Payroll Entry window. You can change this account if the selection was incorrect.

Pay Period End: Enter the closing date for the payroll period.

Weeks in Pay Period: Enter the number of weeks covered by the pay period.

Hours Worked/Salary Amounts: If the selected *Employee ID* is an hourly worker, the bottom half of the screen will display the default for the employee's regular time, corresponding to the *Weeks in Pay Period* entry. You can make changes to the number of hours or enter overtime hours for the period. For salaried employees, this section will display the employee's regular salary for the pay period.

Peachtree will automatically calculate *Gross Pay*. It will show the deductions and net pay. You can make changes if there is an exception from the default. When you have verified that the amounts are correct, then select **Save**.

For your reference, this is how to complete the end-of-chapter activities:

Step 1 Open the Payroll Navigation folder.

Step 2 Select the **Payroll Entry** icon.

Step 3 Select the *Employee ID*; press Enter.

Step 4 Enter the *Date* of the paycheck.

Step 5 Verify that the Payroll Checking account number is displayed in the *Cash Account* field.

Step 6 Enter the *Pay Period End* date; press Enter.

Step 7 Enter the number of *Weeks in Pay Period*; press Enter. Enter the regular and overtime hours for hourly employees.

Step 8 Select the **Post** icon.

Step 9 Select **Close** or **Print.**

PAYING A GROUP OF EMPLOYEES

Most employees receive a salary (or work the same number of hours from one payroll period to the next). In that instance, your paying a *group* of employees is a more efficient way to process payroll checks. You can pay all (or some) of the employees or sales reps in a two-step process: first by filtering and then by selecting the employees to be paid.

These steps pay a group of employees:

Step 1 Choose **Select for Payroll Entry** from the Payroll Navigation folder (Figure 12-2 will appear).

Step 2 Select the pay frequencies you want to include in the payroll.

Step 3 Select whether you want to pay hourly or salary or both groups of employees.

Step 4 Select whether you want to pay a range or all employees.

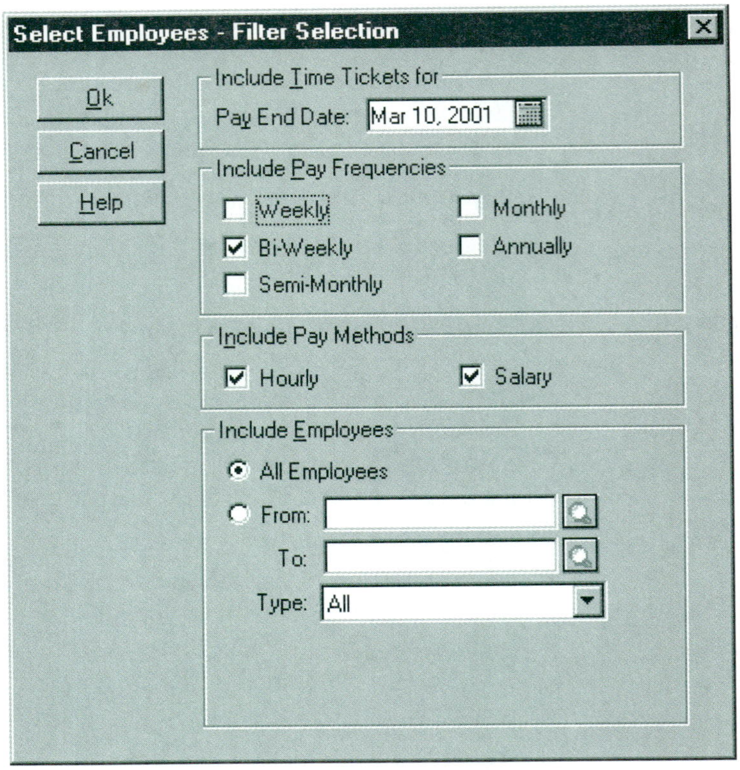

Figure 12–2 Determine which employees to pay

Step 5 Select **Ok** when you are finished. After selecting the filter options, the Select Employees to Pay window will display (Figure 12–3).

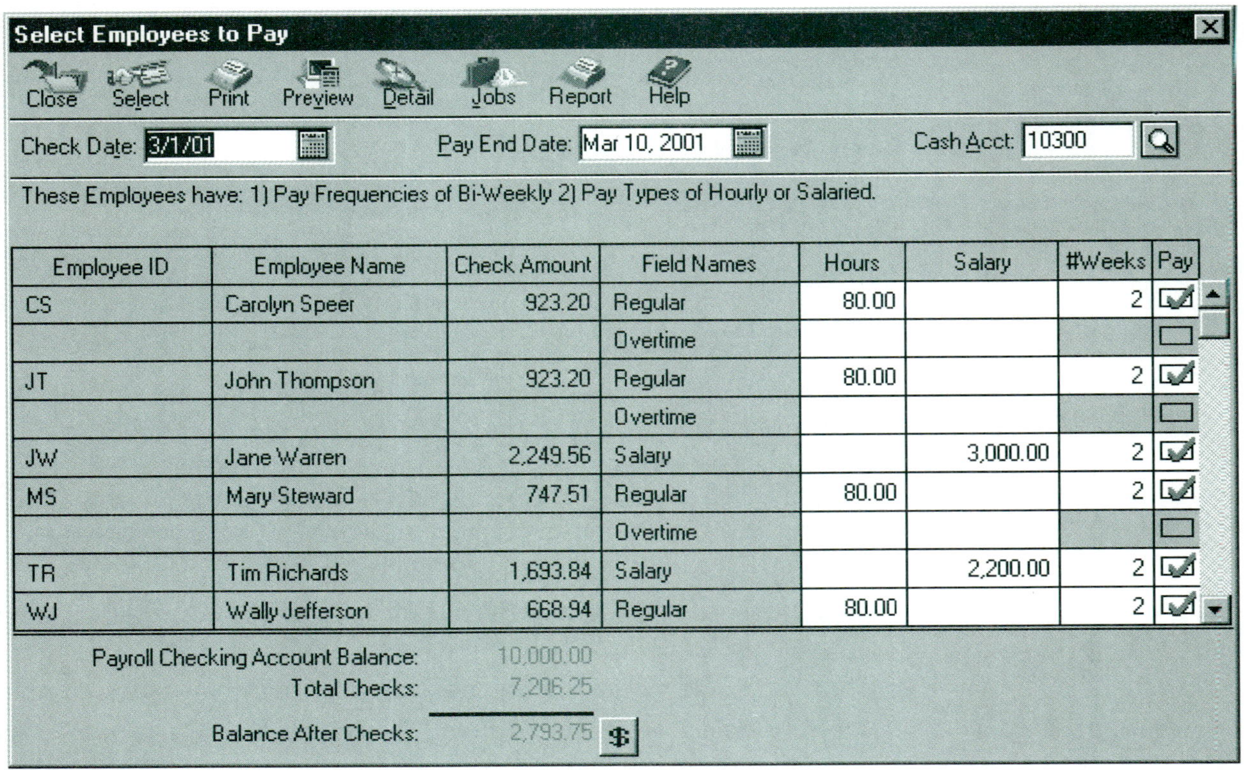

Figure 12–3 Select employees to pay

Step 6 Enter the *date* to print on the check and verify the *Pay End Date.*

Step 7 Verify that the payroll checking number appears in the *Cash Acct* field.

Step 8 You can change deductions or allowances by selecting the **Detail** icon after you highlight an employee.

Step 9 You can make changes to the *Hours, Salary,* and *# Weeks* fields.

Step 10 For any listed employee who you do not want to pay, uncheck the *Pay* box.

Step 11 Select the **Print** icon to print the checks. You will select a check style and enter the first check number.

Step 12 When you indicate that the checks printed properly, you will see a message indicating that the Payroll Journal is now being posted.

PRINTING PAYROLL CHECKS

Peachtree provides three options for printing payroll checks. You can print each check as it is created in the Payroll Entry window. You can print a batch of checks using the Payroll Reports window. Finally, you can print checks using the **Select for Payroll Entry.**

Follow these steps to print a batch of checks that were posted from the Payroll Entry window without check numbers.

Step 1 Open the Payroll Navigation Aid.

Step 2 Select **Payroll Reports**. The Select a Report window will display (Figure 12–4).

Step 3 Scroll through the Report list and double-click the Payroll Checks folder.

Step 4 A list of check forms will display below the Payroll Checks folder; double-click on form PR 7. The screen shown in Figure 12–5 will appear.

Step 5 Enter the check number for the first check.

Step 6 Enter the date for the checks.

Step 7 Select **Ok.**

Step 8 When prompted, enter the first check number.

Step 9 Verify that the checks printed properly. If an adjustment is necessary, select **Align** to make adjustments.

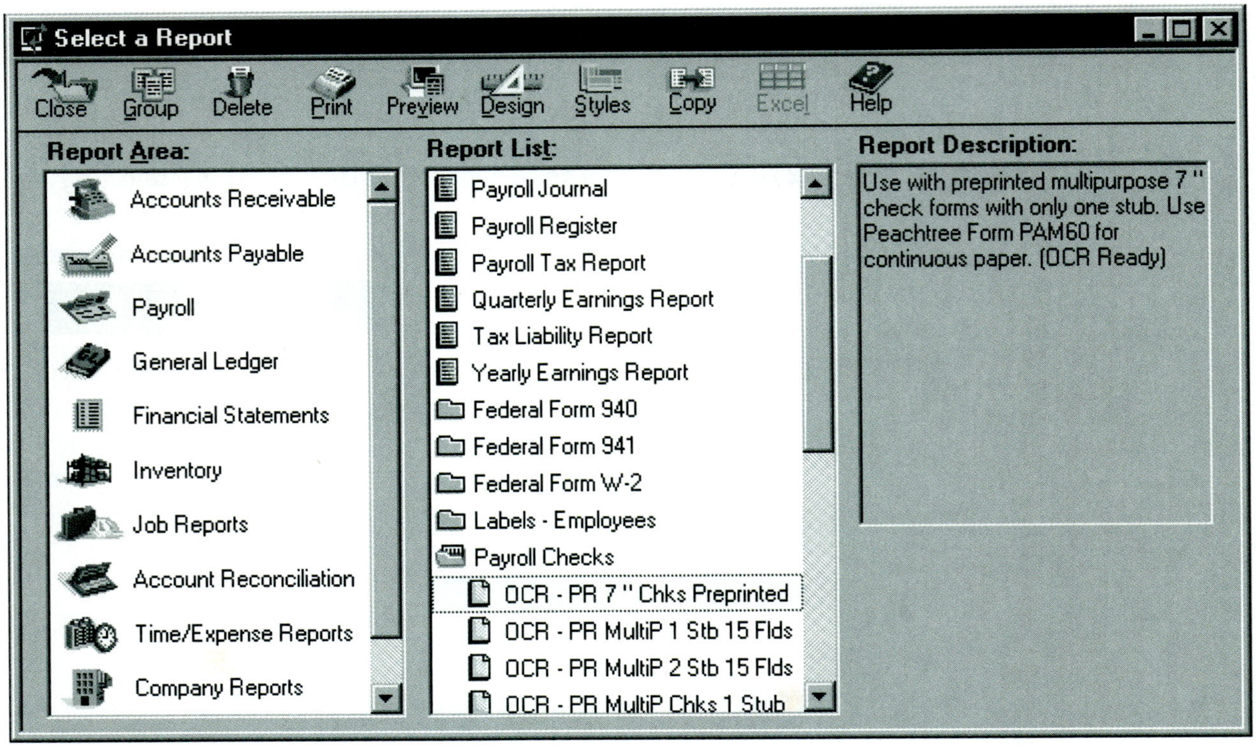

Figure 12–4 Print payroll checks from Reports

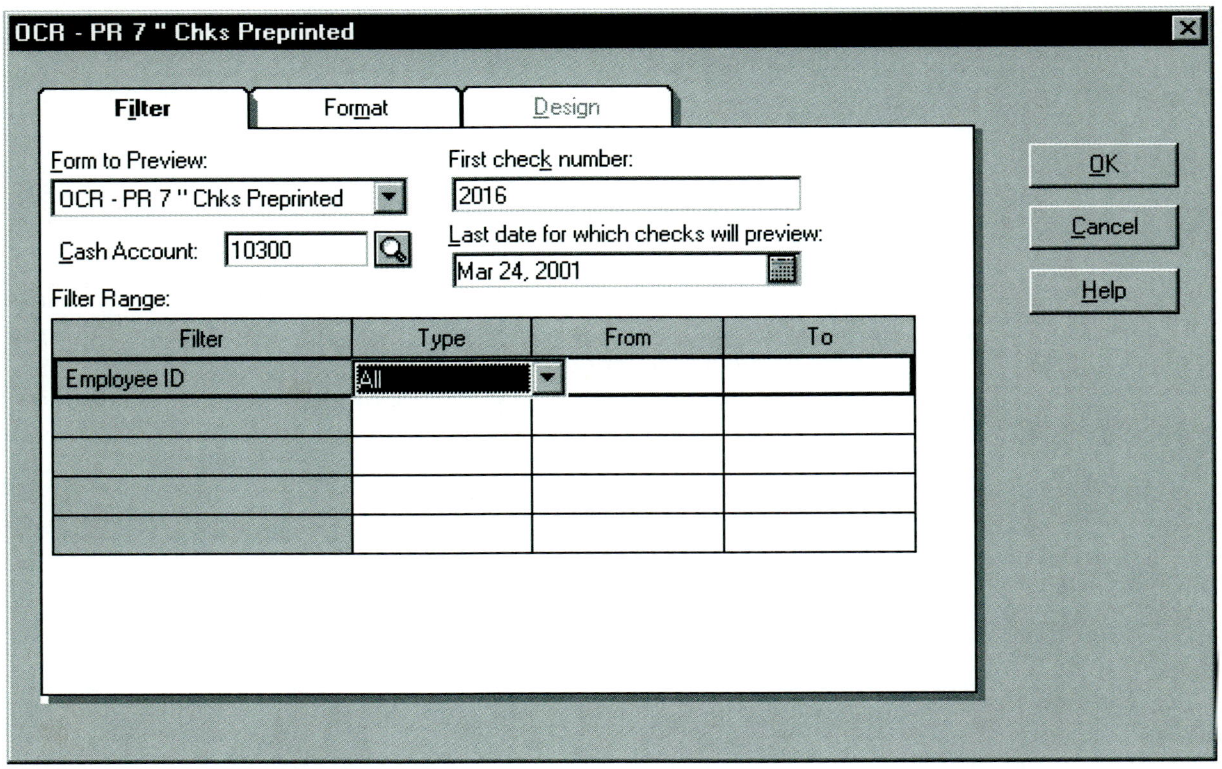

Figure 12–5 Print multiple checks for Payroll Entry selections

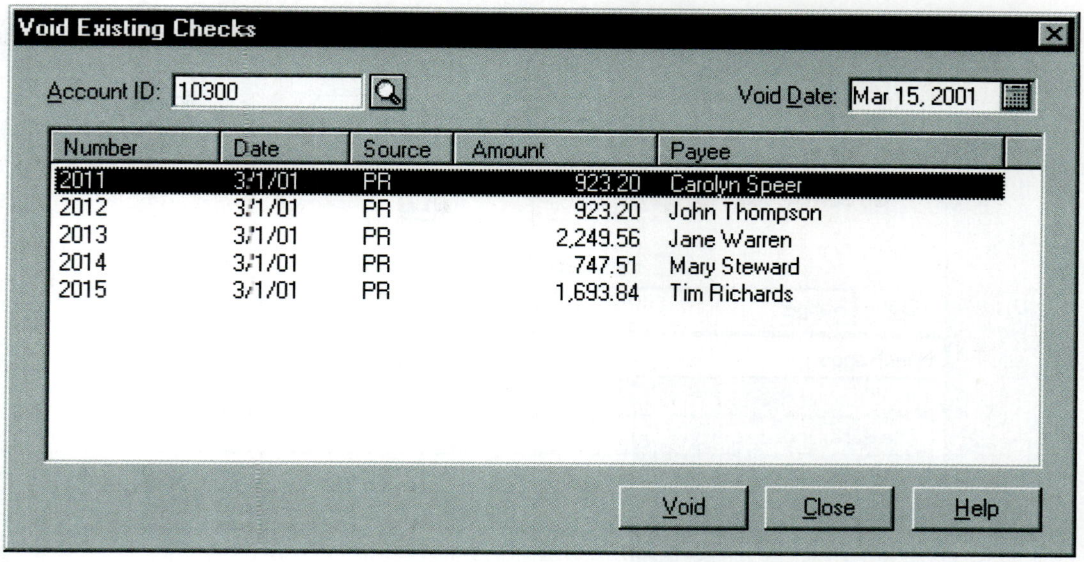

Figure 12–6 Void a paycheck

VOIDING A PAYCHECK

> **Note**
> You can void only paychecks that have a check number.

You can void paychecks like you void disbursement checks entered in Accounts Payable. When you void a payment, *Peachtree* creates a General Ledger entry that reverses the payment. During Account Reconciliation, both the original payment transaction and the voided payment are automatically cleared.

Follow these steps to void a paycheck.

Step 1 Open the Payroll Navigation Aid.

Step 2 Select **Void Checks.**

Step 3 Select the *G/L Cash Account* used on the paycheck to be voided. The Void Existing Checks window will display (Figure 12–6).

Step 4 Enter the date on which you want the check to be voided.

Step 5 From the Existing Checks list, highlight the payment you want to void.

Step 6 Select the **Void** button.

Step 7 Select **Ok.**

Step 8 Repeat this process for each payment you want to void.

Step 9 Select **Close** when finished.

PRINTING A PAYROLL CHECK REGISTER

The Payroll Check Register is similar to the regular Check Register report you generated in Chapter 8. It lists all paychecks, whether or not they have been printed. The Check Register displays the reference number assigned to the paycheck (if it has been printed or a manual check

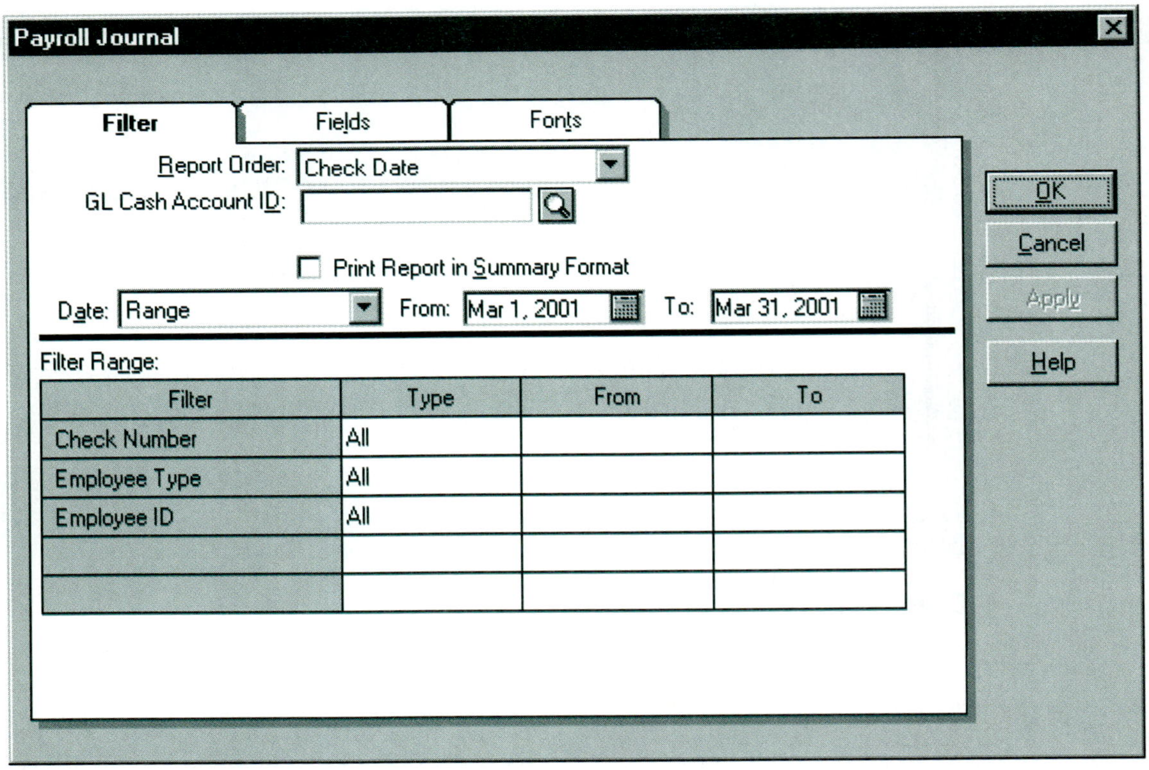

Figure 12–7 Print the Payroll Journal

number has been entered). The Register also shows the date the transaction was posted to the General Ledger, the employee's name, and the net amount of the paycheck. The procedure for printing a Payroll Check Register is as follows:

Step 1 Open the Payroll Navigation Aid.

Step 2 Select **Payroll Reports** (Figure 12–4 will appear).

Step 3 Select Check Register from the Payroll Report List.

Step 4 Select **Preview**.

Step 5 Set the ending date on the report filter. The Check Register will be displayed.

PRINTING A PAYROLL JOURNAL REPORT

A Payroll Journal report allows you to reconcile paychecks and verify General Ledger postings. You can edit a payroll transaction listed on the report by double-clicking on it. You can choose to print the report in detail or in summary. The report can be sorted by check date, check number, or G/L Account.

Step 1 From the Payroll folder, select **Payroll Journal**.

Step 2 Verify that Check Date appears in the *Report Order* field.

Step 3 Verify that the *G/L Cash Account ID* shows the Payroll Checking Account number.

Step 4 Verify that the *Date* field has This Period identified.

Step 5 Select **OK** (Figure 12–8 will appear). If you display the report now, it will contain no data. After you process the payroll entries at the end of this chapter and generate this report, you will select the **Print** icon or you will select **Close** to return to the Report Listing screen.

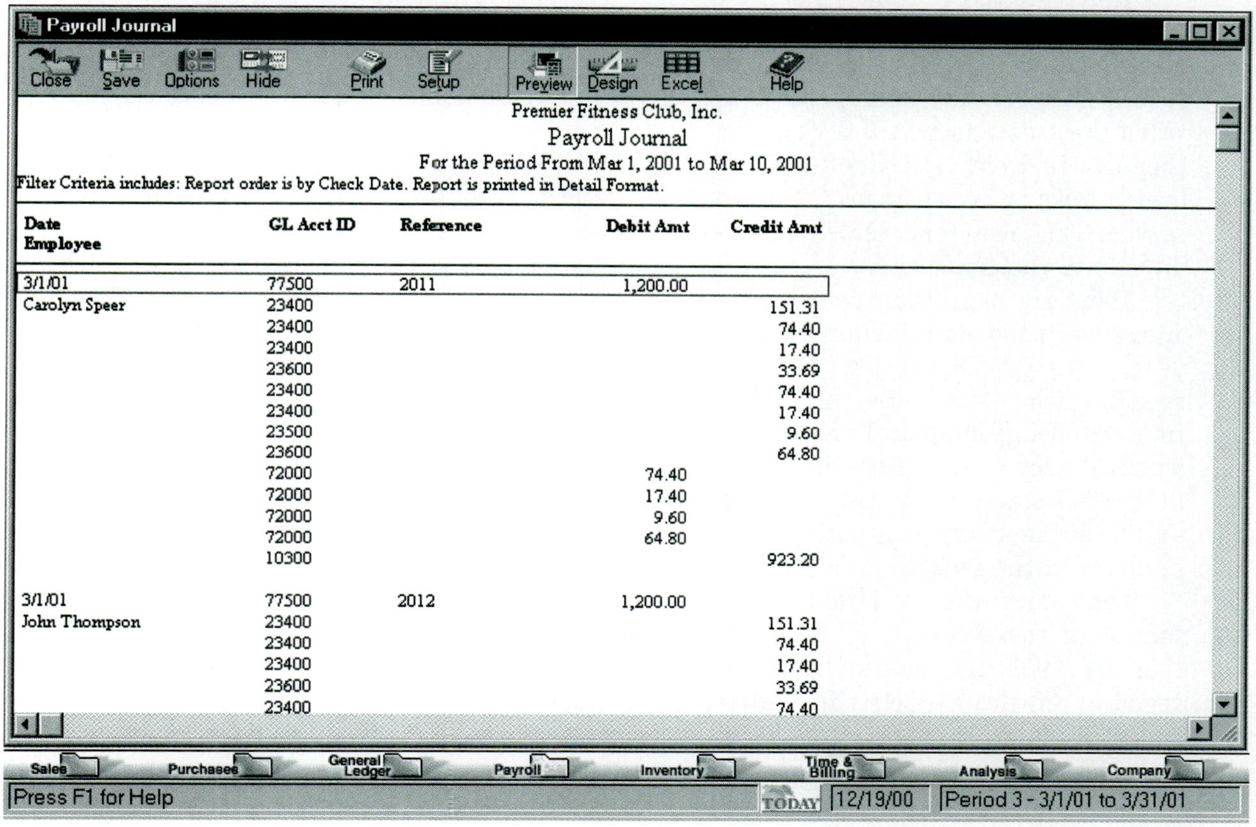

Premier Fitness Club, Inc.
Payroll Journal
For the Period From Mar 1, 2001 to Mar 10, 2001
Filter Criteria includes: Report order is by Check Date. Report is printed in Detail Format.

Date Employee	GL Acct ID	Reference	Debit Amt	Credit Amt
3/1/01	77500	2011	1,200.00	
Carolyn Speer	23400			151.31
	23400			74.40
	23400			17.40
	23600			33.69
	23400			74.40
	23400			17.40
	23500			9.60
	23600			64.80
	72000		74.40	
	72000		17.40	
	72000		9.60	
	72000		64.80	
	10300			923.20
3/1/01	77500	2012	1,200.00	
John Thompson	23400			151.31
	23400			74.40
	23400			17.40
	23600			33.69
	23400			74.40

Figure 12–8 Payroll Journal Report

Get a Job

Technology has begun to help job-seekers and prospective employers find the perfect match. Numerous job-search sites appear all over the World Wide Web.

These sites post listings that are essentially electronic help-wanted ads. Employers place their job descriptions on the site. Job seekers then can sort through these listings. When they see a specific one that they like, they can find out more information by following links to the company's Web site. Job seekers can also send an e-mail message directly to the employer.

There are more than two thousand job sites advertising more than 28 million jobs a year. Some specialized sites list jobs in a specific field. Most sites include listings from various geographical areas. This setup makes it easy to find a specific type of job in another state or country—or to look up all the different types of positions that are available in the seeker's local area.

Companies who are hiring see the usefulness of these sites, too; it is estimated that by 2003 the average company will spend one-fifth of its classified advertising budget on line.

Another service many job-search sites offer is résumé-posting. In this option, a job seeker creates an electronic version of his or her résumé and places it on the site. Prospective employers search through these postings and call or e-mail the job seekers who interest them.

If you are looking for a job, even if you pass on electronic résumé-posting, it is a good idea to make sure you have an active e-mail account before you begin your job search. E-mail allows you to reach employers—and be reached—more quickly than by any other means.

Finally, there is one other way that technology is affecting the way people find and get jobs—and most people aren't even aware of it. Many companies (especially large ones) now use computers to help screen applicants. Paper résumés will be electronically scanned for certain words—that may identify necessary skills, particular personality traits, or even preferred degrees—before any human being ever reads them. Writing a computer-friendly résumé is somewhat complicated, but there are many books and Web sites dedicated to explaining how to do it.

SUMMARY OF KEY POINTS

1. *Peachtree* will calculate, process, and post payroll information based on defaults and employee information.
2. You can generate payroll checks weekly, bi-weekly, semimonthly, monthly, or annually.
3. You can print paychecks individually as they are entered, or you can group checks and print them through the Reports menu.
4. Use the Select for Payroll Entry option to pay a group or all employees.

interNET CONNECTION

No-nonsense, how-to information about bookkeeping can be found at **http://www.onlinewbc.org/docs/finance/bkpg_basic2.html**, a site that includes sample cases about beginning accounting. At that same site (address ending: **basic3.html**) there is a list of fundamental owner responsibilities regarding reviewing the accounts.

Name ______________________________ Date ________________

CHAPTER REVIEW AND APPLICATIONS

Completion

In the space provided, write the word (words) that best completes each statement.

1. You can print payroll checks from the Payroll Navigation Aid or from the ____________________ menu.
2. The ____________________ report provides you with a way to check earnings and tax amounts before you print paychecks.
3. The ____________________ report allows you to reconcile paychecks and verify General Ledger posting accuracy.
4. Only payroll checks that have a ____________________ can be voided.
5. If a payroll check contains an error, you should ____________________ the check rather than delete the entry.

Problem 12–1

Follow these instructions to process the February paychecks. Then answer the Analyze Your Work questions.

Instructions

Step 1 Restore the Premier Fitness Club, Inc. file from Chapter 11.

Step 2 Open the Payroll Navigation Aid.

Step 3 Choose **Select for Payroll Entry.**

Step 4 Enter the Pay End date of March 10, 2001.

Step 5 Make appropriate filter selections.

Step 6 Select **Ok.** The Select Employees to Pay window will open.

Step 7 Enter the check date of March 10, 2001

Step 8 Make any necessary changes to hours, salary, or number of weeks.

Step 9 Uncheck the pay box for any employee who will not receive a check this period.

Step 10 Select **Print.** Choose the first check form on the list.

Step 11 Select **OK.**

Step 12 Enter 2011 as the first check number.

Step 13 Print and verify the Payroll Journal and Payroll Register reports for the March 10 payroll.

Step 14 Print the Check Register for the Payroll Checking Account.

Step 15 Back up the file for use with Problem 12-2.

Name ______________________ Date ____________

Please process the payroll for the bi-weekly pay period ending March 10. The hourly employees all worked 40 hours each week of the pay period:

Jane Warren
Tim Richards
John Thompson
Carolyn Speer
Mary Steward

Analyzing Your Work

Answer the following questions in the space provided.

1. What amount was debited to Wages Expenses for the March 10 payroll.

____

2. What is the net pay for Tim Richards for the pay period ending March 10?

____

3. What amount does Premier owe for FUTA for the March 10 payroll?

____

4. What is the total federal tax liability for the March 10 paryroll?

____

5. What amount was debited to Salary Expense for the March 10 payroll?

____

Problem 12-2

Process the payroll entries for March 24. Follow the steps outlined in Problem 12-1.

Instructions

1. Process payroll for the pay period ending March 24 for the following employees. Employees who did not work 80 hours for that biweekly period are noted.

   Jane Warren
   Tim Richards
   John Thompson (5 hours overtime)
   Carolyn Speer (72 hours regular time)
   Mary Steward
   Wally Jefferson (40 hours regular time)

2. Print the Payroll checks. Enter March 24 as the check date. Enter 2016 as the first check number.
3. Print the Payroll Register for this payroll only.
4. Print the Payroll Journal for this payroll.
5. Transfer (Payments or Write Checks window) for the sum amount of the 3/24/01 payroll from the regular checking account to payroll checking.
6. Print the Check Register for the Payroll Checking Account for this payroll.

Analyzing Your Work

Use the Payroll reports to answer the following questions.

1. What is the gross pay for John Thompson for the pay period ending March 24?

   ____

2. What is the net pay for Mary Steward for the pay period ending March 24?

   ____

3. What was the SUI liability for the March 24 payroll?

   ____

4. What was the decrease in the payroll checking account for the two March payrolls (before transfer)?

5. What was the increase in account number 77500 for the March 24 payroll?

   ____

Chapter 13
Budgets

OBJECTIVES

When you have completed Chapter 13, you should be able to:

1. Describe the budgeting process.
2. Enter annual budget amounts.
3. Allocate annual budget to each accounting period.
4. Edit a budget entry.
5. Print the Income Statement with Budgets.
6. Define terms used in the chapter.

A budget assesses the efficiency of the organization's operation. Budgets forecast future events and compare predicted with actual performance. The forecasting phase is the company's operating plan, expressed in monetary units. The comparison phase is an objective measure of whether or not a firm has met its financial goals.

On the Budgets tab of the Maintain Chart of Accounts window, you can assign budget dollar amounts for each account for the current and next fiscal periods. Once you determine the budget for an account for the year, you can enter the amount, and *Peachtree Complete Accounting 8.0* will distribute it to each monthly accounting period, allocate the total to each accounting period, and determine your success in holding to your budget.

ENTERING A BUDGET

You will enter revenue and expense projections for Premier Fitness at the end of the chapter. Use the instructions and illustrations provided within the chapter to complete those activities.

To enter budget amounts, open the General Ledger Navigation Aid. Select the **Maintain Chart of Accounts** icon. The window opens with the General tab active. Select the Budgets tab (a window like Figure 13–1 will open).

On the Budgets tab, you can enter (assign) a dollar budget amount for each account, for each fiscal period during the *current* fiscal year and the *next* year. Enter or select an *Account ID* in the window's header area. If you enter amounts in the various periods, the total amount (below the Period Ending dates) will be calculated. If you enter the total amount in the box beside the **Allocate** button and then select the **Allocate** button, *Peachtree* will divide and distribute the total equally into all periods for the year. Budget amounts are rounded to two decimal places; odd pennies are placed in the last accounting period.

You can copy budget information from one year to the next. Simply use the copy button in the center of the screen, between the two Budget years. With any accounting period highlighted, click **Copy** and the amounts become automatically entered as next year's budget amounts. The following steps describe the process for entering a budget amount.

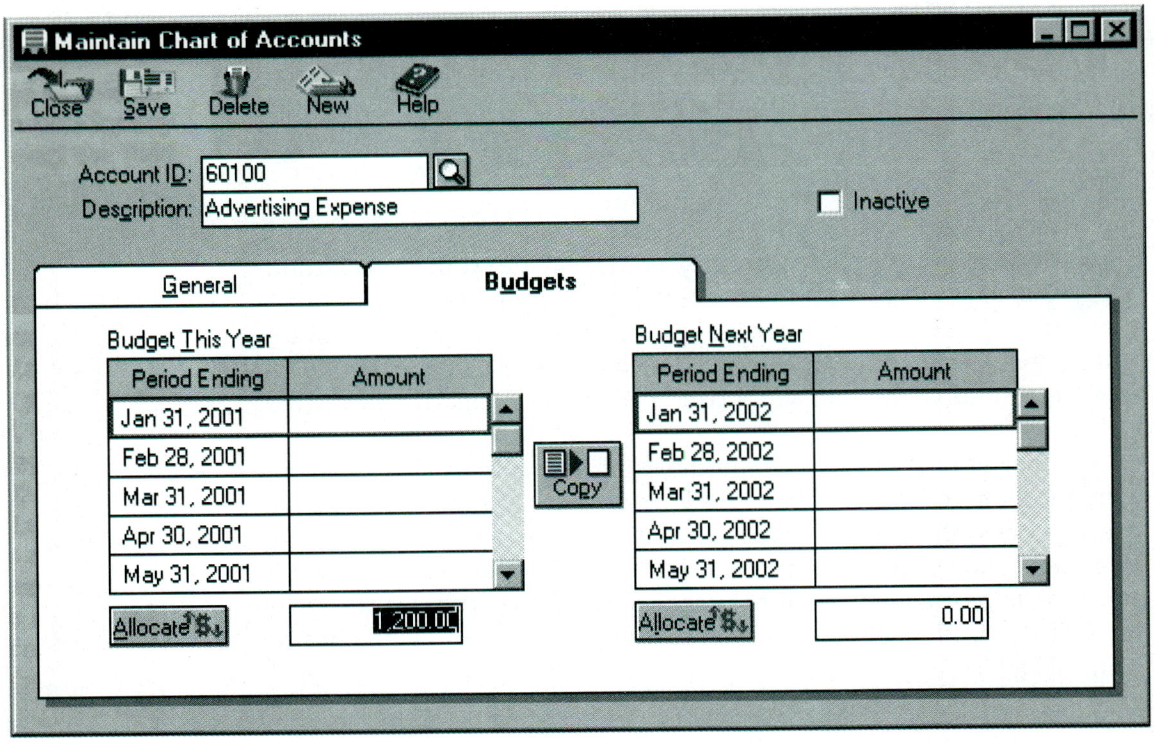

Figure 13–1 Enter budget amounts

ALLOCATING ANNUAL BUDGET AMOUNTS

Step 1 Open the General Ledger Navigation Aid (or use the **Maintain** menu).

Step 2 Select **Chart of Accounts.**

Step 3 Select the Budgets tab.

Step 4 Use the lookup box to select the account to which you want to enter a budget amount. In this case, use 60100, Advertising Expense.

Step 5 In the box to the right of the **Allocate** button, enter $1,200, which is management's annual budget amount for Advertising Expense for the year.

For accounts with debit balances, enter a positive amount. Enter a minus (–) in front of the amount for all accounts that have normal credit balances. For revenue accounts, for instance, enter negative amounts.

Step 6 Click the **Allocate** button to divide the amount among the accounting periods for the year.

Step 7 Select **Save.**

> **Note**
> When *Peachtree* allocates amounts to all periods, it will place any odd pennies in the last period.

EDIT A BUDGET ENTRY

The procedure to edit or adjust budget amounts after they have been entered is essentially the same as the entry process. Use the Maintain Chart of Accounts screen to display the amount to be edited.

In the preceding example, you allocated $1,200 to the annual Advertising Expense budget (*Account ID* 60100), which was distributed equally over 12 accounting periods (see Figure 13-2). Each year in May, your company helps out the local high school. The band sells advertisements in the annual musical production program, and Premier normally buys a $100.00 ad in the program. This expense is in addition to Premier's normal monthly advertising expenditures. You will need to increase the allocation for advertising for May.

Complete the following steps to make an adjustment to the budget.

Step 1 Open the General Ledger Navigation Aid.

Step 2 Select the **Chart of Accounts** icon.

Step 3 Select the Budgets tab on the Maintain Chart of Accounts window.

Step 4 Select the *Account ID* that you want to change (Account 60100, Advertising Expense).

Step 5 Select the Period Ending date to be changed (May 31, 2001).

Step 6 Highlight the field and change the amount to 200.00.

Step 7 Select **Save.**

> **Note**
> Notice that the total allocated amount has changed to 1,300.

> **Note**
> The budgeted amount can be edited to 0.00 if no budget is allocated for that period. Do not use the **Delete** icon, which will delete the entire account!

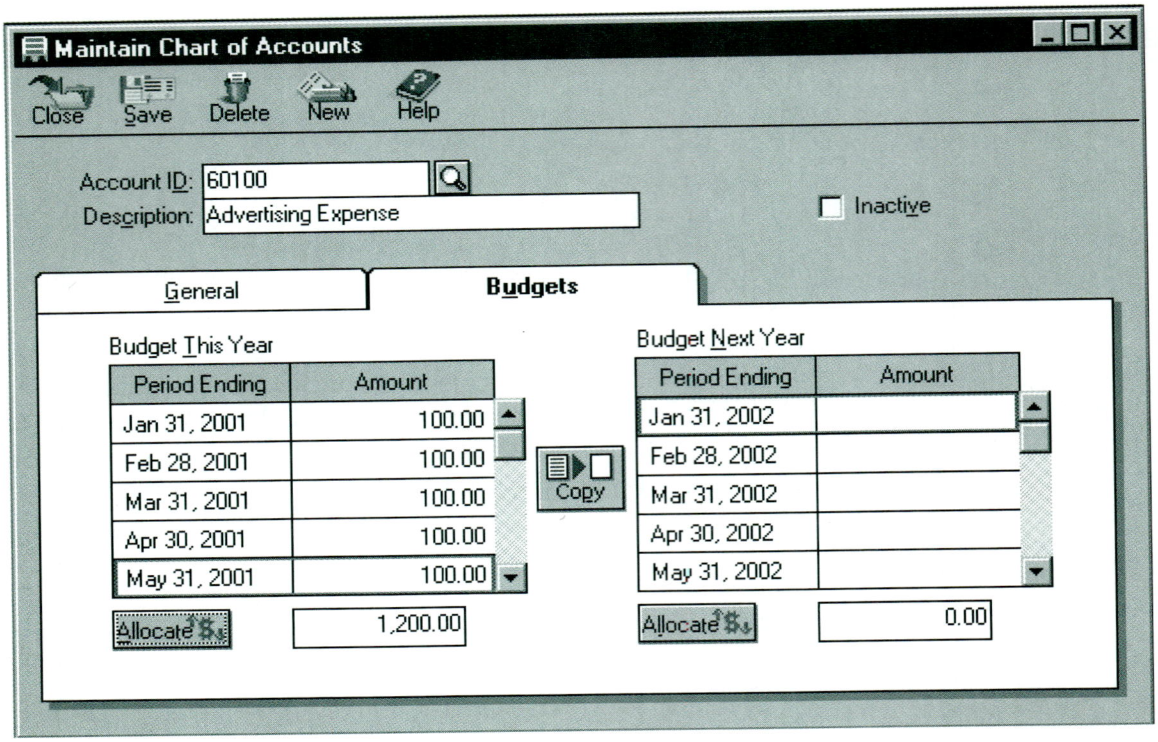

Figure 13–2 Edit budgeted amounts

INCOME STATEMENT WITH BUDGET AMOUNTS

The Income Statement: Budgets compares actual income and expense activity compared to budgeted amounts for a specified period of time. Print or display the Income Statements with Budget figures by completing the following steps.

Note

The amounts in Figure 13–5 reflect 6 months' budget allocation only. Actual amounts have not been entered yet.

Step 1 Open the General Ledger Navigation Aid.

Step 2 Select **Print Financial Statements.** The screen shown in Figure 13–3 will appear.

Step 3 Select Income/Budgets.

Step 4 Select **Preview** to display the Options window (Figure 13–4).

Step 5 Verify the time frame and the time periods. Make any necessary changes.

Step 6 Select the **Ok** button to display the report (Figure 13-5).

Step 7 Select **Print.**

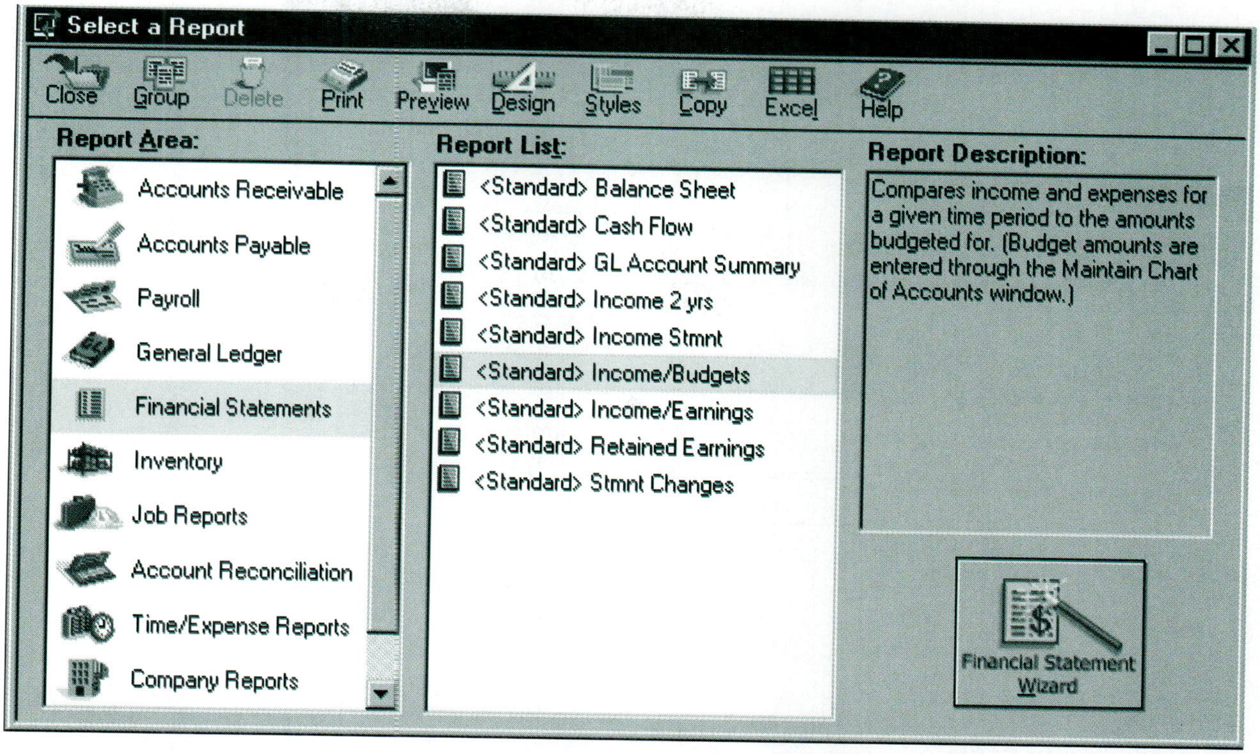

Figure 13–3 Print an Income Statement with budget

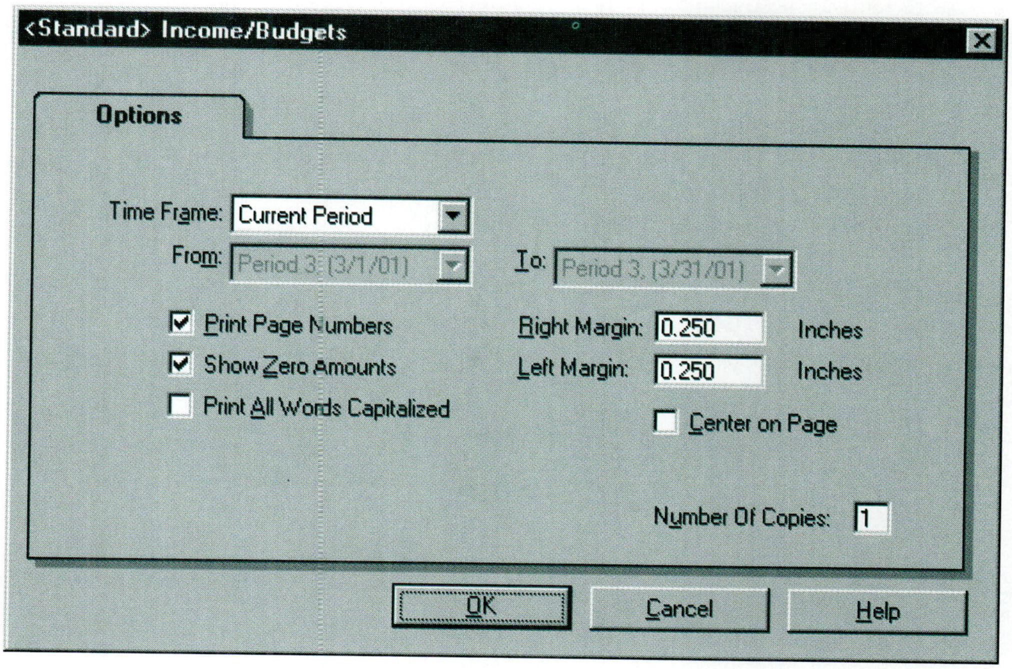

Figure 13–4 Set filters for the Income/Budgets report

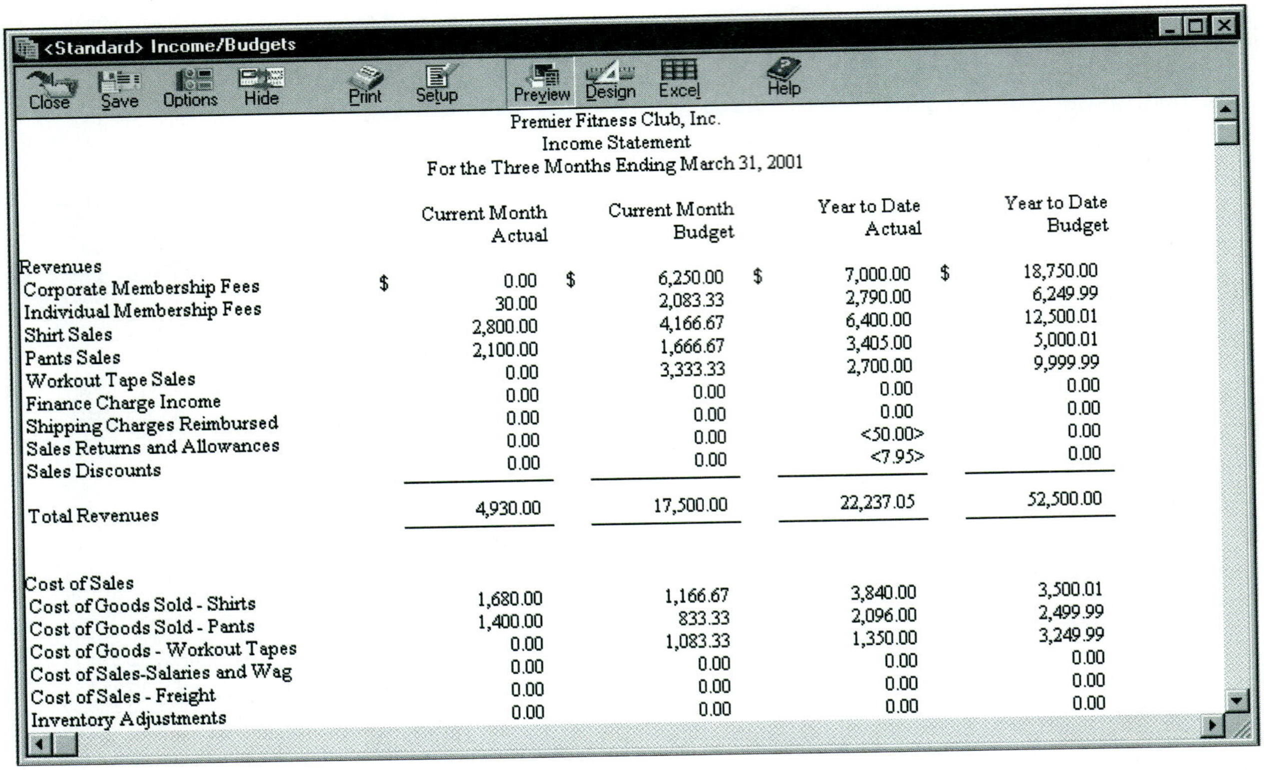

Premier Fitness Club, Inc.
Income Statement
For the Three Months Ending March 31, 2001

	Current Month Actual	Current Month Budget	Year to Date Actual	Year to Date Budget
Revenues				
Corporate Membership Fees	$ 0.00	$ 6,250.00	$ 7,000.00	$ 18,750.00
Individual Membership Fees	30.00	2,083.33	2,790.00	6,249.99
Shirt Sales	2,800.00	4,166.67	6,400.00	12,500.01
Pants Sales	2,100.00	1,666.67	3,405.00	5,000.01
Workout Tape Sales	0.00	3,333.33	2,700.00	9,999.99
Finance Charge Income	0.00	0.00	0.00	0.00
Shipping Charges Reimbursed	0.00	0.00	0.00	0.00
Sales Returns and Allowances	0.00	0.00	<50.00>	0.00
Sales Discounts	0.00	0.00	<7.95>	0.00
Total Revenues	4,930.00	17,500.00	22,237.05	52,500.00
Cost of Sales				
Cost of Goods Sold - Shirts	1,680.00	1,166.67	3,840.00	3,500.01
Cost of Goods Sold - Pants	1,400.00	833.33	2,096.00	2,499.99
Cost of Goods - Workout Tapes	0.00	1,083.33	1,350.00	3,249.99
Cost of Sales-Salaries and Wag	0.00	0.00	0.00	0.00
Cost of Sales - Freight	0.00	0.00	0.00	0.00
Inventory Adjustments	0.00	0.00	0.00	0.00

Figure 13–5 Income statement with Budget report

You Inc.

It is not hard to start a business. All you need is an initial investment, a product or service you believe in, and a lot of determination. There is also some paperwork you will need to take care of: You need to incorporate.

In the eyes of the government and the law, a corporation is like an individual in several ways. It can be sued. It can take out loans. It can enter into contracts with other corporations and individuals.

The advantage of a corporation is that its finances remain separate from those of its shareholders—even if there's only one (you)—so if your corporation goes bankrupt, for example, its shareholders (you) will not necessarily follow suit.

This advantage isn't necessarily available with other forms of organization, such as partnerships or sole proprietorships.

Another benefit to a corporation is that shares in a corporation can be transferred from one person to another. Thus a corporation can "outlive" its shareholders, and the new shareholders can assume control over part or all of the shares. In this way, a corporation, if it can find interested investors, can constantly generate new operating funds.

Is there a catch? Well, corporations are subject to requirements on how they are organized and administered, which other businesses are able to avoid.

There are two types of corporations: "C" corporations and "S" corporations. The difference between them mostly has to do with the way they are taxed.

In a "C" corporation, the profits of the company itself are first taxed by the government. The shareholders take their share of the after-tax profits. Then each shareholder pays taxes on those dividends.

An "S" corporation's profits, on the other hand, are not taxed before the shareholders take their dividends; so the profits are taxed only once.

Why, then, would anyone want to incorporate as a "C" corporation instead of an "S" corporation? The reason is because "S" corporations can have no more than 35 shareholders. Large companies need many more shareholders than that in order to raise enough money to stay in business. Also, there are still a few states that do not permit "S" corporation arrangements.

Sorting out state regulations can be one of the most confusing parts of the incorporation process. Some states are lenient (Delaware, for example); others are, in comparison, strict.

Many states permit businesses to organize as a limited liability company (LLC), which is a partnership that is taxed like an "S" corporation and whose members are protected from some legal actions.

Some companies search for the state that has the most convenient set of regulations, but most firms simply incorporate in the state where they do most of their business. Companies that incorporate outside the state in which they work may find themselves subject to taxes in both states.

SUMMARY OF KEY POINTS

1. The budgeting process predicts future revenue and expenses.
2. The Maintain Chart of Accounts window is used to enter budget information.
3. You can enter budget amounts for each accounting period, or you can enter an annual budget and allocate the amount equally to all periods.
4. Budget amounts can be edited after the total has been allocated.
5. The Income Statement with Budget report compares the actual revenue and expenses with the budgeted amounts.

*inter*NET CONNECTION

This beginner's site cuts through the mystique of budgeting for a small business: **http://www.onlinewbc.org/docs/finance/budget1.html**. It covers how to plan for increased profit, fixed and variable expenses, revenue, and the idea of periodic feedback and control.

Name ______________________________ Date ____________________

CHAPTER REVIEW AND APPLICATIONS

Completion

In the space provided, write the word or words that best complete each statement.

1. The ____________________ Navigation Aid allows you to complete the budgeting activities.
2. Use the ____________________ button to divide the annual budget amount and apply the amount to all periods equally.
3. The ____________________ report compares actual and budgeted amounts.
4. Use the ____________________ button to enter the same budget amounts for *next* year as well as for the current year.
5. To display a report to the screen, use the ____________________ button.

Problem 13

A budget is an objective, monetary measurement of whether the company has met its financial goals. Please enter the following budget transactions on page 212 for this fiscal year. Allocate each budget amount evenly throughout the year. Once you have completed entering the budget transactions, please print an Income/Budgets report. Answer the Analyzing Your Work questions for Problem 13–1 from your printed report.

Instructions

Step 1 Analyze the budget data.

Step 2 Restore the backup file from Problem 12-2 for Premier Fitness Club, Inc.

Step 3 Enter the budgets for the accounts listed on the following page.

Step 4 Allocate each budget amount evenly throughout the year.

Step 5 Print an Income/Budgets report for March 1, 2001 to March 31, 2001.

Step 6 Back up the file as Premier 13-1.

Step 7 Answer the Analyzing Your Work questions on the following page.

Transactions

Account #	Budget Amount	Account #	Budget Amount
40000	$75,000.00	66000	$500.00
40100	$25,000.00	66500	$2,500.00
40200	$50,000.00	67000	$3,000.00
40400	$20,000.00	67500	$200.00
40600	$40,000.00	68500	$3,000.00
50000	$14,000.00		
50500	$10,000.00	70000	$1,200.00
51000	$13,000.00	71000	$600.00
60100	$10,000.00	72000	$12,000.00
61500	$100.00	74000	$15,000.00
62000	$100.00	76000	$1,500.00
63000	$1,000.00	77000	$62,400.00
64000	$500.00	77500	$44,000.00
64500	$100.00	78000	$1,500.00

Analyzing Your Work

Answer the following questions in the space provided.

1. What is the budgeted cost of sales for the quarter?

2. What is the total amount budgeted for expenses for the current month?

3. What is the budgeted net income for January 1 through March 31?

4. What is the budgeted revenue for January 1 through March 31?

5. What is the budgeted gross profit for the current month?

Name ______________________________ Date ______________

Step 8 Edit the budget for the following accounts.

Account #	Budget Amount
40000	$70,000.00
40200	$45,000.00
40400	$25,000.00
77500	$40,000.00

Step 9 Print a revised Income/Budgets report.

Step 10 Answer the following Analyzing Your Work questions based on the revised budget.

6. What is the budgeted amount for cost of sales for the current month?

____

7. What is the amount of budgeted expenses for the quarter?

____

8. What is the budgeted net income for January 1 through March 31?

____

9. What is the budgeted revenue for the current month?

____

10. What is the budgeted gross profit for January 1 through March 31?

____

Step 11 Back up your files as Premier 13-2.

Chapter 14

Business Analysis

OBJECTIVES

When you have completed Chapter 14, you should be able to use:

1. Cash Manager.
2. Collection Manager.
3. Payment Manager.
4. Financial Manager.
5. Terms used in the chapter.

Peachtree Complete Accounting 8.0 business managers offer you several options for analyzing various aspects of your business. The managers allow you to choose graphic or numeric analysis and list all transactions that make up the analysis. They also provide access to transaction details for a specific record (customer or vendor) or to the original transaction as it was entered in the Tasks window.

There are four *Peachtree* business managers.

- Cash Manager
- Collection Manager
- Payment Manager
- Financial Manager

CASH MANAGER

Use the Cash Manager to display expected cash flow for a certain period of time. It projects receipts, payments, payroll, and other cash, broken down by due dates.

Numeric Window

Open the Cash Manager.

Step 1 Open the Analysis Navigation Aid (Figure 14–1).

Step 2 Select the **Cash Manager** icon (Figure 14–2 will appear).

Cash Manager displays (as the default) a numeric table of both current and projected cash amounts for various due dates. The Starting Cash row totals all General Ledger accounts with *Cash* as the account type for the specified dates.

As the default, the table columns are divided into weekly forecast periods, starting from the current system date. You can change the range of dates shown in each column by using the drop-down list in the *Forecast* field. You can select Weekly (the default), Bi-weekly, or Monthly.

The **Add** section lists Sales to Collect for each date category. This list contains all posted sales invoices for customers and any additional adjustments you want to add to the cash projections.

To enter a Cash Adjustment (either plus or minus), move your cursor to highlight the Cash Adjustments row and then double click. An Adjustments window will open. You can enter one or more adjustments.

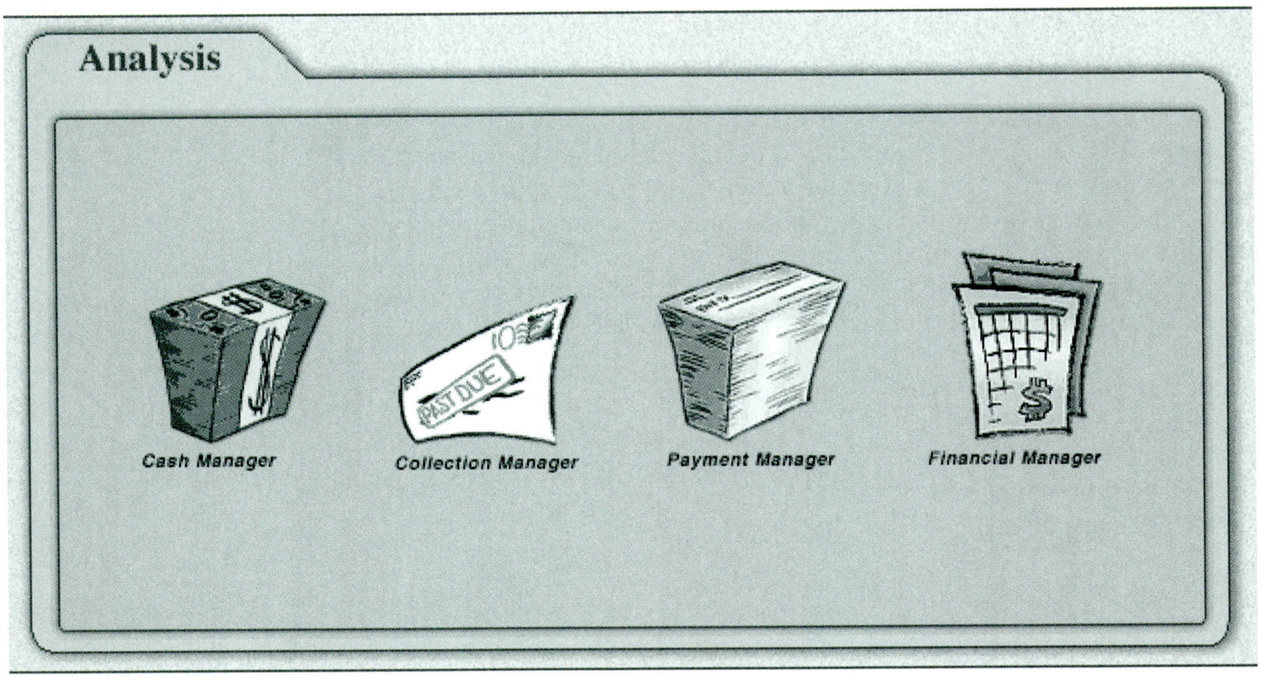

Figure 14–1 ***Peachtree*'s business managers**

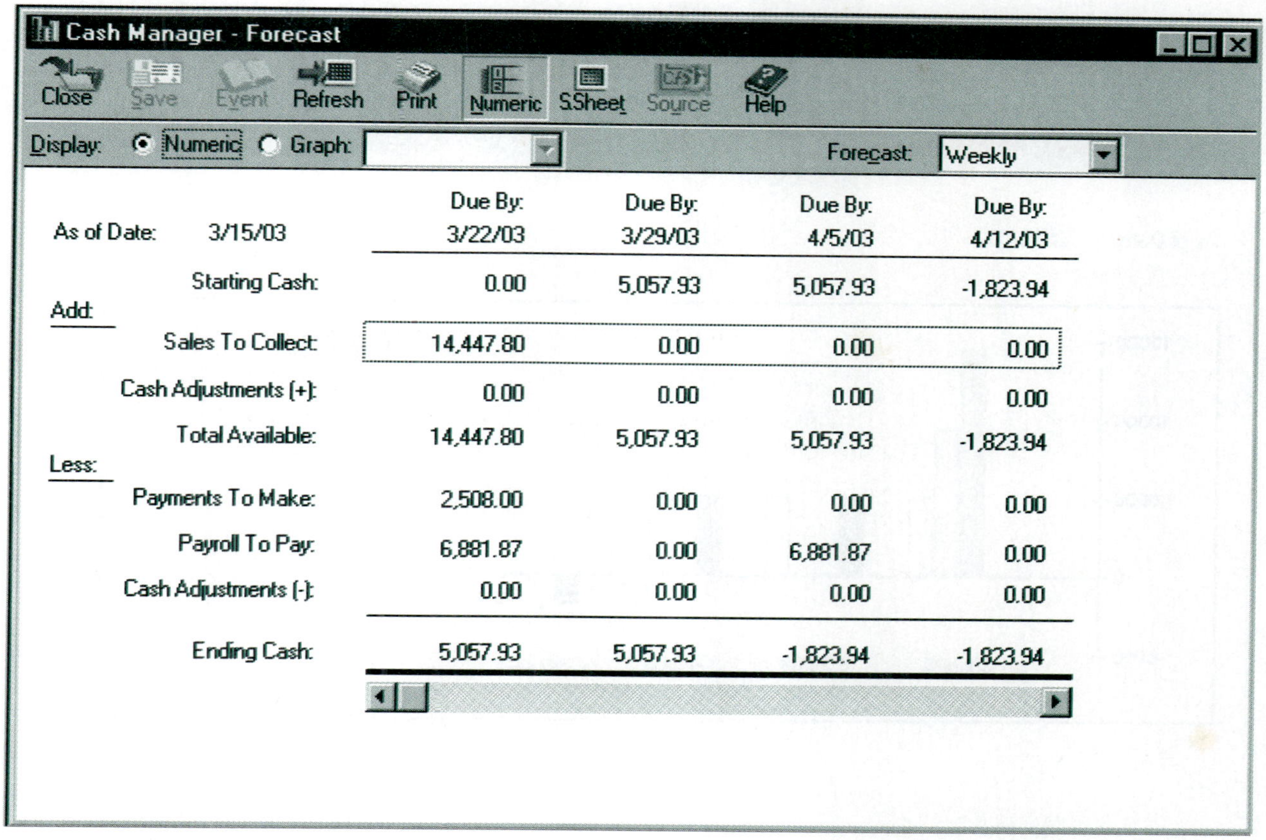

As of Date: 3/15/03	Due By: 3/22/03	Due By: 3/29/03	Due By: 4/5/03	Due By: 4/12/03
Starting Cash:	0.00	5,057.93	5,057.93	-1,823.94
Add:				
Sales To Collect:	14,447.80	0.00	0.00	0.00
Cash Adjustments (+):	0.00	0.00	0.00	0.00
Total Available:	14,447.80	5,057.93	5,057.93	-1,823.94
Less:				
Payments To Make:	2,508.00	0.00	0.00	0.00
Payroll To Pay:	6,881.87	0.00	6,881.87	0.00
Cash Adjustments (-):	0.00	0.00	0.00	0.00
Ending Cash:	5,057.93	5,057.93	-1,823.94	-1,823.94

Figure 14–2 Numeric data for Cash Manager

The **Less** section displays anticipated payments; any unpaid purchase invoices for vendors will appear in this section. All projected payroll checks, based on the pay frequency, are listed. You can open the Adjustments window to enter any cash amounts that you expect to spend by the specified date but that you have not yet entered.

The Ending Cash for each time frame is calculated.

If you enter Adjustments to the Forecast, either (+) or (–), select the **Refresh** toolbar button to update the Forecast. If you open the Cash Manager (after you have entered transactions that affect cash), a Forecast Refresh screen will display. On this screen you can note whether any manual adjustments you made—the last time that you were in the Cash Manager—are included in the new forecast. If you change the system date in order to change the *As of Date* field for the forecast, you will use the **Refresh** button to recalculate the Graphic Forecast.

You can display the numeric information that you see in the numeric table (Figure 14–2) as either a column or a bar graph.

Step 3 When you select the *Graph* option button, the information will display in a vertical column graph (Figure 14–3).

The columns show starting cash, cash in, cash out, and ending cash for each of the forecast periods. A color legend is shown to the right of the columns. Dollar amounts are in thousands.

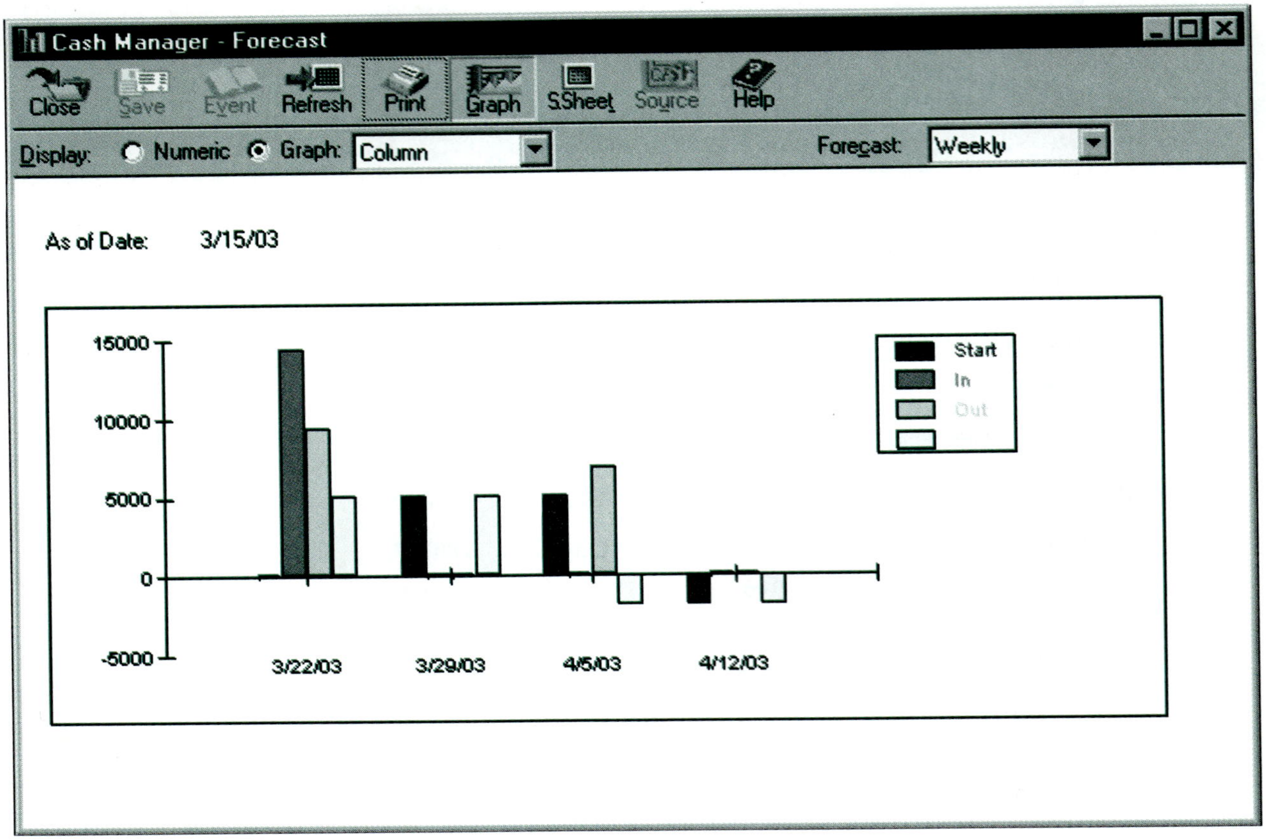

Figure 14–3 Cash Manager presented graphically

Step 4 To change the display to a bar graph, open the *Graph* drop-down list and select *Bar*.

Step 5 To return to the numeric table, select the Numeric button.

Step 6 Select the **Spreadsheet** icon.

COLLECTION MANAGER

Collection Manager provides numeric and graphic analysis of Accounts Receivable (the money owed to you) for a specified time period. This feature allows you to zoom in on various aging brackets in order to see transaction details for certain customers. You can also print collection letters from the Collection Manager. You can choose to have the information displayed as of a date that you enter at the top of the window.

Opening Collection Manager

To open Collection Manager, you will use the following steps.

Step 1 Open the Analysis folder.

Step 2 Select **Collection Manager** (Figure 14–4 will appear).

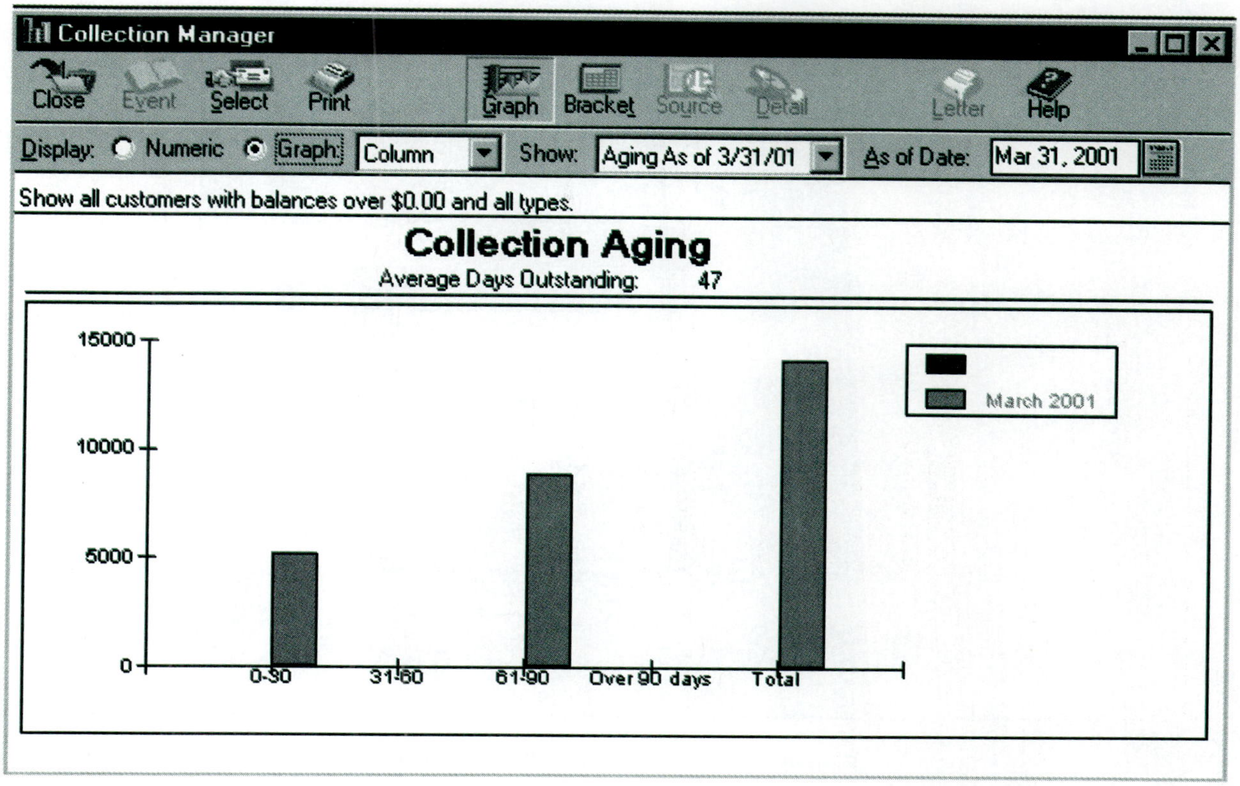

Figure 14–4 Collection Manager

The Collection Manager data includes open invoices for all customers, as well as any payments that they have made. By default, the aging categories are computed from the *As of Date*. The Aging brackets are for the range of days you have already set up in Customer Defaults (Chapter 5).

Step 3 When you open the drop-down list next to the **Graph** option button, the data can be shown as a pie or bar graph.

Step 4 Select the **Select** icon; the filtering window opens.

Step 5 As you can see in Figure 14–5, you can limit the customers or balances that display on the graph or table.

Step 6 Select **Ok** to save your selection criteria.

Step 7 To change the display to the numeric screen, select the **Numeric** button.

Step 8 If you select **Graphic**, the screen will return to a Column graph.

> **Note**
> To find the **Select** icon on the Collection Manager icon bar, go to the third icon from the left.

Perhaps you wish to use only certain data on your Collection Aging report. Perhaps you want at least a range of customers, a beginning date, or a customer type. Use the Collection Selections window to define the information to include.

You can enter the specific range of customers for whom you want data displayed. You can select a customer type code in the *Type Mask* field and thus limit the graph to only those customers of that *Type* code.

You can opt not to view balances *greater than* or *less than* a specified amount.

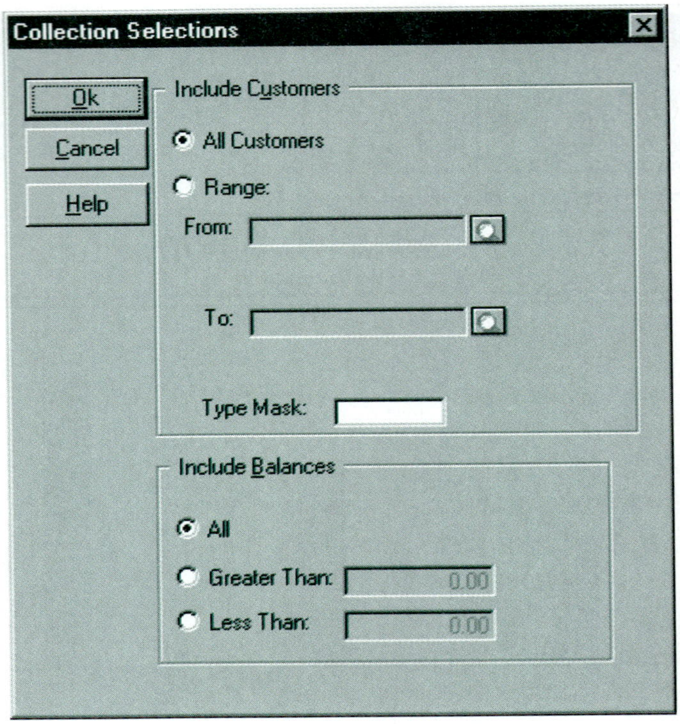

Figure 14–5 Filter for Collection Manager

You can choose to compare the current month to last month, or the current month to last year's current month. To do so, open the drop-down list for the *Show* field (located below the toolbar), and then select which months to compare.

PAYMENT MANAGER

Use the Payment Manager to see the aging status of payments to vendors. You can see details of a balance and then transactions within a balance for a selected vendor. You also select transactions to pay and print the checks from the Payment Manager.

Payments Aging

Payment Manager displays both the total Accounts Payable and the number of open invoices. Aging brackets are determined by the range of days you can set in the Vendor Defaults.

To open the Payment Manager, you will use the following steps:

Step 1 Open the Analysis Navigation Aid folder.

Step 2 Select the **Payment Manager** icon (Figure 14–6 will appear).

Step 3 The graphic display is the default screen. As with the Collection Manager, to change the display to numeric, select *Numeric* as the display. The screen shown in Figure 14–7 will appear.

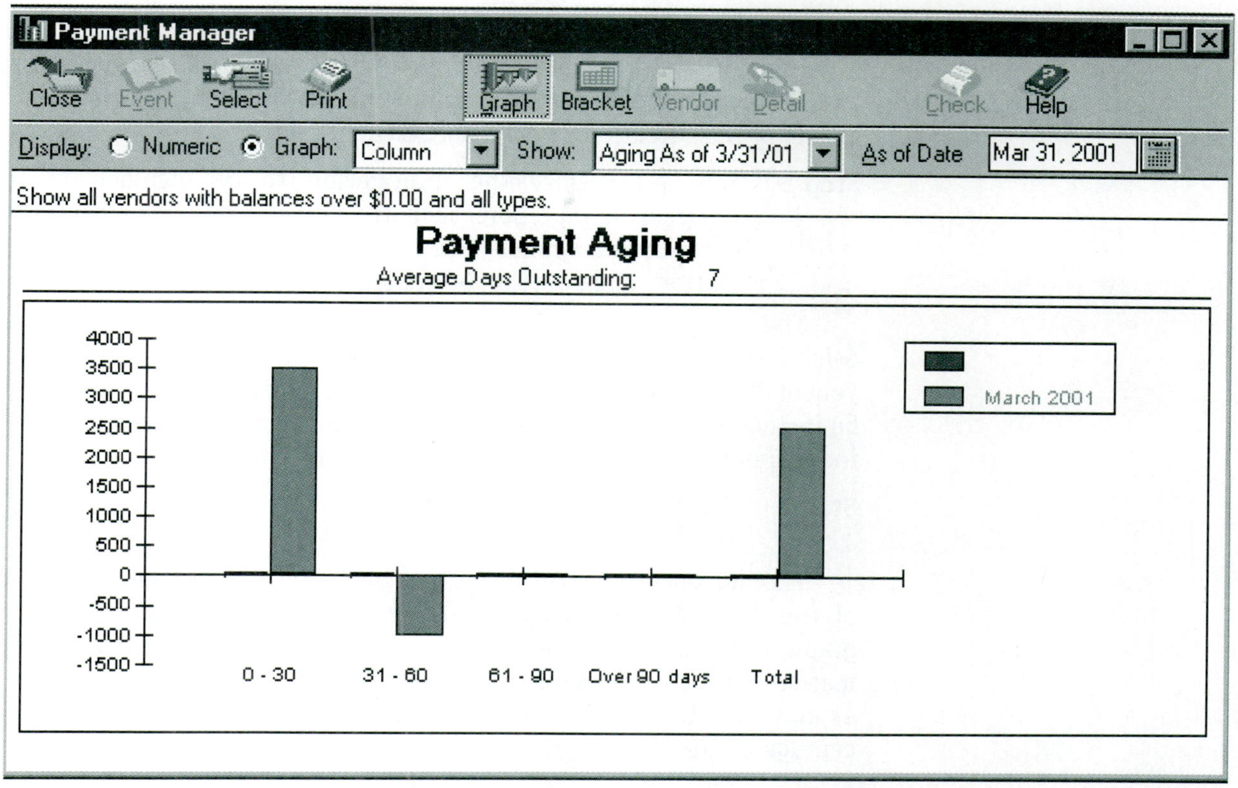

Figure 14–6 Payment Manager

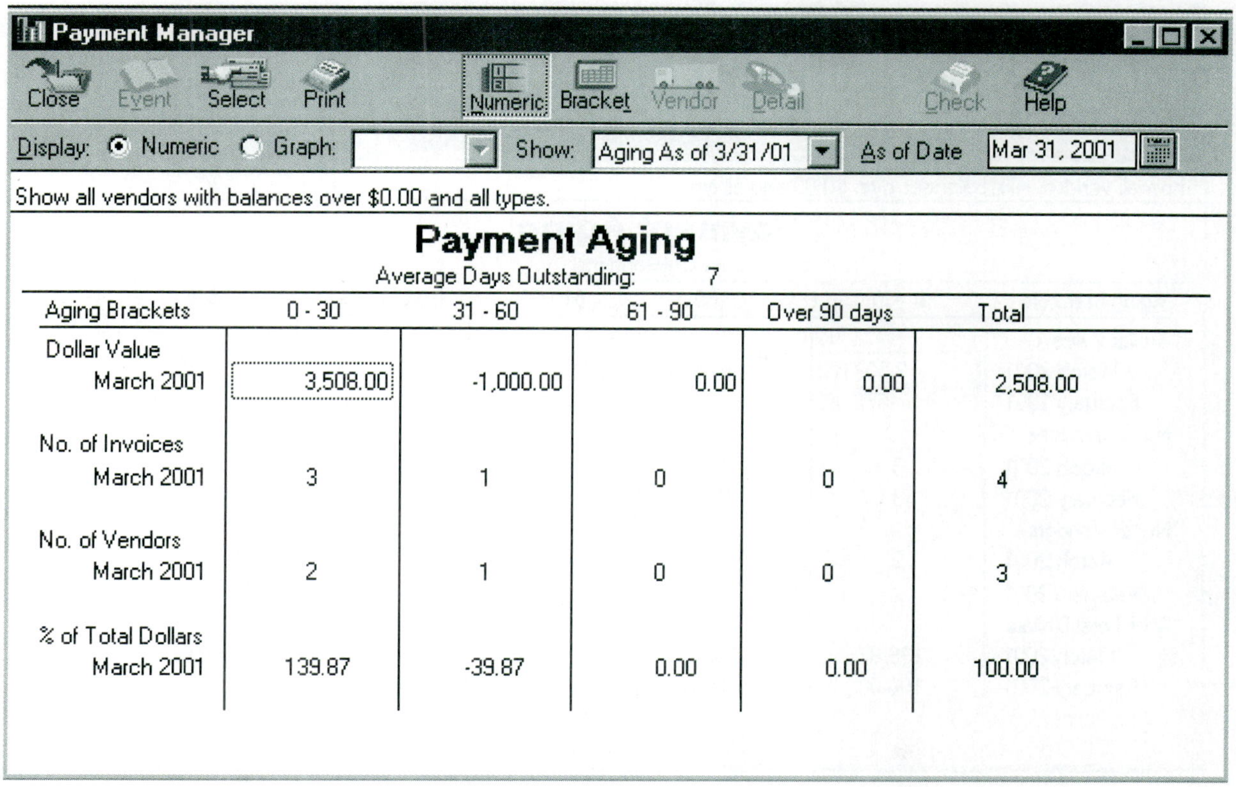

Aging Brackets	0 - 30	31 - 60	61 - 90	Over 90 days	Total
Dollar Value					
March 2001	3,508.00	-1,000.00	0.00	0.00	2,508.00
No. of Invoices					
March 2001	3	1	0	0	4
No. of Vendors					
March 2001	2	1	0	0	3
% of Total Dollars					
March 2001	139.87	-39.87	0.00	0.00	100.00

Figure 14–7 Numeric display for Payment Manager

Step 4 To return to the graphic format, select *Graphs*.

Payment Manager shows any open invoices or invoices with partial payments. *Peachtree* computes aging from the system date (shown in the *As of Date* field). You can change the date.

Step 5 You can specify the information to be included in the Payment Aging report, such as a range of vendors, a beginning date, or the vendor type. To limit the Payment Aging information, click on the **Select** icon.

The range of vendors can be altered by you in the Payment Selections window. To include only vendors of a certain type, enter a Vendor Type Code in the Type Mask field. Only those vendors thus will be included in the report. You can limit the balances included by entering amounts in the *Greater Than* and/or *Less Than* fields.

Step 6 You can display comparative data for two months. Select the months to compare from the drop-down list in the *Show* field.

Making selections in the *Display* fields determines the appearance of the data. You can display data as a bar chart, pie chart, column graph, or in tabular numerical format. Note that some additional information will be displayed in the numerical table: the number of invoices and the number of vendors included in each balance, and the percentage of the total represented by each amount.

Step 7 When you are finished, select the **Close** icon.

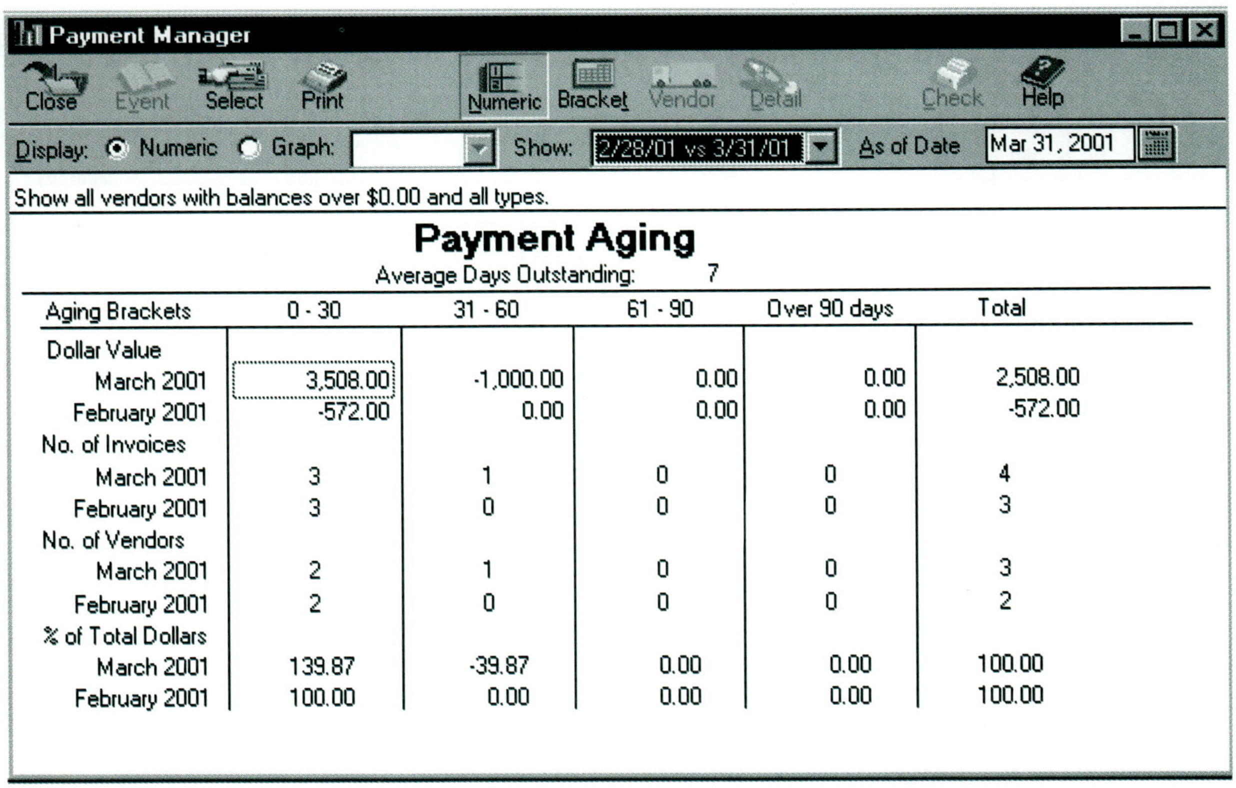

Aging Brackets	0 - 30	31 - 60	61 - 90	Over 90 days	Total
Dollar Value					
March 2001	3,508.00	-1,000.00	0.00	0.00	2,508.00
February 2001	-572.00	0.00	0.00	0.00	-572.00
No. of Invoices					
March 2001	3	1	0	0	4
February 2001	3	0	0	0	3
No. of Vendors					
March 2001	2	1	0	0	3
February 2001	2	0	0	0	2
% of Total Dollars					
March 2001	139.87	-39.87	0.00	0.00	100.00
February 2001	100.00	0.00	0.00	0.00	100.00

Figure 14–8 Comparative data for two months

FINANCIAL MANAGER

The Financial Manager provides an efficient way for the business owner or manager to get a brief, overall financial picture of how the business is performing. Like the other business managers, the Financial Manager is based on multiple levels of analysis.

- A numeric table of a set of business summary data or account balances at a specified point in time.
- A spreadsheet with business summary data or account balances projected for the end of sequential periods for comparison purposes.

To open the Financial Manager, take the following steps.

Step 1 Open the Analysis Navigation folder.

Step 2 Select the **Financial Manager** icon. By default, the first window you see is a numeric table of summary data expressed primarily as business ratios (Figure 14–9).

The *Date* field at the top of the summary window defaults to the current system date if that date is within the current accounting period. Otherwise, the default will be the last day of the current accounting period.

Step 3 To view a numeric table of key account balances, select *Key Balances* below the toolbar on the Financial Manager window. The data includes current balances for key asset and liability accounts. Both current and year-to-date balances are given

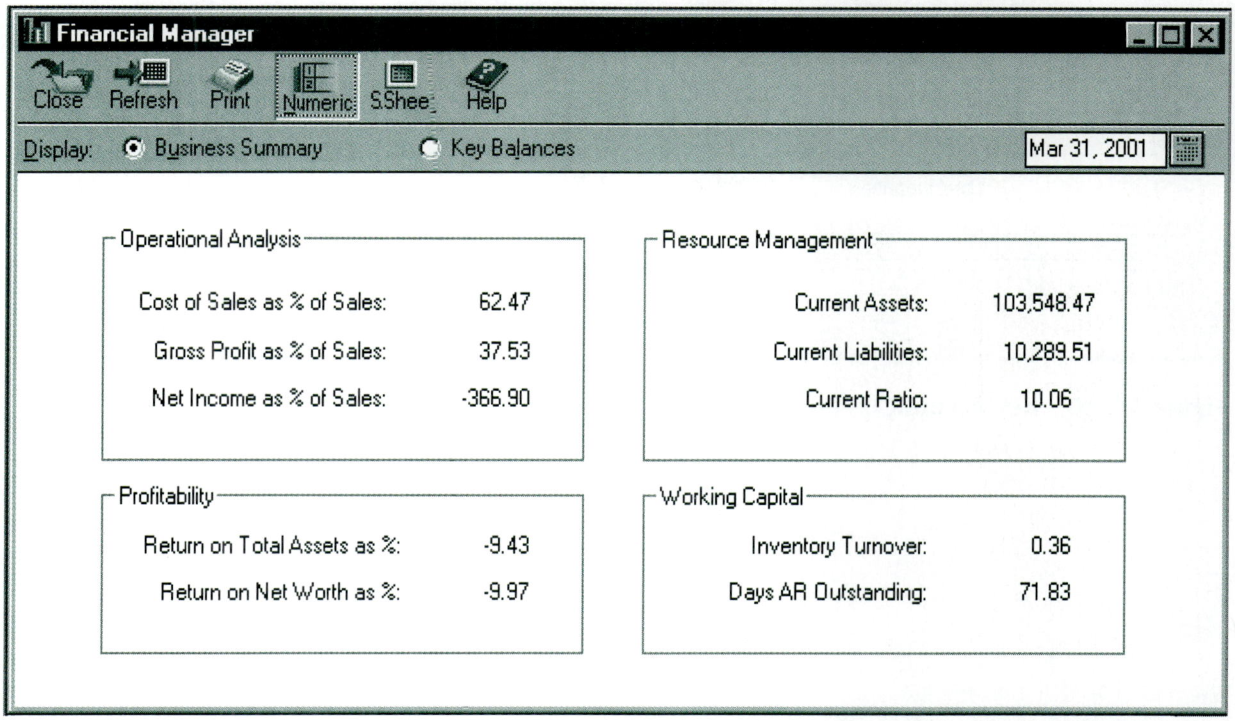

Figure 14–9 Numeric display of summary data

for accounts that reflect the business's profitability (income cost and expense accounts).

All values in the numeric level are computed for the accounting period that contains the date specified in the *Date* field. Only account activity occurring between the first day of the month selected and the day selected is used in calculations. All calculations are rounded to two decimal places. (See Figure 14–10.)

Step 4 To switch to spreadsheet format (Level 2), select the **Spreadsheet** icon.

The number of columns displayed on this window depends on the number of periods defined per fiscal year and the date selected in the *Date* field. You can display up to 36 periods (24 open periods and up to 12 periods in the most recently closed year). The last column on the spreadsheet represents the period that corresponds to the date selected. (See Figure 14–11.)

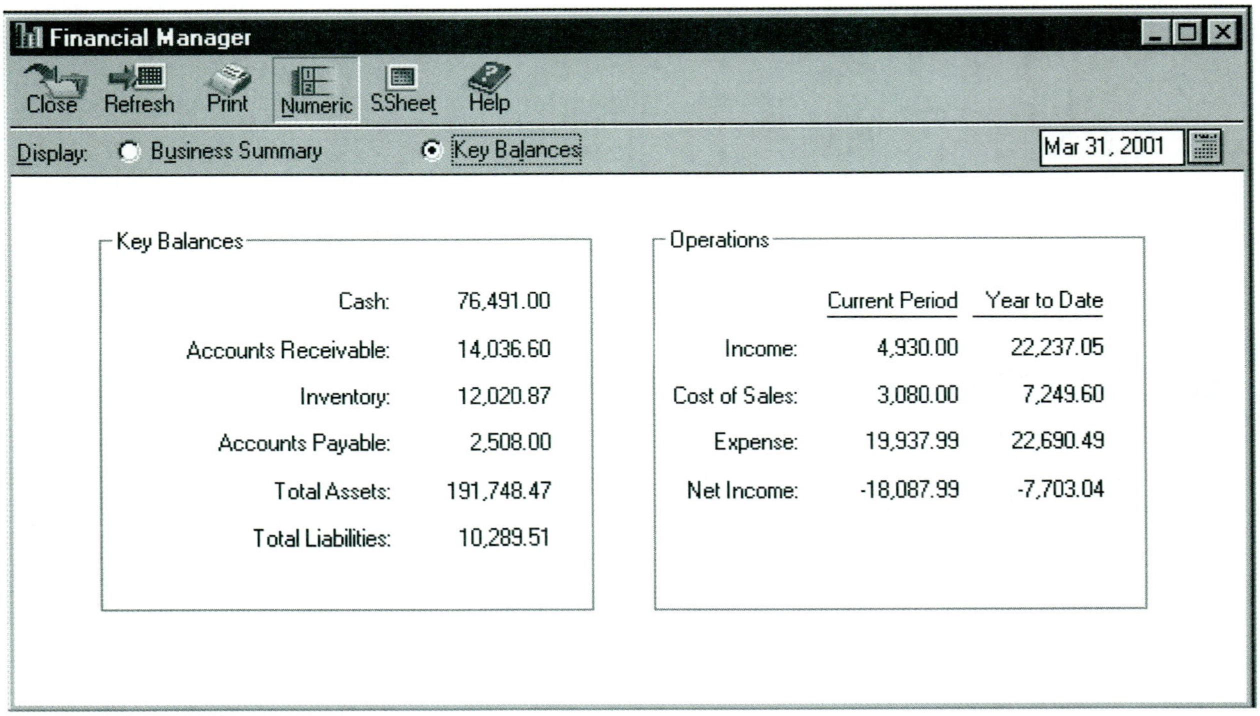

Figure 14–10 Key account balances

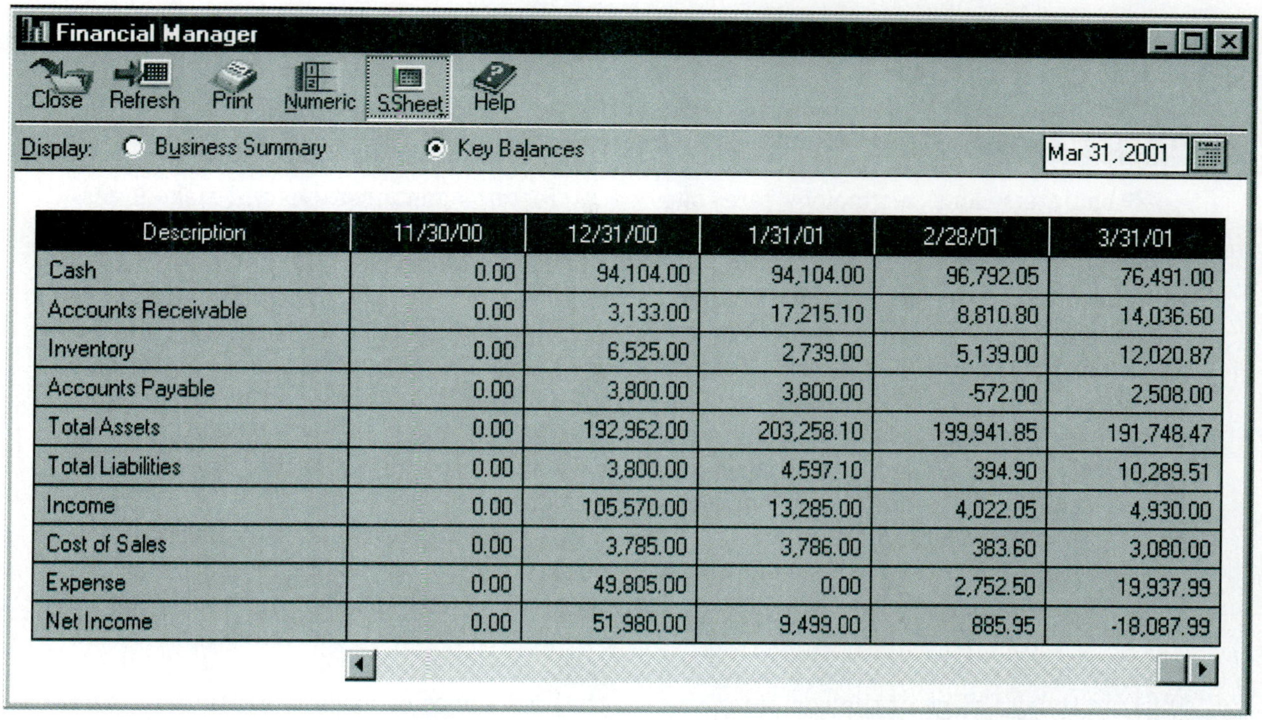

Description	11/30/00	12/31/00	1/31/01	2/28/01	3/31/01
Cash	0.00	94,104.00	94,104.00	96,792.05	76,491.00
Accounts Receivable	0.00	3,133.00	17,215.10	8,810.80	14,036.60
Inventory	0.00	6,525.00	2,739.00	5,139.00	12,020.87
Accounts Payable	0.00	3,800.00	3,800.00	-572.00	2,508.00
Total Assets	0.00	192,962.00	203,258.10	199,941.85	191,748.47
Total Liabilities	0.00	3,800.00	4,597.10	394.90	10,289.51
Income	0.00	105,570.00	13,285.00	4,022.05	4,930.00
Cost of Sales	0.00	3,785.00	3,786.00	383.60	3,080.00
Expense	0.00	49,805.00	0.00	2,752.50	19,937.99
Net Income	0.00	51,980.00	9,499.00	885.95	-18,087.99

Figure 14–11 Spreadsheet of key balances

Take It Easy

Computers and technology are supposed to make work easier for everyone. Gradually this labor-savings has happened. But in the beginning of the age of computers, it took a long time for people to figure out how to use them. During that initial period, hardware and software manufacturers had to devise ways that would make the machines easy to use. It also took some time for clever entrepreneurs and employees to imagine purposes for computers.

Early on, computers were looked at as little more than overgrown calculators. The machines were thought useful only to crunch numbers and spit out results. In contrast, in today's stage of the computer revolution, PCs and similar gadgets are seen primarily as communication devices.

Because computers are changing the way people communicate, there have been major changes in the ways that companies do business. In the coming years, there is much to look forward to; computer networks will continue to expand and proliferate in offices and homes. Ever smaller, more specialized PC-like devices will be used. Most businesses will be connecting their computers via some sort of network. In fact, many homes will soon contain more than one computer, and these, too, will most likely be linked by a network.

Faster communications will make it easier for workers at two different offices—and anyone who works from home—to share files and programs. Furthermore, the wireless communications technology that is now used primarily in cellular phones and pagers will let users stay connected to the network all the time. Much of this technology is possible even now, but it is still very expensive and difficult.

A whole new arsenal of portable digital devices will be available to busy business people. The desktop PC will probably not be completely replaced any time soon because it is extremely versatile and powerful. While they were once considered expensive luxury items, they now are on almost every desk in almost every office, and cost little more than a color TV. But handheld devices that are much less powerful than full-sized PCs, but also much more convenient, are already being adopted by many businesspeople.

Eventually, if all these systems are connected to a network, businesses will be able to streamline their operations significantly. Imagine never having to enter any piece of information more than once, or having all the information about a project or client delivered right to you, wherever you are.

SUMMARY OF KEY POINTS

1. Four Business Manager options are available: Cash Manager, Collection Manager, Payment Manager, and Financial Manager.
2. *Peachtree* provides four levels of analysis in the Cash, Collection, and Payment Manager series.
3. Cash Manager analyzes projected cash flow for a specific time period.
4. Collection Manager analyzes Accounts Receivables.
5. Payment Manager analyzes Accounts Payables.
6. Financial Manager provides an overall analysis of how the business is performing.

*inter*NET CONNECTION

Tips on avoiding common mistakes in making financial projections, cash flow forecasting, and other topics can be found at **http://www.planware.org/finance.htm**. This commercial site by Invest-Tech also lists variables to use to make projected P&Ls (profit and loss statements).

Name ______________________________ Date ______________

CHAPTER REVIEW AND APPLICATIONS

Building Your Vocabulary

In the space provided, write the letter of the item that best matches the description. *(Obj. 5)*

a. **Refresh**
b. Payment Manager
c. Cash Manager
d. *Show* field
e. **Select** icon
f. Collection Manager
g. Analysis
h. Financial Manager

_______ **1.** The analysis option that pertains to the money owed to you.

_______ **2.** The analysis option that pertains to money that you owe.

_______ **3.** The analysis option that determines features of cash flow.

_______ **4.** Use this icon to update the information included in the cash forecast.

_______ **5.** Use this icon to specify data included in the analysis.

_______ **6.** To use the Business Manager options, open this Navigation Aid.

_______ **7.** Select this field to compare two months' collections or payments.

_______ **8.** The analysis option that summarizes the profitability of the business.

Name ______________________________ Date ______________

Problem 14

Follow the instructions to generate a pie chart graph. Show all customers and all balances as of March 31, 2001. Please use your graph to answer the Analyzing Your Work questions.

Instructions

Step 1 Restore the backup file Premier 13-2 for Premier Fitness Club, Inc. from Chapter 13.

Step 2 Open the Analysis Navigation folder.

Step 3 Select the **Collection Manager** icon.

Step 4 Enter March 31, 2001, in the *As of Date* field.

Step 5 Select Graph to generate a Collection Aging Pie Chart.

Step 6 Print the chart.

Step 7 Answer the following questions in the space provided.

1. What percent of receivables have been outstanding for more than 30 days?

____

2. What percent of receivables have been outstanding 31–60 days?

____

3. What is the value of the receivables in the 61–90 days bracket?

____

4. What is the value of receivables that are due within 30 days?

____

5. What is the value of all outstanding receivables?

____

Step 8 Generate a spreadsheet of key balances. If necessary, change the system date to 3/31/01.

Step 9 Print the spreadsheet.

Step 10 Back up the file to your disk.

Step 11 Exit the program.

Step 12 Answer the following Analysis questions.

6. What is the balance of Accounts Payable on March 31?

____

7. What is the Cash balance on March 31?

____

Business Simulations

Problem Sets

TIPS FOR ALL SIMULATIONS

The following information is provided as a reference to be used for all four simulations.

Entering Transactions

Use one of the following methods for entering the transaction.

- You can group the transactions and enter them in the following order: sales, purchases, cash receipts, cash payments, general journal. Simply open the Task window, enter one group of transactions, close that window, and open the next one.
- Open the five Task windows and choose *Cascade* from the Windows menu. The task windows will arrange so that the title bar of each is visible. You can move between the windows by clicking in the title bar of the appropriate window. You can then enter the transactions in chronological order.
- Open the first Task window, enter the transaction, and then minimize the window before opening the next window. You can move between the windows without closing one window to open another one.

Accounting Period

Change the accounting period as soon as you have printed any beginning reports.

- From the **Tasks** menu, select *System* and then select *Change Accounting Period.*
- Select the appropriate period from the drop-down list.
- From the **Options** menu, select *Change System Date.*
- Enter the last day of the month or select that date from the popup calendar.
- Click **OK**.

Sales on Account Transactions

Follow these steps to enter a sale on account.

- Pull down the **Tasks** menu and choose *Sales/Invoicing.*
- Click the **Template** button for the first invoice (sales slip). Select the **Template** icon. Choose Service to display a simplified invoice form that does not show the inventory fields.
- Enter the Customer ID, invoice number (sales slip number), and the date of each transaction.
- Enter the description and the appropriate general ledger number for the type of sale.
- Enter the amount in the *Amount* field.
- Click the **Post** button.

Purchases on Account Transactions

Follow these steps to enter a purchase on account.

- Pull down the **Tasks** menu and choose *Purchases/Receive Inventory.*
- Enter the vendor ID, invoice number, and invoice date.
- Enter the Accounts Payable general ledger number for the first invoice.
- Skip the *Quantity* and *Item* fields.
- Enter the description and the appropriate general ledger account number, i.e., Purchases, Office Supplies, Office Equipment.
- Enter the purchase amount in the *Amount* field. (Skip the unit price field.)
- Click the **Post** button.

Purchase Returns and Allowance Transactions

Follow these steps to enter a purchase return or allowance.

- Pull down the **Tasks** menu and choose *Purchases/Receive Inventory.*
- Enter the vendor ID.
- Enter a credit memo reference in the Invoice # field.
- Record the transaction date.
- Skip the *Quantity* and *Item* fields.
- Enter a description.
- Record the *Purchases Returns and Allowances* account number in the *G/L Account* field.
- Enter the purchase return as a negative (–) amount in the *Amount* field.
- Click the **Post** button.
- From the **Tasks** menu, choose *Payments.*
- Enter or select the vendor ID.
- Find the negative invoice (Credit Memo) and check the *Pay* box next to it.
- Find the invoice you want to apply the credit to and pay it the amount of the credit (as a positive amount)
- The check amount should be zero (0.00).
- Click **Post**.

General Journal Entries

Follow these steps to enter a general journal transaction

- Pull down the **Tasks** menu and choose *General Journal Entry.*
- Enter the date of the transaction and the reference (i.e., NSF).
- Enter the GL account number and the description.
- Enter the amount in the debit column.
- Repeat the previous two steps for the credit amounts.
- Click the **Post** button if your debits equal your credits.

Cash Receipts Entries

Follow these steps to enter a cash receipt from a customer as payment on account.

- Pull down the **Tasks** menu and choose *Receipts*.
- Enter a Deposit Ticket ID. Use the date of the receipt.
- Look up the Customer ID.
- Enter a reference—use the receipt number (i.e., R343).
- Check to see that the appropriate cash account GL number is used (i.e., Cash in Bank).
- Enter the transaction date.
- In the *Apply to Invoices* section enter the amount paid by the customer or mark the check box.
- Click the **Post** button.

Follow these steps to enter cash sales or other cash receipts.

- Pull down the **Tasks** menu and choose *Receipts*.
- Enter a Deposit ticket ID. Use the date of the transaction.
- Leave the *Customer ID* field empty.
- Enter a description, i.e., Cash Sales, in the *Name* field.
- Enter a reference such as the receipt number or the cash register tape number.
- Check to see that the appropriate cash account GL number is used (i.e., Cash in Bank).
- In the *Apply to Revenues* section enter the description, the GL account number(s), and the amount. Do not use the *Unit Price* column.
- Enter the sales tax payable as a GL account if applicable. Use the sales tax area at the bottom of the screen for the Floor Store only. For Creamy Delight and Book Worm, the sales tax has been calculated by the cash register on each individual sale, and the total of the combined sales is key-entered as part of the transaction.
- Click the **Post** button.

Cash Payments Transactions

Follow these steps to enter a cash payment applied to an expense.

- Pull down the **Tasks** menu and choose *Payments*.
- Skip the *Vendor* field.
- Enter a payee.
- Enter the check number and the date.
- Check to see that the appropriate cash account GL number is used.
- Skip the *Quantity* and *Item* fields.
- Record a description, the GL account number(s), and the distribution amount(s). When making the payroll entry, show the credits for the various tax liabilities by using a minus in front of the amount.
- Click the **Post** button.

Follow these steps to enter a cash payment applied to an invoice.

- Pull down the **Tasks** menu and choose *Payments*.
- Enter a vendor number, check number, and the transaction date.
- Check to see that the appropriate cash account GL number is used.
- Check to see that the correct GL number for discounts is used.
- Record the discount (if applicable) and the amount paid for the corresponding invoice.
- Click the **Post** button.

Adjusting Entries

- Use a copy of the Working Trial Balance to determine the adjusting entries.
- Enter the adjusting entries in the general journal.

Print Reports

Print the general journal.
Print the Adjusted Trial Balance (General Ledger Trial Balance).
Print an Income Statement and a Balance Sheet.

Close the Fiscal Year

Follow these steps to have the *Peachtree* program automatically generate the closing entries.

- Pull down the **Tasks** menu, choose *System,* and then select the *Close Fiscal Year* option.
- Indicate that you do not want to print the invoices, checks, or other reports.
- Creamy Delight: Click **OK** to accept the "retained earnings" account to be used for the closing process.
- The Book Worm: Click **OK** to accept the "retained earnings" (partner's equity) account to be used for the closing process.
- When the Accounting Period dialog box appears, press **OK** to continue.
- Click the **Yes** button to purge the old transactions.
- Print a Post-closing Trial Balance (General Ledger Trial Balance).

CREAMY DELIGHT
(Sole Proprietorship)

You will now have the opportunity to review and apply what you have learned as you complete the accounting cycle for Creamy Delight.

Objectives

When you have completed this simulation, you will have

1. Printed the chart of accounts and the customer and vendor lists.
2. Analyzed business transactions.
3. Used the accounting software to input all journal entries.
4. Printed the journals.
5. Printed the general ledger and the customer and vendor ledgers.
6. Printed the check register.
7. Printed a general ledger trial balance.
8. Completed adjusting entries.
9. Printed the general journal including the adjusting entries.
10. Printed financial statements.
11. Completed the closing process.
12. Printed the post-closing trial balance.
13. Analyzed the financial statements.

Creamy Delight

The H. S. Eldredge family owns and operates a franchised, fast food restaurant in Lexington, Massachusetts, which is organized as a sole proprietorship. The business, called Creamy Delight, is a restaurant with seating (tables and chairs) and a drive-thru window. It specializes in ice cream products. The menu includes items made from ice cream or yogurt; food items, such as hamburgers, hot dogs, chicken sandwiches, and french fries; and a variety of soft drinks. Sales for each of the three categories—food, drinks, and ice cream—are recorded separately on the cash registers. Change totaling $750.00 is kept in the cash registers; it is listed as Cash on Hand in the Chart of Accounts.

Although cash sales are recorded and deposited intact daily in this type of business, for expediency in this simulation problem, cash sales are recorded each Friday in the Cash Receipts Journal and then deposited in the bank. Cash sales are also deposited at the conclusion of the last day of the month. Charge sales are recorded on the day the sale is made. Charges are made only to churches, schools, and other non-profit organizations. These organizations are exempt from sales tax. Checks received on account are deposited on the date they are received.

Creamy Delight leases the building and is responsible for maintenance and repairs as well as any remodeling on the building. The furniture and fixtures belong to Creamy Delight. The initial amount paid for the franchise is considered an asset. The franchise agreement requires that eight percent of sales will be paid each month—four percent for royalties and four percent for national advertising—to the franchisor, International Creamy Delight, Inc.

Salary expense is charged to the Salary Expense—Restaurant account except for the assistant manager and the part-time accounting clerk. Their salaries are charged to the Salary Expense—Management account. The owner, who is also the manager, withdraws money each month. Since most of the people work only part time (students and retired persons), they make minimum wage and consequently pay very little in federal income tax.

You have just been hired as the part-time accounting clerk for Creamy Delight. Although Creamy Delight is open for business 7 days a week, you will work only 20 hours a week from Monday through Friday. You will begin work on December 1.

Instructions

1. Start the accounting software.
2. Restore the Creamy Delight problem set.
3. Print the Chart of Accounts, the General Ledger, the Trial Balance, and the Customer and Vendor Ledgers.
4. Change the accounting period to Period 12, December 1–December 31, 2001.
5. Change the system date to 12/31/01.
6. From the **Options** menu, select *Global,* then remove the check from any of the choices for *Hide General Ledger Accounts*. You can also set the decimal method you prefer in this window.
7. Enter the transactions for December.
8. When you open the Receipts window, choose Cash in Bank as the cash account.
9. When you open the Sales/Invoicing Task window, select the **Template** icon and choose the *Service Invoice.*
10. Since not all food sales are taxed, you will simply credit Sales Tax Payable for the amount of the tax recorded on the cash register tape rather than use the sales tax feature in *Peachtree*.
11. Creamy Delight uses real time posting. After each transaction has been entered, select the **Post** icon.
12. Print the sales, purchases, cash receipts, and cash disbursements journals.
13. Print the Customer Ledgers.
14. Print the Vendor Ledgers.
15. Print the Check Register.
16. Print the Working Trial Balance.
17. Calculate and then record the adjusting entries in the General Journal.
18. Print the General Journal including the adjusting entries.
19. Print the General Ledger.
20. Print General Ledger Trial Balance.
21. Print the financial statements—Income Statement and Balance Sheet.
22. Complete the closing process when you are sure that all reports are accurate.
23. Print another Trial Balance.
24. Complete the analysis questions.

Transactions

December

1 Received $191.57 interest from bank for average daily balances in bank account, Receipt 842.

1 Wrote Check 6675 for $2,096.32 to Bay State Products less discount of $41.93 to pay Invoice B20340. Since checks are written manually, you will need to enter the check number for such transactions.

1 Issued Check 6676 to Action Computerized Accounting Service for $150.00. Charge to Computer Services Expense.

1 Purchased merchandise on account, Invoice M4930, from O'Maley Beverages for $29.00, terms net 30.

1 Cash sales for Friday, December 1 are summarized on a cash register tape which shows the following totals: Ice cream/yogurt, $499.26; food, $272.37; and drinks, $44.22. The total deposit is $856.18. The difference between sales and the deposit is due to cash short of $.46 and sales tax collected of $40.79, Tape 82.

3 Sold yogurt to St. Paul's Youth Group on account, $32.75, Sales Slip A1687. Remember that products are sold on account only to sales tax exempt organizations, so no sales tax is collected.

4 Received a check for $29.30 on account from St. Paul's Youth Group in payment of Sales Slip A1682, Receipt 843.

4 Bought $83.99 of office supplies from Boston Office Supply on account, Invoice S5788, terms net 30.

4 Paid Seashell, Inc. for rent for December for $3,000.00. Check 6677.

4 Wrote Check 6678 to First National Bank for employment taxes—Employees, Federal Income Tax, $1,001.94; Social Security Taxes, $1,737.26; Medicare, $406.30; a total of $3,145.50.

4 Wrote Check 6679 to MA Dept. of Revenue and Taxation for employees, state income tax for $700.54.

4 Issued Check 6680 to MA Workers' Comp. Ins. Agency for $318.04.

4 Issued Check 6681 to MA Employment and Security Com., $84.06, for state unemployment tax.

4 Purchased merchandise on account, Invoice C360296, from Vermont Creamery for $578.23, terms net 30.

5 Paid New England Communications $253.38 for telephone expense. Check 6682.

5 Wrote Check 6683 to City of Lexington for water, sewer, and garbage expense for $281.21. Charge to Utilities Expense.

5 Prepared Receipt 844 for check in amount of $61.50 from East High School Pep Club in payment of Sales Slip A1681.

5 Received a check from West High School Student Council to apply on account, Receipt 845 for $42.50 for Sales Slip A1683.

6 Paid Chen's Laundry for $287.64 for laundry expense, Check 6684.

6 Sold ice cream to West High School's Student Council on account, $54.00, Sales Slip A1688.

6 Purchased merchandise on account, Invoice B24475, from Bay State Products for $1,885.82, terms 2/10, n/30.

6 Wrote check 6685 to MA Nurse's Association for advertising in convention program, $80.00.

6 Purchased merchandise on account, Invoice G30919, from Langone Baking for $71.76, net 30.

6 Paid $25 to Atlantic Exterminating, Check 6686. Charge to Miscellaneous Expense.

7 Received a check for $63.00 to apply on account from Oceanridge School PTA in payment of Sales Slip A1684, Receipt 846.

7 Issued Check 6687 to Bicknell's Fire Extinguisher Service for $25.32. Charge to Maintenance Expense.

7 Purchased merchandise on account, Invoice P8580, from Lopez Produce for $308.73, terms net 30.

7 Wrote Check 6688 to Crown Plumbing for repair, $219.21. Charge to repairs expense.

7 Issued Check 6689 for $100 to City of Lexington for license to operate restaurant. Charge to Licenses and Permits Expense.

7 Wrote Check 6690 to Bay State Products for $1,984.17 less discount of $39.68 to pay account, Invoice B20582.

8 Wrote Check 6691 to International Creamy Delight, Inc. for a total of $3,611.56; $1,805.78 for license fee royalties and $1,805.78 for national advertising.

8 Issued Check 6692 for $1,833.90 to MA Department of Revenue and Taxation for sales tax payable.

8 Sold yogurt to East High School's Pep Club on account, $54.80, Sales Slip A1689.

8 Received a check for $84.50 on account from Arlington's Swim Team in payment of Sales Slip A1686, Receipt 847.

8 Purchased merchandise on account, Invoice M5001, from O'Maley Beverages for $69.80, terms net 30.

8 Wrote Check 6693 for $71.76 to Damon Lock and Key for changing locks—charge to Miscellaneous Expense.

8 Wrote Check 6694 to U.S. Post Office for stamps for $39.35—charge to Postage and Box Rental Expense.

8 Paid Chelsea's Coffee & Tea Supply $85.98 on account, Invoice T10087, Check 6695.

8 Wrote Check 6696 to O'Maley Beverages for $1,329.15 to pay account, Invoice M4821.

8 Check returned by bank for insufficient funds. It was written for a cash sale in the amount of $11.19. Use NSF1 as the reference.

8 Cash sales for December 2–8 are summarized on a cash register tape which shows the following totals: Ice cream/yogurt, $4,117.30; food, $3,804.79; and drinks, $548.94. The total deposit is $8,889.33. The difference between sales and the deposit is due to cash short of $5.25 and sales tax collected of $423.55. Tape 83.

11 Prepared Receipt 848 for check in amount of $55.00 from Lincoln High School's basketball team in payment of Sales Slip A1685.

11 Wrote Check 6697 to Boston Office Supply on account, $25.45, Invoice S5621.

11 Purchased merchandise on account, Invoice C366036, from Vermont Creamery for $528.65, terms net 30.

11 Paid Vermont Creamery $3,738.05 on account, Check 6698, Invoice C355852.

12 Issued Check 6699 to W & B Glass for repair of glass for $148.05. Charge to Repairs Expense.

12 Wrote Check 6700 to Langone Baking for $540.13 to pay on account, Invoice G29812.

12 Wrote Check 6701 to Lopez Produce to pay on account $622.68, Invoice P7198.

13 Sold ice cream to West High School's Student Council on account, $45.70, Sales Slip A1690.

13 Wrote Check 6702 for $110.17 to Atwood's Electric Repair for electrical repairs.

13 Purchased merchandise on account, Invoice B26125, from Bay State Products for $1,840.23, terms 2/10, n/30.

13 Issued Check 6703 to Lexington High School for $150.00 for a banner. Charge to advertising expense.

13 Purchased merchandise on account, Invoice G31713, from Langone Baking for $164.53, net 30.

13 Wrote Check 6704 to Bay Kids Soccer for uniforms for $350.00—charge to Advertising Expense.

13 Check returned by bank for insufficient funds. It was written for cash sale in amount of $9.14.

14 Sold yogurt to Oceanridge School PTA on account, $71.50, Sales Slip A1691.

14 Sold meals on account to Watertown's swim team, $83.40, Sales Slip A1692.

14 Purchased merchandise on account, Invoice P8650, from Lopez Produce for $28.05, terms net 30.

14 Wrote Check 6705 to Barclay Paper Company for restaurant supplies such as napkins and wrap for sandwiches, $83.62. Charge Restaurant Supplies.

15 The payroll accounting procedure requires that a check on the regular checking account be written to the First National Bank—Payroll Account. Then special payroll checks are written to each employee. The total of each of these payroll checks will equal the total of the check written and deposited in the First National Bank—Payroll Account. Issued Check 6706 for the total net pay due employees—$5,336.58. Gross earnings for the pay period are $4,883.23 for restaurant salaries, $1,760.00 for management salaries. The following amounts were withheld: employees' federal income tax, $466.26; employees' state income tax, $332.16; Social Security tax, $411.89; and Medicare, $96.34.

15 Recorded the employer's payroll liabilities as follows: Social Security tax, $411.89; Medicare, $96.34; federal unemployment tax, $21.99; state unemployment tax, $39.86. Use Payroll Tax Expense.

15 Sold yogurt to East High School's Pep Club on account, $56.30, Sales Slip A1693.

15 Purchased merchandise on account, Invoice M5035, from O'Maley Beverages for $83.00, terms net 30.

15 Wrote Check 6707 for $1,885.82 less discount of $37.72 to Bay State Products on account, Invoice B24475.

15 Cash sales for December 9–15 are summarized on a cash register tape which shows the following totals: Ice cream/yogurt, $4,502.70; food, $3,984.83; and drinks, $619.85. The total deposit is $9,559.25. The difference between sales and the deposit is due to cash short of $3.50 and sales tax collected of $455.37. Tape 84.

17 Sold yogurt to St. Paul's Youth Group on account, $35.50, Sales Slip A1694.

17 Sold meals on account to Lincoln High School's basketball team, $85.75, Sales Slip A1695.

18 Purchased merchandise on account, Invoice C366505, from Vermont Creamery for $492.08, terms net 30.

18 Collected $11.19 for the NSF check which was returned on December 8. (Reverse the entry made on December 8.)

19 Wrote Check 6708 to Hampshire Inn for $747.73 for annual Christmas party. Charge to Employee Benefits.

19 Issued Check 6709 to Eastern Light, Fuel, and Power for $955.32 for utilities expense.

20 Purchased merchandise on account, Invoice T10259, from Chelsea's Coffee & Tea Supply for $132.31, terms net 30.

20 Sold meals on account to Arlington's swim team, $83.65, Sales Slip A1696.

20 Purchased merchandise on account, Invoice B34969, from Bay State Products for $1,665.34, terms 2/10, n/30.

20 Wrote Check 6710 for $114.25 to Atwood's Electric Repair for repairs.

20 Purchased merchandise on account, Invoice G32410, from Langone Bakery for $83.61, terms net 30.

20 Bought additional computer equipment on account from Boston Office Supply for $2,005.47, Invoice S6438, terms net 30. (Use Office Equipment account.)

21 Wrote Check 6711 for $20.00 to Kelley Security Systems for monthly monitoring. (Use Miscellaneous Expense)

21 Purchased merchandise on account, Invoice P8989, from Lopez Produce for $145.65, terms net 30.

21 Issued Check 6712 to General Cash Register, Inc. for the maintenance contract for 24 months on an additional cash register, $1,560.00. Charge to Prepaid Cash Register Maintenance.

22 Issued Check 6713 to Reese Trophy and Awards for trophies for a fund raiser for $45.00. (Advertising Expense.)

22 Sold ice cream cakes to St. Mark's Youth Group on account, $56.00, Sales Slip A1697.

22 Wrote Check 6714 for $75.00 for advertising in Lexington High School's yearbook.

22 Wrote Check 6715 for $1,840.23 less discount of $36.80 to Bay State Products on account, Invoice B26125.

22 Check returned by bank for insufficient funds. It was written for cash sale in amount of $4.64.

22 Cash sales for December 16–22 are summarized on a cash register tape which shows the following totals: Ice cream/yogurt, $4,764.84; food, $3,910.98; and drinks, $649.16. The total deposit is $9,791.68. The difference between sales and the deposit is due to cash over of $0.45 and sales tax collected of $466.25. Tape 85.

22 Purchased merchandise on account, Invoice C366543, from Vermont Creamery for $393.86, terms net 30.

22 Purchased merchandise on account, Invoice M5143, from O'Maley Beverages for $85.20, terms net 30.

27 Purchased merchandise on account, Invoice B41258, from Bay State Products for $1,924.15, terms 2/10, n/30.

27 Wrote Check 6716 to Ferrari Cleaning Services for window cleaning for $122.00. Charge to Cleaning Expense.

27 Purchased merchandise on account, Invoice G33413, from Langone Bakery for $103.52, terms net 30.

27 NSF check for $9.14, returned on December 13, was collected.

27 Bought restaurant supplies for cash from Brown's Janitorial Supplies, $465.20, Check 6717.

28 Purchased merchandise on account, Invoice P9470, from Lopez Produce for $76.50, terms net 30.

28 Issued Check 6718 to Bay State Products to pay on account, $1,665.34 less discount $33.31, Invoice B34969.

29 Purchased merchandise on account, Invoice M5371, from O'Maley Beverages for $297.10, terms net 30.

29 Sold yogurt to St. Mark's Youth Group on account, $38.50, Sales Slip A1698.

29 Cash sales for December 23–29 are summarized on a cash register tape which shows the following totals: Ice cream/yogurt, $4,247.09; food, $3,109.66; and drinks, $498.41. The total deposit is $8,247.32. The difference between sales and the deposit is due to cash short of $.60 and sales tax collected of $392.76. Tape 86.

29 Purchased merchandise on account, Invoice C367577, from Vermont Creamery for $320.90, terms net 30.

31 Issued Check 6719 to the First National Bank—Payroll Account for the total net pay due employees—$5,455.66. Gross earnings for the pay period are $5,058.07 for restaurant salaries, $1,760.00 for management salaries. The following amounts were withheld: employees' federal income tax, $499.94; employees' state income tax, $340.90; Social Security tax, $422.73; and Medicare, $98.84.

31 Recorded the employer's payroll liabilities as follows: Social Security tax, $422.73; Medicare, $98.84; federal unemployment tax, $20.90; state unemployment tax, $40.91.

31 Recorded the workers' compensation insurance liability, $305.57, for the December payroll.

31 Issued Check 6720 to H. S. Eldredge for personal use, $3,500.

31 Cash sales for December 30–31 are summarized on a cash register tape which shows the following totals: Ice cream/yogurt, $1,420.46; food, $1,258.21; and drinks, $260.13. The total deposit is $3,082.87. The difference between sales and the deposit is due to cash short of $2.87 and sales tax collected of $146.94. Tape 87.

31 Bank service charges for December are $12.96.

Adjusting Entries

Calculate and record the adjusting entries in the general journal using the balances from the trial balance with the following information:

- The value of the ending merchandise inventory on December 31 is $9,432.86.
- The restaurant supplies on hand on December 31 are valued at $435.50.
- The office supplies on hand on December 31 are valued at $173.25.
- The amount of the premium which expired on the insurance policy for the year is $2,394.00.
- The amount of the maintenance which expired on the two-year cash register maintenance contract for the year is $2,337.50.
- The depreciation expense for building improvements is $4,192.28.
- The depreciation expense for store equipment is $6,394.43.
- The depreciation expense for office equipment is $1,120.00.

Name ______________________________ Date ______________

ANALYSIS QUESTIONS

Creamy Delight

INSTRUCTIONS:

Use your completed document to find the answers to the following questions. Write your answers in the space to the left of each question. Write the test-question number on your printouts adjacent to the answer found.

_______ 1. What were the credit terms offered to Creamy Delight by Bay State Products?

_______ 2. What is the amount of the monthly rent expense?

_______ 3. What was the total amount of restaurant supplies purchased during December?

_______ 4. What was the total cash received from charge customers during December?

_______ 5. What was the total dollar amount of cash discounts that Creamy Delight took in December?

_______ 6. What was the total amount of payroll tax expense recorded on December 15?

_______ 7. What was the total of the columns of the trial balance prepared on December 31–prior to adjusting entries?

_______ 8. What was the total dollar amount of checks written in December?

_______ 9. What was the pre-closing balance of the purchases discounts accounted on December 31?

_______ 10. What was the total amount of cash received in December?

_______ 11. What was the total paid on account in December?

_______ 12. What was the total spent for utilities expenses for the fiscal year?

_______ 13. What was the total amount of merchandise purchased from Bay State Products during December?

_______ 14. What amount was debited to salaries expense–restaurant on December 31?

_______ 15. How much was the bank service charge for the month of December?

_______ 16. What was the amount of the total liabilities after all December transactions were recorded and posted?

_______ 17. What was the gross profit on sales for the fiscal period?

_______ 18. What were the net purchases for the fiscal period?

_______ 19. What were the total operating expenses for the fiscal period?

_______ 20. What was the total spent for repairs expenses for the fiscal period?

_______ 21. What was the December 31 balance in Oceanridge PTA account?

_______ 22. What was the net income for the fiscal period?

_______ 23. What was the total amount owed to creditors on December 31?

_______ 24. What was the total net pay on December 15?

_______ 25. What were the net sales for the year?

_______ 26. Which of Creamy Delight's creditors has the largest balance on December 31?

_______ 27. What was the total amount of merchandise purchased for resale during December?

_______ 28. What was the total amount of cash sales, excluding sales tax, for December?

_______ 29. Which operating expense was the highest percentage of net sales?

_______ 30. Which operating expense was the second highest percentage of net sales?

_______ 31. What percentage of net sales was net income?

_______ 32. What was the total of the columns of the post-closing trial balance?

_______ 33. What was the balance of office supplies on December 15?

_______ 34. How many customers had a balance owing on December 31?

_______ 35. How many vendors did creamy Delight owe on December 31?

_______ 36. What was the amount of total assets at fiscal year end?

_______ 37. What was the total of the owner's equity on December 31?

_______ 38. What was the amount of the adjustment for office supplies at fiscal year end?

_______ 39. What was the balance of accounts receivable on December 31?

_______ 40. What is the percentage of total expenses to net sales?

_______ 41. What was the book value of Creamy Delight's store equipment at the end of the fiscal period?

Name ______________________________ Date ______________

THE BOOK WORM (PARTNERSHIP)

You will have the opportunity to review and apply what you have learned as you complete the accounting cycle for The Book Worm.

Objectives

When you have completed this simulation, you will have

1. Printed the chart of accounts and the customer and vendor lists.
2. Analyzed business transactions.
3. Used the accounting software to input journal entries.
4. Printed the journals.
5. Printed the general ledger and the customer and vendor ledgers.
6. Printed the check register.
7. Printed a general ledger trial balance.
8. Completed adjusting entries.
9. Printed the general journal including the adjusting entries.
10. Printed financial statements.
11. Completed the closing process.
12. Printed the post-closing trial balance.
13. Analyzed the financial statements.

The Book Worm

C. W. Reese and G. J. Hummer own and operate a book store located in Greeley, Colorado, which is organized as a partnership. Each partner owns 50 percent of the business. Net income or loss is shared equally. The Book Worm carries books, magazines, greeting cards, postcards, stationery, music, calendars, maps, and a variety of candy and popcorn. These are four sales accumulators on the cash register–books, magazines, cards (greeting cards, postcards, and stationery), and miscellaneous (music, calendars, maps, candy, and popcorn).

Change totaling $150.00 is kept in the cash register; it is listed as Cash in Register in the Chart of Accounts. Although cash sales, including credit card sales, are recorded and deposited intact everyday, for expediency in this application problem, the cash and credit card sales are recorded each Tuesday, Thursday, and Saturday in the Cash Receipts Journal and then deposited in the bank. On the deposit ticket, the cash and credit card sales are shown separately. The sum of the cash and credit card sales is shown as The Book Worm's total deposit. The bank treats the credit card slips the same as cash. The bank charges a monthly fee based on a percentage of the total credit card charges during the month. This fee is deducted from The Book Worm's bank account and is listed on the monthly bank statement. The use of open-account-charge sales are limited to a few schools, the public library, and government agencies. They are recorded individually the day the sale is made. These organizations are exempt from sales tax.

The Book Worm leases the building and is responsible for its maintenance and repairs as well as any remodeling. The furniture and fixtures belong to The Book Worm.

Salary expense is charged to the Salary and Wage Expense account. The partners withdraw money each month. You have just been hired as the accounting clerk for The Book Worm which is a part-time job. You will begin work on September 1. The Book Worm is open for business seven days a week. The fiscal year is October 1, 2000 to September 30, 2001. You will be completing the end-of-year procedures.

Name ______________________________ Date ______________

Instructions

1. Start the accounting software and open The Book Worm problem set.
2. Select Restore from the File menu.
3. Print the Chart of Accounts, General Ledger Trial Balance, and the Customer and Vendor Ledgers.
4. Change the system date to 9/30/01.
5. Enter the transactions for September 2001.
6. The first time you open the Receipts and payment task windows, the Select a Cash Account window will open. Choose Cash in Bank.
7. When you open the Sales Invoicing task window, select the **Template** icon. Choose the *Service Invoice.*
8. Since sales tax is calculated and included on the cash register tape, credit Sales Tax Payable rather than using Peachtree's automated tax feature.
9. The Book Worm uses real time posting. After each transaction has been entered, select the **Post** icon.
10. Print the journal reports.
11. Print the Customer Ledgers.
12. Print the Vendor Ledgers.
13. Print the Check Register.
14. Print the Working Trial Balance.
15. Calculate and then record the adjusting entries in the General Journal.
16. Print the General Journal including the adjusting entries.
17. Print the General Ledger.
18. Print General Ledger Trial Balance after the adjusting entries are complete.
19. Print the financial statements–Income Statement, Statement Changes, and Balance Sheet.
20. Complete the closing process when you are sure that you have completed this simulation correctly.
21. Print another Trial Balance.
22. Follow these steps to divide the partner's equity between two partners.
    - Debit the amount which is in the partner's equity account.
    - Credit one-half of the amount to each partner.
    - Print the general journals.
    - Print a General Ledger Trial Balance.
23. Complete the analysis questions.

Transactions

September

1 Paid Alpine, Inc. $1,600.00 for September's rent. Check 3506.

1 Sold books to Mountain View High School on account, $23.62. Sales Slip S1687.
Remember that no sales tax is collected since schools are tax exempt.

1 Wrote Check 3507 for $40.81 to replenish petty cash–$19.14 for maintenance expense and $21.67 for postage expense.

1 Wrote Check 3508 to Harvard Insurance Health Plan, $739.96 to pay for employees' health insurance liability.

1 Issued Check 3509 to Pacific Publications, Inc. for $330.43, less discount $6.61 to pay account, Invoice P40460.

1 Issued Check 3510 to Hyatt Insurance Agency to pay workers' compensation insurance liability for $317.49.

1 Issued Check 3511 to Colorado Employment and Security Commission, $290.17 for State Unemployment Tax.

1 Wrote Check 3512 to Colorado Department of Revenue and Taxation to pay employees state income tax for $210.10.

1 Paid Ryan Distributors $1,403.39 for Invoice R8321, Check 3513.

2 Cash sales for September 1-2 were summarized on a cash register tape which shows the following totals: Books, $1,765.85; magazines, $551.12; cards, $173.15; miscellaneous sales, $600.08. The total deposit is $3,275.40. The difference between sales and the deposit is due to cash over of $3.34 and sales tax collected of $181.86. Tape 171. Note, the bank will show the cash deposit and the credit card deposit separately on each deposit ticket and on the monthly bank statement. However, in The Book Worm's accounting record, you will debit the amount of the total deposit to the Cash in Bank account.

4 Wrote Check 3514 for $86.65, less discount $1.73 to Pacific Publications, Inc. to pay accounts, Invoice P40485.

4 Purchased merchandise on account, Invoice P20395, from Marilyn Bean Publishing, Ltd. for $685.70, terms net 30.

4 Purchased merchandise on account, Invoice F3715, from Artfolio for $88.22, terms net 30.

4 Purchased merchandise on account, Invoice P10935 from Paper Whales for $449.70, terms net 30.

4 Received a check for $64.95 on account from U. S. Forest Service in payment of Sales Slip S1683, Receipt 358.

Name ______________________________ Date ______________

5	Collected cash for a NSF check for $11.55 which was returned on August 20. Record a General Journal entry debiting Cash in Bank and crediting Loss on NSF Checks.
5	Purchased merchandise on account, Invoice A3185, from Western Distributors for $4,407.52, terms net 30.
5	Cash sales for September 3-5 were summarized on a cash register tape which shows the following totals: Books, $3,165.07; magazines, $755.71; cards, $306.17; miscellaneous sales, $839.77. The total deposit is $5,409.67 (cash–$4,102.56 and credit cards–$1,307.11). The difference between sales and the deposit is due to cash over of $45.85 and sales tax collected of $297.10. Tape 172.
6	Issued Check 3515 for $8,948.89 less discount of $268.47 to Engstrom Periodicals to pay account, Invoice N5376.
6	Sold books to Colorado Community College on account, $19.95, Sales Slip S1688.
7	Cash sales for September 6-7 were summarized on a cash register tape which shows the following totals:Books, $1,401.74; magazines, $481.46; cards, $206.90; miscellaneous sales, $669.40. The total deposit is $2,866.44 (cash–$2,418.36 and credit cards–$448.08). The difference between sales and the deposit is due to cash short of $53.55 and sales tax collected of $160.49. Tape 173.
7	Issued Check 3516 to Mountain States Light, Fuel, and Power for $288.80 for utilities expense.
7	Paid Mountain West Communications $169.96 for telephone expense. Check 3517.
7	Prepared Receipt 359 for check in amount of $141.79 from Mountain View High School in payment of Sales Slip S1684.
7	Purchased merchandise on account, Invoice M49612, from Maps, Inc. for $773.95, terms net 30.
7	Wrote Check 3518 to City of Greeley for water and sewer expense for $25.75. Charge to utilities expense.
8	Check returned by bank for non-sufficient funds which was written for cash sale in amount of $13.75.
8	Wrote Check 3519 to CFI Industries for trash collection for $33.00. Charge to utilities expense.
8	Wrote Check 3520 to Greeley Post for Invoice F7460.
8	Wrote Check 3521 to Klein Enterprises for Invoice K9453.
8	Issued Check 3522 for $1,758.27 to Colorado Department of Revenue and Taxation for sales tax payable.
8	Issued Check 3523 for $1,404.94 to City of Greeley for sales tax payable.

8	Issued Check 3524 to Sunset Publications, Inc. to pay Invoice I92330.
8	Wrote Check 3525 to Colorado Concession Supply, Inc. for $532.50 to pay Invoice C00378.
8	Wrote Check 3526 to First National Bank for employment taxes–employees federal income tax, $485.85; Social Security taxes, $827.08; Medicare, $193.42; a total of $1,506.35.
8	Wrote check 3527 to Marilyn Bean Publishing, Ltd. for Invoice P13697.
9	Cash sales for September 8-9 were summarized on a cash register tape which shows the following totals: Books, $1,655.04; magazines, $418.59; cards, $174.15; miscellaneous sales, $510.61. The total deposit is $2,911.41; cash short, $7.01; and sales tax, $160.03. Tape 174.
11	Purchased merchandise on account, Invoice E3069, from Elizabeth Gerhardt for $1,395.45, terms net 30.
11	Purchased merchandise on account, Invoice R9399, from Ryan Distributors for $83.59, terms net 30.
11	Purchased merchandise on account, Invoice A3232, from Western Distributors for $4,019.81, terms net 30.
11	Purchased merchandise on account, Invoice T16622, from Trail Guide for $308.35, terms 2/10, net 30.
12	Wrote Check 3528 for $254.25 to the Pioneer Historical Society for Invoice H3295.
12	Cash sales for September 10-12 were summarized on a cash register tape which shows the following totals: Books, $2,485.89; magazines, $599.93; cards, $283.20; miscellaneous sales, $891.64. The total deposit is $4,510.16; cash over, $3.36; and sales tax, $246.14. Tape 175.
13	Check returned by bank for non-sufficient funds which was written for cash sale of $44.20.
13	NSF check for $13.75 which was returned on September 8 was collected.
13	Paid $35.00 to KFCC, Check 3529. Charge to Donations Expense.
13	Paid annual dues to Greeley Chamber of Commerce, $100.00, Check 3530. Charge Dues and Subscriptions.
13	Purchased supplies on account, Invoice S81678, from Desk Drawer Office Supplies for $304.22, terms net 30.
13	Sold books to Colorado State University–Education College on account, $40.23, Sales Slip S1689.

Name ______________________________ Date ______________

14	Cash sales for September 13-14 were summarized on a cash register tape which shows the following totals: Books, $1,378.72; magazines, $566.96; cards, $270.84; miscellaneous sales, $581.20. The total deposit is $2,959.14; cash over, $0.09; and sales tax, $161.33. Tape 176.
14	Purchased merchandise on account, Invoice I92348, from Sunset Publications, Inc. for $784.12, terms net 30.
14	Purchased merchandise on account, Invoice X15193, from Music Box, Inc. for $427.89, terms net 30.
14	Received a check from East High School–Speech Department to apply on account, Receipt 360 for $143.18 for Sales Slip S1685.
14	Wrote Check 3531 for $164.76 to Frontier Graphics on account, Invoice G25209.
15	The payroll accounting procedure requires that a check on the regular checking account be written to the First National Bank–Payroll Account. Then special payroll checks are written to each employee. The total of the payroll checks will equal the total of the check written and deposited in the First National Bank–Payroll Account. Issued Check 3532. Gross earnings for the pay period are $3,121.31. The following amounts were withheld: employees' federal income tax, $239.83; employees' state income tax, $98.30; Social Security tax, $193.52; Medicare, $45.26; health insurance, $159.63.
15	Issued Check 3533 to Greeley Post for $105.63 for advertising in newspaper.
15	Purchased merchandise on account, Invoice N5431, from Engstrom Periodicals for $4,249.87, terms 3/10 net 30.
15	Record the employer's payroll liabilities as follows: Social Security tax, $193.52; Medicare $45.26; federal unemployment tax, $24.97; state unemployment tax, $87.40. Charge to Payroll Tax Expense.
15	Wrote Check 3534 to Apex Insurance Company, Trustee for The Book Worm's employee 401K savings plan for $88.13. Charge Salary Expense.
16	Cash sales for September 15-16 were summarized on a cash register tape which shows the following totals: Books, $2,043.95; magazines, $461.31; cards, $205.90; miscellaneous sales, $387.99. The total deposit is $3,291.42 (cash–$2,612.43 and credit cards–$678.99). The difference between sales and the deposit is due to cash over of $25.38 and sales tax collected of $166.89. Tape 177.

18	Purchased merchandise on account, Invoice I23962, from Artwork for $164.28, terms net 30.
18	Paid Desk Drawer Office Supplies for Invoice S81601.
18	Purchased merchandise on account, Invoice A3280, from Western Distributors for $4,891.19, terms net 30.
18	Purchased merchandise on account, Invoice P11356, from Paper Whales for $166.51, terms net 30.
18	Purchased merchandise on account, Invoice X15284, from Music Box, Inc. for $1,787.14, terms net 30.
18	Received a check for $10.00 to apply on account from Colorado Community College in payment of Sales Slip S1686, Receipt 361.
18	Wrote Check 3536 for $320.00 to Frontier Graphics for Invoice G25304.
19	Cash sales for September 17-19 were summarized on a cash register tape which shows the following totals: Books, $3,440.50; magazines, $587.52; cards, $411.86; miscellaneous sales, $925.71. The total deposit is $5,585.83; cash short, $89.08; and sales tax, $309.32. Tape 178.
20	Issued Check 3537 to Action Plumbing Service for $97.66. Charge to Maintenance Expense.
20	Wrote Check 3538 to Trail Guide for, Invoice T16622, less discount.
21	Cash sales for September 20-21 were summarized on a cash register tape which shows the following totals: Books, $1,877.70; magazines, $395.68; cards, $242.33; miscellaneous sales, $531.55. The total deposit is $3,245.68; cash over, $20.75; and sales tax, $177.67. Tape 179.
21	Sold books to East High School–Speech Department on account, $20.35, Sales Slip S1690.
22	Check returned by bank for non-sufficient funds which was written for cash sale in amount of $4.64.
22	Purchased merchandise on account from Fanucchi for $331.62, Invoice H17882. Terms net 30.
22	Issued Check 3539 to Western Distributors to pay account $2,121.85, Invoice A3159.
22	Wrote Check 3540 for $243.35 to Maps, Inc., Invoice M49570.
22	Issued Check 3541 to Elizabeth Gerhardt to pay Invoice E3052.
22	Wrote Check 3542 to Music Box, Inc., Invoice X15110.

Name ______________________ Date ______________

23	Cash sales for September 22-23 were summarized on a cash register tape which shows the following totals: Books, $1,585.39; magazines, $354.63; cards, $271.05; miscellaneous sales, $430.68. The total deposit is $2,873.45; cash over, $90.41; and sales tax, $141.29. Tape 180.
25	Issued Check 3543 to Engstrom Periodicals for $4,249.87 on account less discount $127.50, Invoice N5431.
26	Purchased file cabinet on account from Desk Drawer Office Supplies for $241.93, Invoice S81844. Charge Furniture and Fixtures.
26	Purchased merchandise on account, Invoice A3294, from Western Distributors for $3,514.24, terms net 30.
26	Cash sales for September 24-26 were summarized on a cash register tape which shows the following totals: Books, $3,573.25; magazines, $643.76; cards, $374.91; miscellaneous sales, $1,104.85. The total deposit is $6,043.91; cash over, $14.62; and sales tax, $332.52. Tape 181.
28	Cash sales for September 27-28 were summarized on a cash register tape which shows the following totals: Books, $2,110.93; magazines, $353.94; cards, $286.61; miscellaneous sales, $598.92. The total deposit is $3,536.90; cash short, $9.57; and sales tax, $196.07. Tape 182.
28	Purchased merchandise on account, Invoice H3365, from Pioneer Historical Society for $408.75, terms net 30.
28	Purchased merchandise on account, Invoice K9742, from Klein Enterprises for $325.95, terms net 30.
29	Sold books to West High School–Business Department, $40.35, Sales Slip S1691.
29	Issued Check 3544 to Clyde Custodial Services for window cleaning for $35.00. Charge to Miscellaneous Expense.
29	Purchased merchandise on account, Invoice F7491, from Greeley Post for $78.00, terms net 15.
29	Purchased merchandise on account, Invoice P41523, from Pacific Publications, Inc. for $802.14, terms 2/10, net 30.
29	Purchased merchandise on account, Invoice W8048, from Mountain Country News for $14.00, terms net 30.
30	Bank Charges for credit cards for September are $438.55. Charge to credit card expense.
30	Cash sales for September 29-30 were summarized on a cash register tape which shows the following totals: Books, $1,924.62; magazines, $397.17; cards, $175.65; miscellaneous sales, $655.88. The total deposit is $3,285.43; cash short, $52.51; and sales tax, $184.62. Tape 183.

30 Issued Check 3545 for the total net pay due employees–$2,509.18. Gross earnings for the pay period are $3,282.75. The following amounts were withheld: employees' federal income tax, $254.87; employees' state income tax, $103.37; Social Security tax, $203.53; Medicare, $47.60; health insurance, $164.20.

30 Issued Check 3546 to C. W. Reese for personal use, $1,500.00.

30 Issued Check 3547 to G. J. Hummer for personal use, $1,500.00.

30 Record the employer's payroll liabilities as follows: Social Security tax, $203.53; Medicare $47.60; federal unemployment tax, $26.27; state unemployment tax, $91.92.

30 Record the workers' compensation insurance liability for the September payroll, $305.07. Charge to workers' compensation insurance expense.

30 Recorded the employer's share of the employee health insurance liability for September, $421.18.

30 Wrote Check 3548 to Apex Insurance Company, Trustee for The Book Worm's employee 401K savings plan for $97.21. Charge Salary and Wage Expense.

Adjusting Entries

Calculate and record the adjusting entries in the general journal using the balances from the trial balance with the following information.

- The value of the ending merchandise inventory on September 30 is $110,789.00.
- The supplies on hand on September 30 are valued at $257.42.
- The amount of the premium which expired on the property insurance policy for the year is $1,898.40.
- The depreciation expense for leasehold improvements is $190.00.
- The depreciation expense for furniture and fixtures is $1,874.00.
- The amount of property tax expense which expired for the year is $2,056.68.

Name ______________________________ Date ______________

ANALYSIS QUESTIONS

The Book Worm

INSTRUCTIONS:

Use your reports to answer the following questions. Write your answer in the space to the left of each question.

_____ 1. What were the credit terms offered to The Book Worm by Engstrom Periodicals?

_____ 2. What is the amount of the monthly rent expense?

_____ 3. What was the total amount of supplies purchased during September?

_____ 4. What was the total dollar amount of cash discounts that The Book Worm took in September?

_____ 5. What was the total amount of payroll tax expense recorded on September 15?

_____ 6. What was the total of the columns of the trial balance prepared on September 30–prior to adjusting entries?

_____ 7. What was the total dollar amount of checks written in September?

_____ 8. What was the pre-closing balance of the purchases discounts account on September 30?

_____ 9. What was the total amount of cash received in September?

_____ 10. What was the total paid on account in September?

_____ 11. What was the total spent for utilities expense for the fiscal year?

_____ 12. What was the total amount of merchandise purchased from Klein Enterprises during September?

_____ 13. What amount was debited to salaries expense on September 30?

_____ 14. What was the amount of the total liabilities after all September transactions were recorded and posted?

_____ 15. What was the gross profit on sales for the fiscal period?

_____ 16. What were the total operating expenses for the fiscal period?

_____ 17. What was the cost of merchandise sold for the fiscal period?

_____ 18. What was the September 30 balance in Colorado Community College account?

______ 19. What was the net income for the fiscal period?

______ 20. What was the total amount owed to creditors on September 30?

______ 21. What were the net sales for the year?

______ 22. Which of The Book Worm's creditors had the largest balance on September 30?

______ 23. What was the total amount of merchandise purchased for resale during September?

______ 24. What were the total assets on September 30?

______ 25. Which operating expense was the highest percentage of net sales?

______ 26. What percentage of net sales was net income?

______ 27. What was the total of the columns of the post-closing trial balance?

______ 28. How many customers had a balance owing on September 30?

______ 29. What was the amount owed to Artfolio on September 30?

______ 30. What was the book value of leasehold improvements at fiscal year end?

______ 31. What was the total of the C. W. Reese, Capital account after closing on September 30?

______ 32. What was the total amount of accounts receivable on September 30?

______ 33. How much was the credit card expense for the month of September?

______ 34. What is the percentage of total expenses to net sales?

______ 35. What was the book value of The Book Worm's furniture and fixtures at the end of the fiscal period?

Name ______________________________ Date ______________

THE FLOOR STORE—A COMPLETE CYCLE FOR A MERCHANDISING BUSINESS (CORPORATION)

You will now complete the accounting cycle for The Floor Store, a merchandising corporation.

Objectives

When you have completed this application, you will have

1. Printed the chart of accounts and the customer vendor lists.
2. Analyzed business transactions.
3. Used the accounting software to input all journal entries.
4. Added Customers.
5. Printed the journals.
6. Printed the general ledger and the customer and vendor ledgers.
7. Printed the check register.
8. Printed a general ledger trial balance.
9. Completed adjusting entries.
10. Printed the general journal including the adjusting entries.
11. Printed financial statements.
12. Completed the closing process.
13. Printed the post-closing trial balance.
14. Analyzed the financial statements.

The Floor Store

George Downey manages a merchandising business organized as a corporation. Of the 3,000 shares of common stock authorized at $100 par value, 1000 shares have been issued. The Floor Store is located in Laramie, Wyoming. It sells and installs floor coverings including carpet, tile, and vinyl flooring. Customers include home builders, commercial builders, non-profit organizations, and individuals. State sales tax of 5% is collected **only** on the cost of materials **not** on the cost of installation. Non-profit organizations do not pay sales tax. The money received from cash sales is recorded each Friday in the journal and then deposited in the bank. The Floor Store is open Monday through Friday. Charge sales are recorded individually the day the installation is completed and customers are given 30 days to make final payment.

The Floor Store's employees include the manager, the assistant manager, office workers, and sales people; all employees are paid semimonthly. The State of Wyoming does not have a state income tax. The installation of floor coverings is subcontracted to individuals who specialize in the installation of each specific type. These subcontractors are paid when the job has been completed and accepted by the customer. The Cost of Goods Sold section of the income statement includes the subcontractor installation costs as well as the cost of floor covering, equipment rental, and freight-in.

The Floor Store owns the building and land. Curtis Crockwell, the previous accounting clerk, has completed the accounting work through November. You have been hired to complete the transactions for December and the end-of-year work.

Name ______________________________ Date ______________

Instructions

1. Start the accounting software and open The Floor Store problem set.
2. From the File menu, select Restore.
3. Print the Chart of Accounts and the Customer and Vendor Lists and the General Ledger Trial Balance.
4. Change the system date to 12/31/01.
5. Change the accounting period from 12/01/01 to 12/31/01.
6. Enter the credit limits for existing customers.
7. Enter the transactions for December 2001.
8. When you open the Sales Invoicing task window, select the **Template** icon. Choose the *Service invoice.*
9. The Floor Store uses real time posting. After each transaction has been entered, select the **Post** icon.
10. Print the journal reports.
11. Print the Customer Ledgers.
12. Print the Vendor Ledgers.
13. Print the Check Register.
14. Print the Working Trial Balance.
15. Calculate and then record the adjusting entries in the General Journal.
16. Print the General Journal including the adjusting entries.
17. Print the General Ledger.
18. Print the General Ledger Trial Balance after the adjusting entries are complete.
19. Print an Income Statement, a Statement of Retained Earnings, and a Balance Sheet.
20. Complete the closing process when you are sure that you have completed the simulation correctly.
21. Print a post-closing Trial Balance.
22. Complete the analysis questions.

Maintaining Customer Accounts

Before you enter the December transactions, enter the following credit limits for existing customers.

Customer	Credit Limit
Alexander, Inc.	2,000.00
Antelope Ridge Homes	105,000.00
Anton Ferreira	8,000.00
Avallon Interiors	5,000.00
Buffalo Valley Homes	78,000.00
Cahill Travel Agency	3,000.00
Community College	5,000.00
Constance McGrath	29,000.00
Deer Mountain Homes	82,000.00
Donovan & Associates	1,500.00
Elk Meadow Homes	27,000.00
F. E. Warren Air Force Base	2,000.00
Four Seasons Restaurant	8,000.00

H Bar V Ranch	5,000.00
Homestead Manor	10,000.00
John Hirshberg	6,000.00
Leong's Restaurant	9,000.00
Lopez, Inc.	25,000.00
Maldonato Interiors	25,000.00
Monroe Brothers, Inc.	4,000.00
North Side School	8,500.00
Padilla Apartments	9,000.00
Reese Rentals	7,000.00
Sampson Construction	85,000.00
State of Wyoming	100,000.00
University of Wyoming	68,000.00
Walsh & Holland	23,000.00

Step 1 Pull down the **Maintain** menu and choose *Customers/Prospects.*
Click on **Sales Defaults.**
Enter the customer ID.
Click on **Terms.**
Click on **Use Standard Terms** (the box should be blank).
Key the *Credit Limit* and then click **OK.**
Click **Save.**

Step 2 Continue to enter credit limits for the remaining customers; however, since you are in the **Sales Default** screen, you will follow the sequence beginning with the customer ID each time.

When adding new customers to the customer file, the following information needs to be entered: Customer ID, Name, and the GL Sales Account. Accept the default credit limits.

Transactions

December

1 Issued Check 510 for $9,472.20 to Wyoming Department of Revenue and Taxation for sales tax payable. Choose Cash in Bank as the Cash account to use for the transaction.

1 Issued Check 511 for $11,227.76 to L. J. Brooks, a creditor, on account for Invoice V353 less discount of $229.14.

1 Issued Check 512 for $75.00 to Cheyanne Security Systems for security expense. Charge Miscellaneous Expense.

1 Wrote Check 513 to E-Z Rental for $2,059.80 for equipment rental.

1 Charged Joseph Goldman $527.60 for materials and $325.25 installation upon completion of contract for a total of $879.23, Invoice/Sales Slip A699. Since Joseph

Name ______________________________ Date ______________

	Goldman is a new customer, you will need to input his account data into the customer account file.
1	Received a check on account from Antelope Ridge Homes in payment of Sales Slip A678, Receipt 358.
1	Wrote Check 514 to The Timberline Insurance Agency for $15,432.00 for insurance for 12 months. Charge to Prepaid Insurance.
1	Recorded cash sales for December 1—Sales $12,237.50 plus sales tax, Tape 91.
4	Issued Check 515 to J & B Industries for Invoice C110 for $9,205.63 less 3% discount of $276.17.
4	Wrote Check 516 to Rollins Industries in payment of Invoice K3467 for $33,369.20 less 5% discount of $1,668.46.
4	Received a check for $20,668.00 on account from Deer Mountain Homes in payment of Sales Slip A679, Receipt 359.
4	Issued Check 517 to Cochran Supplies for Invoice N1230 less 2% discount.
5	Wrote Check 518 for $19,298.36 for subcontract to Dependable Flooring. Charge to Subcontractor Installation.
5	Charged Antelope Ridge Homes upon completion of contract (materials, $18,999.60, installation, $11,716.30). Sales Slip A700.
5	Wrote Check 519 to Thompson Tile for invoice A6417 of $3,905.40 less 2% discount of $78.11.
5	Purchased sheet vinyl from Sherman Brothers on account, Invoice U5419 for $4,713.77. Terms are 5/15, net 30.
5	Paid Pioneer Bank $1,480.00, $867.41 for mortgage payable and $612.59 for interest expense, Check 520.
5	Wrote Check 521 to Finnigan Floors for $5,683.70 for completed subcontract.
6	Paid Swartz Supply with Check 522 for Invoice F3925.
6	Purchased $15,213.15 of padding from L. J. Brooks on account, Invoice V470, terms 2/20, n/30. Charge to purchases.
6	Issued Check 523 to Laramie Newspapers for $450.00 for advertising.
6	Returned merchandise $95.32, purchased on account from Kendall, Inc., Invoice B683. Debit memorandum 102.
7	Paid American Catalog $120.00, Check 524. Charge to Dues and Subscriptions.

7	Received a check for $24,570.00 on account from the Maldonato Interiors in payment of Sales Slip A680, Receipt 360.
7	Charged Anton Ferreira upon completion of contract (materials, $4,267.80, installation, $2,631.81). Sales Slip A701.
7	Purchased Sheet Vinyl from Swartz Supply on account, Invoice F5317 for $29,776.86. Terms are net 30.
8	Paid Wyoming Office Products for Invoice L4321 for $564.37, Check 525.
8	Wrote Check 526 to Inkslingers for $317.22 for advertising expense.
8	Wrote Check 527 to Mountain States Communications for $1,208.70 for telephone expense.
8	Paid Plains Oil and Gas $708.19, Check 528 for vehicles. Charge to Gas and Oil Expense.
8	Paid the employment taxes with Check 529 to Pioneer Bank—employees federal income tax payable, $3,137.88; Social Security tax payable, $2,240.97; Medicare, $524.10.
8	Wrote Check 530 to Wyoming Unemployment Commission for state unemployment tax, $361.45.
8	Issued Check 531 for $5,317.43 to Paragon Ceramic Tile, for Invoice D8536 less 2% discount of $108.52.
8	Recorded cash sales for December 4–8—Sales $15,759.00, plus sales tax. Cash short $1.00. Tape 92.
8	Wrote Check 532 to City of Laramie for water, sewer, and garbage expense for $89.23. Charge to Utilities Expense.
8	Issued Check 533 to Western Light, Fuel, and Power for $392.74 for utilities.
11	Charged Deer Mountain Homes upon completion of contract (materials, $36,136.80; installation $22,284.24). Sales Slip A702.
11	Purchased sheet vinyl from Sherman Brothers on account, Invoice U5480 for $1,738.19. Terms are 5/15, net 30.
11	Issued Check 534 to Dickson Distributing, Invoice M3215 of $15,987.25 less 3% discount of $479.62.
12	Received a check for $8,940.00 on account from Padilla Apartments in payment of Sales Slip A681, Receipt 361.
12	Wrote Check 535 to Litton Installers for $2,438.50 for completed subcontract.
12	Wrote Check 536 to Mariah Stanton for $6,985.00 for completed subcontract.
12	Charged O'Leary Enterprise upon completion of contract (materials $308.40; installation $190.15). Sales Slip A703. O'Leary Enterprise is a new customer. You will need to input their account data in the customer file. Address is 1478 Gershwin Drive, Laramie, WY 82074.

Name ______________________ Date ______________

12	Received a check for $25,400.00 on account from Sampson Construction in payment of Sales Slip A683, Receipt 362.
12	Received a check for $1,756.00 on account from F. E. Warren Airforce Base in payment of Sales Slip A682, Receipt 363.
12	Issued Check 537 to Kendall, Inc., Invoice B683 (less return).
13	Check returned by bank for NSF check which was written for cash sale in amount of $123.85. Charge to Miscellaneous Expense.
13	Purchased adhesive from Kendall, Inc. on account, Invoice B831 for $21,694.92. Terms are net 30.
13	Charged Avallon Interiors upon completion of contract (materials, $2,558.20; installation $1,577.52). Sales Slip A704.
13	Wrote Check 538 for $1,202.10 for to Palumbo Maintenance. Charge to Repairs and Maintenance Expense.
13	Returned merchandise purchased on account for $400.29 from Sherman Brothers, Invoice U5419. Debit Memorandum 103.
14	Purchased sheet vinyl from L. J. Brooks on account, Invoice V520 for $11,743.32. Terms are 2/20, net 30.
14	Purchased $239.25 of office supplies from Wyoming Office Products on account, Invoice L5432.
14	Issued 40 shares of $100 par value common stock at $100 a share, Receipt 364.
14	Received a check for $7,556.00 on account from State of Wyoming in payment of Sales Slip A684, Receipt 365.
15	Wrote Check 539 to Dependable Flooring for $482.90 for completed subcontract.
15	Charged Buffalo Valley Homes upon completion of contract (materials, $25,833.00; installation $15,930.31). Sales Slip A705.
15	The payroll accounting procedure requires that a check on the regular checking account be written to the Pioneer Bank—Payroll Account. Then special payroll checks are written to each employee. The total of each of these payroll checks will equal the total of the check written and deposited in the Pioneer Bank—Payroll Account. Paid the semi-monthly salaries by issuing Check 540 for the total net pay due employees. Gross earnings for the pay period are $9,036.15. The following amounts were withheld: employees' federal income tax payable, $1,568.94; Social Security tax payable, $560.24; and Medicare, $131.02.

15	Recorded the employer's payroll liabilities as follows: Social Security tax, $560.25; Medicare, $131.03; state unemployment tax, $180.73; federal unemployment tax, $72.29. Total $944.30.
15	Paid Note #1 for $5,000.00 and the interest expense which was $225.00 to Pioneer Bank, Check 541. The note was for 180 days (assume a 360-day year) at 9 percent interest.
15	Recorded cash sales for December 11–15—Sales $18,182.00, cash short $4.00. Tape 93.
18	Purchased carpet from Rollins Industries on account, Invoice K3812 for $34,203.43. Terms are 5/15, net 30.
18	Charged Constance McGrath upon completion of contract (materials, $16,558.80; installation, $11,211.36). Sales Slip A706.
18	Paid $72.95 to U.P.S. for shipping charges, Check 542. Charge to Freight-In.
18	Wrote Check 543 to Finnigan Floors for $2,077.90 for completed subcontract.
18	Wrote Check 544 to U.S. Post Office for stamps and postage meter for $216.30—charge to Postage Expense.
18	Wrote Check 545 for $15,525.37 to Franciscan Carpets to apply to Invoice M899. (Not paid in full.)
18	Purchased computer equipment for cash from The Electronics Company for $2,380.00. Charge to Machinery, Equipment, and Vehicles. Check 546.
19	Received a check for $33,600.00 from Buffalo Valley Homes in payment of Sales Slip A687, Receipt 366.
19	Received a check for $1,205.12 from Donovan & Associates in payment of Sales Slip A688, Receipt 367.
19	Wrote Check 547 to Litton Installers for $9,240.00 for completed subcontract.
19	Wrote Check 548 to Mariah Stanton for $331.41 for completed subcontract.
19	Issued Check 549 for $4,313.48 to Sherman for Invoice U5419 of $4,713.77, less return and discount. Be sure that the discount is applied to both the invoice and the return.
19	Purchased formica tile from Thompson Tile, Invoice A6543 for $4,003.03. Terms are 2/15, net 30.
20	Purchased carpet from Franciscan Carpets, Invoice M1123 for $16,238.27. Terms are 2/15, net 30.
20	Charged Sampson Construction upon completion of contract (materials, $32,501.00; installation, $20,042.16). Sales Slip A707.

Name ______________________________ Date ______________

20	Check returned by bank for NSF check which was written for cash sale in amount of $24.15.
20	Wrote Check 550 for $651.77 for Christmas banquet to Little Deer Inn. Charge to Travel and Entertainment Expense.
20	Paid $3,655.00 for shipping charges to DFL Freight Lines, Check 551.
21	Charged Alexander, Inc. upon completion of contract (materials $1,103.60; installation $680.55). Sales Slip A708.
21	Paid Associated Contractors $665.40, Check 552. Charge to Professional Dues.
21	NSF check for $123.85 which was returned on December 13 was collected.
21	Received a check for $9,807.80 on account from Homestead Manor in payment of Sales Slip A689, Receipt 368.
22	Charged University of Wyoming upon completion of contract $14,353.50 (exempt from Sales Tax), Sales Slip A709.
22	Wrote Check 553 to Dependable Flooring for $2,697.15 for completed subcontract.
22	Purchased carpet from Dickson Distributing, Invoice M3320 for $16,386.93. Terms are 3/15, net 30.
22	Notified that John Hirschberg's bankruptcy proceedings have been closed. We received a check for $1,500.00 from the Court. Write off the rest of the account.
22	Received a check for $4,100.52 from the Community College in payment of Sales Slip A692, Receipt 369.
22	Recorded cash sales for December 18–22—Sales $11,725.50 plus tax, cash over, $7.94. Tape 94.
22	Issued Check 554 to Swartz Supply on account for Invoice F4836.
26	Received a check for $52,995.00 from the University of Wyoming in payment of Sales Slip A693, Receipt 370.
26	Received a check for $4,577.32 from H Bar V Ranch in payment of Sales Slip A695, Receipt 371.
26	Wrote Check 555 to Finnegan Floors for $1,127.64 for completed subcontract.
26	Wrote Check 556 to Litton Installers for $1,258.76 for completed subcontract.
26	Issued Check 557 to L. J. Brooks for Invoice V470 less 2% discount.
26	Issued Check 558 to Sherman Brothers on account for Invoice U5480 less 5% discount.

27	Purchased underlayment from Cochran Supplies on account, Invoice N1278 for $7,641.72. Terms are 2/10, net 30.
27	Purchased metal stripping from Swartz Supply on account, Invoice F5574 for $3,948.57. Terms are net 30.
27	Charged Walsh & Holland upon completion of contract (materials $12,820.40; installation $7,906.07). Sales Slip A710.
28	Charged Four Seasons Restaurant upon completion of contract (materials, $4,307.00; installation, $2,652.75). Sales Slip A711.
28	Purchased ceramic tile from Paragon Ceramic Tile on account, Invoice D8729 for $5,561.60. Terms are 2/10, net 30.
28	Wrote Check 559 to Mariah Stanton for $1,688.74 for completed subcontract.
28	Received a check for $6,140.88 from Lopez, Inc. in payment of Sales Slip A696, Receipt 372.
29	Received a check for $26,020.00 from Elk Meadow Homes in payment of Sales Slip A698, Receipt 373.
29	Wrote Check 560 to Finnegan Floors for $2,327.55 for completed subcontract.
29	Charged Lopez, Inc. upon completion of contract (materials, $10,185.00; installation, $6,280.75). Sales Slip A712.
29	Received a check for $8,463.80 from North Side School in payment of Sales Slip A697, Receipt 374.
29	Recorded cash sales for December 26–29, Sales $21,195.25 plus tax, cash over $2.00. Tape 95.
29	Issued Check 561 to the Pioneer Bank—Payroll Account for the total net pay due employees. Gross earnings for the pay period were $9,036.15. The following amounts were withheld: employees' federal income tax, $1,568.94; Social Security tax, $560.24; Medicare, $131.02.
29	Recorded the employer's payroll liabilities as follows: Social Security tax, $560.25; Medicare, $131.03; state unemployment tax, $180.73; federal unemployment tax, $72.29.
29	Wrote check 562 for $110.40 to the Laramie Collection Agency. Charge to Collection Expense.
29	Paid Albany County Treasurer for 3 months of property taxes, Check 563. Charge Property Tax Expense for 1 month, $2,429.60; and property tax payable for 2 months, $4,859.20.
29	Record the bank service charge for December, $382.10.

Name ______________________________ Date ______________

Adusting Entries for December 31, 2001

- The value of the ending merchandise inventory on December 31 is $555,216.13
- The office supplies on hand on December 31 are valued at $1,287.04.
- The amount of the expired premium for the property insurance policy for the year is $15,571.60.
- The amount of the premium which expired for prepaid life insurance for the year is $7,013.60.
- The percentage of accounts receivable method is used to estimate bad debts expense. Based on past experience bad debts is calculated to be 5.5 percent of accounts receivable.
- The depreciation expense for building and improvements is $8,231.34.
- The depreciation expense for furniture and fixtures is $1,435.34.
- The depreciation expense for machinery, equipment, and vehicles is $10,551.45.
- Calculate the accrued interest expense on the $15,000 borrowed from the bank on a note issued on October 2 for 180 days at 9.25 percent. Use a 360-day year.
- Calculate the accrued interest expense on the Long Term Notes Payable for $287,608.00 borrowed from the bank at 9.75 percent. It has been 75 days since the last interest payment was made. The interest expense is paid every 90 days.
- The board of directors declared a cash dividend of $70 a share payable on January 31, to stockholders of record on December 31.
- The estimated federal income taxes for the year are $50,566.84. Remember to check the trial balance to determine how much has already been paid.

Name ______________________________ Date ______________

ANALYSIS QUESTIONS

The Floor Store

Instructions

Use your completed documents to find the answers to the following questions. Write your answer in the space to the left of the question.

______ 1. What were the credit terms offered to The Floor Store by Dickson Distributing?

______ 2. What was the total amount of office supplies purchased during December?

______ 3. What was the total dollar amount of cash discounts that The Floor Store took in December?

______ 4. What was the total of the columns of the trial balance prepared for December 31 after the adjusting entries?

______ 5. What was the total dollar amount of checks written in December?

______ 6. What was the pre-closing balance of the purchases discounts account on December 13?

______ 7. What was the total amount of cash received in December?

______ 8. What was the total debited to the Accounts Payable account in December?

______ 9. What was the total spent for utilities expense for the fiscal year?

______ 10. What was the total amount of merchandise purchased from L. J. Brooks during December?

______ 11. What amount was debited to salaries expense on December 31?

______ 12. What was the amount of the total liabilities after all December transactions were recorded and posted?

______ 13. What was the gross profit on sales for the fiscal period?

______ 14. What were the net purchases for the fiscal period?

______ 15. What were the total operating expenses for the fiscal period?

______ 16. What was the cost of the merchandise sold (cost of sales) for the fiscal period?

______ 17. What was the total spent for repairs and maintenance expense for December?

______ 18. What was the December 31 balance in the Paragon Ceramic Tile Account?

______ 19. What was the total amount owed to creditors on December 31?

______ 20. What were the net sales for the year?

______ 21. Which of The Floor Store's creditors had the largest balance on December 31?

______ 22. What was the total amount of merchandise purchased for resale during December?

______ 23. What were the total assets on December 31?

______ 24. Which operating expense was the highest percentage of net sales?

______ 25. What percentage of net sales was subcontractor installation?

______ 26. Which operating expense was the second highest percentage of net sales?

______ 27. What percentage of net sales was net income?

______ 28. What was the total of the columns of the post-closing trial balance?

______ 29. How many customers had a balance owing on December 31?

______ 30. What was the balance of Allowance for Uncollectible Accounts on December 31—after the adjusting entry?

______ 31. What was the balance of Swartz Supply's account on December 31?

______ 32. How many vendors did The Floor Store owe on December 31?

______ 33. What was the amount owed to Wyoming Office Products on December 31?

______ 34. What was the amount of total assets at fiscal year end?

______ 35. What was the book value of machinery, equipment, and vehicles at fiscal year end?

______ 36. What was the total amount of accounts receivable on December 31?

______ 37. What is the percentage of cost of merchandise sold to net sales?

______ 38. What is the percentage of **total expenses** to net sales?

______ 39. How much were the gross earnings for all employees for the year?

Name ______________________________ Date ______________

______ 40. What was the net income after federal income tax for the year?

______ 41. What was the balance of retained earnings after the closing entries on December 31?

______ 42. What was the book value of The Floor Store's building and improvements at the end of the fiscal period?

Name ______________________ Date ______________

TUMBLEWEED FAST FOOD, INC.

Payroll Problem

Objectives

When you have completed this payroll simulation, you should be able to:

1. Edit the employees account file.
2. Enter the payroll data.
3. Print the payroll register report, payroll checks, and other reports.

The Charles Crockwell family owns and operates a franchised, fast food restaurant in Cheyenne, Wyoming, which is organized as a corporation. The business, called Tumbleweed Fast Food, is a restaurant with seating (tables and chairs) and a drive-thru window.

Restaurant employees' earnings are charged to the Salary Expense—Restaurant account. The accounting clerk's salary is charged to Salary Expense—Accounting. Since most of the employees work only part time, they make minimum wage and consequently pay very little in federal income tax. Employees are paid bi-weekly—every other Friday. Employees receive payment on the Friday following the end of the payroll period. For example, employees will be paid on January 22 for the payroll period ending January 15.

After the payroll has been verified, the total amount paid to employees is transferred from the Regular Checking Account to the Payroll Checking Account to ensure that sufficient funds are available for the next payroll. This simulation includes the first quarter of 2001.

Key-Enter the Payroll Information

Follow these steps to enter new payroll information for the Tumbleweed simulation.

- Pull down the **Tasks** menu and choose *Payroll Entry*.
- Enter the Date for the check (the period-ending date) below the check number.
- Enter the Date for the *pay period end*.
- Enter the number of weeks in the pay period.
- Enter or select the Employee ID.
- Enter the number of hours for the hourly employees. Keep in mind that any hours over 80 bi-weekly are overtime hours. The program automatically calculates the amount of earnings and deductions.
- Verify the information the screen displays (number of hours or salary, deductions and allowances, calculated amounts).
- Click the **Post** button.

Instructions:

1. Start the *Peachtree* software.
2. Load the Tumbleweed Fast Food, Inc. problem set.
3. Print the list of employees.
4. Process the semi-monthly payroll.
   a. Add any new employees.
   b. Enter any changes for current employees
   c. From the Payroll folder, choose **Payroll Entry**.
   d. Leave the Check Number blank.
   e. Enter the regular and overtime hours.
   f. **Post**.
5. Back up the payroll files.
6. Print the Payroll Register report. Filter the report to reflect the payment date as the beginning and ending date.
7. Print the payroll checks if directed by your instructor.
8. Write a check to the Cheyenne National Bank to transfer the total of the employees' net pay from the Regular Checking Account to the Payroll Checking Account.
9. Print the Check Register report.
10. Print other payroll reports as indicated by your instructor.
11. Print the Quarterly Earnings report after the final payroll has been entered.
12. Complete the analysis questions.

Name ______________________________ Date ________________

Employee Information

Employee name	Marital Status	Withholding Allowances	Soc. Sec. No.	Rate
Jane N. Bixby 5713 Education Drive	Single	1	520-33-6809	5.15
Jamie Bruce 3617 Duff	Single	0	324-25-7482	5.15
Melissa Jo Brown 208 Bradley	Married	2	520-36-2167	5.60
Michelle Bruce 617 Artesian Road	Single	0	520-91-7351	5.15
Mackenzie Ann Caldwell 4325 Pathfinder	Single	0	520-51-0748	5.25
Jennifer Dowling 3506 Bonita	Married	0	520-89-7312	5.70
Jessica Elliott 4701 Arapahoe	Single	1	520-31-4588	5.15
Scott Esquibel 3220 Colina	Single	0	520-32-0976	5.15
James E. Fontana 706 Duna	Married	3	508-25-0567	1,760.00 bi-weekly
Brian Scott Garcia 1522 Hidalgo	Married	0	520-71-5112	6.30
Shawn Garcia 1522 Hidalgo	Married	0	520-51-7924	6.10
Mary Lou Huang 1607 Espinada	Married	0	585-11-0583	5.70
Kelly Jacobs 3201 Escalara	Married	0	520-87-4342	6.00
Justine Jung 2316 Inca	Single	1	520-63-2705	5.15
Steve Lopez 3215 Cheyenne Drive	Single	0	520-91-3909	5.15
Kristina Mendoza 3829 Colina Drive	Married	2	520-68-5806	5.80
Michael Munoz 7304 Frontera	Single	0	520-51-2954	5.25
Kim Padilla 1610 Pinion Drive	Single	0	542-67-8187	5.15
Shane Quezada 2345 Inca	Single	0	520-20-4518	5.15
Kendra Marie Rossi 302 Vista Drive	Single	0	808-86-7726	5.15
Rose Salazar 4319 Cherokee Drive	Single	0	520-51-3815	5.15
Brandon Taylor 3315 Mohawk	Single	1	520-25-2245	5.15

David N. Weber 1212 Ponderosa	Single	0	520-49-7161	5.90
Kenya Wade 1618 Custer	Single	0	418-21-4532	5.25
Sherry West 2123 East 17th	Single	1	520-74-3962	5.15
Mike Zimmerman 3622 Pine	Single	1	203-65-0692	5.15
Accountant	Single	0	383-87-2376	700.00 monthly

Name ______________________________ Date ______________

Transactions

January

15 The payroll transaction data for the pay period ending January 15 follows. Employees will be paid (Check date) on the following Friday, January 22.

Employee Name	Total Hours	Salary
Jane N. Bixby	18.27	
Jamie Bruce	51.21	
Melissa Jo Brown	59.71	
Michelle Bruce	36.63	
Mackenzie Ann Cadwell	52.18	
Jennifer Dowling	67.84	
Jessica Elliott	22.77	
Scott Esquibel	25.98	
James E. Fontana		1,760.00
Brian S. Garcia	102.13	
Shawn Garcia	23.74	
Mary Lou Huang	13.01	
Kelly Jacobs	32.10	
Justine Jung	41.28	
Steve Lopez	16.25	
Kristina Mendoza	57.00	
Michael Munoz	33.35	
Kim Padilla	33.40	
Shane Quezada	14.41	
Kendra Marie Rossi	9.65	
Rose Salazar	32.27	
Brandon Taylor	9.23	
David N. Weber	67.86	
Kenya Wade	6.06	
Sherry West	26.75	
Mike Zimmerman	81.17	

January 29

The payroll data for the pay period ending January 29. Employees will be paid on February 5. Kenya Wade terminated on January 16.

Employee Name	Total Hours	Salary
Jane N. Bixby	11.26	
Jamie Bruce	39.16	
Melissa Jo Brown	57.76	
Michelle Bruce	4.18	
Mackenzie Ann Cadwell	31.78	
Jennifer Dowling	58.94	
Jessica Elliott	13.16	
Scott Esquibel	29.39	
James E. Fontana		1,760.00
Brian S. Garcia	92.41	
Shawn Garcia	33.95	
Mary Lou Huang	21.22	
Kelly Jacobs	30.07	
Justine Jung	44.60	
Steve Lopez	17.45	
Kristina Mendoza	57.00	
Michael Munoz	38.94	
Kim Padilla	44.61	
Shane Quezada	26.06	
Kendra Marie Rossi	15.92	
Rose Salazar	27.98	
Brandon Taylor	19.94	
David N. Weber	80.57	
Sherry West	29.19	
Mike Zimmerman	83.51	
Accountant (You)		700.00

Name ______________________ Date ____________

February 12

The payroll data for the period ending February 12 follows. The check date for this payroll is February 19.

Michael Munoz and Kendra Marie Rossi did not work during this pay period. Michelle Bruce terminated on January 30.

Employee Name	Total Hours	Salary
Jane N. Bixby	20.28	
Jamie Bruce	29.85	
Melissa Jo Brown	67.85	
Mackenzie Ann Cadwell	41.80	
Jennifer Dowling	68.35	
Jessica Elliott	24.37	
Scott Esquibel	38.38	
James E. Fontana		1,760.00
Brian S. Garcia	101.08	
Shawn Garcia	24.76	
Mary Lou Huang	29.34	
Kelly Jacobs	29.18	
Justine Jung	32.34	
Steve Lopez	6.22	
Kristina Mendoza	57.00	
Kim Padilla	39.96	
Shane Quezada	30.26	
Rose Salazar	31.50	
Brandon Taylor	19.18	
David N. Weber	72.37	
Sherry West	28.47	
Mike Zimmerman	86.09	

February 26

The payroll data for the period ending February 26 follows. Payroll payment date will be March 5.

Employee Name	Total Hours	Salary
Jane N. Bixby	10.84	
Jamie Bruce	37.05	
Melissa Jo Brown	61.68	
Mackenzie Ann Cadwell	40.49	
Jennifer Dowling	59.61	
Jessica Elliott	13.49	
Scott Esquibel	21.69	
James E. Fontana		1,760.00
Brian S. Garcia	103.12	
Shawn Garcia	28.29	
Mary Lou Huang	25.94	
Kelly Jacobs	32.79	
Justine Jung	38.98	
Steve Lopez	19.44	
Kristina Mendoza	56.00	
Michael Munoz	16.34	
Kim Padilla	21.78	
Shane Quezada	20.68	
Kendra Marie Rossi	2.73	
Rose Salazar	26.85	
Brandon Taylor	17.63	
David N. Weber	62.72	
Sherry West	22.48	
Mike Zimmerman	96.14	
Accountant (You)		700.00

Name ______________________________ Date ________________

March 12

The payroll transaction data for the period ending March 12 follows.

Vanessa Killion (520-35-4328) is a new employee beginning March 1. Her address is 4376 Hart Boulevard. She will make $5.15 per hour. She is single and is claiming "0" dependents.

Steve Lopez, Michael Munoz, and Kendra Marie Rossi terminated employment on February 26.

Employee Name	Total Hours	Salary
Jane N. Bixby	27.06	
Jamie Bruce	39.62	
Melissa Jo Brown	58.05	
Mackenzie Ann Cadwell	27.94	
Jennifer Dowling	55.31	
Jessica Elliott	22.75	
Scott Esquibel	28.21	
James E. Fontana		1,760.00
Brian S. Garcia	94.43	
Shawn Garcia	19.99	
Mary Lou Huang	27.94	
Kelly Jacobs	20.10	
Justine Jung	31.16	
Vanessa Killion	26.95	
Kristina Mendoza	57.00	
Kim Padilla	22.37	
Shane Quezada	24.40	
Rose Salazar	31.02	
Brandon Taylor	28.37	
David N. Weber	72.03	
Sherry West	19.94	
Mike Zimmerman	82.00	

March 26

The payroll data for the period ending March 26 follows. Jessica Elliott did not work this pay period.

Employee Name	Total Hours	Salary
Jane N. Bixby	8.96	
Jamie Bruce	24.86	
Melissa Jo Brown	57.15	
Mackenzie Ann Cadwell	19.49	
Jennifer Dowling	55.73	
Scott Esquibel	37.05	
James E. Fontana		1,760.00
Brian S. Garcia	99.29	
Shawn Garcia	20.69	
Mary Lou Huang	29.63	
Kelly Jacobs	19.59	
Justine Jung	26.33	
Vanessa Killion	27.49	
Kristina Mendoza	57.00	
Kim Padilla	19.18	
Shane Quezada	24.13	
Rose Salazar	13.38	
Brandon Taylor	13.83	
David N. Weber	78.89	
Sherry West	25.43	
Mike Zimmerman	5.25	
Accountant (You)		700.00

Name ______________________________ Date ______________

ANALYSIS QUESTIONS

Tumbleweed Fast Food Payroll

INSTRUCTIONS

Use your complete reports to find the answer to the following questions. Write your answer in the space to the left of each question.

______ 1. What was Jessica Elliott's net pay for the January 15 payroll?

______ 2. What was the total amount of deductions withheld from Brian Garcia's earnings for January 15?

______ 3. What was the total amount of the employees' federal withholding tax deductions for the January 15 payroll?

______ 4. How many overtime hours were worked for the pay period which ended January 15?

______ 5. What was the total gross earnings of all employees for January 29?

______ 6. What were Mackenzie Ann Cadwell's gross earnings for January 29?

______ 7. What was the amount withheld for Social Security from all employees for February 12?

______ 8. What was the amount due for federal unemployment taxes for the February 12 payroll?

______ 9. What was the employer's payroll liability for the February 12 payroll?

______ 10. How much did the employer owe for the employer's share of medicare tax for the February 26 payroll?

______ 11. What was the employer's contribution to FUTA for the first quarter?

______ 12. What is the employer's Medicare tax for the quarter?

Appendix

Icon Descriptions

This appendix includes descriptions of some of the icons available to you in *Peachtree Complete Accounting 8.0.* These icons appear in a toolbar across the top of the window and can be selected by:

- clicking with a mouse.
- pressing the ALT key plus the underlined letter of the word on the icon.

The icon descriptions are listed in alphabetical order.

Add Selecting this icon adds:

- an invoice to Customer or Vendor Beginning Balances.
- sales tax codes in Sales Tax Codes.
- a record of a sale to a customer in Sales/Invoicing.
- a line to distribute hours to jobs when you use the Jobs icon in either Select for Payroll Entry or Payroll Entry.
- a record of payment from a customer in Receipts.
- a transaction in the General Journal Entry.
- an adjusting transaction in Account Reconciliation.
- a report to a group in the Select a Report window.
- an alert to the Set Alerts window.

Adjust This displays on the Account Reconciliation window. It allows for making adjustments to an account for errors and service charges that need to be entered to keep the bank account balanced.

Alert This displays in the Alerts tab section of Action Items. Selecting this allows you to set alerts for employees, vendors, customers, inventory items, and general ledger accounts that meet certain criteria. You can set a different alert for each line.

All This displays on the Account Reconciliation window. Selecting this icon will mark all your transactions as cleared.

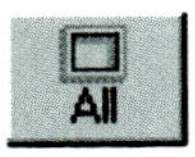

All (None) This displays on the Account Reconciliation window. Selecting this icon will unmark any transactions you marked as cleared.

Cancel Selecting this icon exits a window without saving any entries.

Change ID This displays on the Maintain Vendors and Maintain Customers windows. This allows you to enter a new ID and/or name for a vendor or customer and retain all entries in the account.

Close This closes the window without saving any work that has been entered since the last save.

Copy Use this report to copy a financial statement from a different company. This is especially useful for companies that are part of a conglomerate.

Delete If you select this while you're using a selection from the Maintain menu, the record (customer, vendor, etc.) you're working with will be deleted. When you're finished deleting, select Close, not Save, in order to delete the records.

If you select this while you're working with a selection from the Tasks menu, the transaction (invoice, receipt, etc.) you're working with will be deleted. This differs from Remove, which removes a line from the distribution box.

Design Select this icon to design forms and statements, and reformat reports. This icon displays when you select a form, report, or statement.

Detail This button is used on several windows, including the Create an Event, the Manager Series (Collection Manager, Cash Manager, and Payment Manager), Select for Payment, and Select for Payroll Entry windows.

Edit If you are in a real-time module, this dialog box allows you to select a transaction to edit even though it's been posted. You may select a transaction by highlighting and clicking it. This edit is made both to the general ledger and to the other ledger (for example, customer, vendor, employee, etc.). When you're through making the edit, select the Post icon.

You use this to edit entries within the current period for:

- Sales/Invoicing
- Receipts
- Purchases
- Payments
- Payroll Entry
- General Journal Entry
- Inventory Adjustments

You can sort the list by date, reference (i.e., invoice or quotation number), or record (Customer ID). You can select a prior period in which to correct a transaction by selecting from the list next to Show.

If a transaction has a Y underneath *Qte?*, it means it's a price quotation, not an actual sale or purchase.

Event This allows you to schedule an event for an employee/prospect, vendor, or employee/sales representative. You can also use it to see detail on system generated events.

You can choose to have events display or not display in Action Items. Events you schedule to display will appear on the Events tab of Action Items on the date you schedule them.

You can use this to log notes about telephone calls, meetings, letters, or any other type of activity. You can use this to create a listing of future activities as well.

Excel This icon displays on the Select a Report window. Reports can be displayed as an Excel worksheet. Selecting this icon will launch Excel and display the report.

Filter This icon displays on the Action Items and Event Log windows. You use it to select the types of activities and events you want to display.

This icon also displays for filtering information for Reports, Forms, and Financial Statements, with the information it filters varying with each type.

Format This displays only when you design financial statements using the Reports menu. It allows you to print a listing of the types of fields you've included on your financial statement. It will label the fields such as Text-Header, Text-Body, Column Desc., etc. This is useful if you have a long form, and you want to be able to see how you formatted all the lines.

Graph If you're displaying a subsequent screen, selecting this displays the main screen for Collection Manager and Payment Manager.

Group This icon displays at the top of the Select a Report window. It allows you to group reports, financial statements, and views together so that you can print them in a batch if you select this icon for any report area other than Report Groups.

If you select this icon when report groups are displaying in the reports list, it will open the report group that is highlighted so that you can add or delete reports.

Help This displays on most windows. Selecting this gives you information specific to the current window. The fields of the window are often listed at the bottom of the message.

Hide Titles This displays on reports that you print to the screen. Selecting this hides the title at the top of the screen and frees up more space. To see the titles again, select this icon again.

Jobs This allows you to apply costs, sales, and employees' salaries to up to 10 different Job IDs. You set up jobs using the Jobs selection on the Maintain menu.

For hourly employees, you may change the hourly fields and the hours worked. For salaried employees, you can change the salary fields and the amounts distributed.

New When you're working with maintenance programs, this will clear the record displaying and allow you to enter a new one. This can be used with Customers/Prospects, Vendors, Employees/Sales Reps, Chart of Accounts, Inventory Terms, and Jobs.

Note You can enter up to 250 characters. To enter a note, select the large text box, or press TAB until the cursor is in the box, or press ALT + T. While typing, do not press ENTER at the end of each line, as the words wrap to the next line for you. If you do press ENTER, it will end the entry and return to the main screen.

Use this to keep messages about your customers and vendors.

Important: If you are using the Note feature with the Sales/Invoicing selection, be aware that it prints out on the invoice to your customer. You can choose to print the note either before the line items or after the line items. Use this to print a personal note to the customer.

Numeric This displays the cash flow figures for the Cash Manager. You can set this display also as a graph.

OK This saves information you entered in the window and then closes the window.

Post If you're using the real-time method of posting, this will save and post your entries for your journals.

Preview Select this button in the *Select a Report* window to display the highlighted report, financial statement, or form on the screen. Select this button from task window, the *Forms Design* window, or the *Financial Statement Design* window to display a form on the screen.

Print This icon allows you to print reports, forms, or financial statements.

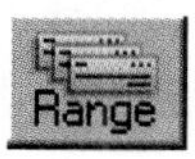

Range This icon displays on the Account Reconciliation window. It allows you to select a range of transactions to mark as cleared. If you have checks you need to mark as cleared, then you can enter a range of check numbers. If any deposit reference numbers fall into this range, those will also be marked as cleared.

Recur This allows *Peachtree* to set up fixed journal entries for a transaction for future months or accounting periods. You can change or delete a recurring entry at any time.

This works with:

- Sales/Invoicing
- Payments
- General Journal Entry

Refresh This displays on the Cash Manager. Use this to make sure that your information is up to date. This includes transactions saved or posted since the last time you refreshed. When you update, you are given the choice of updating the figures and overwriting any manual adjustments you might have made to the spreadsheets, or updating and not overwriting the spreadsheets.

Remove Select this button to delete the selected line item in the displayed window. The Remove button appears only in selected windows. To remove a selected transaction in a window from the Edit menu, choose Remove Line.

Save (Record) This icon saves information such as addresses, telephone numbers, contacts for vendors, customers, and employees.

Save (Journal) If you're using the batch method of posting, this saves information without posting it. If you're using the real-time method of posting, the Save icon does not display; the Post icon displays.

Select (Payment and Collection Manager) Allows you to include all customers or vendors—or to set a range to include in the report. You can also filter the report to include all balances or only those greater or less than a specific amount.

Source This displays in the Cash Manager for the Sales to Collect and Payments to Make spreadsheets. It allows you to see detail on the specific sales or payments. This shows all of the payments or invoices due for a specific vendor or customer on a certain date. Double-clicking a highlighted entry displays the originating transaction where you can edit it.

Spreadsheet This displays in the Cash Manager and in the Financial Manager. You can select the spreadsheet for the following fields in the Cash Manager:

Cash Adjustments—This is where you can enter a positive cash adjustment. Add a description and any adjustments you want to make for up to two years.

Cash Adjustments(–)—This is where you can enter a negative cash adjustment. Add a description and any adjustments you want to make for up to two years. You can add a note to any of these.

Payments to Make—This displays the Vendor, the due date, the amount, and the amounts that are due by the as-of date for every month for up to two years. You can adjust the amount, as well as the amounts for the following months.

Payroll to Pay—This displays the Employee, the due date, the amount, and the amounts that are due by the as-of date for every month for up to two years. You can adjust the amount, as well as the amounts for the following months.

Sales to Collect—This dislays the Customer, the due date, the amount, and the amounts that are due by the as-of date for every month for up to two years. You can adjust the amount, as well as the amount for the following months.

Template Selecting this in Sales/Invoicing or Purchase/Receive Inventory will allow you to change between a service invoice and a product invoice. The product contains fields for Ship Via, Ship Date, Quantity, Item, and Unit Price. These fields do not appear on the service invoice.

Glossary

account data information recorded for new accounts and changes made to existing accounts

account ID a unique identifier for a general ledger account

accounting date the date in a company's fiscal period when transactions are recorded (entered into the company's records)

accounting system the process of recording and reporting financial events or transactions

account maintenance the process of recording information for new accounts and of changing or deleting existing accounts

account name describes the account and prints out on financial statements and activity reports; cannot have more than 30 alpha-numeric characters

account number unique number assigned to each account

accounts payable a promise to pay cash for goods or services received

accounts receivable a promise to receive cash from customers to whom a business has sold goods or services

accrual accounting method of accounting in which sales revenue is reported when the sale is made

action/event log used to display activities that you need to track, such as when to call a vendor or customer or when a letter needs to be sent to a customer or vendor

adjusting entries entries made to update or adjust the general ledger

aged receivables shows outstanding receivables, aged by invoice date or due date

aging reports summary of accounts by the length of time they are past due

alpha-numeric field a field that accepts letters, numbers, or symbols

asset an economic resource owned by a company or an individual

back up a routine that creates a copy of files

balance sheet financial statement listing assets, liabilities, and equity at a specific time

batch posting transactions are saved and posted as a group.

bill document that lists the details of a sale and total amount due; also called *invoice* or *sales slip*

calendar year period of time beginning and ending with the dates conventionally used to indicate the beginning and end of a year

cash basis accounting method of accounting in which you postpone reporting sales revenue until payment is received

cash disbursements used to keep track of all cash payments

cash discount discount that may be offered as an incentive for prompt payment; also called *sales discount*

cash flow report a listing of the cash used in the business for the current month and year-to-date

cash management used to enter and track all banking transactions; also used to consolidate customer and vendor cash transactions

cash receipts journal a list of all cash receipts in detail or summary format

chart of accounts list of accounts and their account numbers; basis for allocating business transactions

check register a routine that provides a method of checking earnings and tax amounts before printing paychecks

collection letters a letter sent to a customer to inform him or her that the account is past due, and that additional action may be taken if the account is not brought up to date

computer software the programs that instruct the computer to perform desired functions; also called simply *software*

corporation company owned by persons who have purchased shares of stock in the business; a separate legal entity from its owners

credit right-hand column of account; a transaction that decreases the customer's balance

credit memorandum document issued as evidence of a credit to a customer's or vendor's account for a return or allowance; also called *sales return slip*

CTRL key allows you to select items from the main menu

customer company or individual to which a business sells goods or services

customer statement statement that lists all of a customer's transactions with a company

debit left-hand column of an account; a transaction that increases the customer's balance

deductions amounts of money subtracted from an employee's pay

deposit ticket ID identifies all sources of cash included in one deposit

destination drive letter of disk drive (and path) where information will be stored

discount date the last date a discount is available

draw salary based on expected earnings

drop-down list an arrow pointing down to the left of a field which accesses a menu of selections or options

due date the date by which an invoice should be paid

dunning message a friendly reminder (for overdue accounts) that you can have appear on your statements when they are sent out

employees people who work for a company performing a variety of tasks for which they are compensated

end-of-period activities tasks performed on a regular basis and in a specific order, such as closing accounts

Enter key computer key used to accept data

estimated expenses an estimate of what expenses might be incurred for a fiscal period or for a particular job

estimated revenues an estimate of what revenue is expected for a fiscal period or from a particular job

expense cost associated with doing business

federal ID number number given to a business by the federal government; sometimes referred to as Employer Identification Number (EIN) or employer ID

FICA Federal Insurance Contributions Act

FICA tax a tax imposed on employees earnings designated percentage of gross income. Commonly called Social Security tax; the same percentage is paid by the employer.

field an input area for text or numbers

finance charges interest on the unpaid balance of a charge account

financial reports provide management with information necessary to make important business decisions

fiscal year an accounting period of twelve months, which may or may not correspond to the calendar year

fixed asset economic resources that a company owns and that have a life expectancy of more than one year

form 941 quarterly federal tax return that tracks the amount of tax paid by an employer

401K a special kind of savings plan that many companies offer where the savings are deducted from gross pay before federal income taxes are computed

function keys keys (on the computer keyboard) beginning with F and followed by a number, such as F1, F2, etc.; useful in executing operations within software programs

FUTA federal unemployment tax

general journal a unique journal in which you can enter debits and credits for transactions that do not fit in any other journal

general ledger simplest and most common kind of accounting ledger, in which all types of business transactions can be recorded; maintains all account balances in the system

general ledger trial balance a listing of the current balance for each GL Account

graphics an alternative (to text) for reviewing and presenting data

hardware physical components of a computer system, such as monitor, disk drives, and keyboard; also called *computer hardware*

income statement lists revenues and expenses, and indicates the profit (or loss) for the period, as well as for the year-to-date; also called *profit/loss statement*

input forms used to organize accounting information and prepare it for data entry

integrated modules modules of a computer package linked together through a menu system

invoice document that lists the details of a sale and total amount due; also called *bill* or *sales slip*

invoice register a listing of all invoices entered into the system

job ledger report lists the job ID, the customer, customer activity, as well as balance and status of a job

job list provides job ID, description, starting and ending dates, and the customer ID

job master file list reports all information on a particular job

job profitability report gives a detailed view of performance

job register gives an overview of the job performance

journal record of business transactions shown in order by date

key to type data into a field entry

keyboard function keys keys (on computer keyboard) beginning with F and followed by a number, such as F1, F2, etc.; useful in executing operations within software programs

liabilities (in payroll context) obligations of the employer for taxes and other withholdings

liability debt, or amount owed by a company or an individual

magnifying glass an icon used to access a menu of options or choices

master control account used to sum a range of subsidiary accounts

Medicare tax levied on both the employee and employer to provide medical benefits to the elderly

navigation aids a graphical flow of the tasks in each feature of *Peachtree Accounting*

numeric field field that accepts only numbers and the decimal point

offsetting transaction made to correct a previous incorrect transaction

open P.O. # the default number that will appear on the customer's invoices

order cancellation notice sent to notify vendor that a purchase order has been canceled

original date issue date of a transaction; used for aging purposes

partnership company owned by two or more people, with each owner having individual investment and withdrawal accounts

past due report lists accounts receivable in which the customer is late in payment

payment manager provides you with a method of analyzing accounts payable for a specific time period

payroll current earnings shows total for the quarter-to-date and year-to-date earnings and deductions for each employee

payroll feature the employee and employer information is entered into this feature

payroll journal a report that lets you reconcile paychecks and verify general ledger posting accuracy

payroll periodic operations tasks performed at certain times of the year and not related to everyday processing

payroll register provides a method for checking earnings, tax amounts, and deductions before printing paychecks

period end end of a specific accounting period

posting process that updates current files; transfers totals from modules to the general ledger

price reduction reduction in price granted to a customer for accepting damaged but usable merchandise; also called a *sales allowance*

product code one-digit code representing the kind of goods or merchandise sold

profit/loss statement lists revenues and expenses, and indicates the profit (or loss) for the period, as well as for the year to date; also called *income statement*

promissory note written promise to pay a specified amount of money at a specified date

prospects potential clients

purchase allowance price reduction provided by vendor in exchange for acceptance of inferior merchandise

purchase journal a record of all purchases made

purchase on account to purchase merchandise or services on credit

purchase order used to order merchandise or service from a vendor; lists the details of a purchase on account

Purchase Order (P.O.) date usually the date found on a purchase order, not the current date on the calendar

purchase order register lists the details of all open purchase orders

purchase return merchandise returned to a vendor for full refund or credit

purge remove transaction details from files

real-time posting transactions are posted as you save them

receipt record of cash received by a business

reconciliation method used to track outstanding, cleared, and voided checks

recovering data files routine to restore files that have been corrupted

reference number unique identifiers for a transaction

revenue income earned by a company

reverse transactions a transaction that reverses another transaction created in a previous period

salary money paid to an employee for services performed

sales allowance price reduction granted to a customer for accepting damaged but usable merchandise

sales discount discount that may be offered as an incentive for prompt payment; also called *cash discount*

sales on account product or service received by a customer but not paid for until a later date; the sale of merchandise or service on account

sales receipt a record of the payment in a cash transaction

sales return merchandise returned by a customer for a full refund or credit

sales return slip document issued as evidence of a credit to a customer's or vendor's account for a return of merchandise or allowance; also called *credit memorandum*

sales slip document that lists the details of a sale and total amount due; also called *bill* or *invoice*

shortcut keys keys that, when used in conjunction with the ALT or CTRL key, can quickly and easily access various commands

simple copy method of copy which assumes all of your data will fit onto one floppy disk

Social Security tax term commonly used for FICA tax, the designated percentage of gross income withheld from employee wages and matched by employer contributions

software programs that instruct the computer to perform desired functions; also called *computer software*

sole proprietorship company owned by one person; investments, withdrawals, and net income are merged into a single account at the end of an accounting period

source code a code in the general ledger that indicates which module a transaction came from

source documents paper records of transactions, such as purchase orders, invoices, or receipts

source path location of files to be copied or backed up

statement of changes report a financial statement that identifies the condition of your company by showing the current month versus year-to-date changes in sources of working capital

status bar gives a brief explanation of the current field or text box when you are currently working

SUTA state unemployment tax paid by the employer

Tab key computer key used to accept data or move from one field to the next

Taxable/Exempt Sales report a report showing what sales tax must be paid to each taxing authority

tax expense account the expense account used to track tax expenses

tax liability account liability account used to track your (employer) tax payments and employee taxes withheld

1099 form standard form required by the Internal Revenue Service for reporting the earnings of contract labor vendors

terms the time interval for payment for purchases or sales on account

transaction record of a business event

trial balance a report showing all debit and credit balances of general ledger accounts

unit price the amount paid for each unit of a product is entered in this field

vendor individuals or companies from whom purchases are made

wages money paid to an employee for work performed

working trial balance lists account numbers, descriptions, and ending balance; includes blank columns for documenting changes to accounts through adjustments

W-2 form statement of employee's annual (calendar year) earnings and any withholdings; must be filed with employee's federal income tax return

year end end of a business fiscal year

year-end closing the closing of accounts at the end of the year

Index